**National Strategy in a Decade
of Change**

A Report on a Symposium Sponsored by

the

Stanford Research Institute

and the

Foreign Policy Research Institute

Airlie House

Warrenton, Va.

February 8-11, 1973

National Strategy in a Decade of Change

An Emerging U.S. Policy

Edited by
William R. Kintner
Richard B. Foster

Lexington Books
D.C. Heath and Company
Lexington, Massachusetts
Toronto   London

Library of Congress Cataloging in Publication Data
Main entry under title:

National strategy in a decade of change.

"A report on a symposium sponsored by the Stanford Research Institute and the Foreign Policy Research Institute, Airlie House, Warrenton, Va., February 8-11, 1973."
1. United States—Foreign relations—1969-   —Congresses. I. Kintner, William Roscoe, 1915-   ed. II. Foster, Richard B., ed. III. Stanford Research Institute. IV. Foreign Policy Research Institute.
E840.N36   327.73   73-9757
ISBN 0-669-90480-5

Contents

List of Figures

List of Tables

Preface

In February 1973 the Strategic Studies Center of the Stanford Research Institute and the Foreign Policy Research Institute cosponsored the second symposium on "National Strategy in A Decade of Change." The symposia brought together distinguished experts from within and without the United States government to discuss a wide range of global problems. Whereas the first conference in February 1972 focused on the implications of the evolving Nixon Doctrine for the position of the United States in international affairs, the second probed programmatic aspects of the Nixon Doctrine in search of an answer to the question of how the general philosophy of that doctrine might be translated into operational policy. Accordingly, the 1973 symposium sought to integrate the key ingredients of a comprehensive national policy, including: national resources and economic strategy, the problem of building a domestic consensus, the demands of détente diplomacy on U.S. government bureaucracies, and the requirements of military posture and technology strategy.

This second symposium, held February 8-11, 1973, at Airlie House, in Warrenton, Va., drew on participants from academic institutions, research organizations, and appropriate departments of the United States government. In addition, several distinguished experts from Europe and Asia assessed the changing international environment in various regions of the world.

This book makes available to a wider public thirteen papers written for the 1973 symposium—some of which were subsequently revised and updated—and includes a summary of the discussion. One consistent theme throughout the symposium was that fundamental alterations in the international environment are compelling the United States to assess the nature of the new milieu while devising a new national strategy. The United States not only must seek to adjust to the changing system but must help shape it in such a way that the oft-proclaimed "generation of peace" may become a reality. It is the editors' hope that this book contributes to the process of public reflection and debate that is a prerequisite to fulfilling American responsibilities in an unsettled era.

Many persons provided able assistance in the preparation and administration of the symposium on "National Strategy in a Decade of Change II: An Emerging U.S. Policy." It is a pleasure to acknowledge the support of Mr. William M. Carpenter of the Stanford Research Institute, who served as the coordinator of the symposium. He was aided by Gordon Boe, also of SRI. Other members of the participating staff were: Bettie Bowman, Norman Furth, Dee King, Kay MacCormack, Gail Patelcuis, Sheldon Rabin, and Tricia Ross, of the Stanford Research Institute and Donna Brodsky, Judy Cole, and Nils Wessell of the Foreign Policy Research Institute. Primary responsibility for preparing the summary of the symposium discussion was shared by Dr. Wessell, Mr. Carpenter, and Mr. Boe under the direction of the editors, who remain responsible, of course, for any shortcomings of this volume.

A special word of appreciation is gratefully offered the Carthage Foundation, without whose generous support the symposium could not have been held.

Richard B. Foster **William R. Kintner**
Arlington, Va. Philadelphia, Pa.
April 16, 1973 April 16, 1973

Introduction

When the Nixon Administration took office in 1969, it was confronted with both the opportunity and the necessity to redefine the role of the United States in international affairs. The entire pattern of postwar international politics was undergoing fundamental change. The bipolar domination that had characterized the era of confrontation still prevailed on the level of nuclear weapons, but below this level new centers of power were emerging. The postwar economic recovery and increased political vitality of Western Europe and Japan presented the Western alliance system with an opportunity to readjust the roles of these partners relative to that of the United States.

The communist world no longer consisted of a monolithic bloc posing a unified ideological and military threat to the West. The Soviet Union and the Peoples Republic of China had become engaged in a great power struggle for leadership of the communist movement. In Eastern Europe, the facade of unity had been shattered by the invasion of Czechoslovakia in August 1968. There was also some evidence that the USSR was undergoing its own internal stresses of change, necessitating at least some realignment of its economic and social priorities in order to ease the tensions building up among its peoples. All these changes gave the Administration the chance to open up new avenues of dialogue and negotiation with America's adversaries.

A new look at the Third World was appropriate by 1969; the situation was changing within the underdeveloped countries, and the attitudes of the great powers toward the Third World were still being shaped by the experiences of the 1960s. This area had been the scene of vigorous competition between the superpowers during much of that period. The use of direct economic and military aid was designed to gain influence in the underdeveloped countries and to promote their economic and social growth. By 1969, however, it was recognized that the allegiance of these countries could not be purchased by the great powers. Attempts to impose development strategies on the poorer nations had failed to solve such intractable problems as overpopulation and lagging industrial growth. A new approach was needed that would benefit from the lessons learned in the past decade.

In addition to opportunities abroad for new directions in foreign policy, the changing American domestic situation made it necessary to remold U.S. policy. The domestic consensus that had sustained an activist American foreign policy since World War II had visibly eroded. The frustrations of the Vietnam war, combined with increasing concern over the urban and social crises of the late 1960s, had resulted in a serious questioning of national priorities. The United States was experiencing a crisis of belief in its institutions and in its national purposes more serious than at any time in recent history. The American people had become weary of international involvement and were inclined to turn back to domestic concerns, although there was no consensus on domestic priorities. A redefined role for the United States in the international arena was needed to rebuild the American consensus.

While the United States was locked into a long and costly war in Southeast Asia during most of the 1960s, the Soviet Union had emerged as a major global military power, seeking and finally obtaining strategic parity. It had also expanded its naval capability to the point where the Soviet fleet was challenging the American Navy in the world's oceans. The Soviet challenge, however, was not solely represented by its increasing military power. While American national strategy planners were emphasizing force-to-force comparisons of military capability during the 1960s, the Soviets were concentrating on the integration of all the elements of total national power—political, economic, psychological, diplomatic, technical, as well as military. By taking this approach, the Soviet Union became more adept at using its military power within an overall political strategy designed to achieve its goals without going to war. The challenge to the United States had thus shifted from military confrontation to a more complex arena involving the interaction of total national strategies.

Meanwhile, the Western alliance system had undergone crisis during the 1960s. American involvement in Vietnam distracted this country's attention from the security needs of Europe and Japan. Increasing Soviet military capability, along with decreasing allied belief in the credibility of the American strategic deterrent, resulted in a loss of common purpose and lack of cohesiveness in the alliance. This *malaise* of the spirit made a restatement of American alliance policy imperative.

Faced with these domestic and international realities, the Nixon Administration had the difficult task of redefining the role of the United States while maintaining a responsible U.S. involvement in international affairs and protecting national interests at a level sustainable by the American public. The nature of the world had changed; the nature of the threat had changed; the mood of the American people had changed. It was necessary that U.S. foreign policy be adjusted to these realities.

To meet this need, the Nixon Doctrine was formulated. It posed three general tasks for U.S. foreign policy: to maintain adequate national strength; to create more equitably shared and more effective partnerships with U.S. allies; and to move from an era of confrontation to an era of negotiation with America's adversaries. Within this framework, the first years in the evolution of the Nixon Doctrine were spent redefining American national interests and reordering national priorities in order to give U.S. foreign policy a coherence and clarity it had previously lacked.

To weigh the effectiveness of the Nixon Doctrine in meeting the needs of the United States in a changing world, the first symposium on "National Strategy in a Decade of Change" was held in February 1972.[a] The symposium adopted a broad approach, focusing on the forces of political, military, social, and economic change that will shape the events of the present decade. These broad

[a]See appendix for the summary report of the 1972 symposium.

subject areas were examined as a prelude to assessing the problems the Administration had faced in forging a domestic consensus capable of supporting the new foreign policy.

The events of 1972 and early 1973 confirmed the relevance of the subjects discussed at the first symposium. The President's trip to Peking opened up new opportunities for a dialogue between the United States and China. His visit to Moscow in May 1972 and the signing of the SALT I agreements and the Basic Principles of Relations helped to codify the process of negotiations between adversaries. These trips suggested that it might be possible for the United States to have better relations with both the USSR and China than either could have with the other.

Yet the advances made in negotiating with adversaries have caused serious concern in Europe and Japan. Many West Europeans believe that the arms limitation agreements between the United States and the USSR may signal the decoupling of the American strategic deterrent from the defense of Europe. They are, moreover, concerned about the lack of Western unity, which they fear may lead to harmful concessions to the Soviet Union in the Conference on Security and Cooperation in Europe and the talks on Mutual and Balanced[b] Force Reductions. The Japanese, too, have raised questions about the credibility of the American nuclear guarantee, especially in view of the U.S.-China *rapprochement* and the decreased American military presence in Asia.

These concerns have been aggravated by the recent international monetary crises in the West. The United States closed the gold window on August 15, 1971, and has been forced to devalue the dollar twice since then. In March 1973, several major Western nations agreed to float their currencies in an effort to find an acceptable solution to these recurrent crises. In the area of international trade, American industry is facing stiff competition from a resurgent Japan and the recently expanded European Economic Community. The deterioration of the U.S. economic position is a matter of grave concern to Washington. America's allies fear that the search for solutions may lead the United States to overemphasize the economic issues to the detriment of the alliance's common political and security interests. Washington is concerned that the Common Market countries may do the same.

In the Middle East, the Arab-Israeli dispute smolders with little hope of a negotiated settlement. This problem, however, is being overshadowed by the rising importance of the Persian Gulf, which contains over sixty percent of the world's known oil reserves. Europe already depends upon countries of the Middle East and the Gulf for over two-thirds of its oil supply; Japan imports 90 percent of its oil needs from this area; and by the end of this decade, the United States will be importing close to 50 percent of its oil, with half of these imports coming from the Persian Gulf. The economic, political, and strategic consequences of the impending world energy crisis and the dependence of the industrial nations on this unstable area for the bulk of their petroleum supplies

[b]At the time of the symposia the United States and NATO referred to the objective of the talks as mutual and *balanced* force reductions. During Brezhnev's visit to the United States in June 1973 the term "balanced" was dropped.

will be among the most important determinants of policy toward the Middle East during the 1970s.

A key event of early 1973 was the ceasefire settlement in Vietnam and the subsequent termination of direct American military involvement in that war. The U.S. foreign policy community could then begin to focus on other high priority issues in Europe, Asia, and the Middle East.

These and other issues were examined in depth at the second symposium on "National Strategy in a Decade of Change" held in February 1973. The discussion at this second meeting centered on how the Nixon Doctrine might be made operationally specific. U.S. policy should be flexible enough to strengthen ties with allies without jeopardizing the climate necessary to negotiate with adversaries.

The Nixon Doctrine is a beginning rather than the end of the quest for a policy to fulfill America's role in the decade. It is necessarily a mixture of continuity and innovation. As one participant stated in the final session of the 1972 symposium, "We are not here to write on a *tabula rasa* a new and fresh policy. This is not done too simply in the real world. But we are here, I believe, each in his own responsible way, to see how we can be helpful with regard to that policy or one which—in our individual estimation—has greater content or meaning." It was in this spirit that the participants in both symposia approached their task of examining a national strategy adequate to meet the challenges America faces in the future.

Part I:
The New International Milieu

In the following chapter, Mr. Richard B. Foster examines the impact on the world environment resulting from the complex interaction of the two structurally different superpowers. Mr. Foster is the founder and Director of the Strategic Studies Center, Stanford Research Institute. He has been engaged in extensive analytical work over the past two decades in the field of strategy and national security policy, especially in politico-military policy, arms control, missile defense, and tactical nuclear weapons policy.

An innovator in the development of intellectual interaction with research organizations in Western Europe and the Soviet Union, Mr. Foster is the author and co-author of many SRI studies in the field of national strategy undertaken for the U.S. Government.

1

The Nixon Doctrine: An Emerging U.S. Policy[a]

Richard B. Foster

A "Generation of Peace" is the unifying theme in all of President Nixon's foreign policy statements. To many of his critics the phrase has been dismissed as a part of the Nixonian rhetoric directed at U.S. domestic political opinion to enlist support for his winding down of U.S. involvement in Vietnam ("Peace with Honor"). Yet from the viewpoint of a strategist, the concept of a "Generation of Peace" may be usefully treated as a positive concrete goal of U.S. global policy. The objective is derived from the strategic necessity of preventing nuclear war without at the same time either abandoning U.S. allies or surrendering U.S. global interests in a retreat to a neo-isolationist policy. It is the thesis of this paper that implicit in the Nixon doctrine is a radical approach to international relations. The traditional concepts of a balance of power are modified by the requirement that an international structure must be based on agreement—made possible by a new kind of international politics—between all nuclear states to prevent nuclear confrontations between them.

In the 1950s and 1960s the United States tended to overemphasize the quantitative aspects of nuclear strategy and to neglect the political, economic, and the other non-military elements affecting international relations—including the requirement for a domestic political consensus for U.S. foreign policy. Vietnam punctured some of the overblown and somewhat romantic perspectives of America's role in the world and of the utility of direct use of American military power to solve deep-seated political problems in Asia. The new realism is leading Americans to a new understanding of international politics, as well as of the indirect political value and strategic utility of nuclear weapons.

In the 1960s the United States stressed the negative utilities, both political and strategic, of nuclear weapons—those of deterrence based on "assured-destruction-only" concepts. Arms limitations policies were predicated on the assumption that if the nation tried hard enough, nuclear weapons could be removed from consideration of international politics and be reduced to strategic

[a]This paper incorporates material from a previous paper entitled "Strategic Interactions" presented at the first Airlie House Symposium on "National Strategy in a Decade of Change" on February 17, 1972. It is a condensation of elements of a longer study entitled "A DIAlectical MOdel of the Nixon Doctrine" (acronym "DIAMOND"). The author reserves the right to publish some of this material in another form. The views in this paper are entirely those of the author and do not reflect those of any client of the Stanford Research Institute nor of the Stanford Research Institute as a whole.

nullity through parity. This strategic parity was expressed in terms of quantifiable outcomes: both sides, the United States and the Soviet Union, would have about the same fatalities in their cities as the other side no matter which side struck first; both sides were assumed to share this view of nuclear weapons. The emphasis was on the technologies that would lead to this result—namely, that any nuclear war, no matter how limited in the beginning, could escalate to mutual suicide. Hence, nuclear weapons would lose their political value to the United States and the USSR, and to Nth powers as well. The quest for strategic nuclear options short of destruction of the opponent's cities in a second strike mode was considered to be a self-defeating quest, since it would have the opposite effect, namely, of making nuclear war more likely.

One of the great accomplishments of President Nixon and his chief foreign policy advisor, Dr. Henry Kissinger, has been to reintroduce political understanding into the strategic nuclear deterrence equation. This new appreciation of nuclear politics provides the basis for erecting a global order based on a new international politics derived from the strategic necessity of preventing nuclear war—equally applicable to the United States and to the Soviet Union because deterrence is mutual in the era of strategic parity.

The "Era of Negotiations"

The U.S. foreign policy for the 1970s outlined in President Nixon's three foreign policy reports to the Congress[1] stresses the necessity for converting the post-World War II era of U.S.-Soviet confrontation into an "era of negotiations." The Nixon Doctrine has been characterized as "the Strategy for Peace," supported by the "National Security Strategy of Realistic Deterrence," described in the annual Defense Reports[2] of the Secretary of Defense. Two elements of the President's strategy for peace—strength and partnership—are presented as making possible the third: meaningful negotiations. Thus the central focus of the Nixon Doctrine can be characterized as a sustained U.S. effort to alter the Soviet-American strategic competition in nuclear arms to less dangerous forms of competition.

This focus of U.S. national security policy is not entirely new. Presidents Eisenhower, Kennedy, and Johnson, as well as Khrushchev and his successors in the Kremlin were agreed that some form of relatively "peaceful competition" between the two opposing social systems had to be substituted for nuclear confrontation policies by both sides.

A New Realism in U.S.-Soviet Strategic Interactions

But what is new, this paper contends, is a much greater U.S. sensitivity to the dynamics of change on a global scale of all kinds of factors—sociological, political, economic, technical, military—accompanied by a radically different perception of, and respect for, the political stability and economic staying power of both great communist states. Communist Russia is now the USSR, and Communist China is now the PRC in the official U.S. lexicon. This is not simply a change in rhetoric; it implies the acceptance by the United States of realistic limits to U.S. power and influence; it signals a change in underlying U.S. philosophy in both describing and seeking to influence the strategic interaction process between the two superpowers. While President Nixon's initiatives to normalize U.S.-PRC relationships take advantage of the Sino-Soviet split, the goal of preventing nuclear war applies both to U.S. policies *vis-à-vis* Sino-Soviet relations and to U.S.-Soviet relations.

America and Russia formulate and carry out their national strategies with respect to each other in different ways, using methodologies appropriate to their histories and political institutions. It is not surprising that they have different military strategies and doctrines, with different perceptions of the political value and strategic utility of nuclear weapons. What is surprising is the length of time it has taken for the United States to accept the full consequences of these basic differences, and to cease "mirror-imaging" U.S. strategy by imputing U.S. strategic concepts and doctrine to the Soviets. Sun Tzu long ago taught that the most desirable objective of one's own strategy should be the defeat of the opponent's strategy without resort to the actual use of military force. But this implies that the aims and the strategy of the adversary have to be studied with an attitude of respect not only for his military weapons and forces (such as ICBMs, SLBMs, and bombers), but also for his intellectual processes and the way that he formulates his strategy and his doctrine.

Needed: An Improved Methodology

If this first step is taken, that is, studying the Soviet method of formulating strategy as well as the substance of that strategy, a beginning can be made toward developing a more adequate theory of strategic interactions between the United States and the Soviet Union. What is needed is a methodology that describes and explains the dynamics of the interactions of strategic decisions made by both sides with respect to one another, and the influence of strategic doctrine on these decisions. In turn, since the United States and the Soviet Union use different approaches to arrive at their non-symmetrical strategies, this interaction methodology should be able to take into account the different national approaches. This effort requires a broad understanding of the philosophical, political, institutional, cultural, and sociological framework in which the Soviets formulate their strategic doctrine. A description of those aspects of the Soviet system—including their institutions and organizations that formulate and disseminate their military strategy and doctrine—can be found in other studies.[3] Some major conclusions of these studies are relevant here.

Soviet Concepts of Doctrine and Strategy

There are at least two areas in which the Soviets are rather explicit about the political utility of the growing power of their military establishment. First, the Soviets see the relative rise in their strategic nuclear power *vis-à-vis* the United States and NATO as limiting Western strategic and policy options out of fear of the consequences of Soviet capabilities. The evolution in Western (NATO) strategy from "massive retaliation" to "flexible response" with a "conventional emphasis" is considered (by the Soviets) to be the result of this process. Second, the Soviets see their growing military capabilities as providing the umbrella under which they can perform their "international duty" of aiding and abetting "national liberation" and "anti-colonial" wars with increasingly less danger of facing escalation to a level of conflict that would threaten the Soviet homeland itself. In the Soviet view, these indirect attacks on the West will be effective in the long run.

Moreover, it can be argued, somewhat more inferentially than on actual statements, that the Soviets see what they call the growing "militarization" of Western societies as a long-run trend working to their advantage, even if it tends to increase somewhat the short-run dangers of war. In the Soviet view, "militarization" intensifies the internal contradictions inherent in "capitalism" and "imperialism," contradictions that eventually will lead to the replacement of these social systems with a Soviet-type social structure. Meanwhile, short-run dangers and tensions can be offset by the American fear of growing Soviet strategic nuclear power.

The destructiveness of nuclear weapons is such that Lenin's dictum on the inevitability of war between "socialist" and "capitalist" camps was modified by Khrushchev in 1956 when he declared nuclear war was not "fatally inevitable."[b] This is to say that deterrence of an American nuclear attack on the USSR is possible but can by no means be guaranteed. Hence, the USSR military establishment must be prepared to fight a nuclear war as a last resort. Soviet military strategy does not envisage a premeditated surprise attack on the United States designed to hasten the historically determined demise of capitalism, because the expected damage to the USSR from the U.S. retaliatory blow is too great.

The Soviet doctrine for "just" wars has been applied equally to Vietnam and to the Near East. In both cases, USSR political, economic, and military aid to the "just" belligerents does not appear to be an accident, or even the result of a

---

[b]Although the idea was popularized by Khrushchev in his speech delivered at the 20th Party Congress in 1956, it had been foreshadowed four years earlier at the 19th Party Congress by Stalin, who argued that the contradictions (likely to lead to war) within the capitalist camp were greater than those between the capitalist and the socialist camps. Neither the military nor the civilian leaders have given any indication of wanting to modify this particular tenet of Soviet doctrine, even if Khrushchev is no longer given personal credit for it.

process of incremental decisions that have led the USSR to a depth of involvement not originally contemplated. The Soviet leaders may well have had their eyes wide open throughout the process even if they proceeded cautiously, testing reactions and evaluating the implications each time they made an additional commitment.

Strategic Superiority and Superior Strategy

In the Soviet view, strategic superiority depends as much on having a superior strategy as it does on having a superior military force. As a consequence of this view, the Soviets stress professionalism in their military strategic planners; the United States does not nourish a trained cadre of professional strategic planners who have continuity. The Soviets have a carefully graduated system of awarding higher academic degrees—through the doctoral level—in their research institutes and their major military academies; the United States' higher military schools and the research institutes do not directly award higher academic degrees. Consequently, there is a need to correct in the United States an overemphasis on the purely technological and quantitative aspects of the strategic arms competition with the Soviet Union. Americans tend to give too little weight to the quality of Soviet strategic thought. A more humanistic and sophisticated appreciation of Soviet strategic thought is necessary if the United States is to develop an adequate theory of the dynamics of U.S.-Soviet strategic interactions.

A Proposal: A Dialectical Model of
U.S.-Soviet Interactions

In order to understand the dynamics of future U.S.-Soviet strategic interactions, a better methodology is needed to explain the post-World War II history of such interactions. Whatever its limitations, the Marxist dialectic of history provides the Kremlin leadership and the Soviet military-intellectual establishment with a general methodology for explaining history and for predicting future outcomes of strategic interactions. The dialectic as a logic of history—first enunciated by Hegel—is not the exclusive property of the Marxists and the communist world. The dialectical method, described as the resolution of opposites through conflict into a higher synthesis, can be useful in analyzing the interactions of strategic decisions of adversary states. For example, an application of dialectical methodology is that which describes the U.S.-Soviet historical relationship as consisting of both opportunities for cooperation and of possibilities of conflict, often with one nullifying the other. Because it is in the interest of both the United States and the Soviet Union to prevent a nuclear war between the two powers, a dialectical necessity exists to cooperate to prevent confrontations that might lead to nuclear conflict. This strategic necessity in turn may lead to a higher synthesis—a new international politics underpinning a global order—arising out of the conflict between the two social systems, but a conflict that stops short of all-out nuclear war.

A word of caution is necessary. In the 1960s, the United States tended to avoid approaches requiring long, hard, patient research and analysis that would integrate the historical, political, military, scientific, technological, economic, sociological, cultural, psychological and other factors necessary to meet the global strategic challenge of the Soviets. However, in the reaction to the overemphasis of the 1960s on highly theoretical quantitative models of the strategic interaction process, one must avoid throwing away the capability to make rigorous cost-effectiveness analyses of alternative weapons systems and military force postures. Such quantitative analyses are a necessary counterpart to the integrative, multidisciplinary approaches that consider the qualitative social, political, and cultural factors together with the quantitative economic factors and the technical and tactical elements of a military force structure in devising and evaluating alternative national strategies.

In this paper "dialectics" is a logic of the history of interstate interactions.[c] The dialectical method is the resolution of opposites through conflict into a higher synthesis. The reverse process may also be true. The use of a synthesis is either to reconcile opposites or to control the nature of the conflict that resolves differences. It is a useful method to analyze the interactions of strategic decisions of adversary states. As such, it may provide an added dimension to the U.S.-Soviet dialogue in the era of negotiations. The Nixon Doctrine is interpreted by this means in furtherance of this aim.

In the remainder of this paper, the Nixon Doctrine will be illustrated in a series of triangles. Five charts will illustrate the emerging global structure of the international system. The fundamental framework of the international system is the strength (S) and the partnership (P) with allies that the United States will negotiate (N) with the Soviet Union (and with the Peoples Republic of China to bring about a more peaceful world in which the prevention of nuclear war is a high aim of policy.

It is assumed that the international system now and in the foreseeable future will be based on an evolution of nation-state relationships. Within those nation-state relationships, the possibilities exist for cooperation and for conflict, but conflict no longer can be taken to its ultimate resolution through general war. Hence competition is moderated. In each of the following diagrams, the

---

[c]The current general definition of dialectics in the Soviet Union is not limited to a doctrinaire economic determinism concept. In the "Short Political Dictionary" (Moscow, 1971, p. 70), dialectics is defined as:

"The study of the most general laws of the development of nature, society, and thought. The dialectic examines objects and phenomena thoroughly, in their contradictions, their operations and their development, in concrete historical conditions and in connection with social practice."

primary partnership lines, the primary negotiating lines, the primary nuclear guarantee commitments, and other relationships are explained in a legend on the upper left hand side.

An Independent Europe: The Cornerstone of the Global Structure of the Nixon Doctrine

Figure 1-1 illustrates the dialectical relationships among the United States, Western Europe, and the Soviet Union. From the very beginning, President Nixon has stressed the primacy of Europe and the maintenance of an independent, strong, and stable Western Europe as the foundation of any global order in which U.S. interests can be maintained. Europe is here defined as "NATO-plus"; that is, all the Western European states including those neutrals that gain their security and maintain their independence under the protection of the American nuclear umbrella—Sweden, Switzerland, Austria, and Spain in Western Europe, and Yugoslavia in Eastern Europe. In order to maintain this nuclear umbrella, the United States has by necessity coupled its strategic nuclear deterrent to the defense of Europe. This coupling has given a nuclear guarantee to the NATO nations to prevent Soviet coercion either by nuclear arms or by conventional forces. This "extended deterrent" has been an extremely difficult problem to solve and every few years a review of NATO strategy has taken place. The current strategy of flexible response includes a direct conventional phase as well as a role for tactical nuclear weapons, theater nuclear weapons, and the U.S. strategic nuclear force; the strategy is based on a concept of balanced force among all of these elements.

However, the problem is that the credibility of the nuclear guarantee and the confidence that the Europeans have in it have been gradually eroded as the Soviet Union has attained strategic parity with the United States. United States negotiations with the Soviet Union, particularly in the first phase of the Strategic Arms Limitation Talks (SALT I), have tended to undermine European confidence in the U.S. nuclear umbrella. Thus the United States is caught in a contradiction: how to reduce the nuclear confrontation between the United States and the Soviet Union and at the same time to extend the nuclear deterrent for the protection of Europe from Soviet coercion. The nuclear power of Britain and France is insufficient to provide a credible deterrent to the Soviet nuclear might poised against Europe. Moreover, both the French and the British lack tactical nuclear weapons that could replace the several thousand such weapons in the American arsenal based in Europe. Hence there is a continuing requirement for the U.S. nuclear guarantee and its coupled strategic deterrent to be reconciled with the aim of entering into "peaceful competition"—or in the Soviet lexicon, "peaceful coexistence"—with the USSR. However, a new concept is arising out of the situation of mutual deterrence.

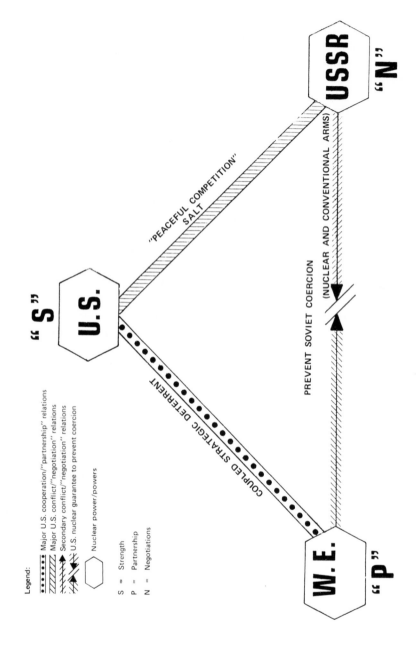

Figure 1-1. Basic Dialectic of Nixon Doctrine: U.S. Strength, Partnership with Western Europe, and Negotiation with USSR

Prevention of Nuclear War as a Limit
on International Relations

Figure 1-2 illustrates the pragmatic or dialectical necessity of preventing nuclear war that operates equally on the United States and the Soviet Union (and on the Western European nations as well). In this concept a basic aim of preventing nuclear war is assumed to be common to all the Western nuclear powers. It sets limits to the use of military force and on the aims of nation states:

1. It sets limits on sovereignty. For example, the Soviet historical insistence on secrecy concerning its military forces has been abridged by the SALT I agreement of May 1972. In this agreement, the United States and the Soviet Union agreed to non-interference with outside means of inspection, which in effect abridges the sovereignty of both states by agreeing to limits on secrecy concerning each other's nuclear forces.

2. It sets limits on expansionist aims of states, particularly in the use of force. In this sense, the dictum of von Clausewitz that "war is an extension of politics by other means" must be modified; there is a requirement for a new international politics that would prevent nuclear war by agreement among all nuclear powers.

Because the nuclear deterrent equation is independent of social systems; i.e., because nuclear war would mean the probable end of the politics of either capitalism or communism, there is no ideological advantage in such a war for one system over another. The Soviet economic system, population, and political system would just as surely be destroyed as those of the United States in an all out nuclear exchange. Hence the aim of preventing nuclear war can be removed from the ideological arena.

Also shown in Figure 1-2 is the concept of mutual assured destruction (MAD) as an historical condition that present strategy has created between the United States and the Soviet Union if all-out nuclear war should occur. However, this historical condition need not commit the two nuclear superpowers to the essentially rigid strategy of MAD; it creates a need for a more stable strategy based on a political concept of mutual assured survival and security (MASS). The MASS concept is therefore necessary as a negotiating (political) aim of the Strategic Arms Limitation Talks (SALT), of the Mutual Balanced Force Reduction (MBFR) talks with respect to forces in Europe, and the Conference on Security and Cooperation in Europe (CSCE). At the root of the MASS concept is a most fundamental statement of self-interest: "I can only assure my own survival and security by assuring you, my adversary, of your survival and security." Such a general concept is necessary as a common negotiating aim between the United States and the Soviet Union and between the Western European powers and the Soviet Union. This is true because no state can

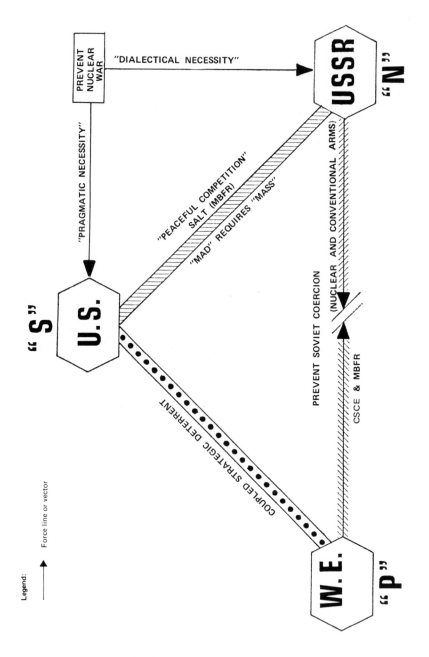

Legend:

——▶ Force line or vector

PREVENT NUCLEAR WAR

"DIALECTICAL NECESSITY"

USSR

"N"

"PRAGMATIC NECESSITY"

"PEACEFUL COMPETITION" SALT (MBFR)

"MAD" REQUIRES "MASS'

"S"

U.S.

PREVENT SOVIET COERCION

(NUCLEAR AND CONVENTIONAL ARMS)

CSCE & MBFR

COUPLED STRATEGIC DETERRENT

W. E.

"P"

Figure 1-2. Dialectical Necessity of Preventing Nuclear War

negotiate its own destruction as a permanent condition or aim of policy; rather it must negotiate the dialectical opposite; namely its own survival and its security. Thus the very destructiveness of nuclear weapons can bring about a new international political order based on a concept of mutual self-interest and mutual survival.

The United States has tended in the past to treat its relationship with the Soviet Union as if the two nation states were two giant weapon systems engaged in a nuclear arms race for superiority. It is now evident that decisive strategic nuclear superiority of one side over the other is no longer an achievable goal if both sides stay in the game. Given this situation, the primary element affecting the outcome is new technology. SALT I in effect codified the basic problem of the arms race; namely, that it had no specific goal except that of denying the other side a strategic superiority that might arise out of a technological breakthrough. Thus both sides have been pursuing essentially a negative or denial strategy; that is, that of preventing the other side from achieving unilaterally an exploitation of new technology. Since neither side has a clear idea of how to formulate or of how to control the so-called technological arms race, it is even more important to concentrate on the development of a new international politics to prevent nuclear war and to avoid confrontations between the major powers that might lead to nuclear war. Thus the Conference on Security and Cooperation in Europe offers an opportunity for both the United States and the Soviet Union to extend the principles of relations between states.[4]

These principles, including those of non-interference between states, provide the basis for a broader set of principles affecting U.S.-Soviet/NATO-Warsaw Pact relations in West European-East European evolution.

In pursuing the goal of mutual assured survival and security, the United States is attempting to strengthen its political-economical and cultural ties with Western Europe, although this situation is fraught with many difficulties: the U.S. imbalanced payments, the problem of stabilizing the international monetary system, the increasing competition from Japan to both the West European and United States economies, international trade, the entrance of Great Britain into the European Economic Community, and other "destabilizing" factors. At the same time, the United States is attempting to enter into economic and trade agreements with the Soviet Union and East European states. Initiatives by other Western states also affect the situation; for example, the Federal Republic of Germany has pursued its *Ostpolitik* and has sought additional bilateral political and economic relations with the USSR.

Vietnam, Eastern Europe, and the Middle East

Figure 1-3 illustrates these three elements as they relate to the U.S.-West European-Soviet triangular relationships.

14

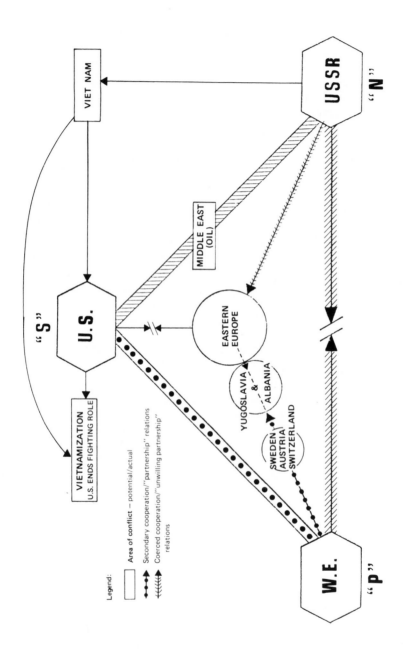

Figure 1-3. Position of Vietnam, the Middle East, and Eastern Europe in U.S.-Soviet Interactions

1. **Vietnam.** The gradual withdrawal of U.S. forces from Vietnam over the past four years in the course of Vietnamization of the defense of South Vietnam, and the end of the U.S. fighting role following the ceasefire agreements of January 1973, removed a major impediment both to the negotiations with the Soviet Union and to the improvement of U.S. relations with its West European partners. Much has been said about Vietnamization and the Vietnam experience, but it is important to make two points in this model of the Nixon Doctrine:

a. While the United States has removed its ground forces from South Vietnam, some capability has been retained for conducting air strikes in Southeast Asia. It is therefore still an area of potential conflict in which forces could be engaged, as in the post-ceasefire bombing of Cambodia. Hence there is a continuing problem in U.S.-Soviet relations as well as in U.S.-Chinese and Chinese-Soviet relations with respect to Southeast Asia and Vietnam. Thus Southeast Asia continues to be an unsettled conflict area in which the interests of the great powers are involved.

b. The profound effect of the Vietnamese war on U.S. domestic politics and on the U.S. view of its role in the world is yet to be fully felt. The Vietnam experience led to the concept of the all-volunteer army and the reduction of the U.S. armed forces. The U.S. Army in particular is undergoing a major reduction in force; this may well affect the stability of the Western European strategic deterrent, since the ground forces are perceived by the Europeans and the Soviets as a major link in the chain of deterrence. A strong effort is being made by the Nixon Administration to overcome the tendency toward neo-isolationism and withdrawal from the world that the American force reduction may suggest. Since the European strategic balance is crucial to the stability of the entire global system envisaged in the Nixon Doctrine, it is imperative that the reduction in force take place in a gradual and well-planned fashion with some corresponding reduction in Soviet forces as well. Hence the necessity for the concept of mutual and balanced force reduction outlined in Figure 1-2.

2. **Eastern Europe.** As illustrated in Figure 1-3, the Soviet Union has given a nuclear guarantee to Eastern Europe *vis-à-vis* the United States, although such a guarantee is not needed inasmuch as the United States long ago gave up the notion of "liberating the satellites" by use of military force. This should be obvious even to the Soviet Union following the non-intervention of the United States in the Hungarian revolt of 1956 and the Soviet occupation of Czechoslovakia in 1968. To a very large extent the East European nations in the Warsaw Pact remain in fact coerced partners with the Soviet Union. Yugoslavia and Albania have undertaken independent foreign policies; Yugoslavia has pulled out of the Warsaw Pact entirely, and the Albanians have aligned themselves with Communist China. In recent years, Romania has also shown an increasing independence in its foreign policy, although it remains internally very much a communist state. It can truly be said that President Nixon's road to Peking led

through Bucharest. Romania's independence is further illustrated by the 1972 invitation to Prime Minister Golda Meir of Israel to visit Bucharest.

Illustrated also in Figure 1-3 are some of the neutrals, particularly Sweden, Austria, and Switzerland, shown in close cooperation relationship with Western Europe. It may be that a neutral position will provide a non-bloc alternative to East European nations that may wish to loosen their ties with the Warsaw Pact without joining NATO. The independent communist states thus may have some "place to go." The possibilities of trade and technical cooperation with the West provide a strong incentive for these states to seek an accommodation with the West without necessarily challenging the security of the Soviet Union. So long as the Soviets see the East European nations as a buffer zone necessary to their security, they may look on Western efforts to establish relations with Eastern Europe as a form of political aggression. Nevertheless the free political movement of the East European states is an intricate and inherent part of the Nixon Doctrine.

3. **The Middle East.** Shown also in Figure 1-3 is the Middle East as a potential conflict area with a parenthetical "oil" shown on the figure. The reason for this is the gradual realization that the possibility is remote that the Arab-Israeli conflict might draw the United States and the Soviet Union into confrontation. On the other hand, the Persian Gulf—with the problem of the competition for oil between the United States, Western Europe, and Japan—might become a source of potential conflict, particularly if the Soviets enter into close relations with other Arab states as they have with the Iraqis. The Middle East is shown on the negotiating line between the West and the Soviet Union and, like Vietnam and Southeast Asia, may become an actual conflict area at any time. Therefore, the Middle East requires constant attention and highly skilled negotiations with the USSR at least into the foreseeable future.

4. **China, Japan, and the Pacific Basin.** Figure 1-4 shows the addition of China as the remaining nuclear power in its negotiating relations with the United States and with the Soviet Union. The Chinese have been genuinely concerned about the possibility of a Sino-Soviet war, particularly the threat of a Soviet nuclear strike. Although the Soviet Union denies any such intent, it certainly has the capability, at least, for a nuclear disarming strike. This is the third area of potential world conflict, in addition to the Middle East and Southeast Asia. It is by far the most dangerous because such a conflict would be between nuclear powers. Yet, in the interpretation of the Nixon Doctrine as developed in this paper, the United States places as much emphasis on the prevention of nuclear war between the Soviet Union and the Peoples Republic of China as it does on a nuclear war in Europe. No one knows whether a Chinese-Soviet conflict could be limited to those two countries. Perhaps it could not. Hence the Peoples Republic of China must be brought into the entire spectrum of negotiations leading to

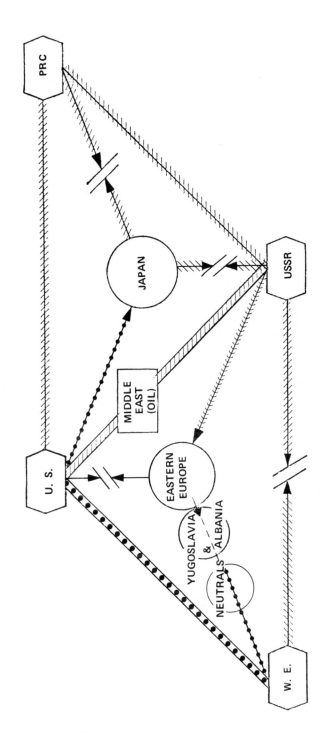

Figure 1-4. PRC and Japan as Part of U.S.-Soviet Negotiations: Multipolarity Begins

an international strategic structure and a new international political system designed to prevent nuclear war and eventually to eliminate the possibility of a nuclear confrontation between the United States and the Soviet Union or between any and all nuclear powers. Since the United States apparently is in a closer relationship with China than China is with the Soviet Union, and because neither Washington nor Peking believe that an American-PRC nuclear confrontation is likely, the potential for an American-Chinese understanding with respect to minimizing the chances of nuclear war between China and the USSR would seem to be greatly improved.

Finally in Figure 1-4, shown within the triangle of relationships among China, the United States, and the Soviet Union, is Japan, with a partnership relationship with the United States and a U.S. nuclear guarantee against both the USSR and the PRC. This nuclear guarantee places Japan in the enviable position of being a major power (part of the multipolar world of five powers described by President Nixon), gaining its international political strength through economic and trading power without the necessity for a large military force, and without an independent nuclear deterrent. Japan (like India) has not signed the non-proliferation treaty and is thus keeping its options open with respect to acquiring a nuclear force in the future. However, Japan has the advantage of being able to play off the United States against Europe and Communist China against the USSR at very little military risk to itself. Japan has a further advantage of being the major source of potential economic capital for both China and the Soviet Union as well as the underdeveloped states in the rest of the world. Hence the two great communist powers are competing for Japanese capital and technological assistance.

Japan has one overwhelming vulnerability in its economic system—that of dependence on Middle East oil and a long sealine of communication without any means to protect the tankers. Japan is dependent on the U.S. naval presence to protect its lifeline from the Persian Gulf through the Indian Ocean to the Eastern Pacific to its own shores. This points up an interesting anomaly; namely, that the two great naval powers, the United States and the Soviet Union, are not the major maritime and trading powers; Japan and Western Europe, which do not have strong navies, are.

**Multipolarity Extended: Latin America, Africa,
Pacific Basin, Indian Subcontinent and
Southeast Asia**

Figure 1-5 shows the general global model of the multipolar world. The lesser developed countries are shown external to the triangular relationships between the nuclear powers, with the existing relationships and certain new ones emerging. They are:

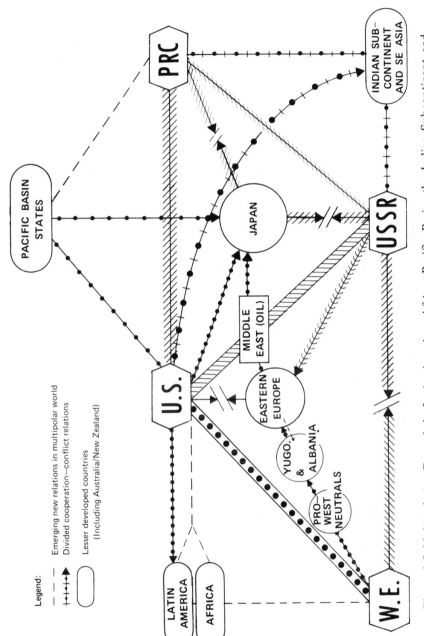

Figure 1-5. Multipolarity Extended: Latin America, Africa, Pacific Basin, the Indian Subcontinent and Southeast Asia

1. **Latin America and Africa.** The chart shows the partnership relationship between Latin America and the United States and the emerging new relationships that Latin America and Africa can and should have. The burden of both of these two continents should be shared with the Western Europeans—and perhaps with Japan—in the interest of providing some form of strategic stability to these underdeveloped areas. The fundamental racial problems in Africa, exacerbated by the inability of the African states to transform themselves from tribal entities into modern states in a single generation, will remain a potential source of conflict for many decades to come. Aside from the strategic importance to the West of the Horn of Africa and the growing Soviet influence over the North African states on the Mediterranean littoral, there are no basic problems in terms of conflicts of interests between the superpowers to bring about a major nuclear confrontation. This situation would also seem to be true for the foreseeable future in Latin America, with the possible exception of the Caribbean. But even here, America has learned to live with communist Cuba. On the positive side, the growth of Brazil's economy is a potential source of stability in the South American continent, particularly if capital from Japan and Western Europe is made available to the Brazilians to supplement their own and U.S. capital. The approach of the Nixon Doctrine is to take a low profile in these areas, with very little implied need to utilize military force to solve political problems.

2. **Pacific Basin States.** With the exception of Australia and New Zealand, the Pacific basin states have severe economic and political problems, particularly the two politically volatile and strategically important island nations of the Philippines and Indonesia. South Korea has shown a marked ability to sustain a high economic growth, but it has also undergone severe internal political stresses as President Park Chung Hee increases his autocratic control. The internal politics of all these Pacific Basin states have been affected by the normalization of U.S. relations with Communist China, formerly regarded as the "enemy" of these lesser states. As the "threat" began to recede, the internal politics of Japan and the other Pacific Basin states radically changed. The martial law imposed on the Philippine government by President Marcos paralleled that of President Park's centralization of power in South Korea. America has found, as did Britain in an earlier day, that parliamentary democracy based on constitutional government is a perishable export to Asia.

3. **The Indian Subcontinent and Southeast Asia.** The lines of divided cooperation and conflict relations with China, the Soviet Union, and the United States are shown. This area of the globe has plagued the United States with its unresolved civil wars, increasing problems of scarcity of resources, such as in India and Bangladesh, and its problems of inherent political instability in all the ex-colonial states, including Pakistan. President Nixon, by his efforts to prevent India from launching total war against Pakistan during the Bangladesh crisis, not

only reinforced his relations with China but set certain limits on the expansionist dreams of the Indians who were emboldened by the support from the Soviet Union. India's nuclear appetite may well grow, as it loses confidence in the Soviet or in the American nuclear guarantee against China, the colossus to the North. China has had one great advantage over India—the Chinese have maintained a social-political system that has been able to cope with poverty in a more organized fashion than the Indian political-economic system has. While the Indian subcontinent and Southeast Asia will remain a potential source of conflict between the great powers, it is probably already tacitly agreed that the Southeast Asian situation cannot be allowed to bring about a confrontation between any of the nuclear powers who have interests in the Pacific and Indian Oceans.

It should be noted in this model that Figure 1-5 illustrates a set of emerging partnership relations between Western Europe, Eastern Europe, and Japan, all connected through their Middle East oil interests and the natural trading relationships that are emerging. For example, Japan may find it to its interest to trade with East European countries and perhaps even to invest in joint enterprises—for example, in Romania. The Nixon Doctrine strongly emphasizes the evolution of international trade and technological exchange carried out through cultural and scientific programs. The development of a strong partnership between Japan, Eastern Europe, and Western Europe is probably actively encouraged by this set of policies.

The Dynamics of the Nixon Doctrine

This global model of the Nixon Doctrine and its dialectical interpretation begs one question: that is, is there such a thing as "victory" for the United States and the free world in its competition without war with the communist world led by the Soviet Union? This is a question that is relevant only when seen in the context of long term prospects for free societies in a world increasingly beset by problems of overpopulation and hunger in the least developed countries, as well as pollution and the decline of the availability of natural resources in the developed countries. The spread of nuclear technology and its availability to many countries, including such small nations as Israel, Switzerland, and Sweden, and the temptation that such nations may have to resort to independent nuclear forces to "protect themselves," may give a different perspective on the meaning of "victory." If some sort of a stable world order—in dynamic equilibrium and still permitting political change, particularly among the underdeveloped nations—can be achieved by cooperation among the Western powers and the Soviet Union and China, then it may be possible to provide for the security of the free nations of the West. In this sense, the Nixon Doctrine, with its goal of a generation of peace, is a shift in emphasis from the U.S. policy of containment through deterrence to a policy of mutual deterrence stressing interactions, where the balance of power and deterrence would be arrived at through a new concept of coexistence. The underlying motivator of the new rules of coexistence would be the mutually perceived requirement to prevent nuclear war.

Prospects for the Future

The 1960s saw America come of age. The limits of U.S. power were learned in Vietnam; Americans learned also that there was a limit to the exploitation of natural resources and the pollution of the land and waters of the continent; they learned from the monetary crises and devaluations of the dollar that there are limits to the strength of the U.S. economy in the global arena. But in learning these limits, Americans need not lose their confidence and retreat to a Nuclear Fortress America. Rather, there can be a return to an earlier vision of America's role in the world, that of making the world safe for democracies without attempting to impose democratic regimes on all the nations of the earth. Another part of the American dream that had to be reappraised was that by setting limits to its own expansionist power the United States could help set limits to the expansionist powers of others, as was done to Germany in the two great world wars of this century. However, the realistic balance of power need not be returned to a vision of international relations dictated by the narrowest set of self-interests. The world has witnessed the overwhelming success of the post-World War II U.S. policies; American generosity toward its former enemies—Japan and Germany—has helped them attain the status of truly global economic powers without the use of military force as a part of their foreign policy.

Therefore, that which would constitute successful attainment of the aims implicit in the Nixon Doctrine as interpreted in this paper would be the emergence of a more peaceful multipolar world in which limits are set to the use of force as the ultimate arbiter of the relations between nation states. It will require the continuous examination of the vision of such a world—a world in which several different social and economic systems can coexist, but a world in which imperialism, whether it be Russian or American or Asiatic, is not only an unattainable state of affairs, but becomes an undesirable way of life in the new international milieu.

What is needed in this new international milieu is indeed a new vision of international order. This vision can be energized not only by the fear of the destructiveness of nuclear war, but also by the positive vision of a pluralist society of men in which each nation state pursues its self-interests and its goals within the limits imposed on all nation states. There can be an acceptance of spheres of influence between the two great superpowers, but not dominion; dominion is not necessary or desirable. In the past it had been assumed that the

Monroe Doctrine gave the United States the right to exclude any "foreign" social system from the Western hemisphere; but certainly the acceptance of both the Cuban and Chilean regimes by President Nixon is an indication that the Monroe Doctrine is viewed with a new realism.

At the same time, the pursuit of independent foreign policies in Eastern European states—as in Romania, and even in such independent economic and social systems as in Yugoslavia—indicates that Soviet dominion has broken down, and that the guarantee of security of the Soviet Union can no longer be based on the hegemony of the Soviets over their East European "satellites."

The Conference on Security and Cooperation in Europe gives the United States an opportunity to take the lead in enunciating the great principles that may underlie the new international politics designed to prevent all-out nuclear war. These principles will certainly include the principles of non-interference in internal affairs of nation states; the renunciation of use of force to change national boundaries; the principle of coexistence of differing social and economic systems; the principle of encouraging trade and technological exchange between all nations whether members of economic blocs as in COMECON and the European Economic Community or independent states such as the neutrals in Europe; the principle implied by most favored nation treatment with respect to trade with the United States; the long-term objective of lowering tariffs; and others.

Finally, the concept of the type of international politics appropriate for the new milieu has implications for the design of military forces. The military posture of the Nixon Doctrine is fundamentally defensive. Specifically, it calls for a new and more comprehensive concept of deterrence, or as the Administration characterizes it, Realistic Deterrence. Heretofore the full potential of Free World strength to make deterrence credible and effective has not been realized. America's massive nuclear strength has not been adequately linked with the remainder of its military capabilities. The Nixon Doctrine is designed to remedy both of these shortcomings.

The Nixon Doctrine defense posture is based upon the concept of the indivisibility of deterrence. It postulates, therefore, a balanced force structure of strategic and theater nuclear weapons and adequate conventional force capabilities.[5] Strategic, theater, and conventional capabilities must be coupled so that the role of strategic weapons is not limited to mass destruction. U.S. and allied forces must be linked in an operational sense, and not merely added up on a balance sheet of Free World forces. The goal is deterrence of conflict at all levels, but a readiness to act if deterrence fails.

To implement such a defense posture forces should be designed for flexibility of action to terminate conflict rapidly, to reach negotiating thresholds where there are options other than escalating to all-out nuclear conflict. This concept is consistent with the necessity described above to supplant the historical condition of mutual assured destruction (MAD) by a doctrine of mutual assured survival and security (MASS).

Requirements for war termination, if deterrence were to fail, would be options short of massive destruction of cities, notably tactical nuclear options based upon the most advanced technology available for effecting target precision and for minimizing collateral damage to population and civil values. These general principles, while they relate primarily to conflict in Europe, also have a relevance to the Asian and other theaters. In every case, the timely, flexible response of U.S. and allied forces has the objective of preventing or quickly terminating conflict.

It is clear that the Nixon Doctrine continues to place Europe and NATO at the top of American foreign policy priorities. The thought expressed by Henry Kissinger, long before he became President Nixon's chief foreign policy adviser, continues to be valid for the new milieu: "If Eurasia were to be dominated by a hostile power or a group of powers, we would confront an overwhelming threat, and the key to Eurasia is Western Europe, because its loss would bring with it the loss of the Middle East and the upheaval of Africa."[6]

There are four general principles regarding the NATO force posture that may be drawn from the Nixon Doctrine as interpreted in this paper; these principles for the design of the NATO force may also well be applicable in the long run to the design of the Warsaw Pact forces and might eventually be acceptable by the USSR. They are:

1. NATO policy should be to provide a valid sense of military security in Western Europe without unduly inhibiting constructive political, economic, and other Western initiatives *vis-à-vis* East Europe and the USSR.
2. More explicitly, NATO's policy to defend Europe is based on deterring any war with the Soviet Union in Western Europe, and if war should come, to terminate it without its enlarging in scope or being prolonged.
3. The NATO force posture should be developed so that it will not appear to the Soviet Union to be designed for preemptive offensive operations, but to be clearly in line with the defensive nature of the NATO alliance.
4. The NATO force posture should be designed for endurance over the long haul, not based on an expectation of fundamental convergence of the two systems, but should try to encourage—and certainly not hamper—a political settlement between the United States and Western Europe on the one hand, and the Soviet Union on the other.

The implications of the Nixon Doctrine for the U.S. military force posture in Asia and other areas where U.S. interests are judged vital, are conceptually similar to the principles stated above, although there would be in these other regions a greater emphasis on sea and air forces. As to U.S. ground forces, although the Nixon Doctrine stresses initial reliance on indigenous ground force response to internal or external aggression, U.S. ground units must be ready to respond where U.S. interests and urgency of the situation require. Close coordination is required among U.S. land, sea, and air forces, as well as cooperation with indigenous forces. The doctrine of rapid conflict termination requires some limited capability for rapid and early response in situations short of general war.

At least a minimum network of overseas bases remains essential for forward deployment. The trend seems to be towards joint basing rights, for political purposes, and to encourage U.S.-allied cooperation. The principles of partnership and burden-sharing imply that regional security groupings of Free World nations should be encouraged to enhance a regional sense of security responsibility and capability.

Overall, the military planning implications of the Nixon Doctrine must be interpreted with the understanding that the new American foreign policy was designed to cope with a time of transition as well as with the longer term. Today's security requirements are much more complex than they were in the Cold War era now apparently ending. The new requirement, if America is to stay the course, is for orchestrating all the elements of national strength—political, economic, technological, social, psychological, as well as military—into a composite of total political power for peace.

Notes

1. See Richard M. Nixon, *U.S. Strategy for the 1970s: A New Strategy for Peace*, (Washington, D.C.: U.S. Government Printing Office, February 18, 1970); *U.S. Strategy for Peace: Building for Peace*, (Washington, D.C.: U.S. Government Printing Office, February 1971); and *U.S. Strategy for Peace, the Emerging Structure of Peace*, (Washington, D.C.: U.S. Government Printing Office, February 9, 1972).

2. See Melvin R. Laird, *Fiscal Year 1971 Defense Program and Budget*, (Washington, D.C.: U.S. Government Printing Office, February 25, 1970); *Fiscal Year 1972-1976 Defense Program and the 1972 Defense Budget* (Washington, D.C.: U.S. Government Printing Office, March 9, 1971); *Annual Defense Department Report FY 1973*, (Washington, D.C.: U.S. Government Printing Office, February 15, 1972).

3. See H.F. Scott, *Soviet Military Doctrine: Its Formulation and Dissemination*, Technical Note SSC-TN-8974-27, (Menlo Park, California: Stanford Research Institute/Strategic Studies Center, June 17, 1971); see also, H.F. Scott, *Soviet Military Doctrine: Its Continuity, 1969-1970*, Technical Note SSC-TN-8974-28, (Menlo Park, California: Stanford Research Institute/Strategic Studies Center, June 17, 1971).

4. A Joint Declaration of the U.S. and the Soviet Union of May 29, 1972.

5. Laird, *Defense Department Report FY 1973*, op. cit., p. 24.

6. Henry Kissinger, *Nuclear Weapons and Foreign Policy* (New York: Harper, 1957), pp. 269-270.

Part II:
The New Milieu: The U.S.-
European Partnership

For an assessment of Europe's role in the new international milieu, the symposium co-sponsors turned to three distinguished Europeans: General André Beaufre, Dr. Werner Kaltefleiter, and Air Vice-Marshal Stewart W.B. Menaul.

General Beaufre, French Army, Retired, is the founder and Director of the French Institute for Strategic Studies. His military career included combat command assignments in Europe and Africa in World War II, Indochina in 1947, and Egypt in 1956. A former member of the staff of SHAPE, his last military assignment was as Head of the French Delegation to the Permanent North Atlantic Treaty Group in Washington in 1960. General Beaufre is an internationally recognized French political-military strategist and is the author of many articles and books on strategy and international affairs.

Dr. Kaltefleiter is Professor of Political Science and Director of the Seminar for the Science and History of Politics at the University of Kiel. He is also Director of the Social Science Research Institute of the Konrad Adenauer Foundation. A Research Fellow at Harvard University, 1968-1969, Dr. Kaltefleiter has lectured and taught at the University of Cologne, the University of Saarbrücken, and the University of Kiel. He is a member of several German associations dealing with political science and foreign affairs and has written numerous books and articles dealing with German internal politics and international affairs.

Air Vice-Marshal Menaul, British Royal Air Force, Retired, is Director-General of the Royal United Services Institute for Defense Studies, London, England. His last military assignment, after a long and distinguished career, was as Commandant, Joint Services Staff Corps. Marshal Menaul specializes in planning and projections for strategy.

While their papers contain significant differences in emphasis, General Beaufre, Dr. Kaltefleiter, and Air Vice-Marshal Menaul share a common concern that the fluid situation in Europe at the present poses grave risks for Europe's future. They believe that the opportunities for promoting greater European integration must be seized if the European states are to offset the growing military power and political influence of the Soviet Union.

2

A Study of European-U.S. Cooperation[a]

Gen. André Beaufre

The present period is a most critical one for Western Europe, which is faced with problems in separate yet related areas; important among these are East-West relations, the question of European unity, and relations with the United States. The answers to be found to these problems will help determine the future of Europe.

It is the thesis of this paper that desirable solutions cannot be found to these issues unless the European allies can agree, first among themselves and then with the Americans, upon a joint strategy to achieve a secure and independent Europe.

The Situation in Europe

The European situation is governed by the interaction of three factors. First, the Soviet Union has attained strategic nuclear parity with the United States. The recent SALT agreements officially recognized this strategic situation. The consequence of this development is that the U.S.-Soviet strategic forces neutralize each other. It is becoming increasingly difficult to apply nuclear deterrence for the protection of powers other than the United States and the Soviet Union. For Europe, this means that the extended deterrent of the U.S. strategic forces, which has protected Europe in the past, is now disappearing. Such a situation carries with it the possibility that an adversary might be tempted to seek a political decision in Europe by means of limited aggression with conventional forces aimed at a quick local victory, which could then be exploited psychologically.

Second, the European Economic Community (EEC) has become an economic giant. The recent addition of Britain, Denmark, and Ireland has increased the economic strength of the EEC. At the same time, however, it is a political and military pigmy. The economic strength of the European Community rivals that of the United States and the Soviet Union, yet it is dwarfed by their military and political power.

Third, the Soviets now have a considerable military force stationed in Eastern

[a]The ideas expressed herein are entirely personal and do not necessarily reflect the opinion of the French Government.

29

Europe. This situation, combined with the fact of Soviet attainment of increased overall military strength in nuclear, naval, and conventional forces, makes it impossible, in the near future, for Western Europe alone to counterbalance this provocative military situation.

Hypotheses for the Future

The results of the interaction of these factors are difficult to predict. However, several hypotheses concerning the future of European unity and Europe's relations with the U.S. and the USSR should be considered. The first hypothesis is that Europe will develop along independent lines, becoming a major economic, political, and strategic power, linked with both the United States and the Soviet Union through a collective security system. This is the most desirable future for Europe.

For this to take place, several conditions must be met. Europe must rapidly establish its unity in order to arrive at common policies before international events overtake it. Simultaneously, it must remain linked with the United States. The maintenance of American cooperation in military security is necessary to provide a secure framework for the establishment of European unity. Lastly, this process must be implemented without antagonizing the Soviets. They would never agree to a European unity developing in such a way as to present an immediate and visible danger to the East.

For example, a European unity built on the basis of a revitalization of NATO would have no chance of acceptance by the Soviets. In their view, this would not only jeopardize peace and security, but would create a "rebirth of dangerous tensions." This consideration precludes spectacular measures being taken within the NATO framework. Thus, the development of a desirable European future also depends on a Europe linked with the Soviet Union.

A new formula for West European unity also offers the Soviet Union some advantages. Only a strong and coherent Western Europe can disengage itself from American tutelage, and only this kind of Europe can enter into security accords with the East without fear of "Finlandization."

A second hypothesis for a European future stems from possible European-American economic rivalry. There is a tendency in the United States to emphasize the economic danger of Europe. This is a mistake, because the economic might of the United States is in its internal market, not in its external trade. If economic conflicts are allowed to override other interests, the resulting rivalry would lead to a Europe developing along either of two paths:

(1) The rivalry could result in the economic subjugation of Europe by the United States. If the United States would then continue to maintain a substantial military force in Europe, the American economic and military

protectorate of Europe would be complete. The preponderant economic and military power in Western Europe would be held by the United States. This would probably cause Soviet opposition and a limited return to the Cold War in Europe would seem likely.

(2) Economic rivalry could also result in a quite different development. If economic issues become paramount, and if the United States reduces its military force in Europe because of economic and domestic pressures, Europe would, in whole or in part, slide into the Soviet orbit. The Soviets would be able to exert political pressure backed by military preponderance, and the Europeans, lacking military power and U.S. support, would be forced to accommodate themselves to Soviet demands. The resulting "Finlandization" of Western Europe would be a major success for the Soviet Union and a catastrophe for the West.

The third hypothesis is a variant of the second. Conflict caused by American fears of the European economic threat, combined with Soviet exploitation of European divergencies in the current international negotiations (the European security conference, MBFR, and SALT II), could lead to the following situation: The Soviets would find it possible to exploit the current German *Ostpolitik* to draw West Germany into the Soviet orbit. The Germans, depending upon Soviet good will for the success of their *Ostpolitik*, lacking American military support, and finding little unity in Western Europe, would find it very easy to slide to the East. The Soviets could also exploit the instability in Yugoslavia and draw that nation into its orbit. Greece and Turkey would then be increasingly vulnerable to Soviet pressures.

These events would leave the remaining nations of Western Europe completely disorganized; the hope for European unity and security would be stillborn. The remaining separate nations of Western Europe would become either an American bridgehead, under the protection of an American military umbrella, or a Russian bridgehead—a neutralized zone—subject to the political influence of the USSR. This would be the worst possible future for the United States and for Western Europe; only the Soviet Union would benefit.

The conclusion to be drawn from the preceding hypotheses is that the economic problems posed to the United States by Europe are not as important as the political stake that America has in Europe. Economic problems between Europe and the United States must be relegated to secondary importance. The primary concern of Europe and the United States must be to decide upon measures needed to bring about the realization of the first hypothesis—an independent Europe linked with both the United States and the USSR through a collective security system. Only this future appears advantageous for both Europe and the United States. A future leading toward either an American protectorate of Europe or the "Finlandization" of Europe under the aegis of the Soviet Union would be detrimental to the interests of both Europe and the United States.

Developing a Joint Strategy

To realize a desirable future for Europe, a joint strategy must be adopted by the Western allies. This strategy should focus on three areas: negotiations with the East; Western defense strategy; and the future development of a European defense command designed to take over NATO's responsibilities in Europe.

The most immediate problem facing the West is the need to avoid the present dangers of the present East-West negotiations—the Conference on Security and Cooperation in Europe, talks on Mutual and Balanced Force Reductions, and SALT II. To avoid these dangers, the West must firmly seize the initiative. This needs to be done in order to limit Soviet flexibility in these negotiations and to show the Soviets that a unified Europe need not threaten them. The West should propose a comprehensive set of security agreements on the political level; this would reinforce the relaxation of tensions already achieved in Europe. Europe and the United States can advance proposals on non-aggression, renunciation of the use of force, and non-interference in the internal affairs of other states. These proposals need not be Russian aims; they can also be Western aims. By the same token, the West can propose some type of collective security pact among the European states, a pact which would reflect the Western position, not the Russian position.

These proposals, reflecting the aims and positions of Western Europe and the United States, would increase the flexibility of the Western negotiating position and would deprive the Russians of issues which could potentially divide NATO. The Russians would also be shown that Europe does want to continue the process of détente and that Europe does not present a visible and immediate danger to the interests of the Soviet Union.

In the present negotiations, the focus should be on political issues. Bargaining over force levels in Europe should be avoided or deferred, for this could only lead to the creation of a special status for Central Europe, thereby destroying the prospects for a unified Western European strategy. If, however, the force level question must be dealt with, a substantial reduction in offensive forces (for example, tanks and aircraft) should be given first priority.

In the area of Western defense strategy, it is vital that a system of military deterrence in Europe be rebuilt, a system designed to replace the indirect strategic deterrent of the United States. This indirect strategic deterrent has been almost neutralized by the SALT I agreements. The serious gap in the deterrent in Europe which has now been created is being further aggravated by the prospect of a reduction in the American forces stationed in Europe. Measures are needed to recreate both a tactical and a strategic deterrent in Western Europe.

On the tactical level, a slight modification of the current NATO strategy could help close this gap and rebuild deterrence. The current NATO strategy of "flexible response" is a product of the Kennedy-McNamara years. In an effort to raise the nuclear threshold in the event of conflict in Europe, Kennedy and

McNamara chose a strategy primarily based on conventional defense. This strategy proposed that tactical nuclear weapons would be used only in case of absolute necessity and as late as possible. Such a limited nuclear defense would be territorially limited to Europe. The flexible response strategy still governs the defense of the NATO nations.

Yet it is no longer a sufficient deterrent against limited conventional aggression in Europe. The uncertainty, created by the flexible response strategy, that tactical nuclear weapons would be used at all could lead an adversary to believe that a conventional attack against Europe would not lead to nuclear reprisals. Moreover, the present imbalance of conventional military forces in Europe, especially considering the possibility of a reduced American contingent, gives the Warsaw Pact a great advantage if it decides to launch a limited conventional attack aimed at a quick local victory. It must also be remembered that the nature of conventional warfare nowadays gives the advantage to the offensive. The weaker Western conventional forces could not stop such an attack. The NATO decision to employ tactical nuclear weapons may be taken too late—after the defeat of its conventional forces. The local battle would be won by the Warsaw Pact, and the Soviets could then exploit this victory psychologically to gain political advantage in Europe.

To rectify this situation, NATO should adopt the principle of early use of tactical nuclear weapons in the event of aggression. This should be declared clearly and unequivocally, so that there would be no uncertainty as to when tactical nuclear weapons would be used; that is, that they would be used at the very outset of aggression. The declared intention to use tactical nuclear weapons in this manner, as a defense against aggression, would act as a deterrent against such aggression. The adversary would be denied all expectation of seeking a quick local victory by conventional aggression. He would know that he is embarking on a dangerous adventure and that he could not hope to avoid at the least a limited nuclear confrontation, which would banish all hope of achieving an early and easy success. Thus by the open declaration of this new strategy, the cohesion of tactical deterrence, destroyed by the doctrine of "flexible response," would be reestablished.

A system of regional strategic deterrence in Europe must also be constructed. A European nuclear force could assure this deterrence; however, this is far in the future, for it will take many years to create a sovereign European authority. In the interim, the existing strategic forces of France and Britain can be developed to provide the necessary regional deterrence. It is not necessary to bring all three Western forces under one centralized command. French-British nuclear cooperation outside the American command and control system would permit the creation of a force capable of deterring Soviet use of MRBMs against Europe. The threat of using this strategic force would be more credible than the U.S. threat to use its strategic forces for the defense of Europe, because France and Britain are European nations. By creating the risk of an autonomous use of their forces against the USSR, Britain and France would strengthen the regional strategic deterrence of Europe. Instead of one strategic force under one control, the Soviets would be faced with three forces under three control systems. French and British cooperation in developing their forces would create a visible link between the European and American strategic deterrents. Naturally, the decision to use these weapons would remain national.

A final step that should be taken in the field of military strategy is to establish, as soon as possible, a European center of strategic thinking. This organization, which could be established within the framework of the WEU (Western European Union), would have the responsibility for conceiving and developing a unified West European strategy. It is important that this be done soon, because there is presently no agreement within Europe on a concept of European security.

The West Europeans are entering a difficult period of negotiations with the Eastern bloc, yet they cannot agree upon desirable policies and a common strategy. This can only work to the advantage of the Soviets, who may be able to gain major concessions at these conferences if the West does not come to some agreement on what it wants. Some Europeans cling desperately to the idea of NATO, disregarding the difficulties of this dependent relationship, because they still have confidence in the American nuclear umbrella. Some place their hopes in the development of European nuclear forces, others on the strengthening of conventional forces. There are some who view European integration as a panacea; others view this as a dangerous and unacceptable solution. This diversity of views is dangerous.

The development of a European center of strategic thinking would force these issues into open confrontation, which would dissipate dangerous illusions and allow for a concerted formulation of the necessary solutions to the problems facing all Europeans.

The center would also be responsible for developing concrete programs for European cooperation in security affairs. For example, a common market in armaments is needed in order to standardize military equipment used by the various European allies. Only through standardization of military equipment will Europe be able to obtain the economies of scale necessary for procuring expensive modern weapons systems.

The last element in the development of a joint strategy will take place in the future. At some later stage, the European organ emerging from the evolution of this center of strategic thinking within the WEU would be transformed into a European supreme command, and NATO's responsibilities in Europe would be transferred to this command. This is feasible if Europe attains a sufficient degree of political unity and if a common strategy can be worked out. Such a system would not involve military integration of forces in Europe, except perhaps in certain technological fields, but rather an eventual coordination of national forces. It is possible that at this stage the evolution of relations with the East will permit the organization of a true East-West collective security system, allowing substantial disarmament by reducing the offensive capability of the conventional forces, while reinforcing their defensive capability and maintaining the necessary regional systems of deterrence.

Conclusion

The success of the proposed European strategy rests first of all on agreement among Europeans themselves, and they are now far from such agreement. This is why a European center of strategic thinking is urgently needed.

It also rests on the ability of the Europeans and Americans to agree. Up to now, the relationship between Europe and America has been one of American leadership. This is not the fault of the Americans. In the 1950s, Europeans thought that the guarantees provided by the NATO treaty were so small that they wanted to engage the United States in the defense of Europe to the greatest possible extent. So Europe gave the Americans all the positions, all the commands, all the responsibilities.

But now nothing will be realized without a profound reform of the diplomatic and strategic methods that have characterized relations between the USA and the European allies. The "Partnership," so often acclaimed since Kennedy, was in fact never more than U.S. leadership. Partnership ("association" in French) already exists in NATO. What is now needed is to transform this partnership into real collaboration, or rather cooperation. Decisions of international significance must be based on reciprocal consultations and acceptance of compromise.

Only at this price will the USA and the West European nations be able to avoid the precipitous path of ill-fated decisions and develop a common action to promote the best solutions to the problems facing the Western allies.

3

Europe and the Nixon Doctrine: A German Point of View[a]

Werner Kaltefleiter

In Washington, the second phase in the implementation of the Nixon Doctrine is generally known as the "Year of Europe." Whatever the details of this shift of emphasis in the American world outlook, the United States will be unable to secure its objectives unless it can find partners on the other side of the Atlantic who have the interest, capability, and willingness to respond favorably to the U.S. initiative. An analysis of the European scene suggests that U.S. leaders should be prepared for a disappointing response. The situation differs from country to country. As far as the Federal Republic of Germany is concerned, there is little chance that policies designed primarily to strengthen the Atlantic Alliance will be pursued. This reluctance can be attributed to a combination of three factors: (1) the dependence of the Bonn regime on the "milieu of détente," largely controlled by Moscow; (2) a revival of a "national approach" to foreign policy; and (3) a general decrease in the perception of threat from the East and in the Atlantic orientation of the German electorate, together with a revival of radical socialism in the ruling Social Democratic Party.

Under these circumstances, if the Western alliance is to be strengthened in accordance with the Nixon Doctrine, a prerequisite in the Federal Republic is the creation of a new domestic consensus for an alliance-oriented foreign policy.

The Meaning of the Nixon Doctrine for Europe

With regard to Europe, the Nixon Doctrine, as it has been articulated since 1970, appears to be based on four assumptions:

(1) There is a Soviet threat to Western Europe as well as to the United States.

(2) This threat is more complex and variegated today than it seemed to be in the 1950s and even the 1960s. It affects various cooperative relationships between the United States and Western Europe on the one hand, and between the Soviet Union and associated communist bloc countries on the other.

[a]The author acknowledges the assistance of Marcus Kreis and Barbara Koenitz of the Social Science Research Institute, Konrad Adenauer Foundation, who read an early draft of the manuscript and offered valuable suggestions.

37

(3) Like the United States, the West European countries are interested in taking advantage of the opportunities offered by East-West cooperation. This interest focuses on three objectives: (a) long-term stabilization of foreign trade, particularly for slow-growth industries, through trade agreements with centrally directed economies; (b) budget savings through agreements on arms limitations; and (c) creation of a general "climate of détente" as a precondition for objectives (a) and (b) and partly for reasons of domestic policy and electoral campaign tactics.

(4) The distribution of the defense burden in the Atlantic Alliance will be determined by the performance levels and the benefit expectations of the partner states.[1]

Expressed more simply, the Nixon Doctrine, in its application to Europe, attempts to adapt the old NATO structure to the conditions likely to prevail in 1975—primarily to the altered perception of conflict and to the changes in economic strength, political influence, and military power of the partner states. The analysis of the Western alliance on which this adaptation is based can be traced back to Dr. Henry Kissinger's writings on this topic, especially his book *The Troubled Partnership*, which appeared in 1965.[2] The point of departure for Kissinger's study was an emerging scenario featuring changed power relationships among the NATO countries (mainly with respect to relative economic perform-ances) and growing doubts in Western Europe (partly in reaction to American behavior, partly because of de Gaulle's influence) concerning the willingness of the United States to defend Western Europe at all levels of escalation. Kissinger's answer in 1965 was consistent with his earlier thesis: There is no alternative to West European unification, where unification is not holistically understood but rather is a process of piecemeal engineering[3] growing out of the need to pool military and economic resources in order to achieve a balanced structure in the NATO alliance.

From the American point of view, such a structure would allow for more acceptable burden-sharing in the alliance, and from the European viewpoint, it would redress the unsatisfactory one-sidedness of decision-making in the alli-ance. It would also facilitate the introduction and control of adequate weapons systems, including small and clean nuclear weapons for the defense of Western Europe and the building of a European deterrent force that would be effective in combination with U.S. forces. The Nixon Doctrine describes these goals by putting the terms "strength" and "partnership" side by side, though both must fit within the framework of the new, partially cooperative concert of states in the international system.[4] "Strength" and "partnership" prepare the way for "negotiations," and together these form the three pillars of the Nixon Doc-trine.[5] Nor, even less than at the time NATO was established, when General Marshall defined its objective as one of "negotiating from a position of strength," is strength an end in itself. Rather, strength is perceived as the avenue to successful negotiations.

This seems to be a closed analytical model and at the same time a remarkable example of the translation of social scientific knowledge into political action. However, the implementation of the doctrine raises certain difficulties, for while it is addressed to Europe in the early 1970s, it is based essentially on an analysis that dates to the early 1960s. The European "partners" are no longer the same as they were when they confronted the United States ten years ago. This applies in varying degrees to the individual countries of Western Europe, and particularly to the Federal Republic of Germany.

Domestic Structure and Foreign Policy in the Federal Republic

Elements of Ostpolitik

The Federal Republic is engaged in a policy generally known as *Ostpolitik*. Based on the confirmation of the status quo in Europe, it aims at creating a climate of détente in order to establish a "new order" in Europe under the auspices of "peaceful coexistence" or "cooperation." A glaring defect of the policy, as well as of the analysis on which it is based, is the fact that it employs such vague terms. For example, what is the status quo in Europe? For East Germany "recognition" means an upgrading of its diplomatic status in international law. What does "détente" signify: Is it a goal or an instrument of policy? What are the objectives of the "reorganization of Europe" and "peaceful coexistence"? This is only a sampling of the ambiguous terms used in this context.

Sifting through the ambiguity, we may arrive at the following interpretation: In the postwar period, West German policy toward the "German Question" had employed certain "instruments" to reach its "goals." Among the instruments were (1) nonrecognition of the German Democratic Republic (GDR) and the Oder-Neisse border, and (2) an insistence that the Four Allies exercise effective responsibility for all of Berlin and Germany. The goals were: (1) to achieve the freedom of the German people in the East; and (2) eventually to reunify the two Germanys in a democratic system. These goals have now been abandoned because—as "possession goals"—they did not correspond to the existing situation. They were abandoned for the "milieu goal" of détente in order to achieve a reorganization of Europe, without making clear whether the latter was a "possession goal" or only a continuation of the "milieu goal" of détente.[6] As a first practical result of the détente policy, some improvement in the travel arrangements for movement between the Federal Republic and West Berlin, from West Berlin to East Berlin, and from West Germany to East Germany has been achieved.

The first phase of Bonn's new policy was supported, or at least acquiesced to, by the American government because it promised to remove the burden of permanent crisis in Europe, and the responsibilities and risks connected with crisis, from American shoulders. Understandably, in the United States the responsibilities undertaken in the 1950s had grown to be an encumbrance, and not only for domestic reasons. Moreover, with the apparent lessening of the Soviet threat, the "German responsibilities" assumed by NATO—nonrecognition of Germany's eastern borders, particularly of the Oder-Neisse line, reservations with respect to reunification, the four-power obligations in Berlin, and non-recognition of the GDR—had found even less support in West European countries. Through the first phase of *Ostpolitik*, the Federal Republic has in effect released its allies from these obligations, and clearly Germany's partners see no reason to represent German interests more intensely than the German government itself. At the same time, the steps taken by Bonn were in apparent consonance with the alliance position. To many observers and governments the abandonment of the Federal Republic's traditional position seemed even to expand the alliance's freedom of action in exploiting opportunities for coopera-tion with the Soviet Union.[7] Confirmation of this was seen in the apparent interdependence of the German *Ostpolitik* and Soviet-American negotiations.

Ostpolitik is now a fact of international affairs. Historians will debate who gained the advantage and whether Chancellor Brandt, or any other Chancellor at any other time, could have made a better bargain. But what is important for political leaders today is this question: What are the implications of past *Ostpolitik* decisions for the future of the FRG foreign policy and the Atlantic Alliance?

One possibility is that after the status quo has been recognized *Ostpolitik* will come to its "natural" end with the entry of the two Germanys into the UN. Yet, how long the milieu of détente thus created will last can hardly be controlled by the Federal Republic. Even under the three-cornered political system of the United States, China, and the USSR, control of the détente, as far as Europe and the Federal Republic are concerned, is largely in the hands of Soviet leaders. For example, if the Federal Republic should decide to play an active role in the reorganization of NATO along the lines prescribed by the Nixon Doctrine—say, in the creation of a viable West European defense community—the Soviet Union could easily end (or threaten to end) détente[8] with the charge that such behavior by the Federal Republic represented a reversion to the old "aggressive" ways.[9] Thus far, *Ostpolitik* has consisted of an asymmetrical exchange of "recognition" for "détente"—asymmetrical because in contrast with détente, recognition of the status quo cannot be taken back. "Possession goals" have been traded for "milieu goals."[10]

This asymmetry bears on FRG domestic factors. A successful détente policy is important to the Brandt Government's continued dominance in politics, including the position of the Brandt wing within the SPD. Brandt's electoral success on November 19, 1972, cannot be interpreted as a plebiscite for *Ostpolitik*, but there is no question that the eastern policies contributed considerably to the government's image of competence and credibility among the electorate, and especially the mass media, and diverted attention from domestic problems. As Table 3-1 shows, foreign policy, i.e., *Ostpolitik*, is the field in which the SPD scores best.

For the future, there are tendencies toward sharpening conflicts on the domestic scene—for example, over budgets, tax policy, and codetermination—that will increase the government's political dependence on foreign policy successes, primarily in the area of détente. The upshot may be that the alternative of ending an active *Ostpolitik* and resuming an active alliance policy, at the risk of creating a new climate of tension, is foreclosed for the Brandt government. Maintenance of the climate of détente was promised to the electorate and represents the coalition government's primary claim to continued power. Willy Brandt, describing his government's objectives, defined the milieu of détente as peace when he pointed out: "Peace in Europe has been strengthened through our work. This peace is today as it was yesterday the clear will of the German people and the basic element of our interest."[11] The Federal government will try to avoid any strain on the developing détente—including even the appearance in the German press of articles critical of events in the GDR.[12] This dependence on the milieu of détente can be overcome only by mobilizing public support in other political fields, for instance in successful economic or—this is quite improbable—European policies. However, the German electorate's perception of the ineffectiveness of German parties in solving political problems (see Table 3-1) and the built-in conflict between the coalition partners, the SPD and the FDP (Free Democratic Party), render such a strategy unlikely, at least for the short-term future.

The constellation now obtaining in domestic politics forces the Federal government to pursue *Ostpolitik*. Thus, the question of its likely content becomes critical. It is academic whether a continuation of *Ostpolitik* beyond the exchange of recognition for détente was conceived from the beginning[13] (in German politics there are differing interpretations of *Ostpolitik* and differing "foreign policy schools," particularly within the SPD) or whether continuation of this policy can be explained by the requirements of domestic politics alone.

Table 3-1
Which Party Can Best Solve These Political Tasks? (Figures in Percentages)

	Price Stability		Foreign Policy		Culture, Schools, Science	
	1969	1972	1969	1972	1969	1972
CDU/CSU	24	41	28	26	28	33
SPD	40	19	42	50	35	34

Source: *Allensbacher Berichte*, 1972, No. 30.

The important fact is that the continuation of *Ostpolitik* must be viewed within the framework of a comprehensive concept of European reorganization. That concept is oriented toward a new system of European nations—an "international structure of peace in Europe," as Brandt pointed out.[14]

The linkages with the United States and the Soviet Union can be organized in a variety of ways. Conceivably, the Federal Republic could stay faithful to its declared aim of remaining a loyal member of the Western alliance, which has been underlined by Brandt several times,[15] while at the same time maximizing the possibilities of cooperation with the East. In Brandt's words: "The Alliance . . . provides the support for our policy of détente *vis-à-vis* the East. . . . We will look for broad cooperation in the economic, scientific-technological, and cultural fields with the East European countries."[16] As has been suggested, however, given the political dependence of the Brandt government on détente—and therefore on the Soviet interpretation of détente—it is unlikely that even a "minimum" *Ostpolitik* will allow for strong West German participation in NATO, regardless of the Federal government's wishes.[17]

At the other extreme is the goal, advanced mainly by the left wing of the SPD, of a largely neutral and denuclearized Federal Republic in Central Europe,[18] with its independence to be guaranteed by the United States and the Soviet Union, the American presence far removed, and the Soviet presence almost within reach.[19]

Between the two extremes lies a range of intermediate positions and goals. While it is difficult to determine with confidence just what the present intentions of the Bonn government are, or what may be its precise ideas regarding a reshaping of Europe, there seems little doubt that the reorganization of Central Europe is the chosen arena of German politics.[20] This choice seems to be compatible with the goals of the Soviet Union[21]—at least for the time being—and thus provides the basis for maintaining the climate of détente during the second phase of *Ostpolitik*. What the European political system will look like in the end will be influenced not only by decisions in Bonn, but also by the actions of the Soviet Union, the United States, and the other countries concerned. In theory, there is no inherent contradiction between a West German policy of cooperation with the Soviet Union and the Nixon Doctrine's concept of a U.S.-West European partnership against a Soviet threat. In practical terms, however, the continuation of *Ostpolitik* places an increasing premium on the reorganization of Central Europe as the target arena of German policies, whereas the Nixon Doctrine attaches primary importance to the reorganization of Western Europe as the prerequisite of Atlantic partnership. In practice, therefore, the two concepts are incompatible. Egon Bahr, Special Minister in the new Brandt cabinet and the acknowledged "architect" of *Ostpolitik*, has stated quite openly that the political unification of Western Europe would be inconsistent with the successful conduct of *Ostpolitik*.[22]

This is not to say that the Federal government will leave NATO or take any similarly dramatic steps in the foreseeable future. The strategy, tactics, and declared policies of the Brandt government are characterized by the fact that they aim only at an ostensibly positive goal: a "peaceful order for Europe" (*Friedensordnung für Europa*). There is no need to express negative goals or to exercise a categorical choice between *Westpolitik* and *Ostpolitik*. The NATO alliance can be frozen, and West European political integration be put to sleep, while policy is concentrated in the East—which is quite compatible with progress in West European economic cooperation or even integration. Brandt implied as much when he stated that European unification was not a problem of this century.[23]

To cite another example, the MBFR talks are a round of negotiations involving NATO, but for *Ostpolitik* they represent more than simply the prospect of lessened tensions and accommodation between the two alliances; they represent a step toward a *Friedensordnung in Europa*. The participation of the United States in the Conference on Security and Cooperation in Europe is intended to give Washington the chance to influence developments in Central Europe so that they do not damage U.S. basic interests—and those of the Western alliance—but the continued influence of the United States in shaping these events should not be overestimated. For one thing, trends in the U.S. Congress make it extremely difficult for any U.S. Administration to resist a development in Europe that goes under the name of "peace settlement."

The Revival of a National Approach
to Foreign Policy

Ever since 1948, the debate over the Federal Republic's foreign policy has reflected the clash of two competing prescriptions that may be called the Bismarckian and the Stresemannian concepts.[24] Adenauer pressed Stresemann's concept to its ultimate conclusion when he saw to it that the Federal Republic—much better suited in this respect than the Weimar Republic because of geography and the overwhelming threat to Weimar's constitutional order— became part of the system of free Western nations. An important motive for integrating Germany in the NATO alliance was to prevent for all time a new national definition of Germany's interests, which Adenauer feared might endanger domestic freedom and international peace. The foreign policy orienta- tion was thus determined by the internal constitutional order. The long-term objective was to protect the constitution, which meant, first of all, in the short term, limiting the Federal Republic's policies to the procedural or "instru- mental" aim of equal partnership in Western Europe's society of free nations.[25] Participation in the alliance was the instrument to secure democracy and to exclude a national definition of interests.[26] Toward this end, Adenauer obtained the majority consensus of his country in 1953 and 1957.

These goals of German foreign policy, long-term as well as short-term, seemed to have been achieved with the formal entry of the Federal Republic into NATO. Attainment of the goal of equal partnership was signaled, for example, by the equal participation of the Federal Republic in the formation of the EEC. When the procedural aim was achieved, the long-term goal, namely, the security of the established democratic order, also seemed to be assured. NATO membership was represented as the "guarantee" of Germany's free constitution. But with this accomplished, the question of the objectives of German foreign policy was soon raised again. Adenauer's persistent repetition of the old aims (along with his almost stereotyped warnings that "never has the situation been so serious . . .") became less and less persuasive—all the more so when the Berlin Wall in 1961 seemed to put his whole concept in question. Moreover, the foreign policies then being pursued by important partners in the alliance, particularly by France under de Gaulle and by the United States after Kennedy took office, seemed to throw Adenauer's concept out of date.

The change confronted the entire alliance with a structural problem, but in no country was it as pronounced as in the Federal Republic. The political implication of an alliance-oriented foreign policy is that the respective countries are limited to the pursuit of procedural goals—that is, to active participation in the alliance—while the alliance as a whole determines substantive policy. Since the late 1950s, however, the Western alliance has been stagnating, particularly with respect to the central task of defining policy aims. The United States' unilateral search for cooperation with the Soviet Union on nuclear questions and the American engagement in Southeast Asia, as well as the Gaullist approach to foreign policy, were determining factors in this stagnation. Consequently, the individual member countries had either to accept a state of aimlessness in their foreign policies—a condition that can be maintained for only a short while in the face of domestic political requirements—or to proceed in the direction of a national definition of goals.

There may be objections to this formulation on the grounds that the NATO alliance is not comprehensive enough to have as a goal or a function the definition of its members' foreign policy aims. But it is precisely this restrictive interpretation of the alliance, correct though it may be from the legalistic standpoint, that has given rise to the structural problems of NATO. Security policy is at the heart of foreign policy, and an alliance that is limited strictly to military strategy is likely to be as inefficient in its way as economic integration is when it is limited to sectors.

The United States and France, in differing ways, were the leaders of the trend in the alliance toward a national definition of national interests. The Federal Republic followed, but hesitantly. No other NATO country had integrated its foreign policies into the alliance as fully and fervently as the Federal Republic—a fact attributable to West Germany's exposed position relative to the postwar threat, to the crisis in German *Weltanschauung* caused by Nazism and the

Second World War, and to the political leadership of Adenauer. For this reason no other member country felt the dilemma as sharply as did the Federal Republic. The pressure became painfully pronounced at the end of the Erhard Administration, when faithful adherence to alliance principles and to solidarity with the United States had brought little in the way of rewards (and indeed some rebuffs from Washington), when the Federal Republic seemed increasingly isolated from friends and enemies alike, and when "dead-end street" (*Sackgasse*) was the popular description for the state of West German foreign policy.[27]

A basic reason for this dilemma was the fact that other NATO countries, above all the United States, never really conceived of the alliance as a new framework for the definition of their interests in foreign policy. For the United States, NATO was one arena and instrument among many on a global scale. When the possibility of concerted action with the Soviet Union arose, particularly with respect to limiting the proliferation of nuclear weapons, the United States grasped at the opportunity for a bilateral understanding—ignoring or failing to comprehend that this seriously weakened the underlying principles of the alliance. It is symptomatic that the conflict in American policy between alliance and national interests became most pronounced in relation to the question of nuclear power distribution, and that the United States resolved this conflict in favor of the NPT and at the expense of the MLF concept. No matter how questionable the MLF idea may have been on military grounds, its implications at the least could have served to organize the alliance more in line with its functions—and the Soviet Union probably recognized this more clearly than the NATO countries primarily concerned.[28]

Ostpolitik is in part the German answer to the alliance's inability to define common objectives and to the accelerating tendency among the most important member countries to pursue strictly national interests. As such, it revives the Bismarckian tradition of German foreign policy—which conceives of Germany essentially as a Central European power between East and West—at the expense of the postwar orientation of West German foreign policy according to the constitutional principle of common cause with democratic societies. The reorganization of Europe that *Ostpolitik* aspires to is not based on the association of states in accordance with their internal constitutional orders, but on a geographic or military order—for instance, on a collective security arrangement comprising the non-nuclear countries in Central Europe, irrespective of their political systems.

It is unnecessary here to detail the Federal Republic's drift away from its alliance orientation. Although the most important causes of this drift were lack of leadership in NATO and the rejection by the United States of partnership within NATO in nuclear questions, domestic political issues also played a role. The foreign policy of the Federal Republic proved to be increasingly dependent on the internal processes of decision-making and domestic trends.

The Rise of Popular Support in West
Germany for a "Peaceful Order in Europe"

Not only did the concept of alliance lose its attractiveness, but the CDU/CSU government also began to lose its appeal as an understandable consequence of its long and uncontested tenure in power. Thus the traditional alternative program of the SPD became more persuasive, although the SPD had not clearly articulated it in the 1960s, partly for tactical reasons relating to the structure of the German party system.[29] Moreover, since the early 1950s the third West German party, the FDP, had been trying to formulate an alternative position *vis-à-vis* the CDU/CSU primarily in the field of foreign policy,[30] on the justifiable assumption that in modern industrial nations the electorate gives its parties and government considerable leeway in questions of foreign policy, provided a crisis does not narrow alternatives. In this situation, there developed a policy oriented toward "national interests"—in contrast to the CDU/CSU alliance-oriented policies—a position which "conservative" parties in the Federal Republic cannot adopt because of traditional political norms, but which "socialist parties" can take up.

In addition, there was a confirmation of the old thesis, the substance of which Tocqueville had long ago recognized, concerning the difficulties that face a democracy in pursuing long-term foreign policy objectives. A governmental system depending on party change seems to require a change in foreign policy approach when a new party comes to power—even when the objective situation remains essentially the same. The chance to gain votes through promises of a new "approach" is tempting, especially when the success of the old policy was "only" the safeguarding of the democratic order, now no longer regarded as seriously threatened.[31] Moreover, an attempt to redirect the FRG's policy seemed to be a natural reaction to the growing cooperation between the Soviet Union and the United States: Why should the Federal Republic be left behind, and perhaps overwhelmed, by the new trend toward securing national advantage?

Internal developments in the SPD paved the way for a reorientation of West German foreign policy. From its foundation a hundred years ago, two groups have struggled in the party: the reform-oriented moderate wing and the revolution-oriented radical wing. During its long history, the moderate wing has been able to determine party policy, but the influence of the radical wing has increased from time to time. In those periods when the moderates effectively controlled the party, electoral success often followed, but this also led to the revival of the radical wing. The latest revival of the radicals began in 1966, when the SPD joined the Grand Coalition, and they have been gaining strength ever since. They have managed to bring large portions of the party under their control. About one-fourth to one-third of the rank-and-file SPD members belong to the radical wing, and because the radical members tend to participate more actively in politics than the others, they are represented by about 50 percent of the delegates at party conventions. In the party's parliamentary representation, only about one-fifth to one-fourth belong to the radical wing, but another substantial group comes from local party organizations largely under the control of the radicals.[32] At the last party convention of the SPD in Hannover, April 10-14, 1973, the radical left firmly controlled one-third of the delegates, while the same proportion supported the present leadership. The last third, in keeping with the leadership orientation of the party, went with the leaders whenever they asked for support, but on all other issues they were in agreement with the left.[33] This led to the ambiguous situation of a "double majority": when the party leaders took a stand, they got a majority; when they did not, the radical leftists could demonstrate their majority.

In foreign policy matters, this radical wing attacks the United States as an imperialistic country and shows open sympathy for the "socialist brother parties" in the East. It is important to remember that the members of the radical wing evaluate a country according to its socio-economic factors, not its constitutional order. Under pressure from this opposition, SPD leaders sometimes seem ready to accept at least a verbal radicalism in foreign policy, knowing that radical domestic programs would be a disaster for the electoral politics of the party.

Meanwhile, the new foreign policy has reinforced itself as a sort of self-fulfilling prophecy. Those who always considered the political and ideological differences between the Federal Republic and the Soviet Union to be relative and were attracted to the "socialist achievements" of communist societies interpreted the apparent success of West Germany's bartering with Moscow in achieving détente as a confirmation of their thesis. The slogan of left-wing Social Democrats of the Weimar days, "democracy means little, socialism is the goal," has been revived in the SPD. This tendency is underlined by the proposal, popular in almost all SPD committees at the turn of 1972-1973, to cease German offset payments to the United States as a "sanction" against U.S. Vietnam policy and as an expression of solidarity with the "progressive system" of North Vietnam.[34] Only by hinting that the late December bombings around Hanoi would soon be halted were SPD leaders able to sidetrack these resolutions.

These developments eroded the consensus for Adenauer's alliance policy, increased support for Brandt's *Ostpolitik*, and reduced the Germans' perception of external threat and readiness to strengthen defense forces. Never was there more optimism among the West German population with regard to peace in Europe than in 1972 and early 1973. Trends in public opinion are reflected in Table 3-2. A poll on twenty different political objectives showed that the consolidation of the Western alliance was ranked only fifteenth by West Germans.[35] In 1972, for the first time, a majority in an opinion poll favored a neutrality-oriented German foreign policy.[36] It is true that public opinion is not aware of the potential development of *Ostpolitik* and its implications. But

Table 3-2
Public Opinion Trends in West Germany (all figure in percentages)

The percentage figures below indicate the trend in West German opinion regarding changes in the outlook for general peace in Europe from December 1964 to July 1972.

	Dec. 1964	Dec. 1965	June 1966	June 1967	Dec. 1968	March 1969	Sept. 1969	March 1970	Dec. 1970	April 1971	Jan. 1972	July 1972	Dec. 1972
Better	10	7	9	9	6	10	10	20	13	10	23	25	28
Unchanged	68	65	65	65	77	66	74	66	70	71	65	69	57
Worse	14	19	17	16	9	15	6	6	8	11	10	7	6
No comment	8	9	9	10	8	9	10	8	10	8	1	0	9

Source: *Emnid-Information*, Nr. 1/2, 1973.

"Which country is the best friend of the Federal Republic?"

	1965	1969	1971
USA	59	49	44
France	8	9	16
Austria	3	4	4

Source: *Emnid-Information*, Nr. 7/8, 1972.

"Which country should we cooperate most closely with?"

	Aug. 63	Jan. 67	Nov. 70	Aug. 72
France	70	76	75	63
USA	90	72	86	77
England	65	52	82	55
Russia	27	41	52	48

Source: Institut für Demoskopie, Allensbach (not yet published).

"Are we menaced by the USSR?"

	1952	1958	1964	1966	1968	Sept. 1969	Aug. 1971
Yes	66	51	39	38	56	33	28
No	15	27	37	37	30	55	46

Source: Ibid.

"Which is the reason for the Russians' willingness to cooperate with us?
1. The Soviet Union wishes peaceful cooperation.
2. The Soviet Union wishes to undermine the good relations between us and the US in order to break the FRG out of the Western Community."

	Total	SPD-voters	CDU/CSU-voters
Peaceful cooperation	49%	74%	25%
Break the FRG out of the Western community	29%	15%	50%
No opinion	22%	11%	25%

Source: Allensbacher Berichte No. 17/1973.

within the electorate no resistance to this policy is observable—and there will be no resistance as long as the Soviet Union "plays the game" by avoiding crisis and maintaining the détente milieu in which the Brandt Government has a strong domestic-political investment.

To be sure, the majority of German decisionmakers do not share the feelings expressed in these polls, but among young elites the radical tendencies are much stronger. Communist student groups of different stripes (Stalinists, Maoists, Trotskyites) in coalition with socialists form a clear majority in the student bodies of nearly all universities.

This is the German scene that confronts the Nixon Administration in its efforts to build a new transatlantic relationship based on West European cohesion. Among the pillars of the Nixon Doctrine, "strength" is hardly deemed necessary by the public and is not at all regarded as a prerequisite for negotiations, and "partnership" seems almost outdated. Negotiations are considered to be an end in themselves or a means for a reorganization of Europe that has little semblance to the vision of the Nixon Doctrine. This was proved by the reaction of the Brandt government to the Kissinger proposal of a new Atlantic Charter. The official statements were friendly but cool, and on his way to Stockholm, the strong man of the SPD, Herbert Wehner, after a meeting with Olaf Palme, called it "an outline for a monster." A Swedish diplomatic source said that "Wehner's statement reflects the views held by the Bonn government." The same source added that the proposal "could not be acceptable to West Germany."[37]

A New Consensus for the Alliance

It would exceed the scope of this paper to examine in detail the assumptions of the Nixon Doctrine concerning the East-West conflict. But if we accept its principles as correct, it would follow logically that the Doctrine can be applied to reorganize and improve the relations between North America and Western Europe. In Western Europe, and particularly in the Federal Republic of Germany, however, the conditions required for successfully implementing the Doctrine are lacking. Foreign policy being to a large degree the consequence of domestic decision processes, it is necessary first to create the domestic prerequisites for the adoption and execution of a comprehensive foreign policy. The Nixon Doctrine must offer not only a concept for structuring the international system but also a strategy whereby a domestic consensus favorable to the Atlantic Alliance can be created (or revived) in the member nations.

Such a strategy requires from the United States the willingness not only to assert its leadership of the Western alliance, but also to assert in its policies—particularly in its dealings with the Soviet Union—its own confidence in and loyalty to the alliance. A strategy aimed at creating a new domestic consensus in

Europe does not have to be a heavy-handed effort to interfere in the domestic affairs of allies. Rather, it should be an attempt to convince the West European peoples of the value of an alliance based on effective partnership and striving for peace and the security of the democracies. This strategy will have no chance of success unless the domestic political forces of the West discharge their responsibilities of enlightened leadership. Transnational cooperation is essential. This is precisely where American leadership should be asserted.

For a long time, a major asset of American foreign policy was its loyalty to allies and the principles of democracy. This asset must be restored in order to give the alliance the leadership it needs. For the time being, the "realities" seem to bode against a successful revival of alliance cohesion in the member countries. The alliance is much weaker today than it was ten years ago. The advice that Professor Kissinger proffered in 1965 is all the more valid today: "The West requires nothing so much as men able to create their own reality."[38] The alliance needs leadership.

Notes

1. See *U.S. Foreign Policy for the 1970s: A New Strategy for Peace*, A Report to the Congress by Richard Nixon, February 18, 1970 (Washington: GPO, 1970); and *U.S. Foreign Policy for 1970s: The Emerging Structure of Peace*, A Report to the Congress by Richard Nixon, February 9, 1972 (Washington: GPO, 1972). German language extracts from these two reports were published in *Europa-Archiv*, 7/1970, pp. D150-174, and 8/1972, pp. D189-200. See, also, *Toward a National Security Strategy of Realistic Deterrence*, Statement of Secretary of Defense Melvin R. Laird before the House Armed Services Committee on the FY 1972-1976 Defense Program and the 1972 Defense Budget, March 9, 1971 (Washington: GPO, 1971); German language extracts published in *Europa-Archiv*, 11/1972, pp. 251-268.

2. Henry A. Kissinger, *The Troubled Partnership: A Reappraisal of the Atlantic Alliance* (New York: McGraw-Hill, 1965).

3. For an explanation of these two approaches to political problems, see Karl R. Popper, *The Poverty of Historicism* (New York: Basic Books, 1966).

4. For the general concept, see Henry A. Kissinger, *A World Restored: Metternich, Castlereagh, and the Problems of Peace, 1812-22* (Boston: Houghton Mifflin, 1957).

5. Laird Statement, *Europa-Archiv*, p. 252. Compare Walter F. Hahn, "The Nixon Doctrine: Design and Dilemmas," *ORBIS*, Summer 1972, pp. 361-376.

6. For this difference, see Arnold Wolfers, *Discord and Collaboration* (Baltimore: The Johns Hopkins Press, 1962), pp. 73-76.

7. Concerning the relationship between the new German *Ostpolitik* and Western interests, see Dieter Dettke, "Politische Interessen fremder Mächte: A,

Westmächte" (Political Interests of Foreign Powers: A, Western Powers), in Richard Löwenthal, editor, *Aussenpolitische Perspektiven des westdeutschen Staates: Volume 3, Der Zwang zur Partnerschaft* (West German Foreign Policy Perspectives: Volume 3, The Imperative of Partnership) (Munich, 1972; publication of the Forschungsinstituts der Deutschen Gesellschaft für Auswärtige Politik, Vol. 30/3), pp. 15-68, especially pp. 20-23.

8. The permanent pressure of the Soviet Union on West Berlin that became obvious in Spring 1973 demonstrates these possibilities of the East. See J. Reissmüller: "Mit Eifer gegen Berlin," *Frankfurter Allgemeine Zeitung*, May 7, 1973; F.U. Fack: "Die Praxis abwarten," *Frankfurter Allgemeine Zeitung*, May 12, 1973; Georg Schröder: "An Moskaus Berlin-Politik hat sich nichts geändert", *Die Welt*, May 7, 1973.

9. Compare Gerhard Wettig, *Europäische Sicherheit: Das europäische Staatensystem in der sowjetischen Aussenpolitik, 1966-1972* (European Security: The European State System in Soviet Foreign Policy, 1966-1972) (Düsseldorf, 1972), p. 183.

10. One example of the capacity of the Soviet Union "to take back détente" is the reaction of the GDR to the treaty between the two Germanys (*Vekehrsvertrag*) of September 1972. Under this treaty, a West German can visit East Germany if he is invited by an East German, but after the ratification of the treaty, the East German government initiated a campaign to require all East German citizens to pledge themselves not to invite West Germans. On the effort of the East German regime to restrict contact with the West, see the program issued by the SED Politburo on November 7, 1972, "Agitation und Propaganda," *Archiv der Gegenwart*, p. 17480B. Also see the contribution by Julian Sokol in the May 1972 issue of the newspaper, *Wojsko Ludowe*, for political cadres of the Polish People's Army concerning the ideological dangers of détente and tourism. Ibid., p. 17475A. Other examples are the regulations for Western journalists decreed by the GDR government on March 6, 1973, which will drastically reduce their freedom of movement in the GDR. See *Die Welt*, March 7, 1973.

11. *Frankfurter Allgemeine Zeitung*, January 19, 1973.

12. See F.U. Fack, in ibid., January 5, 1973.

13. See Walter F. Hahn: "West Germany's Ostpolitik: The Grand Design of Igon Bahr," *ORBIS*, Winter 1973, pp. 859-880.

14. On December 7, 1967, when he was Minister of Foreign Affairs, Willy Brandt outlined in the Bundestag his ideas for a European peace settlement: "A European peace settlement signifies more than a security system. It has to be conceived in such a manner that it seeks not only to reduce military power—a most difficult undertaking and one that cannot be done unilaterally— but also to reduce political tensions, adjust interests, create understanding between peoples, and improve the collaboration of states in order to build a solid foundation for a bright European future. Such a peace settlement,

however, presupposes a reduction of military confrontation and its eventual elimination, a recognition of the justified security interests of the European people, and mutual limitations on armaments and the enforcement of control measures by agreements or preparatory agreements." *Bulletin des Presse–und Informationsamtes der Bundesregierung*, December 9, 1967, p. 1227f. Compare also Boris Meissner, editor, *Die deutsche Ostpolitik 1961-1970* (Cologne, 1970), p. 238.

On December 11, 1971, in his address on the occasion of receiving the Nobel Peace Prize in Oslo, Chancellor Brandt mentioned some elements of a European peace pact based on West European unification and partnership with the United States: (1) respect for the sovereignty and territorial integrity of nations and states; (2) renunciation of force in interstate relations; (3) European participation on an equal footing in negotiating agreements on arms limitations; (4) noninterference in the internal affairs of other states, and freedom of thought; (5) new forms of economic and technical-scientific cooperation; (6) economic development evolution in Europe in order to establish the material prerequisites of social justice and liberty; and (7) Europe's worldwide co-responsibility for the establishment of equal opportunities of development for all nations. *Das Parlament*, No. 52 1971, p. 12.

15. The value of such statements, however, must be questioned. The foreign policy of the Brandt government—as is for structural reasons the case with most foreign policies in history—has been accompanied by statements announcing the contrary of what was in fact going on. Therefore such statements are only of limited value for the analysis of foreign policy concepts. As an illustration see Günther Gillessen: "Lesarten der Ostpolitik", in *Frankfurter Allgemeine Zeitung*, May 12, 1973.

16. *Frankfurter Allgemeine Zeitung*, January 19, 1973.

17. For example, Brandt included in his declaration that he will try to strengthen the European part of NATO by means of the Euro-Group, but the Soviet government has made it clear several times that it strongly opposes every concept of European security based on "military blocs" or "balance of power," especially any military organization of Western Europe. See, e.g., "Declaration of the Political Committee of the Warsaw Pact Countries, January 26, 1972," in *Europa-Archiv*, 4/1972, pp. D106-110; V.M. Falin, "Auf dem Wege zur gesamteuropäischen Konferenz," in ibid., 21/1972, pp. 725-732; and *Pravda*, August 25, 1972.

18. In their arguments concerning foreign policy during the Bundestag campaign in the fall of 1972, the Young Socialists, the youth wing of the SPD, used the slogan "anti-capitalistic policy in Western Europe," in addition to supporting the federal government's *Ostpolitik* and requesting a continuation of this policy. Particular emphasis was put on "the trade union's policy of hostility to important U.S. corporations." In the interest of coordinating international struggle in Western Europe, cooperation was requested also with "those left-wing

socialist and communist parties and political groupings willing to cooperate in such a manner, and which represent in Italy and France significant parts of the worker's movement." *Juso-Zeitschrift der Jungsozialisten in the SPD*, No. 9/10, 1972, pp. 14-16.

19. A similar understanding of the European scene is shared by the British government. It was reported that British officials suggested in private that down the road of force-cutting lies the eventual neutralization of West Germany. *Washington Post*, February 2, 1973.

20. See Hahn, op. cit.

21. Wettig, op. cit.

22. Egon Bahr in a television interview on "Zu Protokoll" with Günter Gaus on June 4, 1972,

Gaus: Let us assume that you would have a choice between the Europe of the national fatherlands and the Europe which has left the national units behind. Let us assume this: from the standpoint of sentimental value which, you said, every high-quality political man needs . . . do you decide in favor of the national solution?

Bahr: Yes, of course, because it [the national solution] embraces within it the tremendous progress toward Eastern Europe and toward the East European peoples, whereas to the contrary I fear—that may not be right, but I fear—that the other [the political unification of Western Europe] can be obtained only at the price of renunciation [of *Ostpolitik*].

Gaus: You mean that Eastern Europe will not be able to come along on the other road?

Bahr: Yes!

For the "Atlantic School" in the SPD, see Helmut Schmidt, *Verteidigung oder Vegeltung* (Defense or Retaliation) (Stuttgart, 1968, 5th edition), and *Strategie des Gleichgewichts* (Strategy of Balance) (Stuttgart, 1969).

23. "Important tasks lie ahead of us, and our generation will perhaps only be able to start. But would it be wrong to begin now even if only a future generation will be able to benefit from our efforts? The answer can be only a strong 'no'." *Bulletin des Presse-und Informationsamtes der Bundesregierung*, March 4, 1970, p. 297.

24. For Stresemann's concept of foreign policy, see Werner Weidenfeld, *Die Englandpolitik Gustav Stresemanns: Theoretische und praktische Aspekte der Aussenpolitik* (Gustav Stresemann's Policy Toward England: Theoretical and Practical Aspects of Foreign Policy) (Mainz, 1972). Waldemar Besson, however, sees a continuity from Bismarck to Stresemann in his *Die Aussenpolitik der Bundesrepublik: Erfahrungen und Masstäbe* (The Federal Republic's Foreign Policy: Experience and Scope) (Munich, 1970), pp. 47-49.

25. Besson, op. cit.

26. When Adenauer, near the end of his Chancellorship, feared that effective European integration would not soon be achieved, he signed the friendship treaty with de Gaulle, hoping to head off a German national approach to foreign policy.

27. Compare Besson, op. cit., pp. 361-364; Wolfram F. Hanrieder, *The Stable Crisis: Two Decades of German Foreign Policy* (New York: Harper & Row, 1970), pp. 36ff.

28. Hanrieder, op. cit., pp. 38-40.

29. For details of this development, see Werner Kaltefleiter, "Im Wechsel-spiel der Koalitionen eine Analyse der Bundestagswahl 1969," in *Jahrbuch Verfassung und Verfassungwirklichkeit*, Vol. I, 1970, and "Zwischen Stagnation und Krise" in ibid., Vol. II, 1972. See also Hanrieder, op. cit., pp. 135-200, and Abraham Ashkenasi, *Reformpartei und Aussenpolitik: Die Aussenpolitik der SPD Berlin-Bonn* (Reform Party and Foreign Policy: The Foreign Policy of the SPD Berlin-Bonn) (Cologne, 1968).

30. Compare the Memorandum of the FDP-Bundestag delegate, Karl Georg Pfleiderer, of September 2, 1962, in Hans-Adolf Jacobsen, *Misstrauische Nach-barn: Deutsche Ostpolitik, 1919/1970. Dokumentation und Analyse* (Suspicious Neighbors: German *Ostpolitik*, 1919/1970. Documentation and Analysis) (Düs-seldorf, 1970), pp. 271-279.

31. This must not be interpreted as a substantial criticism of democratic systems. It is a question of being aware of the possibility of dangerous developments in the political system and of being able to counter them when they arise. It is the duty of social scientists as well as the mass media and the political leadership to prevent threats to the democratic order by devising a workable counter-policy. See Karl R. Popper, "Prediction and Prophecy in the Social Sciences," in Popper, editor, *Conjectures and Reputations* (London, 1963), pp. 345 ff.

For more detail, see Hans Kammler, *Die Bedeutung von Ergebnissen der zoologischen Verhaltensforschung für die Theorie internationaler Konflikte* (The Significance of Zoological findings from Behavioral Research for the Theory of International Conflicts), lecture of December 20, 1972, Cologne (unpublished manuscript).

32. The youth organization and some other sectors of the Free Democratic Party are under the control of a leadership whose political orientation is similar to that of the radical socialists.

33. For a similar interpretation see Bruno Dechamps, "Abmarsch aus der Mitte?" *Frankfurter Allgemeine Zeitung*, April 16, 1973.

34. On January 2, 1973, the Chairman of the Bund of the Young Socialists published a declaration in which he described the silence of Chancellor Brandt with respect to the bombing of North Vietnam as a "disturbing fact." By its silence, the Federal Republic objectively became the "promoter of imperialistic aggression." The Federal Republic was requested to take the following action as

a result of Washington's behavior in Indochina: (1) to recognize North Vietnam according to international law; (2) to cease any material and political support of the "puppet government" in South Vietnam; (3) to stop offset payments to the United States; (4) to set up an information bureau for the provisional Viet Cong government. *Süddeutsche Zeitung*, January 3, 1973.

The Young Democrats (the FDP youth organization) of Schleswig-Holstein requested in a resolution at their meeting in Bad Bramstedt that the Federal government should consider whether it can maintain its relationship with the United States in view of the Vietnam war, which was described as "one of the most infamous crimes in the history of mankind." If necessary, Bonn should organize an exclusively European defense community. *Frankfurter Allgemeine Zeitung*, January 16, 1973.

35. By comparison, "To improve the relationship with the East" ranked fourteenth and "To strengthen the defense position of the Bundeswehr" ranked eighteenth. See SFK (Social Science Research Institute, Konrad Adenauer Foundation) poll, autumn 1970. Compare also E.P. Neumann, *Die Deutschen und die NATO*, Allensbacher Schrifte, 10/1969; Lutz Niethammer, "Traditionen und Perspektiven der Nationalstaatlichkeit" (Traditions and Perspectives of National States) in Ulrich Scheuner, editor, *Aussenpolitische Perspektiven des westdeutschen Staates: Volume 2, Das Vordringen neuer Kräfte* (West German Foreign Policy Perspectives: Volume 2, The Emergence of New Forces) (Munich, 1972), pp. 13-107, especially pp. 90-92.

36. Forty-three percent of the respondents chose neutrality; 37 percent chose alliance with the United States. Figures for 1969 were 38 and 50, respectively. *Allensbacher Berichte*, 30/1972.

37. *International Herald Tribune*, April 27, 1973.

38. Kissinger, *The Troubled Partnership*, p. 251.

4

Western Security-U.S./European Partnership

Air Vice-Marshal Stewart Menaul

"Unless this Treaty becomes more than a purely military organisation it will be at the mercy of the first plausible Russian peace offensive."– Senator Vandenberg, at the signing of the North Atlantic Treaty in 1949.

The military alliance that evolved from the North Atlantic Treaty signed in 1949 has ensured the security and stability of Europe and the Western world despite the internal stresses and strains that have characterized its development. NATO has undoubtedly made considerable progress over the years in both the political and military fields, yet it has remained basically a military alliance of independent states with independent foreign and domestic policies. But it could justly be claimed that the impressive progress made towards a more united Europe, symbolized by the enlarged Community of Nine, which now includes Britain, the third major European Power with France and West Germany, has been due in no small measure to the security and stability that NATO forces have provided for nearly twenty-five years. It could also be attributed in part to the unique experience of fifteen nations working together within an organization designed to ensure their collective security from a very real military threat that persisted throughout the 1950s and 1960s, but that today appears less menacing, though its presence is no less formidable.

The balance of power in purely military terms has now shifted perceptibly in favor of the Warsaw Pact, and this cannot be viewed with equanimity by any member of the NATO Alliance or indeed by any of the Western democracies, despite the reduction in tension that has been evident during the last few years. During this period there has also been a noticeable shift in emphasis in the role and strategy of the NATO Alliance, which changed in 1967 from the tripwire strategy of immediate nuclear retaliation to one of flexible response. Today the role of NATO may be described as providing deterrence and defense in an atmosphere of détente, and it is in this environment that the enlargement of the European Economic Community from six to nine members—accompanied by more positive action to achieve greater unity within Europe in economic, monetary, industrial, and political terms—has been proceeding.

The enlarged Community is basically a customs union with an agreed agricultural policy and a common commercial policy. There is as yet no common foreign policy, nor has there been any positive declaration of intent towards

57

defense integration, though the architects of the EEC clearly envisaged such integration. Full economic and monetary union must inevitably produce a measure of agreement on foreign policy and a gradual move towards a greater European identity in defense, despite France's misgivings, and there must eventually be new concepts for the future defense of Western Europe. Indeed it is imperative that this should be so, since it is in the realms of defense and security that progress has been noticeably sluggish in recent years. The current conventional defense requirements considered necessary for the security of Western Europe by the NATO military organization are not being met despite the claims by politicians that they are "just sufficient"; and so long as defense is regarded as a "national" responsibility the situation is unlikely to improve. In the nuclear field there is a better balance, but the United States provides the bulk of the strategic and tactical nuclear weapons deployed by the alliance.

The claim by some observers in Europe that any integration in European defense must await political union is ill-considered, and France's currently expressed view that such integration is impossible is based on an unrealistic concept of security, formulated under a previous French regime, that is now totally outdated. Future events will dictate that closer integration in defense must proceed in step with progress towards complete economic and monetary union to which the Community is committed by 1978-1980. Defense can no longer be considered as apurely national responsibility even within the NATO Alliance. The more sophisticated and expensive weapons systems of the future will have to be provided on a collaborative basis (some already are) and this in turn will demand a realistic U.S.-European assessment of the future threat, agreed strategic and tactical doctrines to combat that threat, and international collaboration to provide the necessary weapons systems, both nuclear and conventional (at least the more sophisticated and expensive ones), to implement the agreed military strategy.

In President Nixon's phrase, confrontation has, for the time being, given way to negotiation. In the forthcoming Conference on Security and Cooperation in Europe (CSCE) and Mutual and Balanced Force Reductions (MBFR), there will be a unique opportunity for the new European Community (of which eight of the nine members are also members of the North Atlantic Treaty, if France is included) to lay the foundations for a new European identity in defense and advance Europe's claim to a stronger voice in world affairs, which should at one and the same time breed a healthier attitude toward security within Europe and fulfill the just demands by the United States that Europe must shoulder a greater share of the defense burden. This does not necessarily mean greater expenditure on defense by European countries, but rather better utilization of the total funds available for defense as percentages of individual Gross National Products, a considerable proportion of which is currently misdirected into national ventures that result in duplication in research and development, asymmetry in design of equipment, lack of collaboration in procurement, and failure to agree on a common tactical doctrine for the future security of Europe.

But the processes of change that are about to be initiated in Europe and that could provide opportunities for a greater European identity in defense and a more meaningful and effective alliance between Europe and the United States have their pitfalls. As national aims and aspirations are modified in the economic, industrial, and political fields, cherished concepts of national security, patriotism, and national defense requirements must also be changed. In terms of defense and security the modern sovereign state in Europe is already exposed as a functional anachronism in the nuclear age of rapidly expanding and increasingly expensive technology and growing industrial consortia. If this situation is not acknowledged and action taken to ensure greater cohesion without the Community even at the expense of national policies, it could lead to a situation that the Soviet Union would be quick to exploit, as witness its hostility to the whole concept of a European Economic Community from its inception. The attitude of both the superpowers will of course have a marked effect on both the rate and the mode of development of the newly enlarged and still growing Community in the next decade.

The Soviet Union has always considered herself as a European Power and has resented what she regards as the intrusion of an external power—the United States—into European affairs. She has been particularly sensitive to the emergence of a more united Europe providing a potentially powerful economic, political, and military bloc on her Western frontier, and her aim will therefore be to frustrate all attempts at unification of Western Europe, though it is already evident that her efforts in this respect will stop short of war. Her short-term aims will be to influence and ultimately to dominate Western Europe, and there seems little likelihood that her long-term political aims of advancing Communist ideology will be modified, much less abandoned.

The beginning of this decade witnessed one of the Soviet Union's greatest achievements—strategic nuclear parity with the United States. She already enjoyed conventional superiority in arms and manpower over the NATO Alliance. As her relations with China deteriorated, it was hardly surprising that she should adopt an active foreign policy offensive in Europe—a "peace" offensive based on military power and an unshakable belief in the ultimate ability of the Soviet Union to determine the future destiny of the European continent. In the current political offensive the Soviet Union has made a number of concessions in her efforts to promote a Conference on Security and Cooperation in Europe and Mutual and Balanced Force Reductions, while at the same time engaging in Round 2 of the bilateral SALT negotiations with the United States.

The success or otherwise of a conference on European Security must in the end depend upon the outcome of discussions on mutual and balanced force reductions, and it is significant that the Soviet Union attempted initially to have these discussions conducted bilaterally with the United States on the lines of SALT I—a move formally rejected by the United States. Soviet aims on MBFR negotiations therefore will almost certainly be, first, to maintain Soviet military dominance over her East European empire (there is little possibility of substantial Soviet troop withdrawals from the territories of her Eastern bloc allies); second, to ensure the defense of her Western frontier; and third, if hostilities should break out in Europe, to be in a position to exploit such developments to her advantage by superior military power. Her longer term aims are to see the withdrawal of U.S. forces from Europe, the end of NATO, and the fragmentation of the European Community. Meanwhile, her broad strategy will be the continued improvement of her military capability in the north, center, and south while expanding her maritime capability—already assuming worldwide proportions, particularly in the North Atlantic, the Mediterranean, and the Indian Ocean—despite political setbacks from time to time.

U.S. policy in Europe has always included encouragement of European integration. Both President Kennedy and President Nixon have referred to Europe as "the other pillar" in an Atlantic partnership designed to ensure European and Western security and stability. But as the process of integration gathers momentum, there are understandably signs of unease in the United States that the new Europe might develop inward-looking policies, including trade discrimination, which would obviously be to the disadvantage of the United States. On the other hand, some U.S. politicians have actively promoted a campaign for the withdrawal of U.S. forces from Europe on the grounds that Europe has sufficiently recovered economically from the ravages of World War II to stand on its own feet. Others are demanding greater financial support from Europe for the continued presence of U.S. forces.

It is unlikely that Europe will develop an inward-looking policy, which would certainly not be to its advantage, and while the United States may be compelled to withdraw some forces from Europe for domestic reasons and irrespective of MBFR negotiations, it is unlikely that she would withdraw all of them in the foreseeable future—and certainly not during the next four years. There could be no question of Europe in the foreseeable future becoming entirely independent of the United States in defense. A superpower Europe, with its own independent nuclear deterrent and conventional forces capable of matching those of the Warsaw Pact, is neither possible nor desirable in the next decade, if at all. Europe still needs the United States as part of the Western Alliance, whether within the existing NATO framework or in some new grouping designed to encourage and permit Europe to undertake a greater share of the defense burden in both nuclear and conventional arms, while at the same time giving Europeans a greater say in the defense policies of the Alliance. The United States must surely have a continuing interest in the security and stability of Europe and in its future prosperity.

The United States must therefore be prepared to discuss matters related to strategic arms limitations, European security and cooperation, and mutual and balanced force reductions in greater detail and on a more equitable basis with her European partners. Equally, the enlarged and developing Community must acknowledge the interests of the United States in Europe and the contribution she has made, and continues to make, to European security and stability. For the time being the NATO Military Alliance is the framework within which Europe must develop its identity in defense, and it must not be deflected from pursuing this objective of strengthening its defense posture merely because the Soviet Union has declared her willingness to take part in discussions on European security and MBFR. Maintaining and improving one's defense posture when one is in an acknowledged position of inferiority is not a provocative act, though too often fainthearted politicians become obsessed with the possible reaction of the Soviet Union to any proposals for strengthening and maintaining European defense. There has never been any noticeable concern by the Soviet Union for Western reaction to the massive buildup in arms, both nuclear and conventional, that the Soviet Union has achieved in recent years, or to its expansionist policies undertaken through the medium of a rapidly expanding maritime capability, particularly in the Mediterranean, Middle East, and Indian Ocean.

The expansion of the Community, to include those members of the North Atlantic Treaty Organization currently outside the Nine, is highly desirable. Already there are agreements of unlimited duration between the Community and Greece and Turkey (two important members of NATO on the southern flank), Norway (which opted out of the EEC by referendum in November 1972), and Portugal. Spain, which is not in NATO, currently has a 6-year agreement that began in 1970. It is only a matter of time before political and economic factors will permit the admission of all these countries to the enlarged Community, followed, one would hope, by Spain taking her rightful place in a new European identity in defense and contributing her not inconsiderable military power to the European defense structure.

Other agreements have been, or are being, concluded with other Mediterranean littorals, particularly those of the Maghreb (Algeria, Tunisia, and Morocco). In the process of negotiating these agreements the European Parliament has already developed some supranational characteristics which are evident in the decisions taken by the Council of Ministers. In some cases these are seen to limit the sovereign independence of member states, and this trend is bound to continue as the enlarged and enlarging Community discusses common economic, monetary, and industrial affairs. Thus, although there is no specific commitment by the Community to adopt a common defense policy, it is inevitable that a common approach should emerge. It is in fact seen in embryo in the European Defense Ministers' meeting of 23 May 1972, held under the auspices of the Eurogroup to survey the progress that had been made towards a European identity in defense within the NATO framework. For the second time the Eurogroup Ministers voted a considerable increase in defense spending to strengthen European defense.

The Foreign and Defense Ministers of the European member countries of the NATO Alliance are conscious of the fact that Europe, in the form of an enlarged Community of nine, possibly rising to twelve, and then to sixteen to include all the European NATO countries, cannot create a "Common Market" on the one hand while continuing to pursue independent national defense policies on the other. This applies particularly in the fields of research and development and arms procurement. A new European Defense Community complementary to the Common Market would be a logical development that need not await political integration, and conditions in Europe today are very different from those that existed when the first attempt to establish a European Defense Community failed.

There are, however, many obstacles to overcome, one of the most difficult being the absence of France from the existing NATO military organization and her apparent dedication to the notion of national defense policies, even in a greatly enlarged and more powerful European Community. If France were to join the Eurogroup it would be one more step towards the creation of a new European identity in defense.

So much for the politicoeconomic features of the new Europe, which made its bow in January 1973. Most European politicians, not least the Defense Ministers of the European NATO nations, acknowledge that some form of integrated defense policy must inevitably emerge in the years ahead and indeed must be formulated in parallel with political issues to be raised in the forthcoming CSCE and MBFR discussions. Those who believe that a choice is open to Europeans to follow individual defense policies are deluding themselves. The momentum of European development will compel future European political leaders to face the harsh reality that national defense is no longer profitable economically, and that politically it is an anachronism.

French attitudes will, it is hoped, change. It is surely in the interests of France and of future European unity, progress, and security that they should. But the rest of Europe will have to accept that these changes may be gradual, though this should not in any way prevent the other members of the Community from taking any measures they consider necessary to strengthen Europe's defense posture, thus preserving and strengthening the Atlantic Alliance either within NATO or in some new and more appropriate grouping that may develop during the next decade.

The Salt II negotiations, European security conference, and MBFR are the tangible results of a reduction in tension brought about mainly by the achievement of strategic nuclear parity by the Soviet Union, détente, and the knowledge that up to now the strategy of deterrence has been effective. There is therefore some hope for limitations in the arms race, though the SALT I agreements do not in themselves provide for a reduction in nuclear armaments; they merely halt the production of certain delivery systems and warheads in offensive and defensive systems, but place no restrictions on further developments and improvements in existing systems.

There is another, and equally important, result of the Soviet Union's expansion and improvement of her nuclear and conventional capability at sea, on land, and in the air. Both superpowers now have the ability to destroy each other in an all-out strategic nuclear exchange. The SALT I agreements only halted the quantitative strategic nuclear buildup that had already advanced well beyond what was required for mutual assured destruction. Neither side has a first-strike capability, and it is becoming increasingly less likely that either side would resort to strategic nuclear attack unless in an extreme emergency, which would be likely only if the homeland of one of the superpowers were threatened directly by the other.

The NATO Alliance is a purely defensive alliance and has no offensive operational plans against the Warsaw Pact countries and certainly none against the Soviet Union. The West has acknowledged the division of Germany and the status quo in Eastern Europe, but the Warsaw Pact countries, led and dominated by the Soviet Union, do not accept that Western Europe in its present form will endure forever. The Soviet aim is to bring Western Europe within the Soviet orbit at a time they would consider to be appropriate, without resort to force if possible, though they do not rule out the possibility that the achievement of this objective could involve the use of armed forces. If it did, the Soviet High Command not only acknowledges that nuclear weapons might be used from the outset of hostilities in the battle zone, but Soviet and Warsaw Pact forces consistently practice the use of both nuclear and chemical weapons in their conventional exercises, most of which are conducted within the satellite countries.

Soviet tactical doctrine stresses the need for waging a swift offensive campaign in Western Europe, and her forces are capable of advancing up to 70 miles per day. Their ground and air forces are poised well forward to implement this doctrine and the terrain on the central region particularly favors such tactics. There is a growing possibility therefore that war in Europe involving the use of conventional and tactical, or battlefield, nuclear weapons is now more likely, especially in the era of new, controlled, and cleaner warheads, while escalation to strategic nuclear exchange in which the United States and the Soviet Union would destroy each other is receding. The high-yield thermo-nuclear weapons of the 1950s and 1960s designed for use in the strategic nuclear role may have outlawed themselves, and many European strategists no longer question whether a future U.S. President would release his strategic nuclear capability in the event of war in Europe, assuming that it started with conventional and tactical nuclear weapons and that events indicated the possibility of strategic nuclear exchange between the United States and the USSR, but accept the harsh reality that a U.S. President might not release his strategic nuclear capability in reaction to a Soviet adventure in Western Europe; the USSR would also be at pains to avoid such an exchange.

The emphasis is therefore shifting towards the more immediate and pressing question of how the new Europe of the Nine with continued U.S. support can so design its defense capability that it will be able to withstand *any* Soviet incursion into Europe by conventional means supported by tactical nuclear weapons. The U.S. strategic nuclear umbrella still forms a vital part of the whole spectrum of deterrence, defense, and détente, but the time has come to look more realistically at likely developments in the next decade and to acknowledge that the concept of flexible response, which envisages the early use of nuclear weapons by the Allies in the event of conventional forces being unable to halt a Soviet advance on the central front, needs modification. The theory that the early use of tactical nuclear weapons would confer an advantage on the defender is no longer credible. What is required is the right balance of conventional and tactical nuclear forces in the right place and under a command and control organization that would guarantee their use at any level appropriate to the scale of attack. Europe must have tactical nuclear weapons under European control fully integrated into their conventional forces. They should be the most modern available and capable of delivery by the most accurate land and air launch systems.

Nobody seriously disputes the fact that in conventional forces on the ground and in the air the balance is clearly in favor of the Soviet Union and its Warsaw Pact allies. Any further reduction in conventional forces in Europe, either by the United States' withdrawing some or all of its forces or by European members of the Alliance failing to honor their present national commitments to European defense, could produce a situation in which the *will* to defend freedom and democracy in Europe would be undermined and might even wither away. There is no room for maneuver by the Western Alliance in discussions on MBFR. There must be no further reductions in conventional forces either before or during MBFR discussions until it becomes evident that the Warsaw Pact defines "mutual" and "balanced" force reductions in terms the West understands.

It is encouraging that the Defense Ministers of the Eurogroup, at their meeting in Brussels on 3 December 1972, signed a joint Declaration of Intent embodying ground rules for collaboration in arms procurement. This represents another favorable development in the European Defense Improvement Program (EDIP) and acknowledges that no individual European nation can provide entirely for its own defense from its own resources, or even provide a fully effective contribution to a joint defense organization except through collaboration between states, and this must include the United States from whom advanced technology and many, though not all, of the advanced weapons systems of the future will have to be acquired for as far ahead as can be foreseen.

Negotiations to buy the Lance tactical nuclear missile for European armies have already begun. Other sophisticated weapons systems are being obtained through collaborative ventures in the procurement field, and the time is not far off when this growing requirement for defense collaboration in procurement will not only dictate greater integration of defense efforts but may hasten the day stands. It is encouraging that the Defense Ministers of the Eurogroup, at their properly designed and equipped to provide maritime defense, not only in the oceans adjacent to the European continent, but on the oceans of the world upon which Europe depends for her raw materials, especially oil, and for trade. The Tropic of Cancer, as an arbitrary boundary of NATO's maritime responsibility, must soon be abolished; there are already signs that it will be. Britain and the Netherlands are for the first time to carry out a joint naval visit to the Indian Ocean later this year. It is essential that Western naval forces and particularly NATO maritime forces should in future be seen in all the oceans of the world.

But it is in the nuclear field that the most difficult problems arise and where discussion produces the greatest emotion as well as the greatest controversy, and once again France is at the center of the argument. On the assumption that Europe cannot do without the United States in maintaining a credible security posture, that the United States has a continuing interest in European security and stability, and that Europe must, in the words of President Nixon, shoulder more of the burden of defense, it is of the utmost importance that the means by which Europe could contribute more in both nuclear and conventional forces be examined. There could be no more appropriate time than the present, as Britain joins her partners in the enlarged European Community, which includes France, to reexamine these problems in detail.

Britain and France are both nuclear powers in their own right, though neither is in the superpower category. Britain derived certain advantages from her special nuclear relationship with the United States, while France, with no such advantage, achieved nuclear power status on her own. Currently, there is no cooperation or collaboration between Britain or the United States and France in nuclear technology, weapons design, or joint targeting. The arguments for and against nuclear forces in Europe have been aired *ad nauseum* for the last fifteen years. Some have involved ingenious theories that were utterly impracticable, while others, motivated by emotion, have tended to ignore that there are two nuclear powers in Europe, that they have nuclear weapons and the means of delivering them, that these weapons systems are under national control (even though Britain's nuclear submarine force is assigned to SACEUR as part of its nuclear strike capability, while France's nuclear forces are entirely under national control and France is outside the military organization of NATO), and that it is unlikely that either country will voluntarily opt out of the nuclear field altogether. Indeed, it would be quite unrealistic and unwise for either of them to do so.

Britain has signed the Non-Proliferation Treaty; France has not, though that in itself does not affect the immediate issue, which is the future of European nuclear forces in a reassessment of future European defense policy.

Though there are different interpretations of the strategic nuclear guarantee the United States provides her allies, it is generally accepted within the NATO Alliance that the U.S. strategic nuclear umbrella, under which NATO has developed its defense policies and which so far has produced security and stability in Europe, is a real and enduring element in the strategy of deterrence, defense, and détente. Control of the U.S. nuclear forces is vested exclusively in the President, and nowhere is it stated that he would or should use these forces in circumstances that were clearly not in the interests of the United States, even if the interests of other members of the Alliance were threatened. The role of the U.S. strategic nuclear force is defined as a deterrent to a deliberate nuclear attack on the United States or its allies. President Nixon reaffirmed this commitment in his Reports to Congress in 1971 and 1972, and it is reasonable to assume that for the next four years, at least, this commitment will be maintained. But what then?

When the United States enjoyed nuclear monopoly throughout the early 1950s, followed by nuclear superiority in the 1960s, the guarantee provided by the U.S. strategic nuclear forces had unquestioned credibility not only among America's allies but in the Soviet Union as well. But in the 1970s, in an era of strategic nuclear parity in which mutual assured destruction has become a reality, it is appropriate to recall former Defense Secretary McNamara's warning in 1967 that in the widening spectrum of lesser forms of political and military aggression "the use of strategic nuclear weapons would not be to our advantage and strategic nuclear weapons cannot by themselves deter." The United States provides the bulk of all nuclear weapons, strategic and tactical, available within the Alliance. Britain makes a contribution (albeit a small one) to the strategic nuclear capability of the West as a whole, but France retains total national control of the production of nuclear weapons systems and the plans for their employment, though it is difficult to imagine a scenario in Europe in which French nuclear weapons would or could be used in defense of purely French national interests.

Britain's nuclear force consists of four Polaris submarines, of which it is possible to maintain only one on patrol at any given time, though there may be occasions on which two boats could be at sea simultaneously. They are equipped with 16 Polaris A-3 missiles, each carrying three reentry vehicles with nuclear warheads of approximately 200 kilotons—a total of about 600 kilotons per missile. With an accuracy of between a half and three-quarters nautical mile CEP, each multiple warhead missile would give a greater percentage guarantee of destroying a city or industrial complex than a single megaton yield warhead with equal accuracy.

Sixteen such missiles, given guaranteed delivery, could therefore inflict considerable damage on the population and industrial capacity of the Soviet Union, but whether this could be considered as "unacceptable damage" is another matter. The force has no first-strike capability and, as in the case of the French nuclear force, it is difficult to imagine a scenario in which British Polaris missiles could or would be used nationally in defense of purely British interests. Those days have gone. Britain is part of Europe, her interests are in Europe, and her defense orientation is almost entirely towards Europe.

The British nuclear submarine force has, however, certain political values out of all proportion to its current military effectiveness, but there are no other British strategic nuclear delivery systems in being—or planned. Britain's limited aircraft delivery capability, by her few remaining Vulcans and by Buccaneer strike aircraft, is confined to a tactical role.

France, by her own efforts, has developed strategic and tactical nuclear forces that, in delivery systems, are greater than Britain's and more varied. France has followed the pattern of the two superpowers in opting for a Triad system of land-based, air, and undersea delivery systems, but her major problem, like that of Britain, is countering obsolescence in all her delivery systems and meeting the dramatically escalating cost of keeping abreast of developments in the nuclear field.

France's air delivery system consists of 36 Mirage 4A supersonic strike aircraft, of which 24 are deployed operationally; the remainder are held in reserve. The aircraft operate on a high-low-profile, with a low-level supersonic dash to the target. The aircraft would, however, require in-flight refueling from KC-135 tankers if operating against major Soviet cities or industrial complexes. Each aircraft can carry one 60-kiloton atomic weapon (usually a free-fall bomb) and would have a reasonable chance of penetrating Soviet defenses at low-level for at least the next three to four years. They operate from dispersed airfields, and a proportion of the total force deployed is on standby alert and capable of being airborne in a few minutes. Whether the warning time of a Soviet missile strike likely to be available even to the quick reaction alert aircraft would be sufficient to enable all of them to get off the ground to escape a Soviet first strike is debatable. Certainly some will escape, and of those which do, more than half could be expected to penetrate Soviet defenses and deliver their nuclear weapons.

France also has eighteen intermediate-range ballistic missiles in hardened silos. Each missile carries a 150-kt. warhead (soon to be replaced with a megaton-yield weapon) and has a range of 1,600 nautical miles. Many major Soviet cities and industrial complexes West of the Urals are within range of these missiles. The hardened silos are of course vulnerable to a Soviet nuclear first strike unless the missiles were to be launched on warning, which in the present state of the art in France would not be possible; the warning of missile attack from the east would have to come from the U.S. and NATO early warning systems. The French silo-based force does, however, present the Soviet Union with additional targeting problems if it ever contemplated a strategic nuclear strike against the West, but it is unlikely that the Soviet Union would single out France in isolation for such an attack.

France's ballistic missile, nuclear-powered submarines are by far the most important and effective element of her strategic nuclear strike system. Similar to the Polaris systems of the United States and Britain, though developed entirely by French technology, each submarine carries sixteen missiles, each with a 500-kiloton warhead and a range of 1,200 nautical miles. The restricted range of the missiles means that the submarines must operate from the North Sea or Mediterranean if they are to cover important targets in the Soviet Union. Four submarines are currently planned, one is already operational and in service, three are under construction, and there is also an option on a fifth boat. Experience has shown that with four boats it is possible to guarantee only one on station at any given moment, though there will sometimes be two, whereas with five boats there will often be three on station.

The recent SALT I Agreement between the United States and Soviet Union, limiting anti-ballistic missile defense systems, effectively improves the credibility and capability of all existing strategic nuclear missiles, and in this respect the British and French nuclear submarine forces have gained a further lease of life. Unless there is a dramatic breakthrough in underwater detection, the nuclear submarine missile system will remain the system least vulnerable to enemy interference, possibly until the end of this decade.

In addition to her strategic nuclear forces, France has also developed her own tactical nuclear weapons. These are in the form of bombs for carriage on strike aircraft and missiles (Pluton) for carriage on tracked vehicles.

One of the most urgent and important problems now confronting Britain and France is the follow-on system to replace existing strategic nuclear delivery vehicles, assuming that both countries decide to remain in the nuclear business, which they should certainly do. The problem is an economic, technological, and political one, and to go into details in each of these fields would be quite outside the scope of this paper; so, at the risk of oversimplification, it could be shown that economically Britain has an advantage over France in that she is more advanced in the nuclear field, and under the 1963 Agreement for the supply of Polaris (less warheads) from the United States there is a clause that would allow for further reequipment with more modern missiles—for example, Poseidon.

In missile technology, on the other hand, France has a clear lead over Britain, since Britain long since opted out of the strategic nuclear missile business with the demise of Blue Streak.

If either country embarked independently on plans to provide a new strategic nuclear delivery system for the 1980s, it would undoubtedly be a long and expensive process that would put a severe strain on the economy of both countries. Together, however, they could achieve this task at much less cost, but cooperation in the nuclear field would require many political decisions, the most important of which would be the approval and assistance of the United States involving amendments to the Atomic Energy Act of 1946 as amended in 1958. This would be by no means an insurmountable obstacle, and if it could be overcome the way would be clear for cooperation between Britain, France, and the United States, not only in the strategic nuclear field but, more importantly, in the development of new tactical nuclear weapons for use in Europe by European forces.

Such a proposal will undoubtedly call forth once again the question of command and control of nuclear weapons in Europe. Throughout the 1960s there was an interminable debate over the control of nuclear weapons in the Alliance generally, and the old cliché about fingers on triggers was raised on every conceivable occasion. In retrospect, the debate was utterly sterile, since throughout most of the late 1950s and early 1960s the U.S. strategic nuclear forces and the British independent nuclear deterrent, the V-bombers of R.A.F. Bomber Command, were under national control, even though the two forces undertook joint targeting and there were regular and frequent exchanges of information on nuclear affairs. There was an elaborate intercommunications system between the Headquarters of Bomber Command at High Wycombe and the Headquarters of Strategic Air Command at Omaha, Nebraska. The two command and control systems (underground and airborne) were exercised frequently, and no problem arose that could not be settled amicably. Cooperation was always of a very high order, generated by mutual trust and understanding.

As soon as France achieved nuclear status, some people in Britain, particularly in political circles, developed spasms of apoplexy at the idea of having three separate nuclear forces, which they claimed would be impossible to control, and argued that all nuclear decisions should be left to the President of the United States. In fact, all three nuclear forces have been controlled quite adequately on a national basis for the last ten years. Why there should have been misgivings that France would be any less capable of controlling her nuclear forces than Britain had been before her has never been explained. France, of course, rejected any idea of American control of her nuclear weapons, and it was this decision which ultimately led to her withdrawal from the military alliance altogether in 1966.

By 1967, after several dismal failures at coordinating nuclear policy within the Alliance, of which the Multilateral Force (MLF) concept was the least attractive in theory and in the event utterly impracticable, pressures from the European members resulted in NATO Ministers agreeing to establish two permanent bodies for nuclear planning: The Nuclear Defense Affairs Committee (NDAC) open to all NATO countries, and the Nuclear Planning Group (NPG) consisting of seven members to undertake detailed day-to-day planning tasks. NDAC is a purely political body that meets infrequently but serves a useful purpose as a forum in which any or all nuclear problems affecting the Alliance can be aired. The important planning work is done in the NPG.

The composition of the Nuclear Planning Group ensures that most of the European members of the Alliance get experience in nuclear planning, though some of the smaller countries are represented on a rotational rather than a permanent basis. Of the nine European Economic Community countries, only Ireland is not a member of the North Atlantic Treaty, and France, of course, is outside the military alliance but still a signatory to the Treaty. Of the remaining seven countries of EEC, six are members of the Nuclear Planning Group and have considerable experience of nuclear cooperation, planning, and targeting within NATO. The NPG has worked well and on the whole has enabled European countries to play a more constructive part in consultation, planning, and control of nuclear affairs.

To expand the NPG in the future should present no insuperable problems. French participation in particular would add immeasurably to the stature and effectiveness of the Group while giving it a greater European orientation, and this need not mean sacrificing national control of nuclear forces but rather coordinating them, especially for targeting, through the Joint Strategic Target Planning staff, with the United States and Britain, thus making nuclear planning in Europe more effective, more economical, and—most important of all—more credible.

The organization for coordination, cooperation, and control of nuclear weapons in Europe already exists within NATO. As the new Europe of the nine develops its own identity in defense, enlargement of the Nuclear Planning Group to include France—and perhaps at a later date other European countries joining the Community—would ensure a greater measure of unanimity on nuclear defense requirements within Europe. The views of West Germany, now that the establishment of two Germanys has been accepted, would be fully catered to within this organization, and the vexing question of the deployment and control of French tactical nuclear weapons, especially the Pluton missile, could be amicably resolved and, with it, the future deployment of French ground forces in Germany.

As already suggested, the possibility of a strategic nuclear exchange between the United States and the Soviet Union, on whatever pretext, is becoming progressively more remote, while the balance in conventional firepower between the Warsaw Pact bloc and NATO has moved, and will probably continue to move, in favor of the Warsaw Pact. This is true not only in weapons systems but in manpower, and by about 1975, as the abolition of conscription becomes increasingly fashionable throughout the Western world, manpower for the Armed Forces will become a progressively scarce commodity that can be made good only by higher technology, greater mobility—particularly for infantry—and the acquisition of highly sophisticated but expensive weapons systems which are manpower-saving.

New tactical nuclear weapons of greatly superior design and performance, the effects of which are partially controllable, are now possible, and since it is clear that if the Soviet Union ever launched an attack against the West, the Warsaw Pact forces would almost certainly use tactical nuclear weapons from the outset, it is vital that Europe should have available an impressive range of new tactical nuclear weapons and the most accurate and modern means of delivery, which would not only increase the deterrent posture of the Western Alliance but, in the event of an attack in Europe, would probably stem such an attack without recourse to strategic nuclear exchange (which would be unlikely anyway) and without destroying civilian life and property on a large scale in the process.

To sum up, the basis of the present strategy of flexible response, which is a purely defensive strategy, is that there will be sufficient conventional forces available to stem anything but a major conventional attack from the East, but no one seems to be confident, except the politicians, that sufficient conventional forces are, or will be, available. Nor is it any longer logical to assume that an attack from the East would be entirely conventional—it would more likely be conventional and nuclear; and with each successive reduction in European forces on the ground and in the air, even assuming there is no large reduction in U.S. ground forces, the credibility of the present concept of the defense of Europe is becoming increasingly questionable.

The threat by NATO to resort to nuclear weapons, following the failure of conventional forces to stem a Soviet incursion into Western Europe, is no longer sufficient to persuade the Soviet Union that the risks in any adventure into Europe would not be worth the objectives they sought to reach. There is no indication whatever that the Soviet Union takes this view, especially now that she has achieved strategic nuclear parity with the United States. On the contrary, all Soviet doctrine is based on the assumption, often put to practical tests, that the use of tactical nuclear weapons would benefit the offensive, and the Soviet Union therefore plans to use nuclear and chemical weapons if necessary from the outset. Furthermore, whatever variations may be possible in weapons and in manpower in the years ahead, there is one factor which will not vary—geography is on the side of the Soviet Union. The idea, prevalent in some quarters, that there may be a return to massive conventional air attacks on the Vietnam model, is equally illusory.

While the concept of a strategy of flexible response is sound and still applicable in the era of strategic nuclear parity, the means to implement it in all areas of the NATO Command are not available in Europe today, and the credibility of this strategy will be further eroded if action is not taken to adjust the balance in firepower between the two blocs consequent upon the achievement of strategic nuclear parity between the two superpowers, and this will involve political as well as military decisions.

To make the strategy of flexible response credible for the future requires action in four main areas. First, Europe must have tactical nuclear weapons in the new range of controlled warheads with the most accurate delivery systems, and this must be part of the overall Western tactical nuclear capability but be under European control. Second, there must be an improved antitank capability, especially with heliborne antitank weapons. Third, European armies must have the ability to move infantry rapidly from one section of the front to another—helicopter mobility. Fourth, the balance of conventional firepower between the Warsaw Pact and NATO must be redressed by the use of more sophisticated weapons, especially airborne weapons, which are also manpower-saving. These requirements will in the future have to be met on a collaborative procurement basis. Only then can the doctrine of deterrence, defense, and détente become credible and the defense of Europe against any Soviet incursion be contemplated by the United States and her European allies with confidence.

Part III:
The New Milieu: The United
States and the Third World

In the chapter that follows, Robert J. Alexander and Walter Laqueur assess developments in the Third World, including the growing North-South dichotomy and the changing significance of the Middle East in the framework of Soviet-American relations.

Dr. Alexander is Professor of Economics at Rutgers University and has been a visiting professor at Columbia University, Atlanta University, the University of Puerto Rico, and the New School for Social Research. He has published fourteen books on Latin America and many articles in scholarly journals. A member of President-Elect John F. Kennedy's Task Force on Latin America, Dr. Alexander has worked on periodic short assignments for the Economic Cooperation Administration, the International Cooperation Administration, and the Agency for International Development.

Dr. Laqueur is the Director of the Institute of Contemporary History and Wiener Library in London. He is also Professor of Contemporary History at the University of Tel Aviv. At various times a guest professor of history at a number of American universities, Dr. Laqueur is a policy advisor to the Center for Strategic and International Studies, Georgetown University. He has published several books and is a frequent contributor to scholarly journals.

5

The Growing Gap in North-South Relations

by Robert J. Alexander

Introduction

In this paper, I shall try to analyze in some detail the nature of the growing gap between the countries of the North and those of the South. However, before entering into this, I should like to make a couple of general comments, or perhaps words of warning.

First, I think that it should be pointed out that it is a mistake to accept the North-South dichotomy too rigidly. There is, for instance, the almost "accidental" case of Australia, which can hardly continue to be labeled "underdeveloped," even though it is still developing, and which is situated rather far to the South, geographically. But more importantly, there is the whole area of Latin America, which during the last generation or so has been experiencing its own industrial revolution. Although there are increasingly great contrasts among the Latin American countries themselves, the group as a whole certainly cannot be placed on a par with most of Africa and Asia in terms of economic development or much of anything else. As I shall point out later on, some of the larger Latin American countries are quite far advanced in their economic development, and one of them at least is likely to become one of the Great Powers within the lifetime of most of us.

Second, I should like to suggest that the growing gap between the North and South of which we are talking is by no means to be looked at as a completely negative phenomenon. In some regards it is quite positive, creating new problems to be sure, but it should not be lamented. Much of it arises from one of the really major hopeful achievements of the post-World War Two world, decolonization.

Third, I wish to indicate that it does not seem to me that the growing gap between North and South is a completely hopeless occurrence. It can be dealt with, the gap can be narrowed, at least to a large degree, if we have the will to do so.

The Gap as a Military Phenomenon

Although I am rather hesitant to discuss military matters, particularly in this audience, it does seem to me that one aspect of the North-South split in the world is a military one. Perhaps this is true in two ways.

In the first place, the contrast in military power between the North and the South is overwhelming. It is still true at this point that only the two great Northern countries, the United States and the Soviet Union, have the power to destroy the world through their weaponry. Western Europe may soon be in the same "enviable" position. The only exception to this Northern dominance is China, which in spite of its geography belongs more to the South than to the North in this discussion.

The Vietnam War has certainly cast doubt on the military invincibility of the North in anything short of an atomic war. But the fact still remains that the countries of the South feel themselves essentially helpless to prevent or do anything about a possible atomic holocaust coming from the Northern Hemisphere, and this gives them much reason to feel separate from and to some degree hostile towards the Great Powers of the North.

On the other hand, the instruments of nuclear war have also, I suspect, reduced the strategic importance of the South insofar as the North is concerned. This is eminently the case in the Western Hemisphere. When Russian atomic submarines are cruising a few score miles off New York City or Washington, the existence of hostile military bases in the countries of Latin America is of much less significance than was the case in the pre-atomic era. Such bases might make the national defense of the United States somewhat more expensive, but I have been told by military men who should know that they would not fundamentally upset the balance of power. This is in strict contrast with the situation as recently as the early years of World War Two, when the presence of German bases in South America would have been a major factor in the military struggle, and was a matter of primary concern to our military planners.

This shift in the military situation has certainly had its impact in other spheres. This is obvious in what has happened to foreign aid during the last decade or more. Both the United States and the Soviet Union quite clearly have felt much less urgency about trying to "buy friends" through extensive foreign aid programs. Unfortunately, this has meant a drastic reduction in such aid on the part of both the superpowers, to the detriment of the nations of the South.

There are undoubtedly other factors that also help to explain this fall in economic assistance from North to South. Disillusionment with the Vietnam struggle, weariness with "assuming the problems of the world," and a new isolationism help to explain this insofar as the United States is concerned. New efforts to try to meet the demands of the consumer in the Soviet Union itself, together with a growing sluggishness in the Soviet economy, explain at least part of the USSR's retreat from foreign aid. Perhaps both countries have shared, likewise, a feeling that the underdeveloped countries were playing each off against the other, and they have developed a common reluctance to be subject to such "blackmail."

The Gap as a Political Phenomenon

The worldwide problem between North and South is to a very considerable degree a political one. And it is in this field that the relationship between the two parts of the world presents aspects that are by no means unfavorable, at least in their origins.

Since World War Two most of Africa, most of southern Asia, parts of Oceania, and even small segments of the American Hemisphere have emerged from colonial status. The British Empire is little more than a memory, and there are only remnants of the French and Dutch empires; the Belgian has disappeared entirely. Even in the case of the United States, which had few colonial possessions in any case, the Philippines were given complete political independence, whereas Puerto Rico and the Virgin Islands have been granted a new status which is in conformity with the wishes of the people of those two areas.

This movement towards decolonization is one of the healthy trends during the last generation. I trust that there is no one here who still believes (if he ever did) in the "white man's burden," or in the right of one country to rule the people of another.

However, decolonization has had, it seems to me, some logical and understandable corollaries that have tended to widen the distance between North and South. With the removal of the controlling influence of aliens from Europe, there has been a resurgence of the culture of the people of the respective ex-colonies now become nations. In some cases, this has been symbolized by the adoption of a native language as the official tongue of the new country in place of English or French. In virtually all cases, it has provoked a process of trying to merge the inheritance from the colonial period with the indigenous culture, and this has sometimes proved to be a difficult process. All elements of the colonial inheritance were not bad, and all parts of the indigenous culture were not good.

The process has by no means been completed in any of the ex-colonial countries. But to an increasing degree it is generating a diversity which creates a gap between even the elite of the developing ex-colonies and their former metropolitan powers. Increasingly large numbers of the elite are being educated in national universities, unlike colonial times, when virtually all those with university education received it in the "mother country." There is a resurgence in many countries of native art and music and the development of a new literature, often in the national language or languages rather than in a European tongue. All this, too, is a source of pride to the people—or a significant segment of them—in these countries. Obviously, in the midst of all of these developments, the cultural bonds that once bound the colonial countries to their respective European masters are being loosened as were the political bonds before them.

A process similar to this has occurred also in Latin America. For a couple of generations, there has been a tendency to reject models from outside, to stop more or less slavishly copying what is done in Europe or the United States, and to look inward for literary and artistic inspiration. There has also been a growing effort to study the economic, social, cultural, and political problems of the respective countries, to try to find indigenous solutions to these problems. Here, too, increasingly large numbers of people are graduating from the rapidly expanding university systems of the various nations and, although one hears cries of "cultural imperialism," the fact is that more and more intellectuals, technicians, and other more or less highly trained people are being turned out by educational systems that are increasingly adapted to their national *milieux* rather than being mere copies of foreign institutions.

These cultural trends both reflect and reinforce the growth of nationalism in the countries of the South. Certainly, the most prevalent ideology in the world today is nationalism. Even if it had its origins in Europe, it is a worldwide phenomenon today and perhaps is strongest in the developing countries. In some of these countries it has to compete for the people's loyalty with regionalism or tribalism, but there are certainly few nations of the South in which it is seriously challenged by any deep feeling of loyalty to an outside power, least of all a former metropolitan power. Even in the communist-dominated countries of the developing area, old ties of party loyalty to the USSR are seriously undermined by nationalism and national interest.

Nationalism stresses the uniqueness of each individual country. Thus, it not only distinguishes each particular nation of the South from its immediate neighbors, but perhaps even more stresses differences with the ex-metropolitan or formerly dominant outside power. Inevitably, the gap between these nationalistic countries of the South and the industrialized ones of the North is reemphasized and extended.

This emphasis on nationalism finds expressions in many fields. I have already commented on its cultural ramifications. It also finds expression, certainly, in the political-diplomatic sphere. Virtually all of the developing countries pride themselves on their "independence" in the United Nations and elsewhere.

Undoubtedly this "independence" often appears to many in Western Europe and here to be objectively "alliance" with the Soviet Union or other communist countries. It certainly frequently results in the majority of the developing nations and the Communist bloc, or blocs, voting together in the UN and elsewhere.

However, it seems to me that this apparent parallelism with the communist nations does not by any means mean subservience to them. For one thing, the communist countries frequently have nothing to lose, when their own national interests are not involved, by siding with the developing nations on issues which are dearest to those nations' hearts. They can engage in a rather cheap kind of international demagoguery, and frequently do so.

In the second place, it seems to me that nationalism has certain peculiarities that are important in this situation. It involves not only the exaltation of one's own country, but frequently the derogation of someone else's. Within this context, it seems to me most understandable that the outsiders of whom the developing countries would be likely to be most suspicious and whom they tend more or less automatically to react against are the ex-metropolitan powers. In the case of Latin America, the United States serves the same role, since for most of this century it has loomed almost as large over the other nations of this hemisphere as the metropolitan powers did over their colonies.

Thus it seems to me logical that the ex-colonies should be found frequently aligned against their former "mother countries" and the Latin American countries often siding against the United States. The only thing I would add is that, given this proclivity on their part, there seems to me to be no reason why the United States and the countries of Europe should follow policies that often seem designed to encourage the tendency.

The Problem of Foreign Investment

Certainly one of the fields in which nationalism finds most frequent expression is that of economics. I shall look, in a later section of this paper, at some other aspects of the conflict of economic interests between the North and the South. But at this point, I should like to concentrate on one particular facet of the problem that is most closely tied to nationalism—private foreign investment.

Economic nationalism finds expression in the countries of the South in a desire to obtain the greatest degree possible of "economic independence." It seems to me that this means, essentially, two things. The first is to have as broadly based an economy as possible, including what Alexander Hamilton (when we were an underdeveloped country) called the three legs of a three-legged stool—that is, agriculture, commerce, and manufacturing—so as to be as independent as possible of economic pressures and currents originating from outside. The second element of economic nationalism is the desire to have as much strategic control of the national economy as possible in the hands of the people of the particular nation. Inevitably, this desire engenders a certain degree of antipathy towards foreign private investment, and towards the countries from which it comes.

To set a background for this problem, I should like to invite you to consider a hypothetical situation in which the United States might find itself. Let us suppose a circumstance in which the railroads, virtually all of the mines, the largest agricultural enterprises, most of the important banks, the telephone and telegraph system, the biggest manufacturing enterprises, and most of the nation's exports were in the hands of foreign firms. Let us suppose, further, that these foreign firms were almost all from one particular country.

Does it seem reasonable to you that the people of this country would be content with such a situation? Would they not resent such control? Would they not consider it a menace to their national sovereignty? Would they not want to move as rapidly as possible to bring such a lamentable state of affairs to an end? I, for one, am convinced that they would want to do so.

Of course, if we look at our own history, there are elements of this picture that in fact did obtain at one time. Our railroads were once largely foreign financed, if not owned, our chemical and pharmaceutical and some other industries once belonged to European firms. And something was done about this situation.

In fact, the United States has been very fortunate insofar as foreign investments here are concerned. We were able to take them away from the foreigners with virtually no resistance from them. In the first place, the European investors in our railroads made the mistake of making their investment in the form of bonds, instead of equity capital. Since most of the U.S. railroads were bankrupt at least once during the late 19th and early 20th centuries, the holdings of the foreign investors were largely liquidated through the bankruptcy courts, in a quite "legal" and "responsible" fashion.

Insofar as other foreign investments here are concerned, we are fortunate to have engaged in two world wars in which the Germans were our enemies and the British and French our allies. In the case of the former, the Germans, we merely seized their holdings as belonging to "enemy aliens" and turned them over to good loyal Americans (some of them with German names). After World War One, at least, the Germans were compensated, in dollars. In the case of the less fortunate British and French allies, they were forced on two occasions largely to liquidate their investments here at bargain prices in order to finance purchases of arms and other war material to prosecute the earlier stages of World War One and World War Two. Somehow or other, such expropriations and forced sale aroused no wave of moral indignation, least of all in this country.

All of this is a prelude to a few quick comments on the investments of firms from the North in the countries of the South today. These investments, rightly or wrongly, are a constant source of friction between the two parts of the world. The Latin Americans, and to perhaps a less degree the Asians and Africans, *do* resent the degree of domination that foreign enterprises have in their economies, and they are determined to do something about it.

Of course, there are all kinds of arguments that can be made on behalf of the foreign investors. Without them, the mineral and agricultural resources of the developing countries would not have been opened up, at least not as rapidly. Without them, the railroads, the public utilities, many of the factories would not have been built, at least not as rapidly. In recent years at least, they have often been meticulous about obeying labor and tax laws to an extent that is the marvel of local entrepreneurs, often including their competitors.

All of this may be true. However, in looking at the relations between the North and the South, it is to a large degree irrelevant. For one thing, there is a past that still looms large in the memories of the people of the developing countries, a past in which the foreign enterprises did not always act in such an exemplary and understanding manner. In the second place, even if there were not that past, the fact still remains that the countries of the South want to control their own economies, they want to determine their own economic policies, they want to feel masters in their own house. I, for one, can understand and sympathize with this. I shall comment further on this question at the end of this paper, when I try to suggest a few ways in which the gap between North and South can be bridged.

Other Clashes of Economic Interest

Whether or not private foreign investments are a conflict of interest between the countries of the North and those of the South, there are certainly other aspects of the economic situation that are. For one thing, the two parts of the world to some degree live at different points in time. The major countries of the North are already in, or are about to enter, what is fashionably called "the postindustrial era." The countries of the South are generally struggling to enter "the industrial era." Inevitably, the different time perspective engenders quite different ways of looking at things.

This conflict of interest has perhaps most clearly been dramatized in the meetings of the United Nations Conference on Trade and Development (UNCTAD). There the very numerous nations of the South have repeatedly urged upon the industrialized countries the need for allowing the developing nations to ship increased quantities of manufactured goods to the countries of the North, and to establish mechanisms for the transfer of large amounts of capital and other resources from the developed countries to the underdeveloped ones. The countries of the North have as insistently—and largely regardless of ideology—answered these demands with a strong "No!" In their turn, the industrialized North has reminded the developing South of other problems, such as the dangers of pollution, the waste of natural resources, and overpopulation, in which at this point in time most of the developing countries have little or no interest.

For close to a decade now, since the issuance of Raul Prebisch's famous report as first Director of UNCTAD, the developing countries have been demanding that the industrialized countries open their markets to the flow of manufactured goods from the nations of the South, particularly labor-intensive ones in which many of the developing countries have now come to have a comparative advantage. However, the United States, Western Europe, and the Soviet Union have been deaf to such pleas. For instance, President Nixon, in spite of a promise made at the beginning of his administration to make such concessions to the Latin American countries, has done nothing to make good on this promise. Indeed, whenever these kinds of imports from the underdeveloped countries begin to take place, cries arise about "cheap labor," and in more than one case "gentlemen's agreements" have been worked out to limit the sale here of textiles, shoes, and other things from the developing countries. In this regard, our record is no worse than that of most of the rest of the industrialized countries.

Nor have we of the North been any more receptive to the requests and demands of the countries of the South for large transfers of capital and other resources. With the possible exception of France, no one of the industrialized countries has within the last decade approached 1 percent of the GNP for such transfers, which was supposedly one of the objectives of the "first development decade." Robert McNamara, as President of the International Bank, has wrestled seriously with the problem of how to make it possible for his institution to extend more loans to countries which are already "loaned up" in terms of the degree to which their balance of payments is burdened with interest and amortization charges. However, little has been heard recently about the anomalous contrast between the aid given largely in grants to the rich European nations after World War Two and the fact that virtually all aid to the underdeveloped countries is in the form of repayable loans.

On the other hand, the underdeveloped countries are for the most part little interested in the problems of pollution, exhaustion of resources, and even overpopulation—problems they are being forewarned of by representatives of the industrialized countries. Indeed, they point out that the conversion of the countries of the North to an interest in these issues is of very recent vintage. The more suspicious among the leaders of the countries of the South see in the insistence of the North on these questions a not-too-subtle attempt to hold back the economic development of the Southern nations.

From here, certainly, these questions appear to be serious ones. We have become acutely aware of the dangers of pollution in our own society—and this awareness is shared by the West Europeans, the Japanese, and the Soviet Union. We in the United States have become increasingly conscious of the exhaustion of some of our own natural resources. We have also become fearful of the effects of a growing population.

Furthermore, as we look at the developing countries, it seems to us as if these problems are serious there. It seems only a matter of time until the cities in that part of the world will have air as polluted as our own—and Mexico City, at least, has already developed a problem as serious as that of any U.S. metropolis. Even resource exhaustion seems to be potentially serious in the South. For instance, the possible dangers of a sudden onslaught on the vast forested regions of the Amazon have aroused words of caution from Northern experts. There is undoubtedly some considerable degree of reason for these kinds of worries, and from this part of the world at least, it seems foolhardy that the leaders and people of the developing countries do not share our concern. To quote Winston Churchill, "Those who don't read history are doomed to repeat it."

Our concern about overpopulation is perhaps somewhat misplaced. But even here, we tend to generalize too much on the subject. I doubt if there are many people who would question that China, India, or Haiti are overpopulated. However, there is good reason to raise doubts as to whether Brazil, Venezuela, or Colombia has reached that state. If I knew more about Africa, I might add a few countries from that continent to this list of nations in which our concern is misplaced, at least for the time being.

Many of the developing countries need more people rather than less. To begin to develop their resources adequately, to have markets forming a sufficient basis for a modern economy, they need to expand their populations. For them, at least, the problem of overpopulation is certainly one of several generations hence, not of the here and now.

In any case, regardless of how appropriate these Northern concerns with population, exhaustion of resources, and overpopulation, they are of secondary interest (except in some countries, the issue of too many people) to the leaders and rank-and-file citizens of the developing countries. Their reply to the spokesmen of the nations of the North is that their first order of business is development, which will give them the resources to deal with the other questions in due time. Even if the North's worries about these issues are not an attempt to prevent the development of the South, argue Southern spokesmen, they are at very least premature.

The Statistical Gap

One aspect of the economic differences between the North and South that is frequently discussed does not seem to me to be as relevant as is sometimes assumed. This is what I would call the "statistical gap." It is frequently pointed out that the GNP of the industrialized countries (or many of them) is increasing more rapidly than the GNP of the developing countries (or most of them). Therefore, it is argued, the economic distance between the two groups of countries is growing rather than narrowing. Depending upon his personality and scale of worries, one who labors this point is likely to make it with a greater or less degree of shrillness and tone of foreboding.

It seems to me that to a large degree this is a case in which, as the old adage would have it, "figures don't lie, but liars figure." Not that the respectable gentlemen and ladies who make this point are lying, but that they are to a considerable degree misinterpreting the figures which they cite.

In arguing against the seriousness of this statistical gap, I should like to make two points. First, I should like to suggest that the situation may be more apparent than real, and second, I should like to raise the question as to whether these figures really matter that much anyway.

It seems to me that much of the rapid growth of the GNP of the industrialized countries is in fact false, insofar as its representing any increase in the real levels of living of the people of those nations. In the case of the United States, and the Soviet Union as well, a substantial part of it represents expenditures on war or preparation for war which do not in themselves result in any real increase in the material well-being of the people of these countries.

In addition, in virtually all of the highly industrialized countries, much of the statistical increase in the GNP results from increases in expenditures on things that may be made necessary by increases in real material levels of living, but do not actually constitute such increases in and of themselves. Most obvious, perhaps, is the growing need to allocate resources for fighting pollution. This is made necessary by increasing numbers of cars, more factories, and electric power, which do represent improvements in levels of living, but antipollution devices themselves are not such improvements. Thus the need for the Russians to spend large amounts of resources on fighting the pollution of Lake Baikal is the result of the sawmills thereabouts making available larger quantities of paper and other products. These products represent an increase in the material well-being of the Soviet people, but the antipollution expenditures are results of the increase in paper and in themselves are not an expansion of the people's well-being.

A perhaps more complicated case is represented by parking lots, traffic signals, and even superhighways. These are made necessary by the fact that every family in this country now has a car and a half, which represents, presumably, an increase in the material well-being of families in the United States. But the parking lots, traffic signals, and superhighways themselves are not improvements in the well-being of the citizenry, they are merely costs we must incur because of the improvements.

Yet all of these things are counted when the GNP is calculated. The cost of a traffic light or an antipollution device is included just as much as a new home, a new car, or a new suit of clothes. In other words, the increase in the GNP in the industrialized nations is to a greater or less degree fictitious insofar as it represents a rise in the real level of living of the people of these countries. To the degree that this is true, the growing statistical gap between the North and South is less real.

However, aside from this point, one can raise the question, I think, concerning whether the statistical gap should really be a matter of prime concern. Are not the real questions, insofar as the people of the developing countries are concerned, those of whether their economies are in fact producing more, whether they are doing so more efficiently, whether the increased output is being more or less equitably distributed, and whether all of this is occurring rapidly enough to meet the rising expectations of the people? In some countries of the South, the answers to these questions would be positive, in others it is certainly negative, but these are the really important questions, or so it seems to me.

Inequality of Development in the South

One other aspect of the economic gap between North and South that is worthwhile to consider is the inequality in development among the nations of the South themselves. One of the troubles with this whole question of the developed versus the developing countries, as I indicated earlier, is that the developing countries are by no means uniform. Some have reached an intermediary stage, others still have most of their people living at subsistence level. Similarly, some are making rapid progress in economic development, and others are lagging very badly behind.

It is also important to note that some countries may well be shifting within the next generation from the "developing" to the "developed" category. Within our lifetimes we have seen this take place in Japan, which almost without being noticed has emerged as the third most potent economy in the whole world. Canada and Australia have also shifted from one category to the other since World War Two. A similar kind of phenomenon is not to be discounted insofar as some of the presently developing nations of the South are concerned.

In Latin America, for instance, there seems to me to be little question that, barring some unforeseen disaster, Brazil, Mexico, and perhaps Colombia and Venezuela will make this transition before the end of the century. Perhaps there are some countries in other parts of the world with which I am less familiar that will make this same shift.

The Case of Brazil

In this connection, I should like for a moment to center attention particularly upon Brazil. This country is largely overlooked by North Americans and the North in general, but Brazil seems to me likely to emerge as not only one of the major industrial nations of the world, but as one of the Great Powers before the end of this century.

Of course, Brazil is geographically the fifth largest country in the world. In terms of population it is the seventh or eighth largest, and the number of its people is expanding with great rapidity. It possesses vast resources, which are largely undiscovered and still largely untapped, including the world's largest iron deposits, greatest forest reserves, large petroleum reserves, deposits of many other minerals, and very extensive agricultural resources that are just now being opened up, let alone exploited.

One may well answer that Brazil has had many of these things for a very long time. A generation ago, many Brazilians were commenting that "Brazil is the land of the future, it always has been, and it always will be." I fear that this picture of the country is still widely prevalent here and elsewhere in the North, but certainly no longer in Brazil itself. The Brazilians are now supremely optimistic about their country, and their optimism is well founded.

The fact is that during the last forty years Brazil has gone through a massive industrial revolution. Passing through various phases in which the country first became self-sufficient in light consumer goods, then in heavier consumer goods, and finally culminating in the spurt of rapid growth under President Juscelino Kubitschek from 1956 to 1961, Brazil entered fully into the phase of development of heavy industry, including machine tools, engines, and other advanced aspects of modern manufacturing.

By the early 1960s, Brazil had a thoroughly integrated industrial economy. That is, it was physically capable of producing virtually anything one might need, from textiles and hoes, through televisions and automobiles, to machine tools, turbines, and all but the largest and most complicated kind of product.

From 1945 to 1961 Brazil had one of the most rapidly growing economies in the world. After a period of economic crisis during the early 1960s, it once again began to expand rapidly, and from 1968 to the present it has again had one of the most rapidly growing GNPs of any country on the globe.

The country will soon begin showing up in the statistics of major producers of industrial goods. By the late 1970s it will be turning out 20 million tons of steel, which will represent a tripling of its output in about ten years; plans for similar expansion are being prepared for the following decade. It is beginning to establish its own base for an atomic industry. It is already the seventh or eighth largest automobile producer in the world.

It is still true that this integrated industrial economy has a narrow base. Physically, it has been largely confined to the littoral, within a few hundred miles of the ocean, and particularly to the southeastern fourth of the republic's area. A considerable proportion of the population is still out of the market—that is, does not receive enough money income during a year to buy substantial amounts of goods. However, this, too, is beginning to change. Massive efforts are being made to develop the impoverished Northeast. The interior of the country, south of the Amazon, was first opened up by President Kubitschek, when he established the new national capital of Brasilia there, and built roads in four directions to connect it with all but the most isolated parts of the republic. The Amazon itself is now being opened up by the Trans-Amazon Highway and various lateral roads that will connect it with the south and central areas of the country.

During the last decade there has begun a highly significant shift, too, in the nature of Brazilian exports. The country is beginning to become a significant seller of manufactured goods to other developing countries and to the highly industrialized ones. I even understand that some African coffee is now being shipped to Brazil to be processed there and sold to the United States and Europe.

Furthermore, the Brazilians are now hard at work building up a technological base for their new industrial economy. They have become acutely aware of the continuing dependence of their country on imported technology. The present administration of General Médici has begun investing very large sums in the development of laboratories, the training of scientists and technicians, and the establishment of other scientific and technical research facilities. The Brazilians are determined to join the technologically advanced as well as the industrially advanced countries.

Although the fact has not yet received much attention in this country, Brazil has begun to act like a Great Power, at least within its own geographical area. It is within this context that Brazilian participation in the intervention in the Dominican Republic in 1965 should be regarded, and various events have subsequently confirmed this Brazilian behavior.

At the time the Brazilians sent troops to join the American Marines and Army soldiers who were occupying the Dominican Republic in April 1965, this act was generally interpreted here, as well as in other Latin American countries—and even in some circles in Brazil itself—as subservience to the wishes of the United States. However, the Brazilian military leaders who made the decision to send Brazilian troops certainly looked at the situation differently.

They felt that Brazil had developed sufficiently to share with the United States the task of "maintaining order" in the Western Hemisphere. They saw it as Brazil's "right" to join the United States in the occupation of the Dominican Republic. They saw Brazil as merely assuming the place to which its growing economic, political, and military importance in the hemisphere entitled it.

More recently, Brazil has been expanding its influence more quietly, both elsewhere in Latin America and outside the hemisphere. It has established economic and technical aid programs, albeit so far modest ones, in neighboring Bolivia, Paraguay, and Guayana, as well as in more distant Nicaragua.

Also, Brazil has been reported as operating on two levels in Africa. The Foreign Office has been establishing close relations with the nations of Black Africa. While the military have been working with increasing closeness with the Portuguese administrations in Angola and Mozambique, the Brazilian businessmen are beginning to become important investors in the Portuguese territories.

Finally, Brazil is reported also to have undertaken its own program of atomic energy development. It has decided to expand beyond the modest type of program sponsored by the United States under the Atoms for Peace program, and to establish its own general program of atomic research and development.

All of this adds up to Brazil's aspiring to a much larger role in world affairs than it has had hitherto. Within another decade it will be difficult to look upon it any longer as an "underdeveloped" country, although it will undoubtedly continue to have within its borders underdeveloped regions. The weight of its economy will be felt throughout much of Latin America and Africa, and manufactured goods will have displaced agricultural products as its principal exports. Brazil will itself be making important contributions to the economic development of the remaining underdeveloped nations.

At least by the end of this century, Brazil will be one of the world's Great Powers. It will have a population of over 200 million and will be one of the globe's major industrial countries. It will in all likelihood be an atomic power. It is hardly likely that Brazil will be content not to use its economic, political, and military power.

Ideological Aspects of North-South Relations

In the foregoing discussion I have largely ignored ideological issues, except in talking about nationalism. Although questions of ideology cannot be ignored in a discussion of North-South relations in today's world, it seems to me that there has generally been a tendency to exaggerate their importance.

In rejecting foreign control, the underdeveloped countries often emotionally reject the ideology that they conceive of as being characteristic of the countries that once more or less dominated them. This is the ideology of liberal capitalism.

Thus, in contrast to liberal capitalism, many of the underdeveloped nations declare their allegiance to "socialism." However, there are almost as many kinds of socialism as there are countries "adopting" it. A few, most recently Cuba, have frankly sought to organize their economies, societies, and policy along Marxist-Leninist lines. But most have sought to evolve their own versions of what they have labeled socialism.

There are such things as the socialism of the long-dominant Congress Party of India. There is African Socialism (which is certainly different in Tanzania from what it is in Senegal). There is Arab Socialism, which has distinct forms (if it has any unity at all) in Tunisia and Egypt. There are still other kinds of so-called "socialism."

A few countries shy away from using the word "socialism," talking of such things as "humanism" or a "cooperative republic," as in the cases of Peru and Guyana. These are not very distinguishable from some of the myriad forms of so-called socialism.

It seems to me that we should not get caught in a semantic trap. I consider myself a Socialist of the old-fashioned Social Democratic variety. But I find little with which I can sympathize in the "socialism" of Stalin, or even those of Khrushchev or Brezhnev—or in those of Fidel Castro or General Amin of Uganda.

In viewing and trying to form judgments upon underdeveloped countries, we should not be misled by the labels their governments give them. There is not much to choose among the sterling capitalist regime of General Stroessner of Paraguay, the African Socialist government of General Amin in Uganda, and the Marxist-Leninist regime of Major Fidel Castro in Cuba.

We should look behind the labels to the realities—economic, social, and political. This should be true, it seems to me, whether in framing our individual judgments or in formulating whatever advice, solicited or otherwise, we may give to government policymakers.

With regard to economic issues, appropriate questions are whether economic development is really taking place, whether resources are being wasted on a grand scale, whether increasingly large elements of the population are participating in the material benefits of economic development. Social questions of significance are whether rigid traditional class lines have been broken down, whether new ones are being established, if the degree of social mobility is expanding. In politics, the important questions are the degree to which the people are allowed to choose their own rulers, the extent of existing civil liberties, whether or not legal opposition is permitted.

We should not seek for perfection in any regime. No country has it. One of the troubles in the world, and in some people's judgment of it, has been the tendency to pardon all kinds of barbarities and excesses when these are carried out by those who claim to be perpetrating them while on the road to Utopia. On the other hand, there is a similar tendency on the part of other people, when they are judging regimes that are doing the same kinds of things in the name of upholding old virtues and principles.

In both cases, such judgments are wrong. Certainly, those of us, including myself, who in recent weeks have for the first time in our lives almost been ashamed of being Americans because of actions of "our" government, should not demand perfection in others.

How to End the Gap Between North and South

I doubt·that I have anything very original to propose in connection with ways in which the gap between North and South might be bridged. However, I would stress that there are things that can be done to this end. We need not resign ourselves to seeing this gap grow to the proportions of an unbridgeable canyon.

First of all, it seems to me that if the countries of the North really expect to prevent the existing gap between them and the developing nations from growing into an enmity of explosive proportions, it is urgent that the industrialized countries frankly accept the need for major transfers of capital and other resources to the nations of the South on a long-term basis. This means not only a renewal of foreign aid by the highly industrialized nations to the developing ones, but the growth of such aid to proportions greater than ever before. There should be acceptance at the very least of something like the transfer of 1 percent of the GNP of the industrialized countries to the developing ones.

This suggestion may seem boring because of its constant repetition for twenty years or more. However, something does not necessarily become untrue because it is oft-repeated. The need still exists for help from the highly industrialized nations so that the developing nations can grow at a pace giving them some chance of keeping up with the revolution of rising expectations. It is perhaps more urgent now than two decades ago, because, having achieved some development, these countries realize better than in the past what they are lacking.

Second, it is urgent that the industrialized nations recognize the degree to which the developing countries have in fact progressed by importing from them manufactured goods that the newly industrialized nations can now produce competitively. It is time that the highly industrialized nations put into practice their declared belief in the law of comparative advantage, a doctrine which they have frequently used to try to convince the developing countries not to adopt measures to foster their industrialization.

From their own point of view, it is self-defeating for the highly industrialized countries to refuse to accept manufactured imports from the developing ones. The more the nations of the South sell to those of the North, the more they will be able to purchase from them. The potential demand of the developing countries for goods from those nations that preceded them along the road to industrialization is gigantic. Just as Japanese demand for goods from overseas vastly expanded as it became a major industrial nation, so will the demand of the presently underdeveloped nations grow as they also industrialize.

Third, the industrial countries should fully recognize the right of the developing nations to run their own economies. This means that the nations of the North must give up their fixation on the issue of treatment of branches of their private firms in the developing nations. This is particularly true in the case of the United States.

The governments and firms of the Northern countries must accept the fact that most nations of the South are no longer going to allow strategic segments of their economies to be in foreign hands: public utilities, major export industries, banking, etc. Also, they must come to recognize that in many cases it will be all but impossible for the countries that take over foreign firms within their borders to "pay back" anywhere near what these firms think to be the full value of their property. It is time, too, for new bases of calculating this value to be accepted by firms and governments of Northern countries. In many cases, these firms will have to be satisfied with the fact that for a longer or shorter period in the past these investments in the developing countries have provided a more or less important proportion of their total profits, and let it go at that, writing these investments off as depleted assets.

It is time, too, for those firms from the North that want to continue to be investors in the countries of the South to use their entrepreneurial imaginations more extensively in working out new ways by which this may be possible in a manner which does not involve their having equity holdings. I have the impression that Japanese firms are taking the lead in working out such arrangements.

It is time that the government of the United States realizes that the interests of particular U.S.-based enterprises are not synonomous with the interests of the United States itself in the underdeveloped countries. When the government of a particular country decides to expropriate a U.S. firm within its boundaries, the U.S. government should not more or less automatically react with reprisals. More often than not such a reaction is counterproductive; it usually will have no effect on the expropriation, and it will merely embitter relations between the country involved and the United States. It is time to recognize the principle that when a U.S. firm invests in a developing country, it does so at its own risk, as supposedly is the case with investments made by the same firms in the United States itself.

The case of Chile at the present time is a good example of what I mean. The action of the United States in seeking to block loans to Chile through international agencies, and other reprisals it has taken against expropriation of U.S. mining firms by Chile, can serve no useful purpose. It certainly will not get Anaconda and Kennicot their mines back. However, it does give President Allende the opportunity to accuse the United States of "blockading" his country, and to make it possible for him to mobilize opinion in many other developing countries against the United States. For example, the Congress of Venezuela on two occasions recently has declared its support of Chile in that country's resistance to U.S. "aggression."

The most important interest of the United States in the Chilean situation should be the maintenance of that country's precious tradition of democratic government. Our Administration should be assiduously trying to avoid any act that would convert the situation in Chile into any appearance of a struggle between "them" and "us"—that is, between the United States and Chile. Such a confrontation can only serve to strengthen those in the Allende regime who wish to push Chile into a Marxist-Leninist totalitarian regime, which is certainly not in the interest of the United States, and will in any case not get the copper companies back their investment.

A fourth requirement for narrowing the gap between North and South is the downplaying of ideological rhetoric. It is necessary to learn to distinguish between nationalism and Marxism-Leninism. It is also urgent that the leaders and people of the developing countries begin to overcome their suspicions of the highly industrialized nations. They must cease seeing in virtually all the activities of the countries of the North some kind of "imperialism."

Finally, it will become increasingly important for the already industrialized countries to recognize the emergence of newly developed nations in the South. They must be given a role in world affairs consonant with their economic development.

Conclusions

As the Cold War, which seemed to dominate international relations during the last generation, recedes, the confrontation between the world's industrialized

North and its developing South becomes increasingly important. In terms of population, the South has constituted the majority of the earth's inhabitants throughout the 20th century. Since World War Two, we have witnessed the emergence of a new self-awareness accompanied in several score cases by attainment of political independence by these nations of the South; we have seen them striking out on the path of economic development and industrialization.

These events certainly result in a more complicated pattern of international relations. They make obvious the fact that there are certain basic conflicts of interest between the countries of the North and those of the South. Accommodations will certainly have to be made, and most of these will have to come from the North, since it is the North that has most of the world's power and wealth. However, I hope that I have been able to suggest that existing conflicts of interest need not be irreconcilable. The fate of the world certainly will depend, during the next two or three generations at least, upon the willingness and ability of the nations of the North to concede some share of their economic and political dominance, and the ability of the countries of the South to learn how to prevent their reach from too greatly exceeding their grasp.

6

The Middle East Problem

Walter Laqueur

Introduction

This paper deals with the Middle East in the wider context of the U.S.-Soviet relations. It refers to internal Middle East problems, of which there are a great many, only to the extent that they have a direct bearing on international relations, and it deals with the past only inasmuch as it is absolutely essential for an analysis of current problems. I am, of course, aware that present-day events can only be understood with reference to the past, but on the other hand the history, and in particular the recent history, of the Middle East has been the subject of an enormous literature, and the knowledge of it in broad outline can be taken for granted. There would be little time left for a discussion of the issues likely to face us in the 1970s if we became involved in disputations, however important and interesting, about the problems of the 1940s or 1950s.

Given these limitations, the first question facing us is the degree of priority that will be given to the Middle East in U.S.-Soviet relations. Any attempt to answer this question has to be based on a number of assumptions extraneous to the Middle East. My assumptions are that there will be a détente of sorts in Europe, that the Sino-Soviet conflict will continue, and that the Soviet leadership will not in the near future radically change its present policy towards the United States. None of these assumptions is certain, but we cannot do better than base ourselves on probabilities. Given these assumptions it appears that the Middle East will be a major factor of instability and of possible friction in U.S.-Soviet relations both because the situation there is intrinsically far more volatile than in Europe and because the Middle East belongs to the "grey zone"; it is part of neither one camp nor the other. It is one of the long-term aspirations of Soviet policy that the Middle East, or at any rate large parts of it, should become part of the Soviet sphere of influence. This has been a constant factor in Russian policy since well before 1917, and there is no reason to assume that it is likely to change. On the other hand it seems fairly obvious that such a policy is conceived in terms of a gradual, long-term process. A sudden change in the balance of power in the Middle East in Russia's favor would almost certainly have far-reaching repercussions all over the globe and would jeopardize the achievement of Soviet aims in other parts of the world.

The United States and the Soviet Union have a common interest in preventing a confrontation as a result of some local Middle East crisis; this will be difficult to achieve unless there is an understanding as to how to control crises that could affect their overall relationship. The perspectives as far as the more distant future is concerned are less reassuring, but inasmuch as the next few years are concerned there is much reason to assume that no determined attempt will be made by any of the big powers to radically change the status quo in the Middle East. The United States (and China) are in no position to effect such a change and, while the Soviet Union is much better placed for a venture of this sort, it would probably involve too many risks.

Present Status

If this were all there is to the Middle East situation our survey could be concluded with this observation; this paper would be one of the most cheerful and certainly the briefest of all. But in actual fact the real complications only start beyond this point for the simple reason that neither the United States nor the Soviet Union is in control as far as events inside the area are concerned. They may prevent local wars or bring them to a speedy end. Whether they will be successful will very much depend on the circumstances; the United States and the USSR are not the only arms suppliers. Perhaps one should not make too much of the danger of a local war at this stage; if there is an understanding between the two superpowers that a local war should be localized it will be over in a few weeks and no lasting damage will be caused, except of course to the unfortunate people who will get killed and wounded in such a war. Every war is undesirable and dangerous but I believe that the possible consequences of a Middle East war have been overdramatized in recent years. It is far more likely that the balance of power in the Middle East will be upset as the result of internal development in one or more countries than as the consequence of a war, which may or may not take place. Both President Nixon and Dr. Kissinger have compared the Middle East situation to that prevailing in the Balkans in 1914 with the apparent implication that the new Sarajevo (or should one say Armageddon) could be located in the Middle East. I doubt whether the analogy is correct. There had been quite a few Balkanic wars before 1914 without causing great excitement outside the countries directly concerned. 1914 caused a catastrophe not because there was yet another crisis in the Balkans but because statesmen in Berlin, Vienna, St. Petersburg, Paris, and elsewhere engaged in miscalculations decided to intervene and to risk a much wider conflict.

Seen from the Western capitals and especially from Washington, the Arab-Israeli conflict loomed until recently as the most important and certainly the potentially most dangerous issue—dangerous not only in the Middle East context but also in the wider framework of U.S.-Soviet relations. I am reasonably certain that this is not how Soviet policymakers now view the Middle East scene. The

Arab-Israeli conflict helped the Soviet Union at a certain stage to establish a foothold in the Arab world, and it has been of some subsequent use. But there have been diminishing returns during the last five years. As a result, Soviet attention has shifted in recent years to other parts of the Middle East—some of them Arab, others non-Arab—rightly, I believe, from their point of view. This has happened partly because these other areas are intrinsically more important—economically, politically, and perhaps even strategically—and because they involve fewer complications.

Turkey and Iran

A good case could be made, I believe, for starting our Middle East survey with the Northern tier—that half of the Middle East which is neither Arab nor Israeli and which is so frequently overlooked because it does not figure prominently in the headlines. But it is in every respect of equal importance. Internal stability in Turkey and Iran has been taken more or less for granted since the end of the Second World War; these nations, unlike the Arabs, throughout their history have never lost their sovereignty and national independence, a fact that has made for greater stability and cohesion in their domestic politics. However, stability is no longer assured in the case of Turkey and, while the situation in Iran seems outwardly very stable, political progress there is certainly lagging behind economic development. Inside Turkey there has been growing tension and polarization; the Demirel government was ousted by the military leadership in March 1971 for failing to act with sufficient vigor against the extreme left and right, and also for failing to carry out pressing needs for agrarian and tax reforms. However, riots, armed clashes, and other forms of unrest have continued since, and a state of emergency has been proclaimed in Turkey's eleven main provinces. While Turkey has made economic progress during the last decade, there is still glaring inequality in wealth and income, inflation, rural unemployment, and absentee landlordism. Industrial progress has been inadequate and the development of the country's many natural resources insufficient. Politically there has been a great deal of radicalization and the authorities have shown little success in counteracting it. Turkey has the second largest army in NATO after the United States insofar as manpower is concerned, but there are doubts with regard to the effectiveness of these forces as the result both of the political situation and of the low technological level of the country. Anti-Westernism, in particular anti-American feeling, has been more frequently manifested, and while those in charge of defense and the conduct of Turkish foreign policy are well aware of the country's essential security problems, this is much less the case with regard to "public opinion." Thus the outlook for Turkey during the years to come is one of internal crisis and further tension; without overdramatizing the extent of the crisis and its possible consequences, it seems virtually certain that Turkey will not be able to play in the area as active a role as befits a country that only a few years ago was soon expected to be promoted to the league of medium powers.

Iran, Turkey's partner in CENTO, is now in every respect better off than in the 1950s, when economic stagnation and acute political crisis threatened its very existence. The rapidly growing oil revenues have been put to good use, and the reform program launched in the early 1960s (the "White Revolution") has had spectacular results. In its foreign policy Iran has mended its fences with its neighbors (with the exception of Iraq); the Shah has been to Moscow more often than any other non-Communist statesman, a fact that has not, however, affected his close relations with the West. But the very success of the "White Revolution" has created certain dangers: political power still rests on a very narrow basis; the emerging middle class, the intelligentsia, and the semi-intelligentsia want a share in power but have not yet received it; rapid urbanization has created social problems; and there is always the danger that fanatical mullahs, terrorists, students, and discontented tribesmen will make common cause in an unholy alliance. Neighboring Iraq has tried to foment unrest inside Iran—without notable success.

Iraq

Of all the Arab countries, Iraq has drawn nearest to the Soviet orbit during the last year, perhaps mainly as the result of its isolation within the Arab world. Iraq is ruled by a military junta in collaboration with civilian leaders of the Iraqi Ba'ath. In contrast to Iran, Iraq has been far less successful in making use of its oil revenues. But it is precisely as a result of this frustration (and of the background of Iraq's disputes with Western oil companies) that the Soviet Union has found it easy to win friends and influence people in Baghdad. Soviet interest in Iraqi oil is well known and need not be further documented, but Iraq is also of considerable strategic importance: once a member of CENTO, the country now provides the Soviet Union with a base in the Persian Gulf. True, close Soviet cooperation with Iraq may create certain problems in Soviet relations with Iran and also with some other Arab countries. But these difficulties may not be insurmountable; at any rate, the new relationship with Iraq has much to recommend itself as seen from Moscow because it involves a much smaller financial and military investment than the alliance with Egypt. The Soviet Union has no intention of putting all its Middle East eggs into one basket: Soviet policy in the Middle East seems to be to diversify its investments.

South Yemen

Iraq, as I said, is important as a door to the Persian Gulf, the area that is thought to contain between 50 and 60 percent of the world's oil reserves. Iraq is also the sole protector and friend of the People's Republic of Yemen—South Yemen.

This country is to all intents and purposes communist ruled (its constitution was drafted by East German experts). It is also a desperately poor and backward country, and it would be quite unimportant but for the fact that it is adjacent to the Horn of Africa, and a base for military action against Oman and other Persian Gulf Emirates. The "Popular Front for the Liberation of the Occupied Arab Gulf" has been acting mainly from South Yemen; the fact that their ideological inspiration seems to be Chinese rather than Soviet should be noted at least in passing, but since in the area as a whole Soviet influence is still so much stronger than Chinese, one should perhaps not attribute to it undue significance for the time being. Of late, attempts have been made to make the South Yemenis return to the Pan-Arab fold, but the chances of a lasting peace seem quite remote. Someone once remarked that a people that fought for a hundred years over the possession of a she-camel by the name of Batul is unlikely to bury the hatchet at a time when so much bigger stakes are involved. The stakes are of course well known: Kuwait is a ministate with 800,000 inhabitants, half of them foreigners; its oil revenues in 1971 were considerably in excess of one billion dollars, a sum which may well treble or quadruple within the next few years. If Kuwait is a ministate, Abu Dhabi is a mini-ministate, for it has 46,000 inhabitants, slightly more than the number of employees in the Department of Justice (but it will have an income of one billion dollars in 1975). Abu Dhabi in turn is big and powerful in comparison with Ajman, which has 4,200 inhabitants—slightly less than the number of those employed in the Executive Office of the President.

Assuming, as the experts do, that oil revenues in the Persian Gulf area will rise between 500 and 1,000 percent between 1970 and 1980, it is easy to see the makings of a highly explosive situation: ministates incapable of defending themselves and disposing of enormous wealth. It is a situation that seems almost to invite aggression: from the outside by bigger powers needing the oil, and from within by all sorts of revolutionaries, genuine and self-styled, who want to get control of the oilfields and the revenues. Since open aggression from outside is no longer the fashion, it seems more likely that there will be aggression by proxy. But since such a great deal of money is involved, and since money means political influence (as the case of Khadafi shows) even in the case of a thinly populated country, the situation in the Persian Gulf will be a highly complex one, in some respects without precedence. There will be in all likelihood a great deal of turbulence, and Iran and Saudi Arabia in their attempts to prop up the existing order will face an uphill struggle. The Soviet Union, in view of its geographical proximity, its base in Iraq, and its naval presence in the Indian Ocean (to be augmented, no doubt), will be in a strong position in the coming struggle for power in the Persian Gulf.

Increasing Energy Crisis

a. Soviet Union. Events in far-away places like Oman or Dhofar assume growing importance in view of the increasing dependence of all industrial countries on

Middle East oil. This refers also to the Soviet Union, albeit to a lesser degree than to the West and Japan. According to official Soviet sources, the Soviet Union may have to import between 10 and 30 million tons in 1980; according to Western estimates, it could be as much as 100 million or more. A deficit of this magnitude would mean a cost of one billion dollars at present prices as far as the Soviet balance of payments is concerned, but since the price of oil is bound to go up, 2 or 3 billion dollars may be a more realistic estimate. This assumption is based on the fact that Soviet oil production is now increasing at the rate of 6 percent annually, and that it will reach about 600 to 620 million tons by 1980. (Production in 1971 was 377 million tons; the target for 1975 is 496 million.) Soviet domestic consumption in 1971 was only 280 million, but since Soviet car output is rising by about 20 percent, since Soviet exports to the Comecon countries are to increase according to plan also by 20 percent, and since Russia may not want to discontinue its exports to certain Western countries, it seems realistic to assume that by the end of the decade the Soviet Union will be among the major oil importers—and the Middle East is the obvious source. Present Soviet imports are relatively small—about one million tons each from Iraq, Algeria, and Egypt and probably the same quantity from Libya. However, as the result of recent Soviet oil deals with Iraq and other Middle East countries, it can be taken for granted that Soviet imports will rise steeply during the next few years.

These calculations do not take into account Soviet exports of natural gas; it is thought that by the end of the decade Russia may cover as much as 15 percent of Western Europe's energy requirements, and if the deals with U.S. firms and with Japan now discussed go through, this will constitute a gain of perhaps 800 million annually to the Soviet balance of trade. However, the flow of natural gas is unlikely to start before the 1980s. Moreover, the hard currency income from natural gas will be needed by the Soviet Union for purposes other than covering the cost of oil imports. To summarize, Soviet oil resources are becoming increasingly stretched and while the Soviet Union as an exporter of oil is interested in higher prices for oil in world trade, as an importer it wants to spend as little hard currency as possible and to base its dealings with the Middle East on a barter basis. With this background, a conflict of interest with Middle East oil-producing countries seems inescapable. For since the United States, Western Europe, and Japan pay in hard currency, it will be undesirable for the Middle East exporters to be paid on a different basis by the Soviet Union once the quantities of oil involved are substantially higher than at present. This dilemma is bound to occur even if political control in some of the main oil-producing countries passes into the hands of revolutionary, anti-Western forces. For whatever the political orientation of the rulers, they will try, needless to stress, to strike the most profitable bargain for themselves; "proletarian internationalism" is a well known ideological slogan, but economic transactions have a momentum and logic of their own. In other words, short of the annexation of some major oilfields, the Soviet Union will have to pay for its oil imports.

b. America and Western Europe. If the Soviet Union and the other Comecon countries face a serious problem with regard to their energy supply, that facing the West is incomparably greater yet. It is estimated that both American and West European consumption will be in excess of 1 billion tons each per year by 1980 and that of Japan 600 million or more. The deficit in the American trade balance for the import of fuels would run at the rate of 30 billion dollars annually (compared with total American exports of around 40 billion at present); the West European deficit would be of a similar magnitude. According to the director of the Office of Economic Preparedness, "the energy crisis is going to replace the cold war as perhaps the most urgent problem America faces in the years ahead." For the Middle East oil producers, the following assumptions can be more or less taken for granted: (1) oil production will be gradually taken over by the governments concerned. This is a matter of national prestige and the fact that the nationalization of the oil companies' installations will not greatly increase the revenues and may even cause temporary loss of revenue will not act as a deterrent; (2) since oil reserves are not unlimited and since the oil-producing countries have few other natural resources, they will try to maximize their profits. According to more or less informed guesses, Arab income from oil, about 5 billion dollars in 1970, will rise to 12 billion in 1975 and 30-50 billion by 1980. According to one estimate, all Middle East countries may have accumulated one trillion (one thousand billion) dollars by 1990.

Possible Alternatives to Middle East Oil

It has been argued that by 1990 the industrial countries of the West and Japan will be totally dependent on the Middle East for their industrial production, and there have been dire predictions as to the political and strategic implications of this dependence. Serious as the situation is, partly as the result of Western neglect in the search for alternative sources of energy, certain basic facts affecting the overall picture should not be overlooked: It is perfectly true that the less populated an oil-producing country, the easier it is to stop the flow of oil. This refers for instance, to Libya, to Abu Dhabi, and to some other countries. The bigger and more populous a country (Iran, Iraq, or Algeria), the greater its dependence for many years to come on oil revenues for its domestic development plans. Furthermore, there are obvious limits to oil price increases. Middle East oil plays at present the important role as chief source of energy because of its advantage over other sources of energy (such as shale oils, tar sands, coal, nuclear power, and solar radiation)—above all, because of its relatively low cost. However, once the price of oil is pushed beyond a certain limit, the industrial countries of the West and Japan not only will intensify exploration of oil outside the Middle East (which, in fact, has already happened), but investments for the development of other sources of energy will be made. These investments should have been made long ago and have been postponed so far only because Middle East oil extraction costs were so low. This refers in particular to nuclear-powered generating stations; their development has been slow because of relatively high costs and various technological problems.

The argument that there is no substitute for oil is correct only for a limited period—ten years perhaps. One school of thought maintains that "for the next decade or two, there does not seem to be a really durable alternative to Middle Eastern and North African oil" (Charles Issawi). Against this it is argued that "in the final analysis the only future in the energy field is 'all nuclear' and 'all electric,' and that the nuclear solution is no longer a scientific question but one of industrial organization" (Paul Delouvrier, Chairman, Electricité de France). It is, therefore, in the last resort "only" a question of money—whether politicians and businessmen will cooperate, act quickly, and decide on massive investments. Such action is not only of utmost importance for the long-term perspective; it will have an immediate sobering effect on the oil-producing countries of the Middle East, which will be less likely to misuse their present advantage if they know that the West has a clear energy policy and that exaggerated demands or political blackmail will be self-defeating.

Prospects

To what extent are Soviet-American relations likely to be affected by the energy crisis? There may be room for cooperation as to the supply of natural gas, but this has nothing to do with the Middle East and is outside the compass of the present survey. U.S. and West European oil imports come largely from countries which belong to the non-revolutionary camp (Iran, Kuwait, Saudi Arabia); Libya's junta claims to be "revolutionary," and it is certainly true that its rulers have strong political ambitions, reaching even beyond the Middle East. They have a great deal of money and are willing to use it to foster their various political aims, which are however often quite inconsistent. Money alone can no doubt cause a great deal of mischief; whether lasting political influence can be bought that way is highly doubtful. Given the general trend of Middle East politics and the particular vulnerability of certain oil-producing countries (such as Saudi), *coup d'états* cannot be excluded; they could bring to power army officers who would replace the present leadership. There is little the West could do to prevent such a takeover. As has already been pointed out, the Soviet Union would not necessarily profit from such revolutionary action, nor would it necessarily make for a common front in the Middle East, for the new rulers would presumably emulate the Libyan example without accepting Libyan leadership. On the contrary, with so much money around to promote political ambitions, existing conflicts may well be exacerbated.

Soviet Aims

For several years the possibility has been discussed that the Soviet Union may want to gain control of Middle East oil; the political consequences need hardly be spelled out in detail. As far as the near future is concerned such an eventuality seems most unlikely. Full control could be established only by annexation; that the Soviet army would prevail over the Abu Dhabi police force goes without saying, but this of course would not be the end of the story. If annexation seems ruled out, it is almost equally unlikely that the Soviet Union will be able to persuade the Middle East oil-producing countries to use its good services instead of the Western oil companies.' The Soviet Union does not have the downstream facilities to carry out this task, and even if it had them, the Middle East producers would be unwilling to deal with Soviet middlemen, thus forgoing part of their profits. The Soviet Union will certainly attempt to make the oil-producing countries coordinate their policies with its own, to establish close relations, and it may well have some success in this respect. But this would not give it any decisive advantages in the near future.

During the past fifteen years Egypt has been regarded in both West and East as the "key to the Middle East." This appraisal was based on an exaggerated view of Egypt's importance; at the time of Nasser's death at the latest it should have been clear that the attempts to restore unity in the Arab world under Egypt's leadership had failed. Most observers now believe that the center of gravity in the Middle East has shifted from Suez to the Persian Gulf. This is not to imply that the Arab-Israeli conflict will soon be resolved and that the superpowers will no longer be involved in it. According to one school of thought in the West, the Soviets have a vested interest in the existence of Israel, because it made Soviet penetration into the area possible. Unable to get sufficient Western help to defeat Israel, the Arabs turned to the Soviet Union and gradually became more and more dependent on it. As a result the Soviet Union outflanked the "Northern tier," established bases in the Mediterranean, and became within a number of years the trusted protector of the Arab cause. The advocates of this thesis claim that if the Arab-Israeli conflict were settled, the presence of the Soviet Union would no longer be needed as far as the Arabs are concerned; "Western missionaries would again get converts, Western businessmen contracts, and Western generals—bases," as one observer somewhat facetiously put it. Proponents of this school also argue that the Soviet Union seems to be only too willing to do its share towards a permanent peace settlement in the area.* But such an assumption seems to be a *non sequitur*, for if the Soviet presence is based on the Arab-Israeli conflict and would have been impossible without it the Soviet Union would clearly go against its own best interest by helping to liquidate the conflict. Nor is there any reason to assume that the Soviet fleet would disappear from the Mediterranean; its presence, anyway, had little to do with the Arab-Israeli conflict.

*Soviet Relationship to the
Arab-Israeli Conflict*

The real significance of the Arab-Israeli conflict for Soviet foreign policy is far more complicated; it constitutes a textbook illustration of what some of those present would call a dialectical process. It is quite true that the conflict provided the Soviet Union with an opening in the Middle East, though sooner or later a similar opportunity would no doubt have arisen as far as the Soviets are concerned; there are a great many conflicts in the Middle East and someone would no doubt have appealed for Soviet assistance at one stage or another. On the other hand, it has been a very expensive venture, in particular when it comes to Soviet involvement in Egypt, and it has also in a curious way inhibited the growth of Soviet influence in the area. For the challenge of Israel has acted as a unifying factor between the various Arab countries and it has given a great impetus to Arab nationalism; this in turn has made it very difficult for the Arab communists to pursue a militant line, for while the conflict with Israel continues they would be denounced as traitors if they pressed a policy deviating from "national unity." It could be argued that there is not today that much unity between the Arab countries, and that communists are now to be found in the Iraqi and Syrian governments and even in Egypt. But these party members are not in key positions, and from the point of view of inter-Arab relations, it seems virtually certain that, but for the conflict with Israel, tension not only between "moderates" and "radicals" but also between states that ideologically are not that far apart, such as Iraq and Syria, would be much higher than at present. It has been one of the side effects of the Arab-Israeli struggle to sweep many inter-Arab conflicts under the pan-Arab carpet. Above all, Soviet involvement in the Arab world has made at least some Arab countries far more aware than they

---

*Senator Fulbright writes in his recent book: "Without Israel the dream of paramount Russian influence in the Middle East and of the Mediterranean as a Soviet lake would go aglimmering. If Israel did not exist . . . the Russians would have to invent it" (p. 132). But two pages later on Fulbright says: "The weight of evidence indicates that the Russians do indeed want a compromise settlement in the Middle East . . . most enticing of all in the Soviet perspective would be the ego-gratifying prospect of a region full of neutralist states more amenable to Soviet than to American 'influence'—whatever that might mean in concrete terms." J. William Fulbright, *The Crippled Giant* (New York: Random House, 1972), p. 134.

were in the past of the dangers of too close an alliance with the superpower geographically nearer to them. In other words, but for Israel the Russians might never have come to Egypt, and they certainly would not be out of Egypt now. This is not to say that the political inoculation that was provided has been of sufficient strength to last forever; it is quite possible that the present leadership in Egypt, in the Sudan, and in Libya will be replaced by another, more amenable from the Soviet point of view. But it is almost certain that the innocence, the naive belief that prevailed in Arab capitals vis-à-vis Soviet policies only a decade ago does no longer exist, and that on the other hand some of the illusions nurtured by the Russians about their prospects in the Arab world have vanished.

The present view in Moscow seems to be that the old theories about the emergence of "national democracy" in the Arab world were at best premature, and that a transformation such as would be desirable from the Soviet view will be at best a longer and much more complicated process than anticipated even a few years ago. The problem facing Soviet policy in the Arab world from the very beginning was to find partners (or clients) who could be trusted and relied upon. They expected that "progressive" military leaders would gradually move from neutralism to a clear pro-Soviet orientation, and that the logic of events would compel them to adopt socialist measures in their domestic policy. These assumptions were, as I said, overoptimistic; the disarray in the Soviet bloc should have taught the Soviet leaders that the nationalization of industries and of banks and the establishment of a foreign trade monopoly are by no means a guarantee for loyalty vis-à-vis Moscow. It would have been far more realistic to assume that the military leaders who rule most Arab countries will pursue a neutralist line, involving no doubt friendship treaties, loans, military aid, and support for the Soviet line in the United Nations and on other such occasions, but at the same time keeping a distance, trying to play the big powers against each other. There will no doubt be more political opportunities for the Soviet Union in the Arab world in the years to come—the special case of Iraq has already been mentioned. But whether any of their partners in the Middle East can really be trusted as seen from Moscow is doubtful, and a startling Soviet breakthrough in the near future seems therefore unlikely.

The Soviet reaction to the Egyptian demand for the removal of most of its "advisers" has been remarkably cool—sensibly so, because a violent reaction giving expression to their anger would have served no useful purpose. Arms supplies to Syria, and to a lesser extent to Egypt, will no doubt continue, but on the other hand, the Soviet Union is now less under pressure to make the Arab cause against Israel its own. Soviet intervention in an Arab war against Israel would involve the dispatch of substantial forces. Even if one ignores for a moment the political and possibly military consequences of such intervention, what gratitude would the Soviet Union earn? According to recent evidence, very little. The Soviet Union will no doubt champion as before the Arab cause in the United Nations and in direct talks with the United States, and perhaps also with

Western Europe, insisting on unconditional Israeli withdrawal from all occupied territories on the basis of Security Council Resolution 242. At the same time, it would certainly be no disaster from the Soviet point of view if the present state of affairs (of no war and no peace) should continue. This would probably mean that the Suez Canal will not be reopened, but its importance for the Soviet Union has been exaggerated; the Russians would of course prefer its reopening but they have existed for five years without it and they could no doubt live for some more years without it. There is the danger that "controlled tension" will go out of control, and that there will be a new round of fighting between the Arabs and Israel. But again there is no reason to assume that this is bound to have a detrimental effect on Soviet interests in the area. Given the present state of relations between Moscow and Washington, crisis control should not be too difficult. An Arab victory seems at present unlikely. An Arab defeat, or even another stalemate, would probably strengthen the influence of the pro-Soviet circles in Cairo that would argue that victory has not been achieved because collaboration with the Soviet Union was not close enough.

American-Soviet Peace Initiative

The prospects of an American-Soviet peace initiative in the Middle East cannot be rated high at the present time. Past experience is not encouraging: after displaying interest in the Rogers Plan, the Soviet Union suddenly and without explanation rejected it. A change in Soviet attitude is of course a possibility, but it is difficult to imagine what might induce Moscow to modify its stand in this respect. It would certainly not earn the gratitude of the Arabs if it would accept anything less than they demand. An American-Soviet peace initiative seems likely only in an extreme situation, in an emergency—if, for instance, a new Arab-Israeli war should break out, and if, against expectations, both superpowers should become directly involved; if, in other words, there were a real danger of global conflagration. In such a constellation, agreement between the superpowers on an imposed settlement would be a possibility. But such a scenario seems at present most unlikely.

From what has been said so far, a fairly confused and contradictory pattern emerges; this, however, is not entirely the fault of the *rapporteur*, for the Middle East situation is inherently confused and contradictory. What does transpire with reasonable certainty is that even in an age of détente the Middle East is likely to remain an area of conflict between the two superpowers; tension also exists elsewhere, but whereas in Europe the danger of a sudden local crisis seems now remote, this is not so in the Middle East. The Soviet Union is in some respects in a superior position, as a result of geographical proximity and of the presence of pro-Communist and pro-Soviet forces in most countries. But active Soviet intervention seems nevertheless unlikely because it would put into question the success of its policy in other parts of the globe. The Soviet Union, as we have noted, probably still hopes that as a result of long-term developments the Middle East will gradually become part of its sphere of influence. This refers to the internal divisions of the area, to its political, military, and economic weakness, and to the inability of present day Middle East leaders to solve the problems facing them.

Guideline for American Policy

What should American policy be in the years to come? America's overall aim can be defined very briefly and in a positive way: the area as a whole should remain independent. The loss of independence would constitute a drastic change in the global balance of power with repercussions far beyond the Middle East. America's interest is furthermore to safeguard the flow of oil from the Middle East during the next critical ten years, while making every effort to lessen its dependence and to shorten this period. America should stand by its friends and not exert itself unduly to appease those who are not its friends in the area. Given the overall objectives it should be a matter of indifference how the various countries in the area wish to organize their political life. As a superpower America admittedly has certain special obligations, and a contribution to the search for peace is one of them. This implies consultation with the Soviet Union and an understanding between the two superpowers not to be drawn too deeply into local conflicts. It may or may not imply independent American initiatives to restore peace between Israel and Arabs. This is not a question of finding an ingenious formula. The point is eventually reached when both sides are psychologically ready for peace. It may take a long time, but invariably happens once both sides realize that the other is unlikely to disappear, that decisive victory is not in sight, and that the cost of pursuing the fight is unacceptable. Once this situation arises, even a "bad" peace will be accepted, whereas before there is such psychological readiness even the fairest, most sensible, and most equitable proposals will be rejected. One should always try to shorten a conflict, but such attempts should be made without illusions and exaggerated hopes.

The prerequisite for a successful American policy (or at least for nonfailure) in the area is a credible military presence. That the concept of a "pentagonal world" is profoundly mistaken appears perhaps nowhere more clearly than in the Middle East. Western Europe has even more vital interests in the area than the United States, but it has found itself quite incapable of asserting them and pursuing an active European policy. The inability of Western Europe to develop a political will—its political and military impotence—is one of the great tragedies of the postwar period. Twenty-five years after the end of the war, Western Europe has virtually abdicated in the Middle East, and this leaves the United States with the main burden. But given the American military presence there is much reason to assume that, despite possible local setbacks, America will be able to assert its interests in the Middle East. Perhaps in some respects its position will be easier in the future than in the past.

To justify this optimistic assessment I would like to quote from the conclusions of a book I wrote five years ago (*The Struggle for the Middle East*), since some of the trends that could only be vaguely discerned at that time have since become somewhat clearer:

> As Soviet pressure grows, the call for a more active American policy is likely to emanate from Europe, Asia, and the Middle East. In the view of many Europeans and Asians, American interventionism and the cold-war mentality used to be the main threat; in future they may come to regard American isolationism as the main danger. Soviet foreign policy is likely to concentrate on the areas adjacent to the Soviet Union in Europe, the Middle East, and Asia. As a result, Americans now feel less concerned about Soviet policies than those geographically nearer to the Soviet Union who have begun to realize that the roles are about to be reversed and that an immediate threat will affect them far more than the Americans. As the Soviet military presence [in the Middle East] becomes more palpable, and its political implications more obvious, America [and Western Europe] may find itself in greater demand than at present as a counter force to Soviet pressure. The Soviet Union was welcomed in the 1950s as a counter force to "Western imperialism." Since then the political scene has radically changed, and it is gradually coming to be understood that the domination of the Middle East by one great power is not in the best interest of any country in the area. In some capitals it will no doubt take a little time to grasp and digest this, and no radical change in attitude can be expected in a few months or years, but there is a good chance that self-interest and the instinct of survival will eventually make most, though perhaps not all, of these countries recognize these basic facts and act accordingly. If this analysis is correct, the political (in contrast to the military) problems facing the West in the Middle East will ease in the years to come.

This analysis may have been overoptimistic in two respects. The assumption that nations and their leaders always act in accordance with self-interest and that the instinct of survival is omnipresent cannot invariably be taken for granted. And it is probably also true that it will take these nations and their leaders even longer than I anticipated at the time to accept some of the basic facts of geopolitical life. But *grosso modo* these are the facts, and facts as Lenin used to say are stubborn things; however unpalatable, in the end they have to be accepted. The nations of the Middle East have an even more vital interest in the presence of a counter force in the area than the United States, for the simple reason that they have more to lose.

Part IV:
The New Milieu: The Emerging
Balance in the Pacific

Jun Tsunoda, who is an Associate of the National Diet Library in Tokyo, raises questions as to the implications of the Nixon Doctrine in Asia and underscores the limitations—many of them a legacy of past American policies—on Japan's ability to assume greater responsibility for peace and stability in Asia.

Dr. Tsunoda is the author of numerous books on international affairs, including *Road to the Pacific War* (eight volumes), edited and translated in part by Professor Nobutaka Ike as *Japan's Decision for War*. He has long been active in fostering greater intellectual interchange between Japanese and American scholars. Much of Dr. Tsunoda's own scholarly attention has focused on the field of maritime strategy.

7

Japan's Role in East Asia: Domestic and Foreign Constraints

Jun Tsunoda

There has recently been prevalent in the Western world a curious fashion to parade a combination of initials which, whatever its intent, tends to overawe the ordinary layman with its impressive mysteriousness: MIRV, GCD, SALT, MBFR, and, last but not least, GNP. Being no scholar in the field of political economy, I have to confess my failure to grasp the full implications of the word "GNP," but certainly I belong to a group of political scientists who try, possibly in vain, to resist the magical influence exerted by that word.

Take these familiar GNP statistics:

Table 7-1 [1]
Comparison of Gross National Product of Japan and USSR

	1957 (A)	1969 (B)	$\frac{B}{A}$	$\frac{D}{C}$	
				1957	1969
Japan (C)	28	167	6.0	7.7	2.3
The Soviet Union (D)	215 (1958)	380	1.8		
(In billions of U.S. dollars)					

As evident in Table 7-1, the gap in the GNP figures of Japan and the Soviet Union has undeniably become much narrower during the last ten to fifteen years, and there are already forecasts in Japan which assume that that figure of both countries will reach rough parity sometime in the 1980s.[a] Should these forecasts prove accurate, as will probably be the case, Japan will be equal in GNP to the Soviet Union and may well then be considered a GNP-superpower.

One can seriously ask, however, whether a GNP index is sufficient to permit a description of Japan as being "super." *Pace* GNP, I think not. The minimum qualifications of superpower status consist of two attributes: national interests

---

[a]The official estimate for 1972 is 305 billion dollars, excluding that of Okinawa, a figure which is proportionately dramatically higher because it is based for the first time on the new central rate of $1=Y308, representing a 17.8 upward revaluation. (The *Asahi*, January 6, 1973 Evening Edition)

and concerns of a global nature, and a full range of nuclear weapon systems. It is absolutely inconceivable that Japan will, or can, develop, in the next ten years or so, a full range of nuclear weaponry at the level that both the superpowers will enjoy throughout the 1980s. Moreover, Japan's growing GNP will of necessity make her even more reliant on foreign natural resources that she must import, and overseas markets to which she must export even for the sake of maintaining her GNP level. Table 7-2 suggests the developing trend.

Furthermore, while Japan would, as now, be utterly dependent on the safety of sea lanes for the transit of her imports and exports, she would surely lack the ability herself to police all the sea lanes of the world on which her trade is carried. To be sure, Japan has and would have worldwide interests and concerns, if not from an overall standpoint, then in terms of trade. Nevertheless, she definitely lacks and would lack the political and military means to guarantee effectively even interests narrowly defined in terms of trade. Consequently, Japan's economic interests and concerns would be more of a liability than an asset, demonstrating how misleading it is to rely on the GNP figure as a calculus of Japan's international power.

Lacking both of the qualifications needed for superpower status, Japan is not and cannot be regarded as "super," and her GNP, even while giving an

Table 7-2[2]
Degree of Japan's Dependency on Imports

	1934-36 (average)	1966	1967	1968	1969	1970
Barley	1.1	38.6	47.3	49.8	55.7	64.8
Wheat	24.4	79.3	80.6	80.1	85.1	90.8
Soya Beans	64.0	91.9	91.9	93.5	95.0	96.3
Sugar	96.0	84.4	83.3	84.5	85.0	86.1
Coal	9.6	27.5	34.9	41.0	48.0	56.5
Crude Oil	90.8	99.1	99.3	99.4	99.5	99.5
Iron Ore	85.6	97.6	98.1	98.5	98.9	99.2
Phosphate Ore	100.0	100.0	100.1	100.0	100.0	100.0
Bauxite	. . . .	100.0	100.0	100.0	100.0	100.0
Scrap Iron	. . . .	100.0	100.0	100.0	100.0	100.0
Cotton	100.0	100.0	100.0	100.0	100.0	100.0
Wool	100.0	100.0	100.0	100.0	100.0	100.0
Hides	67.5	82.7	80.5	80.2	83.2	81.8
Natural Rubber	100.0	100.0	100.0	100.0	100.0	100.0
Salt	67.2	82.0	82.0	84.6	85.1	87.2

(In Percentage)

impression of her increased international weight, ought not mislead one to conclude that there has come about a so-called economic tripolarity in the world, to say nothing of tripolarity in the political-strategic sense.

The present concern for Japan as a global power derives overwhelmingly from her single-minded export drive, which has evoked claims that the invasion of Japanese goods is seriously disturbing the economic stability of other (especially industrialized) countries. These broad-gauged efforts to restrict the expansion of Japanese trade place Tokyo in a vulnerable position, since she must maintain amicable relationships with all trading nations in order to assure the smooth flow of resources and goods. Inevitably, then, Japan will of necessity make some sort of orderly retreat in the spirit of self-discipline. Thus, doubly vulnerable in her economic position relative to the rest of the world, Japan's global role in economic activity is essentially that of a passive and restrained nature.

Regionalism: Economic Dimensions

Japan can, however, play an important regional role in spite of the above limitations. Japan's stand and function in global international politics grows out of her role in East Asia, an area in which she has come to occupy a pre-eminent position, at least economically.

It is evident that Japan now dominates trading relationships with the East Asian region. Even ten years ago, in 1963, she had already surpassed the United States in this regard.

Table 7-3 [3]
Trade of East Asian Countries with Japan as a Percentage of Their Total Trade, 1968 (In Millions of U.S. Dollars)

Country	Exports		Imports		Total		Rank (Total trade)
	Amount	%	Amount	%	Amount	%	
Burma	12.4	15.2	39.3	24.2	51.7	21.3	1
Cambodia	6.6	21.5	20.3	28.0	26.9	26.1	2
China	224.2	16.9	325.5	29.5	549.7	22.6	1
Nationalist China	150.7	19.1	471.7	52.7	622.4	36.9	2
Indonesia	251.9	34.7	146.6	22.1	398.5	28.7	1
South Korea	101.6	22.1	602.7	46.1	704.3	36.5	1
Malaysia	343.4	30.6	104.5	15.9	447.9	25.2	1
Philippines	398.0	48.3	411.1	32.1	809.1	38.5	2
Singapore	61.8	20.6	209.3	21.2	271.1	21.1	1
Thailand	147.0	34.4	365.5	35.8	512.5	35.4	1
South Vietnam	2.7	15.4	199.0	28.1	201.7	27.7	2

As seen in Table 7-3, most Southeast Asian countries[b] have been suffering from a chronic deficit in their trade balance with Japan, and it is therefore not surprising that some of these nations have increasingly expressed dissatisfaction with this imbalance. Nevertheless, given the level of their economic development and the competitiveness of Japanese goods, it is highly probable that this trade deficit will persist in the foreseeable future. Consequently, there will be mounting pressures from these countries on Japan for economic assistance—private or governmental—as a sort of compensation.

Apart from Korea and Taiwan, areas once under direct Japanese jurisdiction, most East Asian nations were occupied by Japan during World War II. In order to prevent any revival of anti-Japanese sentiments rooted in that occupation, Japan would do well to be generous in providing assistance to those countries. Moreover, recent international public opinion, especially in various U.N. organizations where the developing countries form the majority (e.g., General Assembly, UNCTAD, etc.) has seen it as a moral obligation of the developed countries to assist the developing ones. Japan, as a *nouveau riche* among the former, has decided to comply with this sentiment and has already declared a willingness to devote one percent of her GNP to foreign assistance by 1975—with a concentration in East Asia.

Whatever Japan's actual motives may be, one must still ask if the assistance offered can produce the desired result of stability and peace in and among the recipient countries. Postwar American foreign aid policy was apparently rooted in the assumption that assistance would lead to economic growth, which in turn would be conducive to a peaceful international posture by the recipient country. However, in practice a substantial amount of political stability—be it military dictatorship, oligarchy, "guided" democracy or the like—must be present in order that the aid may be even effectively used for economic growth. Whether rapid growth then conduces to domestic political stability and/or international harmony are other, open questions. Hence, there is no sure guarantee that the assistance offered by Japan will actually contribute to peace and stability in East Asia in the long run. This pessimism is justified in terms of many of the American assistance projects as well; and in view of the recently expressed professions of neutralism of ASEAN (Association of Southeast Asian Nations), a pooling of American and Japanese aid might serve to encourage a continuing neutralist posture. Further active participation of China and the Soviet Union in expanding the assistance pool to the region ought to be explored, while cooperation between multinational enterprises—of Japan and the U.S. for example—might be desirable in the case of private investments.

Ultimately, Japan's regional economic contribution might be in the form of solid and steady assistance to facilitate the self-sufficiency of East Asia. Japan can, perhaps more effectively than any other nation, provide real assistance in medical care and services, technical know-how in agriculture and light industries,

---

[b]Malaysia and Indonesia are exceptions, as is the Philippines since 1970.

and in a variety of managerial skills. It seems inevitable that economic assistance on both the large and small scale cannot provide regional peace and stability in the shortrun and the rewards, if they come at all, can be reaped only in the rather distant future.

Regionalism: Political-Security Dimensions

What aspects other than economic aid comprise Japan's regional role in East Asia? We have become dimly aware of the general implications of the Nixon Doctrine regarding the security and stability of East Asia, although there is still considerable uncertainty regarding America's ultimate intentions. To begin with, President Nixon himself openly listed Japan as one of the four "major powers" of Asia in his second State of the World message. Apparently, being "major" in the setting of international politics of East Asia implies Japan's competence to assume a more active, positive and stabilizing role than heretofore. In fact, Japan has consistently been prodded during the last four years to assume such a role by the American Secretary of Defense. *The belief has been manifested that in order to participate fully and permanently in the regional politics of East Asia, rearmament of Japan, hopefully in close concert with the United States, is indispensable. On the other hand, while asking Japan rather openly to assume some sort of military role at the regional level, the Nixon administration throughout its first term has been indeterminate and obscure about the proper and advisable dimension of that role,* leaving the issue of nature and timing of Japan's rearmament utterly undefined.

For example, the exceptionally steady development of the Chinese nuclear weapon systems has hastened the day when China can make a direct strategic strike into the American homeland. To be sure, Chinese weapons would most probably be directed toward Moscow rather than Washington. *However, without nuclear arms capable of neutralizing Chinese weaponry—*be it under unilateral, bilateral, or multilateral controls—*Japan cannot be expected to engage fully in regional politics as a counterpoise to nuclear China.* Yet, it has been American strategic experts who "have shown a notable reluctance to acknowledge and/or confront this development—and who presuppose that Japan will not be confronted with a security threat with which the United States could and would not deal."[4] Is the United States really unclear and unsure what would be desirable in the dimension, nature, and timing of Japan's role for the maintenance of security and stability of East Asia? Or, is the U.S. prepared to leave the questions of timing and scope of involvement wholly to Japan's own discretion? And, more fundamentally, does the United States think the Japanese government can readily comply with such a vague request? Does the United States think it possible to continue asking Japan to be strong in conventional arms and impotent in nuclear ones at the same time? Possibly, the second Nixon administration might be advised to reconsider the practical implications of the Doctrine bearing the name of its President, at least in terms of its relevance to Japan. Seen from across the Pacific, that Doctrine appears to rest on a somewhat overly optimistic and simplistic assessment of the peculiar climate surrounding security issues in Japan. Many of the domestic uncertainties are ironically rooted in two American-made legal structures.

**Japanese Security Policy: The
Constitutional Obstacles**

In 1959, a very important document was published: *Report of Government Section, Political Orientation of Japan: September 1945-September 1948*, by the Supreme Command of Allied Powers. Looking back on four years of Occupation efforts to institute sweeping reforms of demilitarization and democratization, the report declared that the Occupation's fundamental aim had been "to insure that Japan would not again become a menace to the U.S. or the peace and security of the world." Quite recently, Professor Robert Scalapino also pointed out that the first phase of postwar American policy was "initial emphasis upon punishment and reform" with "the vision of a weak, pastoral, pacifist Japan."[5] While demilitarization reforms were of direct consequence in framing the famous Article IX of the Japanese constitution, what is often forgotten is that the democratization reforms were also integrally related.

Demilitarization through democratization meant, in actual terms, that the Occupation authorities drafted a constitution for Japan structured around the most utopian philosophical assumptions underlying the American and French Revolutions. For instance, Articles XI and XII prescribe: "The people shall not be prevented from enjoying any of the fundamental human rights. All the people shall be respected as individuals. Their right to life, liberty and the pursuit of happiness shall be the supreme consideration in legislation and in other governmental affairs."

Twenty-seven more articles follow, defining almost all practical aspects of human rights. In the light of constitutional progress made since the days of those two revolutions, we can probably maintain at present that the sound performance of statecraft requires a fair balance between the rights of the state and the individual. An undue and one-sided emphasis on human rights at the expense of the state's right will only lead to a populist style of direct participation in politics, practicable, if at all, only on the scale of a Swiss canton. When applied to a country like Japan with a population of over one hundred million, this imbalance inevitably renders almost any sort of statecraft impotent. The constitution of Japan, in severely restricting the authority of the state as a legal entity, denies the state indispensable rights to balance against those enjoyed by individuals. Thus, the Japanese state is virtually unable, both administratively and judicially, to deal with the assorted claims for redress of individuals based on the constitution's articles of human rights. Unquestionably the Japanese state exists in name, but in reality it does not function as a normal state. Rather the real Japan is a politically and legally unorganizable society in which every member acts in accordance with his own view of his human rights constitutionally guaranteed. This kind of society is, so to speak, less a state than anarchy in the basic Hobbesian sense of the word. The Japanese governmental system is essentially weak, and therein lies the real cause of its "immobilism."

While democratization took place in a somewhat roundabout fashion, demilitarization was carried out in a more straightforward and forceful way. The Japanese constitution contains the following explicit passages:

We, the Japanese people have determined to preserve our security and existence, trusting in the justice and faith of the peace-loving peoples of the world. (Preamble)

Land, sea and air forces, as well as other war potential will never be maintained. The right of belligerency of the state will not be recognized. (Article IX, Paragraph 2)

With regard to the preamble, reference should be made to Article IV, Paragraph 1 of the U.N. Charter, establishing that "membership in the U.N. is open to all peace-loving states." Hence, the so-called "peace-loving" states or people can be construed as the members of the U.N. inviting us to paraphrase our constitution's preamble in terms of a determination to "preserve our security and existence, trusting in the justice and faith of the members of the U.N." The U.N. organization authorized to guarantee Japan her "security and existence" is undoubtedly the Security Council, which has "primary responsibility for the maintenance of international peace and security" (U.N. Charter, Article XXIV, Paragraph 1). Thus, we may further paraphrase our preamble as a determination "to preserve our security and existence, trusting in the justice and faith of the members of the Security Council, especially its five permanent members" who are given special privilege of veto powers. It was pointed out that throughout the whole period of drafting the U.N. Charter that "it seemed that the dangers to be guarded against were those which Germany and Japan represented and the Charter therefore sought to forge an irresistible weapon to deal with such dangers."[6] While the preamble to Japan's constitution reads like an expression of voluntary "determination" on the part of the Japanese people, in actuality Japan was forced by the Occupation authorities to accept without discussion or amendment the Constitution they drafted. Through this forcible arrangement, the Allied Powers, or "United Nations" in the sense of wartime alliance as was embodied in the "United Nation's Declaration" of January 1, 1942, had Japan "voluntarily" offer a solemn pledge to put herself wholly at the mercy of the Big Five of the Security Council, acting alone or in common. A genuine sense of fear of the Big Five with regard to Japan has long smoldered beneath the surface in the political conscience of many Japanese. This has inevitably become more intense with the admission of the Peking government into the U.N. Security Council as a legitimate member of the Big Five. By making the Big Five in the U.N. Charter identical with the global Nuclear Club, the legal competence of the Big Five over Japan was provided with a new, rather ominous dimension.

The wording of Article IX is precise and unambiguous, leaving little room for interpretation. Implying that Japan is an aggressor and a potential threat to *Pax Americana*, the Occupation authorities forced her with punitive, Carthaginian harshness to renounce "war, threat or use of force," the means which are universally acknowledged as elemental necessity for a state's participation in international politics. Deprived of the inherent light of sovereignty conferred on all modern states by the authority of traditional international law, Japan since has simply been unable to act positively in the world of *Realpolitik*. Herein lies the basic reason why the Japanese have acted as "economic animals" or, collectively, as a kind of trading company, rather than as "political animals" in the Aristotelian sense. Indeed, the Japanese have acted not so much from conscious policy freely chosen but within the parameters of international behavior stipulated in the constitution.

American reformists in the Occupation were motivated by missionary zeal to create a "Wonderland" of their own, not in the U.S. but in Japan. They treated Japan as an experimental laboratory for testing the utopian thesis of the feasibility of unarmed nationhood. Indeed, Japan presented an ideal subject for their proselytism, and they soon became enthusiastic preachers of the new occupational gospel of "punishment-transformed-into-disarmed-pacifism." The Occupation authorities intentionally chose to regard disarmament as pacifism *per se:* they committed Japan to it irrespective of the wishes of her population; they publicly and solemnly gave legal sanctity and symbolic dignity to it; and they colored all practical issues of force, defense, and security with an emotional aura and moral cast in simple black-and-white terms. Further, this punitive pacifism was fed into school curricula and textbooks in all elementary, middle, and high school courses. In time, when students became adults, many consequently saw this sort of American-made pacifism as the sole basis on which Japan could live side by side with the United States.

This perverted pacifism, which attempts to see punishment in the guise of the blessing of disarmament, could logically be valid only so long as enmity is postulated between Japan and the U.S.; and, also, so long as Japan remains isolated in a kind of fantasy-land, excluded from any contact with international politics. Fortunately for Japan, fundamental changes in American policy did subsequently take place, with an emphasis on transforming Japan from yesterday's enemy into an ally. Yet, at the same time, a very serious problem was thereby created for both Japan and the United States, posing a grave obstacle to easy cooperation along the line of alliance between the two countries. Stated plainly, Japan's constitution has outlived America's early occupation policy. Incorporated into the corpus of the basic law of the land in the most solemn way possible, the principles of weak government-through-disarmament-pacifism are very difficult to modify. The Occupation drafters shortsightedly made the process of amendment extremely difficult: a two-thirds majority in each House and a simple majority by national referendum. Consequently, there is simply no prospect that the ruling conservative party can obtain in the foreseeable future the number of seats necessary for amendment. Moreover, a national referendum amending the Constitution would set up a highly moralistic debate on the merits of pacifism vs. militarism with uncertain and potentially explosive results, and it would virtually obviate a pragmatic approach to rearmament.

Japan and the United Nations

We are unreservedly grateful for the basic change of American policy toward Japan, but we are also deeply resentful that the U.N. has continued since its inception to keep Japan in the status of an "enemy." Indeed, the U.N. Charter is quite outspoken in making discriminating references to Japan:

Nothing in the present Charter shall invalidate or preclude action, in relation to any state which during the Second World War has been an enemy of any signatory to the present Charter, taken or authorized as a result of that war by the Governments having responsibility for such action. (Article CVII)

1. The Security Council shall, where appropriate, utilize such regional arrangements or agencies for enforcement action under its authority. But no enforcement action shall be taken under regional arrangements or by regional agencies without the authorization of the Security Council, with the exception of measures against any enemy state, as defined in paragraph 2 of this Article, provided for pursuant to Article 107 or in regional arrangements directed against renewal of aggressive policy on the part of any such state, until such time as the Organization may, on the request of the Governments concerned, be charged with the responsibility for preventing further aggression by such a state.

2. The term enemy state as used in paragraph 1 of this Article applies to any state which during the Second World War has been an enemy of any signatory of the present Charter. (Article LIII)

Governments "having responsibility for" the postwar settlements, e.g., states that signed diplomatic papers relative to postwar settlements, armistice, surrender, and peace agreements can apply at their own discretion a wide range of actions, including those of an enforcement nature, against the "enemy" states.[7] Further, they can authorize other states to act in their stead. No permission from the Security Council is required and that Council cannot act in their place unless requested to do so by the governments concerned. Nor can the Council invalidate or preclude the actions by those governments.

Second, actions taken under regional arrangements or by regional agencies and measures taken in accordance with articles of regional arrangements against "renewal of aggressive policy on the part of 'enemy' states" do not require the Council's permission. Moreover, the right to decide whether "aggression" takes place rests solely in the hands of the governments concerned, and their subjective judgment is deemed sufficient. As a consequence, it is unnecessary to adhere to any of the limitations set on the right of self-defense by Article LI of the U.N. Charter. For the Security Council to assume responsibility in place of the governments concerned, both the unanimous request from those governments and a Council resolution of approval are required; and the latter may of course be blocked by the veto power enjoyed by each of the Big Five in that Council. If no unanimous request is made and/or no resolution approved, the measures taken by the governments against the "enemy" states remain effective on a permanent basis. Finally, measures can be taken "as a result of that war," permitting enforcement actions to be taken against "enemy" states without showing precise justification. Thus, there is an obvious danger of misuse inherent in this loose wording.

On the other hand, even if an "enemy" state should seek relief from the U.N. contending that those measures taken against it violate purposes and principles of the U.N. Charter (Articles I,II), it would be in vain, because both the Security Council and General Assembly have no competence to prevent those governments from acting. In addition, those "enemy state" articles are of unlimited duration, thereby giving the governments concerned a permanent right to control "enemy" states. As permanent outlaws, the enemy states are excluded from the very protection of the U.N. Charter, the purpose of which is nothing short of "maintaining international peace and security." (Article 1, Paragraph 1) It is certain beyond any doubt that this outlawry would make future war against Japan a one-sided game, at least from the legal point of view—a context in which that harsh dictum rejecting for Japan "the right of belligerency of the state" (Constitution, Article IX, Paragraph 2) most properly makes sense.

So much for the legal argument. So long as the U.N. is a legal body that behaves only in accordance with the articles of its own Charter, Japan cannot remain indifferent to the "enemy" status in which she has been forced to remain long after admission in the U.N. Possibly and hopefully, no effective enforcement action will be taken against her on the basis of the authorization provided by those two articles of the Charter. Nevertheless, patent resentment in Japanese political circles against those insulting articles is quite deep and serious, making, naturally enough, any cooperation with the U.N. agencies inevitably colored with a shade of mental reserve. For instance: countries of former Allied Powers who happen to seek aid from Japan may, it is argued, be asked whether it is not thoughtless, impolite, and logically inconsistent for them to continue to treat Japan as a legal "enemy" and still expect that "enemy" to provide aid to its legal opponents. As mentioned previously, Japan has decided to commit by 1975 one percent of her annual GNP to economic aid directed toward developing states. But understandably she has little enthusiasm in doing so under the sponsorship and within the framework of the U.N.

Even if Japan were elected as a permanent member of the Security Council in the future, it will be an empty achievement so long as measures against "enemy" states remain outside the jurisdiction of the U.N. organization itself. Moreover, since Japan is forbidden to maintain any armed forces of her own except—by implication—those of self-defense, it is, to say the least, unclear how she could discharge the obligations of permanent Security Council membership, which require assuming "primary responsibility for the maintenance of international peace and security." The fact that Japan, alone among all the countries in the world, has been and remains under exceptional legal constraints domestically and internationally must be faced squarely. These restraints are basic and formidable barriers for Japan's willing and voluntary assumption of a more positive security role in the world.

Japan's Role

In 1969, an influential literary club, The Cultural Congress of Japan, convened a symposium with the theme: "Is Japan a State?" The majority view which came out of the discussion was rather in the negative. Rightly or wrongly, this underscores that the U.S. should not take it for granted that Japan is simply an ordinary state. After the creators of "Wonderland" went home at the end of the Occupation, the Japanese Alice had to stay in her Homeland-turned-into-Wonderland with no sure prospect of amending her basic legal code in the near future. Since there is no visible prospect of returning to the *status quo ante* of life as an ordinary state, whenever Japanese become concerned about the status of their nation—either in solitary speculation in their study or together with friends after drinking—they invariably find themselves fundamentally irritated, ill-humored, and indignant. It is clear to many that Japan is basically a cripple, a "half-nation" at best. With many Japanese in this state of mind, external pressures on Japan either to assume a more positive security role in East Asia or to close off for good the option of future defense capability with the ratification of the Non-Proliferation Treaty, could provoke a severe domestic reaction. In such circumstances, the development of an anti-American brand of nationalism is a distinct possibility.

By virtue of Japan's emergent economic capacity, all of the great powers have come to expect her to play a more positive role in East Asia (beyond the original and limited role of preserving herself), so far as possible under the constraints of the Constitution. As American policy toward Japan underwent fundamental change during the past decade, successive Japanese governments have sought to defend the gradual expansion of arms against the attacks of the opposition parties. The shift of the conservative governments from the path of pacifism established by the Occupation to rearmament had to be made in the face of rigid and stern wordings of Article IX and in the face of a largely pacifist and indifferent climate of opinion at home. After having to defend most earnestly the principle of thoroughgoing demilitarization during the occupation, the conservatives had to make an abrupt about-face to defend the principle of rearmament in conformity with the change of American policy. Devoid of consistency, and necessarily credibility, they have since lacked the position to move forcefully ahead. Consequently, although their effort to rearm may not have seemed to be in earnest, it could hardly have been otherwise in the light of the circumstances. Moreover, rearmament under a demilitarization Constitution is a *contradictio in adjectio* philosophically and sheer hypocrisy morally. Clearly there are limits in advocating rearmament in utter disregard of the exact phrase of the Constitution, limits that make any transition to positive security responsibilities beyond territorial self-defense singularly hazardous, barring of course the shock brought on by some kind of future international emergency.

In the context of a global balance of power, the problem of East Asia has come under the influence of the progress of the SALT talks between the two superpowers. Another potential force at play is the American expectation of the future success of arms control talks with China, once the latter has developed an ICBM system. Meanwhile, Japan can do nothing but remain a passive spectator at the scene of global negotiations on the issue of war and peace. What really matters is and will remain the issue of a regional balance—provided that balance is somehow preserved between the United States on the one hand and the Soviet Union and China on the other, and so long as it deters the outbreak of open hostilities. To be sure, those two conditions are rather difficult to fulfill; but, at any rate, it is only on the basis of the possibility and expectation of their realization that Japan can continue to act with the United States as representatives of the free world, believing with confidence in the future victory of liberal ideas and economic principles over the communistic ones sponsored by the Soviet Union and China. Japan's role will then be to stand before the countries of East Asia as an example of relative political stability born of parliamentary democracy and of a sound and affluent society born of economic liberalism.

In the long run, Japan's active participation in any program of regional security in East Asia can take place only through a slow process of gradual self-adaptation, with an emphasis on a small-scale but steady increase of maritime self-defense forces. For Japan as a maritime nation, defense of sea lanes near her home waters is in itself a kind of territorial self-defense, and it might be well if Japan's own protective arms were stretched somewhat beyond her territorial waters in order to assure the safe arrival of vital imports—oil, in particular. Another possible program for future development is a loose and *de facto* system of maritime cooperation including Japan, Indonesia, and the ANZUS[c] countries—with Japan sharing the major financial burden—to promote unhindered seaborne trade in the Pacific-Asian waters to the benefit of all participants. Indeed, in the prescient words of Professor Robert Osgood,

---

[c]Incidentally, this proposal may also serve to revitalize the ANZUS treaty, which reportedly is now undergoing severe reappraisal by the newly elected governments of both Australia and New Zealand.

"weapons and equipment or an extended naval role would be most acceptable forms of Japanese assistance"[8] to some of the Pacific countries.[d] Another proposal meriting consideration might be to have Japan make direct financial contributions to the maintenance of American fleet units stationed in the Pacific-Asian waters.

Bold initiatives such as President Nixon's trip to Peking are surely bound to produce both light and shadows in their wake. On the one hand, the Nixon initiative inevitably helped to decrease American credibility in Japan; on the other hand, it induced Prime Minister Chou En-lai to raise a *ballon d'essai* in hinting that China does not now feel threatened by the Japanese-American Treaty, that it also understands and upholds the need for American defense in the Pacific, and that it can conceive of circumstances that would bring it to the aid of Japan together with the United States if the Soviet Union would attack Japan. Short-term strategic calculations of the regional balance have now come to be clarified with the most serious questions centering on the Soviet posture. If the Soviet naval forces should develop overwhelming ascendency in Asian waters then the overall regional balance would be upset beyond repair. Japan's geographical and economic dependence on the seas around her means that she must also be absolutely dependent on any naval superpower in command of those waters, whether be it the United States or the Soviet Union. Moreover, this is true if it is command of the sea in wartime or simply naval presence in peacetime. Should the Soviet Union surpass the U.S. in the Asian waters, Japan would almost inevitably have to accept forceful incorporation into the Russian orbit irrespective of her own wishes, with the attendant result of the disappearance of any regional role for Japan.

Interesting books and articles about Japan's role in international politics have been coming forth in profusion from the pens of American scholars, and we in Japan have been much stimulated in reading them. What I have tried to do here is only to add my own observations, with an emphasis on the meaning of foreign policy problems in the context of Japanese politics, in the hope that they may serve to present a somewhat different perspective for understanding these matters. Personally speaking, I am afraid that we have been somewhat less than frank in presenting differences in perspective and perceptions of objective facts. At the same time, I regret that this paper ends without offering many positive and encouraging arguments, and tends to be rather passive and reserved. If there is anything on which I can still be positive, it is to insist on patience. Patience is vital, because the gradual development of mutual understanding about what can and cannot be expected from the other side at a given stage can only be brought about on the basis of mutual patience. In the final analysis, I would venture to maintain, the relationship between Japan and the U.S. may well prove to be the key to peace and war in East Asia.

---

[d]Similar views are also put forward by Professor Scalapino (op. cit., p. 85) and Zbigniew Brzezinski (*The Fragile Blossom: Crisis and Change in Japan.* New York: Harper and Row, 1972. Harper Torchbook Edition, p. 138).

Notes

1. Donald C. Hellmann, *Japan and East Asia: The New International Order* (New York: Praeger Publishers, 1972), p. 27.

2. Ministry of Finance, *Statistical Monthly on Finance and Banking.*

3. Hellmann, op. cit., p. 38.

4. Hellmann, ibid. p. 131.

5. Robert A. Scalapino, *Asia and the Major Powers: Implications for the International Order* (Washington, D.C.: American Enterprise Institute for Public Policy Research, 1972), p. 65.

6. James L. Brierly, *The Law of Nations.* 6th ed. Waldock, Humphrey, ed. (London: Oxford University Press, 1963), p. 386.

7. In my interpretation of these two articles I have drawn heavily on the work of Professor Hans Kelsen. Hans Kelsen, *The Law of the United Nations.* (New York: Praeger Publishers, 1951), pp. 808, 810-811, 813, 815.

8. Robert E. Osgood. *The Weary and the Wary: U.S. and Japanese Security Policies in Transition* (Baltimore: The Johns Hopkins University Press, 1972), p. 49.

Part V:
The Strategy of Implementation:
Resources and Economics

Although both stronger U.S. partnership with allies and negotiations with adversaries are predicated on national strength as the third pillar of the Nixon Doctrine, defense allocations in the United States have come under increasing criticism at the very time the Soviet Union has been engaged in vigorously expanding and modernizing its strategic and naval forces. In the first paper that follows, M. Mark Earle, Jr. and Robert W. Campbell compare the U.S. and Soviet economies and conclude that in recent years Soviet defense spending has increased at a faster rate than U.S. defense expenditures. In the second paper William A. Niskanen, Jr. examines the economic constraints on the U.S. defense budget and on increasing that portion of it devoted to military preparedness. Finally, John M. Hennessy assesses the international economic circumstances that have raised economic problems to the level of high policy in the United States Government and that will be a major determinant of the future international structure.

Mr. Earle is Senior Economist and Assistant Director, Strategic Studies Center, Stanford Research Institute. He has done extensive work in program and cost analysis, and macroeconomic analysis, especially of the economic potential of the United States, the Soviet Union, and the Peoples Republic of China. His current research is concerned with strategic force options and war termination and comparisons of the U.S. and Soviet economies.

Dr. Robert W. Campbell is Professor of Economics at Indiana University, specializing in Soviet economics, and is a consultant to Stanford Research Institute, the Arms Control and Disarmament Agency, and the U.S. State Department. Dr. Campbell has written many articles and books on the Soviet economy, including: *Soviet Economic Power; Economics of the Soviet Oil and Gas Industry*; and "Management Spillover from Soviet Space and Military Programmes," which appeared in the April 1972 issue of *Soviet Studies*.

Dr. Niskanen is a Professor at the School of Public Policy at the University of California, Berkeley. He has previously served as Staff Analyst at RAND Corporation; Director of Special Studies, Office of Systems Analysis, Department of Defense; Director of the Program Analysis Division, Institute for Defense Analyses; and Assistant Director for Evaluation, Office of Management and Budget. He is the author of *Bureaucracy in Representative Government* and numerous articles on public program analysis and management.

Mr. Hennessey is Assistant Secretary of the Treasury for International Affairs. A graduate of Harvard University, he was associated with the First National City Bank of New York from 1964-1968, serving tours in Bolivia and Peru. From 1968 to 1970 he was a management and economic consultant for the Arthur D. Little Company in Boston. In 1970, Mr. Hennessey joined the Treasury

Department as Deputy Assistant Secretary for Developing Nations. He was appointed to his present position in March 1972.

8 A Comparison of U.S. and Soviet Economics

M. Mark Earle, Jr. and Robert W. Campbell

Introduction

Considerable use is made of U.S. and USSR economic comparison data to support statements about U.S. national and defense policies. Often the use of such data is based explicitly or implicitly on the following reasoning:

1. A larger GNP reflects a greater potential to initiate or expand programs relating to satisfaction of national objectives. Therefore, if Soviet GNP were bigger than U.S. or were increasing at a rate greater than U.S., the USSR could execute options to the comparative disadvantage of the United States.
2. A relationship exists between military capability and expenditures on national security such that higher levels of expenditures result in increased military capability. Therefore, if Soviet NSE were "bigger" than U.S. or increasing at a rate greater than U.S., the USSR would achieve a defense posture superior to the United States whether measured in terms of political utility or warfighting capability.
3. While RDT&E outputs cannot be measured directly, a relationship exists between expenditures on input factors and resultant output such that higher levels of expenditures result in a greater scientific and technological capability. This capability moreover is linked to the deployment of military forces and, in turn, military capability. Therefore, if Soviet RDT&E expenditures were "bigger" than U.S., over time the USSR would have a greater number of force improvement options than the United States and would achieve a defense posture superior to the United States whether measured in terms of political utility or warfighting capability.

Yet, comparison of relative sizes must be used with caution—problems are encountered in developing the estimates, which limits their accuracy, and conceptual problems inhibit their ability to provide the desired policy insights. This paper contributes to the understanding of the above by:

1. Giving preliminary estimates of selected U.S.-USSR economic aggregates;
2. Interpreting them in light of data and theoretical considerations;
3. Commenting on the state of the two economies to provide a basis for interpreting future resource allocation decisions; and finally

4. Presenting observations on what can be drawn from U.S.-USSR comparative economic studies at this time for defense policy analysis.

Estimates of U.S. and USSR
Economic Aggregates

The economic aggregates that are the objects of comparison are defined in brief as follows:

1. GNP (Gross National Product)—the value of output of all final goods and services, as traditionally defined in Western countries.
2. NMP (Net Material Product)—the value of net tangible material output, which is the Soviet conception of national income and which differs from GNP in that capital consumption allowances and certain "unproductive" kinds of services are excluded.
3. NSE—the sum of DOD, AEC, and NASA expenditures or their Soviet equivalents.
4. RDT&E (Research, Development, Test and Evaluation)—expenditures by government and private industry on basic and applied research in the sciences and engineering, including the design, development, test, and evaluation of prototypes and processes, plus expenditures on R&D plant and facilities.
5. National Security Related RDT&E—those RDT&E expenditures, as just defined, relating to national security purposes.

A survey of the comparative economic literature reveals differing estimates of these aggregates, although the lack of consensus is much greater for estimates of USSR economic activity than U.S. Analysis of the underlying methodologies and source data is impossible for most of the estimates due to lack of documentation. Moreover, the time periods covered by the estimates are not uniform, thus further complicating the systematic evaluation of differences between the estimates and interpretation of U.S.-USSR comparisons.

As a result, SRI estimates were prepared, and estimates for selected years are given in the tables following this chapter. The SRI estimates should be treated as preliminary, given the major computational problems encountered in calculating the Soviet estimates. Estimates by others are also included, but no attempt is made to document the differences indicated. Special note should be made of the impact of using different ruble-dollar ratios in converting rubles to dollars, and the different results obtained when comparisons of aggregates are made in rubles rather than dollars.

Interpretation of the Comparison
of Economic Aggregates

The Basic Question Addressed
by the Comparisons

The SRI research has focused to date on the problem of comparing the productive capacity of the two economies. Essentially for GNP the question is—could the U.S. have produced the Soviet mix of goods and services with less resources than were used to produce U.S. GNP in a given year? For NSE the question addressed is—could the U.S. have produced the Soviet mix of military goods and services with less resources than those allocated by the U.S. for national security purposes? A different question must be asked for RDT&E. Since the output of RDT&E is not a product in the sense of a tank or missile, the comparison is made in terms of input resources. Therefore, the question addressed is—could the U.S. have purchased the Soviet RDT&E inputs with less resources than were used by the U.S. to purchase its RDT&E inputs?

Once estimates of the desired economic aggregates have been prepared, two fundamental problems remain: (1) How accurate are the estimates?—which relates to data and computational problems, and (2) What do the numbers mean?—which relates to conceptual problems.

Data and Computation Problems:
How Accurate are the Numbers?

1. Estimating U.S. Economic Aggregates. The U.S. estimates used in the SRI and in most other comparative economic studies are derived from official publications of departments or agencies of the U.S. government. These numbers are generally accepted as accurate reflections of the desired economic aggregates.

However, one of the major limitations in determining total expenditures for defense related RDT&E is the lack of adequate data relating to the funding that may have been contributed by private industry. Preliminary estimates for 1968 have been made of this contribution, using a model developed by SRI for this purpose. These estimates indicate that the sum for that year of DOD, AEC, and NASA expenditures on RDT&E may understate total national security RDT&E by as much as 5 percent.

2. Estimating USSR Economic Aggregates. The USSR does not publish data for GNP, NSE, and RDT&E as defined for this study. Therefore it is necessary to develop methodologies to estimate these economic aggregates using Soviet source materials.[a]

The quality, reliability, and interpretation of Soviet data, as well as the price structure in the Soviet Union, must be taken into consideration in an assessment of the accuracy of the USSR estimates developed. First, only very general information is available on the derivation methods of Soviet data, and Soviet data published in open literature is often lacking in definitive description. Second, a variety of pricing systems are in use in the Soviet Union, a fact that further complicates data interpretation. Third, the applicability of official Soviet indexes for reduction of the data to a common price base, or for the calculation of certain components of the economic aggregates, is questionable. Sufficient evidence is available to indicate a general upward trend in prices, although the Soviets report a declining price index for the Machine Building and Metal Working (M&MW) sector. Moreover, many Soviet and Western specialists question the accuracy of indexes based on so-called "constant 1955 prices," which are a composite of current and constant prices. And, finally, no information is available on the ruble pricing of military and space hardware.

As a result of data and procedural uncertainties, the accuracy of the USSR estimates is thought to decrease as one proceeds from NMP to GNP, NSE, and finally to RDT&E.

3. Estimating Ruble-to-Dollar Conversion Ratio.[1] Once the ruble estimates have been prepared, they must be converted to dollar magnitudes. There are four factors at work to change the ruble-dollar ratios over time. These factors are:

1. Different inflation rates in the two countries.
2. Changes in individual ruble-dollar relatives; i.e., the prices of some goods produced both in 1955 and in 1970 may have changed in response to diverse patterns of resource allocations in the two countries.
3. Changes in the U.S. and Soviet product mix. For example, in 1970 the Soviet mix may contain more goods which had relatively high ruble-dollar ratios than in 1955.
4. Introduction of new products; i.e., the production in 1970 of goods that, because of the state-of-the-art, could not have been produced in 1955. Such new products may have quite different ruble-dollar ratios than the products produced in both countries in 1955.

It should be noted that these four factors may move in the same or in opposite directions as far as the effect on the ruble-dollar ratios is concerned.

The factors for converting these outlays into dollars continue to be based on empirical evidence that is more than fifteen years old. In an attempt to expand

---

[a]The basic SRI methodologies for estimating USSR NSE and expenditures on RDT&E were developed by W.T. Lee.

the data on ruble-dollar ratios, a survey of the Western and Soviet literature on estimates of ruble-dollar ratios was made with the following major findings:[2]

1. With only a few notable exceptions, the methodologies employed by the various authors were not sufficiently documented to permit establishing the requisite set of ruble-dollar ratios for the purpose of this study.
2. Some fragmentary data were found in the Soviet literature indicating that the ruble-dollar ratios for investment and durables were higher in 1955 than Bornstein[3] had estimated, and that the ratios in 1967-1970 may have been higher than in 1955.
3. Soviet and Western sources have raised serious questions about the validity of using Soviet price indexes (particularly those for M&MW) to adjust the 1955 ruble-dollar ratios to other years. The main reservations about Soviet price indexes relate to the methods used in their computation and the limited coverage of the samples.

In the absence of post-1967 ruble-dollar price relatives, no empirically verifiable ratios can be calculated for recent years. The values adopted for the development of SRI estimates are based on plausible quantification of judgmental assessments of the four factors that influence the ruble-dollar ratios over time.

Conceptual Problems: What do the Numbers Mean?

However accurate the estimates of Soviet GNP, NSE, or RDT&E expenditures various researchers produce, and however precise their conversion into dollar magnitudes, there are a number of conceptual ambiguities and methodological crudities, common to all these numbers, that should be kept in mind.

1. The Index Number Ambiguity. When two countries exhibit such differences in the composition of their output and in the relative costs of different kinds of output as do the USSR and the United States, there is an inherent ambiguity in the question how big one country's output is compared to that of the other. Because the two aggregates involve such different mixes of products, it is necessary to interpret the summary comparison represented by "how many dollars worth of output does each produce" as standing for something independent of what combination of things is being produced—some kind of abstract, general, production potential which will serve as a common denominator to which *any* kind of output can be reduced. Because the price stuctures are so different, however, the result of phrasing the question about relative production potential alternatively as "how many rubles worth of output could each country produce" is to show Soviet production potential as much smaller in relation to U.S. potential than did the dollar comparison.[b] It may not even be possible to say unambiguously which country's output represents the larger production potential.

2. Defense Output Measured as a Mixture of Investment and Current Inputs. In comparative studies of U.S. and Soviet output, the convention is to treat the contribution of the defense establishment to the total output of the society (and its drain on production potential) as the sum of (a) additions to its capital stock (i.e., its stock of missiles, submarines, and other such military durables), and (b) its current consumption of such inputs as labor services, fuel, and repair parts. This convention ignores the fact that the defense sector holds a very large stock of capital, the size of which is crucial in determining how much defense or security the defense establishment produces.

3. How Well Do Estimates of GNP Reflect Productive Potential? Apart from the ambiguities of the index number problem, the use of comparative Soviet and U.S. output in some given year as a surrogate for comparative production potential at that point depends on several simplifying assumptions that may not be met.

It is assumed that there is in fact some rather unambiguous upper limit to the amount that either society can produce with its available resources, and that resources are fully employed. But in reality every economy has a certain amount of slack, and there may be quite a differential between the U.S. and the Soviet economies in regard to how close they are to capacity at any given time.

Under the production potential concept, a statement that the Soviet economy is two-thirds as large as the U.S. economy is supposed to hold regardless of how either economy alters the mix of outputs that as they are produced, draw on that production potential. But, in the very short run it may simply not be possible to shift resources from the moon program to producing more beefsteak, and even in the longer run there may be increasing or decreasing returns.

Unfortunately, on either side there is a large area of economic activity where prices and measures for the outputs are lacking, and the practice has been followed of including as output in national totals the cost of the inputs used in these activities. Education, health care, research and development, and defense are all examples.

The Changing Environment for Future Policy Decisions: The State of the Two Economies

The Soviet Economy:
A Period of Transition

The Soviet economy is involved at the present time in a difficult transition, involving a shift in priorities, a shift in the allocation of output and in economic

[b]See for example the Bornstein 1955 dollar and ruble comparisons in Tables 8-1 and 8-2.

structure, and a transition to a new strategy of growth. The traditional Soviet growth strategy has been one of mobilizing big increases in inputs of capital and labor to ensure the continued growth of output. The demographic situation today does not allow the latter, and the former is made unattractive by very high incremental capital-to-output ratios. The high capital requirements under the old strategy made overall growth strongly competitive with military expenditures, and with increases in consumption.

The new strategy has several elements: (a) it alters the composition of output somewhat in favor of consumption; (b) as a first step in that direction, it shifts the composition of the investment program to more investment in industries producing consumer goods and less investment in industries producing investment goods; (c) it places a very heavy emphasis on productivity increases as a source of growth. These increases are in turn dependent on modernizing the technology of the civilian sectors of the economy and on improving the management of the economy.

Increased consumption should help to motivate productivity increases, but another reason for this shift is the lesson from Poland that if significant rises in consumption are not achieved, even a communist regime may be faced with severe worker disturbances. Another possible interpretation worth exploring might be that since the USSR has sharply altered its relative standing in military capital, relative military strength is now less directly related to current spending on procurement of weapons systems (as shown in comparative NSE) and more to existing stocks; it is, therefore, freer to contemplate a diversion of some of the capacity that has gone into producing military hardware into producing more modern equipment and machinery for the civilian sectors. This would mean that the Soviet military planners might also want to use the military RDT&E resources available to them differently than in the past, say to explore more speculative ventures, rather than concentrating them on development of well-defined systems to match and offset U.S. systems.

Also important to the strategy is an emphasis on trade to help ease some of the bottlenecks that accompany this shift in proportions and to help with the modernization goal through importing technology directly in the form of patents and licenses and indirectly as embodied in capital goods.

It is not at all clear how successful the Russians will be in making this transition. It is full of risks and uncertainties. In the past, outside the military sectors, they have never been very successful at innovation and technical progress, either in creating it domestically or in absorbing and mastering it through importation. The system has never been very effective at getting the successful experience of the military and space sectors transferred to the task of rejuvenating the technology of the civilian branches. If the new strategy may ease the competitiveness of military programs with investment objectives, it would seem to exacerbate the competition for R&D resources between military and civilian purposes. Moreover, the Russians are seeking much larger productivity gains than they have hoped for in the past. They imply unprecedented success in the creation and absorption of new technology, radical improvements in managerial behavior, and breakthroughs in what have always been intractable problem sectors in the past, such as agriculture.

The total spending on RDT&E is such that even with a high share devoted to military and space programs the absolute amount left for civilian work is very large. If, of the $28 billion of Soviet RDT&E expenditures in 1970 only 60 percent is military, the remaining $11 billion represents a handsome expenditure on behalf of civilian technology, considering that the analogous U.S. total was about $16 billion for a much larger economy. The obstacles to innovation in the civilian economy would thus seem to be related more to defects in organization and incentives than to the volume of R&D spending. The implications of this proposition are ambiguous, however. To get serious gains in civilian technology it may be necessary to call on the capacity of the organizations and facilities in the military sector that have produced results, in which case the military-civilian competition would be felt very directly and keenly. Alternatively the leaders may conclude that the emphasis should be on organizational and planning changes within the share of resources already allocated to civilian RDT&E. Soviet planning documents and public statements do not as yet reveal how these RDT&E resource allocations problems are being resolved.

The goal of more trade carries with it many dilemmas. The problem of what to export must be a difficult one. The index number problem that bedevils economic comparisons implies as a corollary that there are plenty of export possibilities; the Russians have a comparative advantage in all those areas with low ruble-dollar ratios, such as machinery, investment goods, and industrial producer goods generally. Shifts in priorities also imply excess capacity in some heavy industry branches. It is often held that the Russians are not in fact competitive in this area due to durability problems, but it is interesting they have recently become very aggressive in selling products such as turbines, aircraft, and industrial plant. They also must have a strong commercial motivation to sell conventional weapons around the world to utilize the excess capacity in the branches that have produced the present stocks of these weapons.

The Russians would like to make the program of modernizing the civilian sector through trade more or less self-financing; if so, it need not compete with the military for RDT&E and investment resources. The hope is to create new capacity on a high technical level, on credit, in those sectors where this capacity can provide directly the exports to pay off the debt. Oil and gas are the prime example. This is one of those mixed competitive-cooperative interactions that will tax the ingenuity of policymakers on each side to extract for their side the largest possible share of the gains.

There is also the question of how effectively technology imports can solve the technical progress problem. There already exists a long history of Soviet borrowing of foreign technology, a history that suggests it is a far from costless process. It creates obstacles to learning how to innovate independently. Technological imports may give a much smaller impetus to productivity growth than expected—they may require better maintenance, new skills, and higher quality inputs than the Soviet economy normally supplies.

The risks of this transition strategy are revealed by the experience of the first two years of the Ninth Five Year Plan. The Russians have experienced a drastic failure in agriculture; growth as a whole has been considerably below the levels set in the Five Year Plan for the first two years; they have not succeeded in fulfilling many of the goals for consumer goods output. How the Soviet policymakers will react to these difficulties over the next couple of years is very important for a net assessment of U.S.-USSR relations. The hardline faction within the leadership could take the position that the new strategy is dangerous adventurism, that there must be a return to the old emphasis on heavy industries and defense industries, and that the country must not risk giving up the strong comparative position it has won in the military area and in defense RDT&E by frittering away its production potential on "unattainable" civilian and consumer goals.

As of now, the leadership seems to be holding to the transitional strategy. Faced with a failure in the agricultural program, the Soviets committed half a year's hard currency earnings for grain imports. Kosygin, however, is reported to have cautioned the planners that they must not expect to solve growth problems by big new infusions of capital and that they must stay within the amounts planned. The Central Committee met in December to discuss the Plan and Budget for 1973, and the plan as approved reaffirms the original strategy of the Five Year Plan. It reacts to the agricultural failure by saying that the effort in that sector should be increased; it reiterates the high priority of consumer goals, and the budget for 1973 specifies an allocation for military expenditures at the same level as for 1972. This need not be accepted as the true indication of what will happen to military spending, but this action is a significant symbolic action for internal purposes. They are still vigorously pursuing the trade aspect of the strategy. There are a few contrary indications regarding the viability of the strategy, such as the greater fulfillment of producer-goods industry goals than of consumer-goods industry goals in the last two years, and in a sharp increase in the investment allocation to the steel industry for 1973. These differentials may, however, be explainable as results of the failure of input requirements to decline as hoped for.

The U.S. Economy: A Period of
Accelerated Recovery

If the Soviet economy seems to be engulfed in a set of problems associated with a transition to a new strategy for economic development, the U.S.

economy seems to be recovering from the unsettled conditions of a different kind of transition characterized by inflation, considerable unemployment of resources, fiscal pressures associated with the Vietnam War, and adjustments caused by changing national priorities (e.g., as in government support of research and education).

The transition from the recession of 1969-1971 to the current period of accelerated growth was accomplished through the New Economic Policy (NEP) introduced in August of 1971. The NEP was a revolutionary and unprecedented program of government controls and stimulation for economic recovery. The three main problem areas addressed by the NEP were excessive wage and price increases, poor gains in worker productivity, and a worsening balance of payments.

Phase I of the NEP commenced on 15 August 1971 and was comprised of a ninety-day freeze on all wages and prices, termination of the convertibility of dollars held by foreign governments into gold held by the U.S., imposition of a 10 percent surcharge on all imports, and demands for the reform of the international monetary system. Phase II provided for the establishment of control mechanisms for regulating wage and price increases, tax incentives for stimulating producer accumulation of capital goods, the reduction or elimination of those federally funded programs with low levels of productivity, and negotiations on the devaluation of the dollar relative to the currencies of trading partners of the United States.

Phase III of the NEP was announced on 11 January 1973. It lifts the mandatory wage and price controls of Phase II and substitutes a program that continues government surveillance of product and sector performance and enforces compliance through informal government pressure and the threat of reimposing Phase II controls. Certain "problem" areas (food, health, and construction industries) of the economy will remain under the wage-price controls.

The improved performance of the economy since the introduction of the NEP has been encouraging. Real GNP (at 1958 prices) advanced at a rate of 6.5 percent, compared with the 2.7 percent rate of 1971. The unemployment level fell from the 6 percent-plus rate of 1971 to 5.2 percent by the end of 1972, a 27-month low. The Consumer Price Index at the end of 1972 was increasing at an annual rate of 3.5 percent, somewhat above the Administration's target rate of 3 percent.

1972 was the best year in a decade for industrial peace; i.e., in terms of working days lost due to labor strikes. This stabilizing environment is reflected in the gains registered in labor efficiency, where output per man-hour rose in 1972 at an annual rate of better than 3 percent. By comparison, from the second quarter of 1966 to the spring of 1971, output per man-hour rose at an annual rate of 1.9 percent.

Perhaps the most critical variable in any administration's attempts to bring the economy into a period of full employment, stable prices, and rising real growth is consumer and producer confidence. Housing starts in 1972 (better than 2.3 million units), machine tool orders, automobile production figures, and last-quarter retail sales all indicate rising expectations that the economic recovery begun in 1972 will accelerate in 1973. Corporate profits, a most critical index, were up by 15 percent in 1972, which should contribute greatly to continued confidence in the economy under Phase III.

While progress has been made toward the realization of the objectives of the NEP, there remain several areas where long-run problems persist. These areas are balance of payments, the effectiveness of the federal budget as an instrument for economic stabilization, and the economic implications of changing national priorities.

The stabilizing U.S. prices and increasing productivity coupled with a serious inflationary trend in the West European countries should contribute significantly toward the making of American exports competitive once again. However, the $6.5 billion deficit last year on the current (or trade) account of the balance of payments is due not so much to a slow growth of exports as to a phenomenal increase in the rate of imports. For example, while figures for the first 11 months of 1972 showed exports running 12 percent ahead of the 1971 pace, imports for the same period swelled by 22 percent, creating an 11-month deficit of $5.8 billion. What the Administration proposes to do about this problem will become more clearly defined in Phase III during the Congressional debate over the Burke-Hartke Bill and during the "Nixon Round" of trade talks that will start in September in Geneva.

The second problem area, the effectiveness of the federal budget as an economic stabilization instrument, has become prominent recently as more and more public and private sector economic policymakers have concluded that macroeconomic instruments (those that deal with the management of aggregate demand) such as the federal budget are focusing on the wrong variables. In other words, in fighting inflation and unemployment, post-Keynesian policy instruments such as the federal budget may be far less effective than disaggregated policies dealing with prices, consumer and producer preferences, market structures and the employment problems of individual groups (e.g., young black males). Furthermore, the relatively uncontrollable categories of the federal budget (such as pensions and social security payments) may effectively deny the federal budget's ability to serve as a stabilization mechanism. The federal revenue-sharing plan reflects a growing realization that certain services may be provided more effectively if certain programs are formulated and administered on a regional or local basis. Such an adjustment to the pattern of government expenditures may, however, inhibit federal government anti-cyclical activities.

Traditionally, anticipated real growth such as forecast for 1973 is the basis for formulating new program initiatives. In light of the continuing high deficit levels, however, emphasis is currently being placed by the Administration on the reduction or elimination of domestic programs judged to have had poor performance or to have low priority. Yet, expectations of continued increases in the type and level of government services are generally evident. Thus, until more information on the Administration's domestic strategy becomes available it is difficult to forecast the near-term economic implications of changing national priorities.[c]

Summary Observations on U.S./USSR Economic Comparisons

Despite all the ambiguities in comparisons of economic aggregates, and in the light of the best assumptions that can be made about the interpretation of the preliminary estimates, what can be said at the present time that is responsive to the policymakers' concerns expressed in the introduction?

1. There is no doubt that the Soviet production potential has moved appreciably closer to that of the United States over the years considered by the study. There are two qualifications to this finding, both of which somewhat mitigate the impression the GNP comparisons give of the favorable Soviet situation. First, during the last several years, U.S. GNP has provided an appreciable understatement of production potential. In 1970, for example, there was 6 percent unemployment, and output had fallen by one-half percent from the previous year. Second, the preliminary SRI comparisons have been made in dollars only. If ruble comparisons were made, the ratio of USSR to U.S. GNP would certainly be smaller, although a dynamic comparison would probably still reflect ratios with trends favorable to the USSR.

2. Regarding the validity of published Soviet data:

(a) Soviet budget data on defense expenditures are an unreliable measure of annual resources devoted to military uses. This is not the case with U.S. NSE.

(b) Unlike the figures the Russians release for defense expenditures, the data they publish for total science[d] are a fairly good reflection of the annual resources expended on RDT&E. The major exclusion from the

---

[c]The Administration's domestic strategy as reflected in the 1973 federal budget has two themes: income security and new federalism. The income security strategy means less emphasis on direct provision of public services to people (e.g., urban renewal programs) and more emphasis on efforts to equalize access to private goods and services (e.g., food stamps). The new federalism component of the domestic strategy means that state and local governments will be strengthened through general revenue sharing and by consolidating certain federally funded programs into block grants (known as special revenue sharing).

[d]Total science is defined as "science from all sources including R&D plant."

published data appears to be some, perhaps all, of the expenditures on prototype and other material-intensive R&D activities.

3. What the preliminary comparisons show, with all their data limitations and conceptual ambiguities, is that the Soviet leaders had a strong propensity to devote the new output derived from their expanding production potential to areas that are important for strategic power purposes, especially NSE and RDT&E. This stands in sharp contrast to the recent situation in the United States.

4. Estimated on an annual basis for the period 1955 to 1970, the United States could have produced the Soviet mix of military forces and programs with less U.S. productive potential than was used to produce U.S. national security programs. That is, the Soviet national security program valued in dollars is estimated to have cost less than that of the United States in each year during the period studied. However, comparisons of dollar valuations of national security reflect the Soviet leaders' decision to increase their NSE faster than the United States during those sixteen years; the USSR-U.S. NSE ratio increased from 0.73 in 1955 to 0.90 in 1970.

5. While the precise linkage between expenditures and military capability cannot be documented, this increase surely reflects the fact that they are catching up or have caught up with the United States in terms of military capability. Moreover, the calculated NSE ratios understate the rate at which the Soviets have closed on the United States and, if they continue to use their productive potential allocated to national security to emphasize procurement of durables, comparisons of near-term NSE estimates will understate the additions to military capability being realized by the USSR. Ruble estimates of U.S. NSE are needed before the comparisons can be placed in full perspective.

6. The RDT&E establishment of the USSR employs substantially more individuals than does that of the United States. As a result, dollar valuations of total RDT&E expenditures reflect a significantly greater annual expenditure by the Soviets than by the United States. However, RDT&E figures are measures of inputs, representing the drain on production potential to service this objective. They are not measures of output, the payoff policymakers realize for this commitment of resources. It is, therefore, difficult to settle between two different interpretations of these findings about comparative RDT&E expenditures. First, that the larger Soviet dollar expenditure on RDT&E reflects the burden the USSR is willing to bear to achieve technology objectives *vis-à-vis* the United States. Second, that the larger dollar expenditure reflects significant inefficiencies in the Soviets' ability to generate equivalent RDT&E output. Moreover, it is recognized that these findings are not mutually exclusive.

7. The lack of RDT&E productivity measures prevents the calculation of

net comparisons and interpretation of the meaning of U.S.-USSR RDT&E expenditure differences. The Department of Commerce has released data that indicate that the industrial productivity of the USSR is about 40 percent that of the United States. It is not clear how much the relatively high quality resources in the Soviet RDT&E establishment would increase the USSR-U.S. productivity relationship above that figure.

8. Definitive comparisons of military RDT&E expenditures are not possible at this time using published Soviet data; the breakdown of RDT&E between defense and nondefense is simply not documented. Comparisons can be made, however, by costing USSR RDT&E programs and activities in dollars. Preliminary estimates of USSR military RDT&E based on an SRI pilot study indicate that the Soviets might have expended in 1970 on a dollar basis up to $1 billion more than the United States. Again a ruble valuation of U.S. RDT&E programs and activities is needed to complete the comparative analysis.

9. Beyond the question of productivity in the use of R&D resources lies the question of the comparative ability of the two economies to translate newly available technology in a dynamic way to raise their productive potential. No comprehensive comparative study of this phenomenon is available but it can be documented that the Soviet Union has had more difficulty than the United States in absorbing new technology in such key areas as computers, chemicals, and agriculture.

10. Analysis of the current state of the two economies finds the Soviets in a period of transition in which their basic strategy for economic development and resource allocation has been revised. Because of institutional and structural problems, success of this strategy is uncertain. The United States conversely is entering a period of more stable growth following the transition from a period of high inflation, high unemployment, and dislocations resulting from changing priorities. The near-term opportunities to pursue programs and initiatives represented by this comparative situation probably favor the United States over the USSR.

Notes

1. Material in this section extracted in part from F.W. Dresch, et al, "A Comparison of US/USSR Gross National Product, National Security Expenditures and Expenditures on RDT&E," SSC-TN-2010-1, Stanford Research Institute, Menlo Park, California (December 1972).

2. For further discussion, see A. Woroniak, "Ruble/Dollar Conversion Ratio Survey," SSC-TN-8974-54, SRI, Strategic Studies Center, Menlo Park, California (July 1972).

3. M. Bornstein, "A Comparison of Soviet and United States National Product," in M. Bornstein and D.R. Fusfeld, eds., *The Soviet Economy, A Book of Readings*, (Homewood, Ill.: Richard Irwin Press, 1962, revised edition, 1966), p. 283.

Table 8-1
Comparisons of U.S. and Soviet GNP[1]

Sources		Soviet GNP in Rubles (Billions)	Conversion Ratio (Rubles/Dollars)	Soviet GNP in Dollars (Billions)	U.S. GNP in Dollars (Billions)	Ratio USSR/U.S. (Percent)
SRI	1955	119.3	.65	184	398.0	46%
	1965	246.2	.60	410	684.9	60
	1968	324.3	.61	532	864.2	62
	1970	376.6	.59	638	974.1	66
ACDA	1970	n.a.	n.a.	497	974.1	51
Dept. of Commerce (1971 Dollars)	1968	n.a.	n.a.	497	1001.0	50
	1970	n.a.	n.a.	551	1023.0	54
Bornstein	1955	128.6	.61	212.4	397.5	53

		Ruble Comparison				
Source		U.S. GNP in Dollars (Billions)	Conversion Ratio (Rubles/Dollars)	U.S. GNP in Rubles (Billions)	Soviet GNP in Rubles (Billions)	Ratio USSR/U.S. (Percent)
Bornstein	1955	397.5	1.20	480.2	128.6	27%

n.a. = not available
[1] For source references see notes following Table 8-4.

Table 8-2
Comparisons of U.S. and Soviet NMP[1]

Sources		Soviet NMP in Rubles (Billions)	Conversion Ratio (Rubles/Dollars)	Soviet NMP in Dollars (Billions)	U.S. NMP in Dollars (Billions)	Ratio USSR/U.S. (Percent)
SRI	1958	127.7	0.62	206	283.9	73%
	1965	193.4	0.60	322	422.0	76
	1970	289.6	0.59	491	563.8	87
Central Statistical	1965	192.6	0.78 (implicit)	248	401.0	62
Agency (TsSU SSSR)	1970	289.6	0.76 (implicit)	·381	579.0	66

[1] For source references see notes following Table 8-4.

Table 8-3
Comparisons of U.S. and Soviet NSE[1]

Sources		Soviet NSE in Rubles (Billions)	Conversion Ratio (Rubles/Dollars)	Soviet NSE in Dollars (Billions)	U.S. NSE in Dollars (Billions)	Ratio USSR/U.S. (Percent)
SRI[2]	1955	12.5	.42	29.4	40.2	73%
	1965	22.5	.50	45.5	57.7	79
	1967	29.0	.52	56.3	81.2	69
	1968	32.5	.52	61.9	86.1	72
	1970	39.0	.52	74.3	82.4	90
ACDA	1967	n.a.	n.a.	50.0	75.4	66
	1970	n.a.	n.a.	65.0	77.8	83
SIPRI	1967	14.5	.42	34.4	75.4	46
	1970	17.9	.42	42.6	77.8	55
Cohn	1955	11.5	n.a.	n.a.	n.a.	n.a.
	1967	19.4	n.a.	n.a.	n.a.	n.a.
Boretsky	1968	n.a.	n.a.	84.0	78.0	108
Bornstein	1955	14.5	.4	36.2	38.4	94
Dept. of Commerce	1971	n.a.	n.a.	70.2	70.0	100
Central Statistical	1965	17.1	.5 (SRI)	34.2	57.7 (U.S. Gov.)	59
Agency (TsSU SSSR)[3]	1970	24.5	.52 (SRI)	47.1	82.4 (U.S. Gov.)	57

	Ruble Comparison				
Source		U.S. NSE in Dollars (Billions)	Conversion Ratio (Rubles/Dollars)	U.S. NSE in Rubles (Billions)	Soviet NSE in Rubles (Billions)	Ratio USSR/U.S. (Percent)
Bornstein	1955	38.4	.5	19.2	14.5	75%

n.a. = not available

[1] For source references see notes following Table 8-4.

[2] Soviet NSE in dollars calculated using unrounded ruble/dollar ratios.

[3] Soviet ruble estimates for defense and science converted to dollars using SRI conversion ratios to indicate the possible consequences of accepting published Soviet data.

Table 8-4
Comparisons of U.S. and Soviet RDT&E[1]

Sources		Soviet RDT&E in Rubles (Billions)	Conversion Ratio (Rubles/Dollars)	Soviet RDT&E in Dollars (Billions)	U.S. RDT&E in Dollars (Billions)	Ratio USSR/U.S. (Percent)
SRI	1955	2.0	.39 to .56	3.6 to 5.6	6.7	54% to 84%
	1960	5.5	.44 to .62	8.9 to 12.5	14.6	61 to 86
	1965	9.7	.47 to .66	14.7 to 20.6	21.9	67 to 94
	1967	9.9	.47 to .66	15.0 to 21.1	24.9	60 to 85
	1970	15.3	.47 to .66	23.2 to 32.6	28.2	83 to 116
Kozlowski	1967	8.2	0.33	24.8	n.a.	n.a.
Harvey	1971	13.2	n.a.	n.a.	n.a.	n.a.
	1972	14.4	0.48	30.	n.a.	n.a.
Government	1960	3.8	0.50	7.6	n.a.	n.a.
Acctg. Off.	1965	7.0	0.50	14.0	n.a.	n.a.
SIPRI[2]	1960-1969 Average	2.2	0.35	6.3	n.a.	n.a.
Central	1965[4]	4.3	.47 to .66	6.5 to 9.1	21.9	30% to 42%
Statistical	1970[4]	6.5	.47 to .66	9.8 to 13.8	28.2	35 to 49
Agency	1965[5]	6.9	.47 to .66	10.5 to 14.7	21.9	48 to 67
(TsSU SSSR)[3]	1970[5]	11.7	.47 to .66	17.7 to 24.9	28.2	63 to 88

n.a. = not available
[1] For source references notes following Table 8-4.
[2] SIPRI data is military only.
[3] Soviet ruble estimates converted to dollars using SRI conversion ratios to indicate the possible consequences of accepting published Soviet data.
[4] Ruble data for science.
[5] Ruble data for science from all sources.

Source Reference for Tables 8-1 to 8-4

References for Table 8-1

SRI:	F.W. Dresch, et al., "A Comparison of U.S./USSR Gross National Product, National Security Expenditures and Expenditures for RDT&E," SSC-TN-2010-1, SRI, Strategic Studies Center, Menlo Park, California, pp. V-5, VI-5 (December 1972).
ACDA:	United States Arms Control Disarmament Agency, *World Military Expenditures, 1971*, Washington, D.C., pp. 10, 11 (1972).
Department of Commerce:	P.G. Peterson, Secretary of Commerce, "U.S.-Soviet Communist Relationships in a New Era," Department of Commerce, Washington, D.C., p. A4 (August 1972).
Bornstein:	M. Bornstein, "A Comparison of Soviet and United States National Product," in M. Bornstein and D.R. Fusfeld, eds., *The Soviet Economy, A Book of Readings*, (Homewood, Ill.: Richard Irwin Press, 1962; revised edition, 1966), p. 283.

References for Table 8-2

SRI:	F.W. Dresch, et al., "A Comparison of U.S./USSR Gross National Product, National Security Expenditures and Expenditures for RDT&E," SSC-TN-2010-1, SRI, Strategic Studies Center, Menlo Park, California, pp. V-5, VI-6 (December 1972).
Central Statistical Agency:	Tsentral'noye Statisticheskoye Upravleniye pri Sovete Ministrov S.S.S.R. *Narodnoye Khozyaystvo S.S.S.R. v 1965 Godu. Statisticheskiy Yezhegodnik* Statistika, Moskva, 1966, pp. 87, 589 [The National Economy of the USSR, 1965, Statistical Yearbook].
	——————————, N.Kh. 1970, pp. 85, 533.

References for Table 8-3

SRI:	F.W. Dresch, et al., "A Comparison of U.S./USSR Gross National Product, National Security Expenditures and Expenditures for RDT&E," SSC-TN-2010-1, SRI, Strategic Studies Center, Menlo Park, California, pp. V-5, VI-11 (December 1972).
ACDA:	U.S. Arms Control and Disarmament Agency. *World Military Expenditures, 1971*, Washington, D.C., pp. 18, 19 (1972).
SIPRI:	Stockholm International Peace Research Institute. *World Armaments and Disarmament*, SIPRI Yearbook, pp. 84, 85 (1972).
Cohn and Boretsky:	Joint Economic Committee. *Economic Performance and the Military Burden in the Soviet Union*, U.S. Government Printing Office, Washington, D.C., pp. 168, 220 (1970).
Department of Commerce:	P.G. Peterson, Secretary of Commerce, "U.S.-Soviet Communist Relationships in a New Era," Department of Commerce, Washington, D.C., p. A8 (August 1972).
Central Statistical Agency:	Tsentral'noye Statisticheskoye Upravleniye pri Sovete Ministrov S.S.S.R., *Narodnoye Khozyaystvo S.S.S.R. v 1970 Godu. Statisticheskiy Yezhegodnik* (Statistika, Moskva, 1971, pp. 730 [The National Economy of the USSR, 1970, Statistical Yearbook].
Bornstein:	M. Bornstein, "A Comparison of Soviet and United States National Product," in M. Bornstein and D.R. Fusfeld, eds., *The Soviet Economy, A Book of Readings*, (Homewood, Ill.: Richard Irwin Press, 1962; revised edition, 1966), p. 283.

References for Table 8-4

SRI:	F.W. Dresch, et al., "A Comparison of U.S./USSR Gross National Product, National Security Expenditures and Expenditures for

RDT&E," SSC-TN-2010-1, SRI, Strategic Studies Center, Menlo Park, California, pp. V-5, VI-16 (December 1972).

Kozlowski: J.P. Kozlowski, "R&D in the USSR," *Science and Technology*, No. 87, p. 10 (March 1969).

Harvey: M.L. Harvey, L. Goure, and V. Prokofieff, *Science and Technology as an Instrument of Soviet Policy*, (Coral Gables, Florida: University of Miami Center for Advanced International Studies), pp. xii and xiii.

GAO: The Comptroller General of the United States, *Comparison of Military Research and Development Expenditures of the United States and the Soviet Union* (Washington, D.C., July 23, 1971).

SIPRI: Stockholm International Peace Research Institute. *World Armaments and Disarmament*, SIPRI Yearbook, p. 58 (1972).

Central Statistical Agency: Tsentral'noye Statisticheskoye Upravleniye pri Sovete Ministrov S.S.S.R., *Narodnoye Khozyaystvo S.S.S.R. v 1970 Godu. Statisticheskiy Yezhegodnik* (Statistika, Moskva, 1971, pp. 732, 734 [The National Economy of the USSR, 1970, Statistical Yearbook].

The Problem of Resource Allocation

William Niskanen

More Money for Less Defense

The present U.S. defense budget presents a paradox that will be the basis for a major national debate: after completion of the long U.S. involvement in the Vietnam war, the proposed fiscal 1974 federal budget would increase total defense spending by around 6 percent in current dollars. This is the first time in our history that defense spending has not been substantially reduced after a major war. The proposed defense budget is nearly 25 percent higher *in constant dollars* than the average defense spending between the Korean and Vietnam wars.

On the other hand, we seem to be engaged in a process of unilateral disarmament. In comparison to U.S. forces in 1964, the proposed budget would support one-third fewer strategic bombers, three less division forces, five less tactical fighter wings, eight less aircraft carriers, and less than one-half the number of other surface combatant ships.

An understandable concern about the spending patterns leads some people to conclude that the defense budget is too large. A comparable concern about the reduction in our military forces leads others to conclude that the defense budget is too small. Most Americans, I contend, share *both* concerns, although the opposing conclusions about the defense budget, of course, cannot be reconciled. And any consensus on a "National Strategy in a Decade of Change" must be based on the large group that shares both of these concerns. Both of the smaller groups that would reduce the defense budget regardless of the consequences for national security or that would increase military forces regardless of cost are appropriately isolated from influence in our political system. This paper summarizes my views concerning the appropriate process for developing a consensus on the defense budget and a national security strategy that provides adequate defense at supportable cost.

The Economic and Fiscal Outlook

For many years, the economist's traditional role in such discussions has been to forecast the economic and fiscal conditions over some planning period and to make the expected statements about scarcity of resources and the necessity for hard choices. This paper continues that tradition, but for the primary purpose of dismissing these conditions as relevant constraints on the defense budget. As a matter of record, our forecasting accuracy is not impressive, but this is a minor concern. More important, our defense budget has been determined and should be determined, not in response to the question, "How much can we afford?," but in response to the question "How much do we want to spend?" And there is no historical stability of the relation between the U.S. defense budget and either total national output or the total federal budget, and there is no objective basis for establishing such a relation as a matter of policy.

The 1973 Economic Report of the President forecasts a growth of GNP during calendar year 1973 of 10 percent to an annual level of $1,267 billion. The forecast increase in GNP is expected to consist of a 6 3/4 percent real increase in output and a 3 percent increase in prices: My reading of the record of prior forecasts by the Council of Economic Advisers and of current conditions suggests that their forecast of the increase in GNP in current dollars is only slightly high. My guess, however, is that real growth will be somewhat less and inflation somewhat higher than the (public) forecasts of my friends in the CEA. My primary short-run concern about real growth involves the large number of major wage agreements that must be renewed this year and the probability of some extended strikes in major industries. My primary short-run concern about inflation is based on the recent increases in both interest rates and the money supply, both of which are strong predictors of future price increases.

In the longer run, there are good reasons to expect an annual increase of GNP in current dollars of 8-9 percent and an annual increase of real output of 4-5 percent. My major long-run concerns about real output derive from several conditions: large federal deficits have absorbed resources that would have been committed to private investment, and this may reduce the rate of increase of private productivity. Recent evidence also suggests that the rate of return on education has dropped substantially. And the continued growth of the public sector appears to be associated with a negligible increase in productivity in this sector. My major long-run concerns about inflation derive from two conditions: a failure to develop satisfactory procedures for wage bargaining has led to widespread increases in nominal wage costs in excess of achievable increases in productivity; this, in turn, creates pressures operating through the political process to inflate prices, reduce the real wage increases, and reduce the increase in unemployment that would otherwise result. A continuation of large federal deficits also generates pressures on the monetary authorities to increase the money supply and, consequently, prices. As a rule, I am moderately optimistic about the long run. Americans have demonstrated an extraordinary ability to work out such problems, but it is important to recognize that there is no current consensus on the specific solutions to the above problems.

Our aggregate economic conditions are an important dimension of the well-being of the American community, but they are neither a relevant constraint nor an important determinant of our defense budget. Several comparisons illustrate this assertion: if the United States committed as high a proportion of the forecast 1973 GNP to defense as in 1944, the total defense budget could be $550 billion, and we would still have one of the highest levels of personal consumption in the world. If the United States reserved as much real resources per capita for other than defense as in 1944, the defense budget could be $835 billion. In both cases, the defense budgets could be even larger by a proportion of the increase in GNP that this defense effort would stimulate. Such huge potential defense budgets are an important part of our deterrent against major wars not involving a strategic nuclear exchange, but they are not relevant constraints on the amount of resources we are currently willing to commit to defense. Since World War II, the defense budgets in peacetime years have ranged from less than four percent to over 11 percent of GNP, and this percentage has been declining with some regularity in the peacetime years since the Korean War. In terms of the forecast 1973 GNP, this percentage range represents defense budgets from $50 billion to $143 billion; this range is also much broader than the range of current debate on the defense budget and does not provide a useful basis for establishing a consensus on the defense budget. Although in the long run the United States may be prepared to commit more resources to defense as output grows, for periods as long as a decade the real resources we are collectively prepared to commit to defense appear to be independent of our national output. Any defense budget rule based on a constant percentage of GNP appears to be inconsistent with the historically revealed preferences of the American population.

The Fiscal 1974 Budget of the United States Government proposes an increase of federal spending of 7.5 percent to a level of $268.7 billion. Although this proposed budget is widely regarded as austere, the proposed percentage increase is only slightly less than the average percentage increase in GNP. In addition, the budget history since World War II indicates that the average actual percentage increase has been nearly 4 percent higher than the percentage increase proposed by the President. A continuation of this pattern suggests that the actual increase may be around 11 percent and the actual fiscal 1974 budget outlays around $280 billion.

Proposed defense spending would increase around six percent to a level of $81.1 billion. The proposed percentage increase in the defense budget is smaller than for other major programs, and the proposed defense budget is the smallest proportion of the total budget in any postwar year. Nevertheless, this proposed increase in defense spending will be the basis for one of the major political controversies of this year. Both the population and Congress, for understandable reasons, expected some reduction in defense spending after termination of the U.S. military activities in Vietnam. In addition, defense officials created the expectation that there would be a major reduction in military bases that is not reflected in the proposed budget. Most importantly, the major reduction of social service programs proposed by the President will increase the pressure to make some reductions in defense spending. My expectation, whatever the merit of the case for the President's budget, is that federal domestic spending will be higher and defense spending will be lower than in the proposed fiscal 1974 budget.

For the first time, the proposed fiscal 1974 budget also presents estimates of outlays by function and total outlays for the subsequent year, given approval of the proposed budget. Total outlays are estimated to increase by around seven percent to a total fiscal 1974 level of $288 billion. Defense spending is estimated to increase by around five percent to a fiscal 1974 level of $85.5 billion. For the longer run, given approval of the proposed fiscal 1974 budget, total fiscal 1978 outlays are estimated to be $307 billion. It is interesting to compare these estimates of total outlays with the recent estimates prepared by the American Enterprise Institute of the future outlays for those programs and initiatives endorsed by the Nixon Administration as of fiscal 1973.[1] AEI estimates total outlays of $301.4 billion for fiscal 1975 and total outlays of $346 billion for fiscal 1978. The proposed fiscal 1974 budget indicates how much the Administration has cut back on programs and initiatives it has itself previously endorsed.

The proposed defense budgets for fiscal 1974 and fiscal 1975 suggest that the Administration is *not* setting the defense budget at a constant percentage of either GNP or the total federal budget, as both of these percentages are expected to continue to decline. The rule the Administration appears to be following is to add to the fiscal 1973 defense budget a percentage equal to the expected percentage increase in wage rates in the private sector. This rule has obvious merit as it could provide for a constant level of defense manpower. The major concern about this rule would be the appropriateness of the fiscal 1973 budget as the basis for post-Vietnam budget planning. It should also be recognized that this rule would provide for a continuous increase in total defense capability in proportion to any increase in the productivity of defense manpower.

The general fiscal outlook provides some valuable insights about the short-run opportunities or problems of changing the defense budget, but does not help provide a basis for estimating how much we want to spend for defense. Americans and their political representatives are clearly not prepared to commit a constant percentage of the federal budget to defense. Defense budgets in peacetime years since World War II have ranged from 30 percent to 60 percent of the total federal budget, with this percentage declining rather regularly since the Korean War. Development of a coherent defense program in the post-Vietnam period is dependent on general acceptance of some rule for determining how much we want to spend for defense.

The Selection of a Rule for Determining the Defense Budget

A coherent national security strategy and defense program, I believe, requires the following two steps:

1. *Development of a quasi-constitutional consensus on a rule for determining the total defense budget.*

This rule would be based on our objectives, the general level and character of the relevant military threat, the military forces of our allies, and any relevant conditions in our economy. The government should formulate and explain this rule, seek a broad-based endorsement, and enforce this rule for as long as there is no major change in the above conditions.

2. *Serious sustained attention to the allocation of resources within a known time-profile of total defense budgets.*

The total defense budget may be somewhat higher in each year of the planning period, but the defense budget in each year would not be subject to change as a consequence of allocation decisions in that year. The single most important problem of improving the allocation of defense resources is the current expectation that hard choices can be avoided by a sequential increase in the total defense budget.

On what basis might we establish a defense budget rule that would reflect a consensus of the American population and their political representatives? My suggestion is that we look to the past for guidance, and modify the defense budget levels of a prior period during which there appears to have been a near-consensus by amounts to reflect any major change in conditions since that period. (If looking to the past for guidance types me as a reactionary, so be it.) The most appropriate period on which to base a defense budget rule for the post-Vietnam years, I suggest, is the 12-year period from 1954 through 1965, from the Korean Armistice to the major build-up of U.S. forces in Vietnam. The average defense budget during these years was $65.8 billion in 1973 dollars. Although the range of the defense budget was from $60.3 billion in 1955 to $71.4 in 1962 (both in 1973 dollars), there does not appear to be any significant increase in the total real resources committed to defense over this period, and this permitted a yearly continuous reduction in the percent of GNP committed to defense. These conditions are illustrated on the accompanying chart. Although this period included a temporary buildup of U.S. military forces following both Sputnik and the "missile gap" controversy of the 1960 campaign, the total real resources committed to defense were remarkably stable.

What objective change in conditions since this period would justify a higher defense budget in 1973 dollars? Our national security objectives, if the Nixon Doctrine has any meaning, have been reduced. We have accepted a "strategic sufficiency" relative to the Soviet strategic nuclear forces. We no longer regard China as a major potential adversary. We are less likely to engage in another war like Vietnam, and we are also less likely to commit U.S. forces to such crises as Lebanon, Quemoy and Matsu, Cuba, and the Dominican Republic. The Nixon Doctrine, given other conditions, would suggest a lower defense budget.

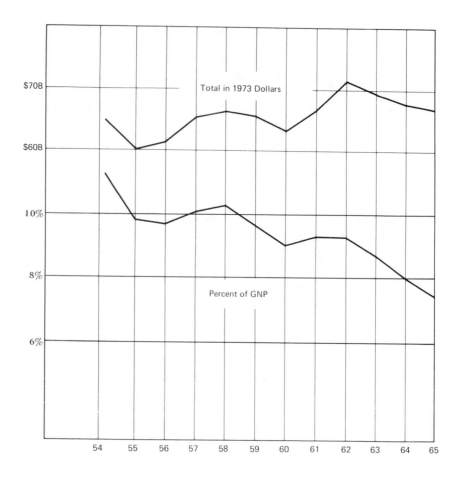

Figure 9-1. U.S. Defense Expenditures from Korea to Vietnam

Moreover, the general level and character of the military forces of the Soviet Union and those of our allies also do not suggest a basis for a larger defense budget. The huge increase in the Soviet strategic nuclear forces represents a major change from the earlier period but, given our current strategic concept, does not require a budgetary response as large as that during the early 1960s. Soviet tactical forces are still formidable but are smaller than their average level during the earlier period. From our perspective, the military forces of our allies are still insufficient but their military forces, their economies, and their political stability are higher than during the earlier period. Neither the gross nor the net threat appears to justify a higher budget.

Three other conditions, however, suggest that the total defense budget, as conventionally measured, should be increased relative to the average budget in 1973 dollars of the period from Korea to Vietnam:

1. The termination of conscription has not increased the real resource cost of defense, but it has transferred these costs from a particularly discriminatory form of tax on young men onto the defense budget, and, consequently, to the general tax base. The best estimate of the budget cost of a volunteer armed forces is around $5 billion; this estimate was made in 1965 dollars and was specific to a total level of military personnel of 2.65 million. Although general prices have increased around one-third since 1965, total military personnel in fiscal 1974 are expected to be only 2.3 million, so this estimate should still be roughly accurate.

2. The proposed fiscal 1974 defense budget still includes $2.9 billion for U.S. military forces in Southeast Asia. As long as these activities continue, this amount should be added to the base-line budget. My own preferences are to add this amount permanently to the base-line budget in order to reinforce the incentive to reduce U.S. military activities in that theater.

3. The third smaller amount derives from an inappropriate accounting of military retirement costs. Current annual outlays for retired military personnel are now around $1 billion higher than the annual increase in military pension liabilities, and this difference is expected to increase over the next decade. This difference should also be added to the base-line budget.

These considerations led me to suggest a basis for determining the fiscal 1974 defense budget that is based on a prior consensus and the above changes in conditions and would provide the basis for future defense planning. This fiscal 1974 defense budget would be based on the following components:

	(1973 Dollars)
Average defense budget 1954-1965	$66 billion
·+ Volunteer armed forces	5
+ SEA costs	3
+ Net retired pay outlays	1
	$75 billion

Although this total is $6 billion less than proposed by the President, my guess is that it is closer to what will finally be approved. A fiscal 1974 defense budget of $75 billion would also represent a slight reduction of the total defense budget after termination of the U.S. military role in Vietnam, a change that is more consistent with historical precedent and the expectations of the American people.

For the future, my preferences would be to increase the defense budget by the expected percentage increase in the general price level plus any increase in the difference between current payments and accrued liabilities for retired pay. As private sector wage rates will continue to increase by several percentage points faster than general prices, this defense budget rule would *not* provide for both a constant level of defense personnel and a constant grade structure. This defense budget rule *and* good management, however, should provide for a roughly constant level of military capability. There appears to be considerable slack in both total personnel and the grade structure, and there is no inherent reason why the productivity of military personnel should not increase as fast as that of private employees. More importantly, a constrained time-profile of defense budgets is probably a necessary condition to provide the incentive to wring out the excess personnel costs and to achieve a continuous increase in productivity.

In the short run, there will be great controversy over whether the fiscal 1974 defense budget should be $75 billion, $78 billion, or $81 billion, and this is appropriate. In the long run, however, I am less concerned about what defense budget within this range is approved for fiscal 1974 than about the acceptance of a budget rule that would establish a constant time-profile of future defense budgets. We should not deceive ourselves that we have the information, the time, and the patience to develop a precisely optimal defense budget in terms of the specific conditions in each year. The only way I know to achieve an effective division of labor between our political and defense management processes is to base the total defense budget on a roughly constant consensus of what we want to spend and to focus the attention of our defense officials on the allocation of resources within this constraint. The question, "How much is enough?" never was the right question for defense officials, let alone systems analysts, to resolve. As in many areas of public policy, a well-chosen rule is preferable to relying on the authority of the most conscientious officials operating on the best available information.

Some Special Resource Allocation Problems

Many external observers of the U.S. defense program are quick to substitute their own judgment on some element of the program for the decision worked out within the government. Although many of these suggested reallocations deserve consideration, they serve to erode the division of labor that is requisite for effective defense management. The single most important problem of defense management in the last decade was a confusion of roles among the major groups contributing to defense decisions: political officials became exercised about detailed personnel policies and the selection of a rifle. Civilian officials intervened at a detailed level in the conduct of a war. And military officers made pronouncements about national strategy and the balance of payments. This confusion of roles has led to a diffusion of responsibility such that every group has avoided the responsibility for the specific activities for which they are charged.

An effective defense management system, as I have argued in several articles, requires a stronger division of labor: political officials would establish firm but rather general guidance on national security policy and the defense budget, assure that the Department of Defense faces the correct resource prices, periodically monitor performance at an aggregative level, and use their powers of appointment to discipline performance. Civilian officials would translate this guidance at a more detailed level and monitor performance at that level. And the armed services would have the dominant responsibility for detailed allocation decisions. Although most of us, including myself, have some suggestions for rather detailed reallocation, the more important challenge is to identify those conditions that would lead the routine defense management processes to consider these suggestions and to make the appropriate allocations.

This final section addresses only one of the major problems that restricts the efficient allocation of resources in the defense program: for a number of important resources, the Department of Defense faces resource prices that are substantially less than the value of these resources in other uses. For any given total defense budget, the underpricing of these resources will cause a relative overuse of these resources. The major resources that are underpriced to the Department of Defense are land and structures, defense personnel, nuclear weapons, the electronic frequency spectrum, and the airspace and air traffic control services.

1. The Department of Defense now "owns" land and structures that are worth around $100 billion in other uses. The annual defense budget includes no "rent" on this real property, and the Department would receive no additional funds if some of this property were transferred, outleased, or sold for other uses. As a consequence, the Department has an incentive to continue using this property as long as its marginal value within the Department is higher than the associated budget costs of managing and using this property. The annual unbudgeted cost of this property is nearly $12 billion, and an appropriate definition of the Defense budget should include these costs.

My suggestion for correcting the underpricing of real property would involve the following steps: any new acquisitions of land and general-purpose structures would be leased, rather than purchased. Thus, the annual cost of newly acquired real property would be included in agency budgets in each year of use, rather than only at the time of purchase. The real property would be retained on the local property tax base, thus avoiding a reduction of local revenues or an increase in federal impacted aid. Budget outlays in the acquisition year would be lower, thus making it easier to finance capital improvements within a tight budget.

For real property now owned by the government and any additional property that is purchased, some form of rental charge system is necessary and to assure that the annual cost of this property is included in agency budgets and subject to periodic review by both the agency and higher authorities. Annual rents would be established on all land and general-purpose structures equal to the total annual value of these resources in other uses. The suggested procedure for incorporating annual real property rents into agency budgets would be to add these rents to the budget outlay ceilings against which the defense agencies prepare their proposed budgets. Agencies would be authorized to increase their direct budget outlays if the sum of these outlays and the rents on real property is within the ceiling on total annual costs. Any real property disposed of by an agency would be maintained by GSA pending transfer to another federal user or disposal to a nonfederal user. This rental charge system should lead to a reduction in direct budget outlays, both by reducing new real property acquisitions and by providing offsetting receipts from the sale or outlease of real property.

2. The major source of underpriced military manpower has recently been eliminated by the termination of conscription. Three other defense manpower pricing problems, however, have yet to be resolved: the underfunding of the Civil Service pension fund, the deferred payments for military manpower in retirement payments, and the deferred payments for military manpower in veteran's benefits.

A 1967 study estimated that the current funding of Civil Service pensions would have to be increased from 14 percent of the civilian payroll to around 21 percent to provide full funding of the expected progressive increase in civilian pensions. For the Department of Defense, this annual unbudgeted civilian manpower cost is around $1 billion, and this amount should be added to the Defense budget to reflect the total annual cost of civilian manpower.

At the present time, military pensions are "unfunded." The annual increase in military pension liabilities, now nearly $4 billion, is nowhere included in the defense budget. The current annual outlays for retired military personnel, now nearly $5 billion, are included in the defense budget, although these payments are in no way related to the current use of military manpower. As the current outlays for retired military personnel are expected to grow relative to the annual increase in pension liabilities for the next decade, the defense manpower budget will become an increasingly inaccurate estimate of the annual cost of current military forces. This problem could be easily resolved by including the annual increase in military pension liabilities and excluding the current outlays for retired military personnel from the Defense budget guidance, without going through the charade of establishing a formal military retirement fund.

The annual increase in federal liabilities due to the expectation of future veteran's benefits is a current cost of using military manpower but is nowhere included in the budget. This increase has not been estimated, and the current Veteran's Administration budget is not a useful basis for making this estimate. My suggestion for correcting this underpricing of current military manpower is to eliminate all veteran's benefits, other than medical care and compensation for service-connected disability, for all *future* entrants into the armed services after the termination of conscription. This would increase the annual budgeted cost of military manpower by an amount equal to the perceived present value of the implied commitment to future veteran's benefits at the time of initial recruitment.

3. The Atomic Energy Commission produces nuclear materials; it develops, tests, and produces nuclear weapons; and it develops and produces nuclear reactors for use by the Department of Defense. Outlays for these activities are included in the AEC budget, not in the Defense budget. AEC directly defends the budget for these activities in the presidential and congressional budget reviews. The Department of Defense establishes the "requirements" for the output of these activities but does not defend the cost of these activities and does not have the opportunity to reallocate spending between the military activities funded in the Defense budget and those funded in the AEC budget. The exclusion of defense-related AEC activities from the Defense budget induces AEC to supply all that is required and Defense to require all that can be supplied, regardless of the value of these resources or the production assets in other uses. The potential allocation problems of this condition are substantially moderated by the presidential and congressional budget reviews, but these reviews are necessarily captive of the information provided by the supplying and using agencies.

In addition, the present stock of nuclear weapons includes a large amount of nuclear materials produced in prior years. This material has a substantial value in other uses, either as reactor fuel or in new weapons. The Department of Defense now pays no "rent" on the value of these materials, and this part of the annual cost of defense is nowhere included in the federal budget. The Department of Defense has an incentive to hoard nuclear materials as long as their value in current use is higher than the small budget outlays for management and storage. The presidential and congressional budget review appears not to have even recognized this problem.

My own estimate of the annual cost of current defense-related AEC activities is around $1.8 billion and the annual rent on the existing stock of nuclear materials is around $1.2 billion, for a total annual cost of around $3 billion. The most direct means to correct the present underpricing of these activities and resources to the Department of Defense is to add this amount to the Defense budget guidance, require Defense to pay AEC for any services and materials it demands, and to permit Defense to reallocate these funds between nuclear and nonnuclear military activities. A somewhat similar proposal has recently been made by the House Appropriations Committee, so maybe this proposal that I have promoted for a decade will no longer be regarded as such a crazy idea.

4. The Department of Defense also uses several important resources—the electronic frequency spectrum and the airspace and air traffic control services—

for which prices are not established either within the government or in the private sector. The proportionate use of these resources can only be estimated in physical terms, as no estimate of the value of these resources has been made.

The federal government, primarily the military, has exclusive rights to around 20 percent of the frequency spectrum 25 and 5,000 megahertz and shared rights to around 30 percent of this most valuable part of the spectrum; this allocation has been remarkably stable since World War II, although the value of the spectrum in other uses has increased rapidly in this period.

The federal government, again primarily the military, uses a significant proportion of the nation's airspace and air traffic control services. Around 22 percent of the controlled en route events and around 6 percent of the terminal events are attributable to government airplanes. The Department of Defense does not pay to use either of these resources, both of which are now allocated by administrative regulation. The best mechanism for allocating these resources is not yet obvious but, as the general demand for these resources increases, some new mechanism to improve their allocation to and within the Department of Defense will be required.

A more detailed explanation of each of the above problems and the proposed solutions is presented in a 1973 study published by the American Enterprise Institute.[2] These problems are complex, however, and my primary purpose is to make the case for the type of serious, sustained effort that is necessary to resolve them.

A Concluding Comment

Although I have counseled outsiders to restraint in making specific recommendations on the allocation of defense resources, I cannot resist the temptation to make some personal comments on a few minor items. In recent months, considerable attention has been given to several aspects of personnel policy—the top-heavy grade structure, flight pay for officers who do not fly and will not fly again, tax exemptions for disability on retirement income for men who are obviously able, and several of the more conspicuous types of perquisites for military personnel. A thorough scrubbing of these items would probably reduce the defense budget by less than $1 billion, but this is not the important aspect of this issue. It is important for the U.S. defense program to *be* lean and tough. It is also important for the defense program to *look* lean and tough. A failure to correct some of these more obvious excesses can destroy the consensus on which an effective defense program must be based, reduce confidence in the ability of the armed services to make more important allocation decisions, and reduce the defense budget by more than any potential savings from these actions. The consensus on which an effective defense program in a democracy must be based is fragile, and the maintenance of this consensus deserves our most serious attention.

Notes

1. David Ott, et al., "Nixon, McGovern and the Federal Budget," American Enterprise Institute, *Domestic Affairs Study 8*, September 1972.

2. William Niskanen, "Structured Reforms in the Federal Budget Process," American Enterprise Institute, April 1973.

10

The United States and the International Economic System

John M. Hennessy

This paper addresses three areas concerning the United States and the international economic system.

First, since my paper falls within the section of this symposium denominated "Strategy of Implementation—Resources and Economics," an assessment of the U.S. international economic position appears in order.

Second, I would like to report on the status of economic reform discussions and comment on the substance of the U.S. proposals for monetary reform and multilateral trade negotiations.

Third, and last, I would like to discuss briefly the interrelationship of monetary and trade reform with the evolution of the international political structure.

The U.S. External Economic Position

The United States has experienced balance-of-payments deficits and a deterioration in its net external reserve position in nearly every year since 1950. For most of the 1950s, these deficits were widely welcomed by countries anxious to strengthen their payments positions and rebuild reserves lost in World War II. The deterioration was at least to some degree a consequence of deliberate U.S. policy.

The beginnings of concern about the deterioration in the U.S. position surfaced in the late 1950s, highlighted by a brief flurry in the private gold market. The 1960s saw continued but moderate balance-of-payments deficits, continued concern both here and abroad, and a variety of U.S. measures and programs to control or correct the problem. But throughout this period, there was a confidence that the situation was essentially short-term, not structural—that if the war in Vietnam could be wound down, if domestic price stability could be restored, the deterioration in our trade position could be reversed and our overall deficit eliminated.

The year 1970 produced the first eye-catching U.S. international payments deficit, one of almost $11 billion on the official settlements basis. In 1971, changes in relative monetary conditions here and abroad led to large capital outflows, and signs of accelerating weakness in our trading accounts became

159

undeniable. Speculation of enormous proportions followed, leading to a record deficit for that year.

The crisis of 1971 led directly to the President's 15 August 1971 measures, the Smithsonian Agreement, and the international economic reform negotiations currently underway. The events of 1971 and their aftermath also led to a new recognition in this country that international economics and finance would require greater attention and higher priority in the years ahead. In earlier years, few had considered the balance of payments more than a minor constraint on our military and aid commitments. Today there is a recognition that our international economic and financial position not only may place a greater constraint on our international activities but also has a very direct relationship to employment and income in the United States.

Last year our international accounts continued to represent an economic problem of major proportions. Despite improvement in our overall position, the trade deficit approached $7 billion and the current account deficit, excluding government transfers, will probably be $6 billion or more. The deterioration in the trade account from the peak surplus year of 1964 to the trough in 1972 was on the order of $13.5 billion.

Focusing inordinately on performance in the year 1972 can, however, give a mistaken impression of pessimism. A good part of the trade decline can be attributed to the initial adverse impact of the Smithsonian realignment. The positive effects of the realignment will be felt more fully in 1973. Another special part of the decline was cyclical factors. The U.S. economy grew briskly in 1972, while a number of our major trading partners managed only moderate growth. In 1973, improvement of both the trade and the current balance should take place. But the fact remains that the magnitude of the required improvement in the U.S. current account is such that the problem of the compatibility of countries' international economic goals is clearly posed. A relevant query is whether other nations will be willing to allow a $15 billion turnaround in the U.S. current account in the next several years, recognizing that most of the offsetting deterioration in others' current accounts will have to occur in their trade accounts. The future difficulty is clear when we see that last year the United States ran a trade deficit with every major region of the world except Eastern Europe.

The $15 billion figure is an approximate one and it is based on a U.S. current account surplus of $9 billion. This is a necessary condition if the world is to have a sustainable international equilibrium, and such a surplus would be only slightly larger than the surplus recorded in 1964. It is not a mercantilist aim or an objective to finance direct investment in Europe. A surplus on current account is the only way the United States can provide aid to developing countries in real goods. It is the only way we can ever pay off, net, the debts we have piled up or, excluding SDR allocations, rebuild the depleted reserve position of the United States. The possibility of political tension increases, of course, during a period of such large economic adjustment.

Work in international economic forums has identified the incompatibility of countries' goals with respect to their trade and current account balances, and discussions on reconciling these are underway. As a group, the developed countries desire a current account surplus with the developing countries of a larger magnitude than they are prepared to finance by aid and other capital flows. Of equal importance, the developed countries tend to take a conservative view of the prospective strength of their underlying positions—today's trade or current account surplus is always a fragile one and the prospect of deficit always looms clearly ahead.

A new factor has been added to the problem of achieving a sustainable U.S. external economic position in the future—our growing needs to import energy and raw materials. Last year we saw the dramatic symptoms of a fundamental problem of energy supply for the U.S. economy. In 1972 alone, oil imports rose by more than $1 billion. Estimates of the increases in energy imports needed in the future vary considerably, but all are in the range of at least an additional import bill of $4 to $5 billion for energy by the end of this decade.

Resolution of apparently incompatible balance-of-payments goals is of paramount importance in the period ahead and has obvious implications for international relations. The alternatives of the way in which the reconciliation can take place are narrow. Solutions can be in the form of ever-increasing controls on the flow of capital and goods—of isolating markets and countries. These actions could be taken only at a high cost to the world's economic and political welfare. The alternative is the present multilateral negotiations that seek market-related solutions.

One clear conclusion to be drawn from the outlook for the U.S. balance of payments is that for some time yet the problem of allocation of our scarce foreign exchange earnings is going to be with us. We may have to consider more carefully how our overseas earnings are to be allocated among competing overseas expenditures. There will be a tendency to view our assistance expenditures, our expenditures for energy imports, our expenditures for security overseas, and other expenditures as alternatives. For example, how will the Third World capital needs for development be fit in? Their needs are increasing while it is clear that our ability to provide even the same relative share has been declining.

Another conclusion is that there is little hope of dealing with these problems in the absence of fundamental reform of the international economic system. The disequilibria have been too prolonged and large, the realities too changed since the system was constructed, to believe that a patchwork reform will be adequate.

International Economic Reform

In September 1972, Treasury Secretary Shultz put forward the principles and ideas which the United States believes should guide reform of the international economic system. The proposals build on those elements of the past system that have served us well, while filling in the gaps that made that system overly rigid and, eventually, inadequate. In particular, they introduce clear disciplines and standards to guide the international adjustment process. Without such standards, it is difficult to imagine resolving the incompatibilities that I discussed earlier. Standards not only help reduce friction among large industrial nations, but would provide equality of help or protection in the system for the smaller nations in a world of greater economic competition.

One standard that the United States has introduced, as a central element of its reform proposals, is the use of movements in international reserves as an indicator of payments disequilibria and need for adjustment. Under such a system, disproportionate reserve increases would signal the need for surplus countries to adjust, just as, under any system of convertibility, disproportionate reserve losses place adjustment pressures on deficit countries. The system of reserve indicators would be supported by appropriate incentives and penalties to insure that needed adjustments were undertaken. The system proposed by the United States is designed to provide even-handed treatment for all countries, imposing special obligations on no one and conferring special rights on no one.

While the United States insists on the need for a system of prompt and effective adjustment, with equal obligations for all countries, it has also provided for maximum national discretion on how adjustment is achieved. Countries can choose from the range of internationally acceptable adjustment instruments those most suited to their particular needs and circumstances. This would seem most appropriate for the new international structure, which will incorporate more diverse economies and groups of countries than perhaps before.

Within the context of a system that stresses adjustment but provides for national choice of the adjustment measures to be undertaken, we believe more flexible use of the exchange rate mechanism is desirable. We have proposed that wider exchange rate margins be made a permanent feature of the system, and that the U.S. dollar be afforded the same potential for fluctuation within the margins as that available to other currencies. While the U.S. proposals assume that most will wish to maintain established values for their currencies supported by convertibility, we also believe that a reformed system should provide for those wishing to float their currencies, either transitionally or for prolonged periods, under agreed international standards.

In 1972, the principal forum and terms of reference for the negotiations on reform were established—in the Committee of Twenty under the general auspices of the IMF. The initial meeting in September 1972 resolved organizational questions and formulated a work program looking toward the possibility of agreement on the main outlines of reform by September 1973. By year's end, detailed talks were well under way in the Committee of Deputies to Ministers.

To date, the Deputies have held initial discussions on several aspects of reform: the adjustment process and the exchange rate regime; reserve assets and convertibility; and the interrelations between monetary, trade, and other matters. A Deputies meeting scheduled for mid-March will take up the question of capital movements and the special interests of the less developed countries in reform. A further Ministerial meeting is being planned for late March or early April.

It is difficult at this stage to make a very useful assessment of the discussions. The issues are complex and closely interrelated—and not all of them have received initial discussion. We are not likely to see countries committing themselves on individual aspects of reform until they are able to view the shape of the whole. At this stage, we are essentially engaged in an education process that seeks to alter patterns of thought that have developed over extended periods of time. I believe that the reactions we have seen to date indicate that this process is accomplishing its intended goal, that countries are focusing on the fundamentals and not being sidetracked by extraneous issues. Development of the main outlines of reform in time for the IMF annual meeting in Nairobi in September 1973 is a reasonable target.

Areas other than monetary reform are receiving increasing attention in the international economy. In the Committee of Twenty, the United States has emphasized the need to recognize and deal with the broader relationships between trade, money, investment, and development. In so doing, we have argued for a consistency in the broad principles governing these areas—for example, the logical counterpart of nondiscrimination in monetary arrangements is most-favored-nation treatment in trade.

Incentives should be built into the rules concerning the adjustment process to encourage trade liberalization, for example, in cases where surplus countries find it more desirable from their own point of view to reduce tariffs or eliminate other restrictions than, say, to put the full weight of adjustment on exchange rates.

Large areas of national economies cannot be isolated from foreign price competition, if adjustment measures such as exchange rate changes are to be effective. There is also need to reach agreement among trade and monetary authorities regarding the use of trade measures in the adjustment of payments deficits.

Another important area for negotiation is constituted by those fiscal measures, subsidies, administrative pressures, and competition in export credit that affect the flow of goods and investment.

Finally, there is the problem of finding organizational arrangements to assure that the problems of the international economy continue in the future to be treated as a coherent whole.

In the past, fragmentation of what is a linked international economic system has placed stumbling blocks in the way of change. Each institution charged with overseeing individual aspects of the world economy has tended to view its responsibility in a narrow context, failing to consider adequately the implications of its decisions on other parts of the system. One familiar example is the GATT prohibition against the use of import surcharges as a balance-of-payments measure while allowing quotas. Monetary specialists tend to the view that when deficit countries find trade measures unavoidable, import surcharges are preferable to quotas.

The two groups have never gotten together to develop agreed rules. The result is that countries often take actions that disregard the outmoded rules, thereby leaving the international community with no effective safeguards. This is a difficult problem to solve not only because of the issues themselves, but also because of the way both national and international bureaucracies work.

In trade, international preparations are underway for multilateral negotiations. At their 28th annual session in November 1972 the GATT Contracting Parties reaffirmed their intention to enter into new and far-reaching trade negotiations. To lay the groundwork for the negotiations, they established a Preparatory Committee to develop the methods and procedures for the negotiations. The Contracting Parties also decided to convene a meeting at the Ministerial level in September 1973 to consider the report of the Preparatory Committee, to establish a Trade Negotiations Committee, and to provide the necessary guidelines for the negotiations.

In international economic affairs a vacuum is quickly filled, and what otherwise might seem to be unimportant becomes critical. This is particularly true in the trade field. Individual actions and practices with little immediate impact multiply and tend to be self-reinforcing. Unless dealt with, they soon become entrenched and reversible only through major political and economic confrontations. This explains some of the apparent paradoxes in the international trade field, where major tension or misunderstandings among nations can arise over apparently inconsequential matters such as grapefruit and tomato paste. These are the symptoms of the breakdown in the use of rules and institutional mechanisms. In trade perhaps even more than in monetary matters, there is a need for effective grievance-resolution procedures. The number and complexity of issues that arise need a process and mechanism to assign them a relative weight of economic importance and work to resolve them promptly. The alternative is not only an inefficient allocation of resources but also increased tension.

In addition to improvements in the trading system, there are numerous substantive issues to be faced in the trade negotiations. Tariffs, non-tariff barriers, and the problems of agriculture are the most well known and most widely debated. Agriculture raises particularly difficult questions of a social and political nature for all countries. At the same time, agriculture is an area in which the United States has a strong competitive advantage and where real trade gains can be realized. The problem is to bring about rationalization in a meaningfully short period of time.

A second major question is the problem of preferences. This encompasses both developed and developing countries. The proliferation of preferences and reverse preferences by the European Community beyond the confines of the customs or trade union is a clear derogation of the most-favored-nation principle. Its importance goes far beyond the initial trade-distorting effects and economic costs it imposes on others. It sets the whole system down a road of economic one-upmanship that is difficult to reverse for it builds in strong national and domestic interest groups behind discrimination.

The other side of the problem of preferences is how to reconcile the desires of the developing countries for tariff preferences in a multilateral, nondiscriminatory system where the developed countries are asking whether tariffs can be reduced or eliminated. You cannot eliminate tariffs without eliminating preferences in the process.

Another problem facing us is that in agriculture the developing countries and some industrial countries have been seeking commodity agreements which allocate markets—with increasing shares apportioned to them and with rigid pricing provisions not responsive to market forces. The United States, on the other hand, has been pressing for a more market-oriented world agricultural structure.

Finally, there is a practical question of how to achieve more effective coordination between international organizations, such as the GATT, the IMF, and the OECD. A start is being made by the C-20, which has a broad mandate encompassing trade, monetary, and investment matters, and is itself taking up those issues of direct concern to the adjustment process and is concerned with the work on these proceeding elsewhere as well as their interrelationship.

In this last section I have set out many questions and provided not many answers, for answers do not yet exist. The GATT has just begun its work; the Preparatory Committee for Trade Negotiation met in early February 1973 to begin working out the agenda and timetable. The difficulties of successful reform in trade are great. In almost every nation, exports are perceived as being more important than international investment as a means of promoting jobs and economic welfare.

Interrelationships Among Economic, Political, and Security Matters

The third subject I wished to discuss—albeit briefly—is the interrelation of monetary and trade reform to the evolution of the international system as a whole, which this symposium has been focusing on. In a recent journal article, Richard Cooper called attention to an often ignored fact—that trade and monetary policy is foreign policy.

Precisely because the postwar agreements of Bretton Woods and GATT were appropriate to the economic conditions prevailing in the early postwar years, international economic matters could be and were relegated to a secondary position in foreign policy. This is clearly no longer the case and, as I have pointed out in the previous sections, there are more and more examples of international economics spilling into the political arena.

While I believe there is broad agreement now that international economic matters can no longer be handled at a level secondary to international political and security matters, it is interesting to note, though, that economics is being discussed here under the "Strategy of Implementation" section. Actually international economics will be much more than a constraint on U.S. policy. In the future it will be a major determinant of the entire international structure.

In addition, there is a fundamental relationship between the objectives the United States is pursuing in the economic field and the quest for a stable, peaceful world. Last year at the International Monetary Fund in a speech of major importance, but one that has received little attention, President Nixon spoke to this point at some length. He drew the connecting ties quite clearly, pointing out that as the danger of armed conflict between major powers is reduced, the potential for economic conflict is increased. He also pointed out that:

- The new economic structure must help and not hinder the world's movement to peace;

- International commerce must become a source of stability and harmony rather than friction and animosity; and

- For this end a realistic code of economic conduct is needed.

The appearance of a President of the United States at an international economic forum to discuss the critical nature of monetary and economic reform was an unusual event. Both the forum and the substance of his speech were uncharacteristic in terms of what Americans had become accustomed to hearing their President discuss in the international economic area over the previous twenty-five years. Point Four, the Marshall Plan, and the Alliance for Progress, yes, but not tariffs and exchange rates.

Economics is here to stay as high foreign policy, and rightly so. In great part the differences being debated and negotiated represent fundamental philosophical ones—the age-old debate of the proper balance between control and competition, between market and managed solutions. At stake is whether nations desire to retain, as a practical operative concept, the principle of nondiscrimination in the conduct of international trade; whether they intend to pursue a liberal economic order in which freer flows of goods, people, and capital strengthen the links among nations operating in a multipolar world; and whether they are prepared to adopt a system in which each nation assumes international rights and obligations equivalent to those of every other country. It is important that the answers to these questions be positive.

Until an international economic system with agreed rules and principles is achieved, there will be continued friction and potential adverse effects to our existing foreign relations. An important part of the emerging international structure will be the economic system. Successful reform will build foundations to provide stability for the system as a whole.

Part VI:
The Strategy of Implementation: Diplomacy and Domestic Consensus

The emerging international structure places an increasing burden on the decision-making capacity of government and requires extensive public education if the United States is to live up to its international responsibilities. Robert R. Bowie points out in the following paper that the increasing complexity of U.S. foreign relations makes new demands on the United States to maintain a coherent set of policies coordinated with its allies. In the second paper Leo Cherne stresses the need for strong leadership in articulating the rationale of a responsible foreign policy if that policy is to generate the public support required to sustain it over time.

Dr. Bowie is the Director of the Center for International Affairs at Harvard University. He is currently a Rockefeller Research Visiting Professor at the Brookings Institution. Dr. Bowie has held several positions in government, including Director of Policy Planning Staff, Department of State, and Counselor, Department of State.

Mr. Cherne is co-founder and Executive Director of the Research Institute of America. He has been active in the area of international cultural and educational affairs, serving in many capacities. Among these are: Chairman of the International Rescue Committee; member of the Board of Advisors of the Industrial College of the Armed Forces; member of the U.S. Advisory Commission on International Educational and Cultural Affairs; and Chairman of the Executive Committee of Freedom House.

11

Implementation of U.S. Foreign Policy in the Decade of the 1970s

Robert Bowie

How should U.S. foreign policy be implemented in the coming decade? In carrying it out, what will be the demands on political leaders, officials, Congress and the public? How should the U.S. work with other nations? How will domestic politics and foreign policy interact? The answers depend, of course, on more fundamental issues. What should the U.S. seek to achieve in international affairs? What should be the purposes of its policy? Under what conditions will it be pursued?

I

The international system is clearly in flux. The situation appears more fluid than it has for twenty-five years, and the major actors are uncertain about their course. Internally they are undergoing significant social and structural stresses under the impact of growing affluence, generational change, technology, and other factors. And each of them is to some degree forced to reappraise the kind of international order that is emerging and its role in that order.

Western Europe certainly displays these features. West Germany, Britain, France, and Italy and other countries are in the midst of very substantial social changes at home, and at the same time, they are trying to create a new community in Europe. With Britain now a member, and France more cooperative after de Gaulle, the Community has regained some of its momentum, but its functions, authority, and structure will still have to be greatly strengthened if it is to be an effective entity for internal or foreign affairs. Whether those changes occur will depend on the political leadership of its members. Moreover, the Europeans are confused and unsure about their relations with the U.S. and with Eastern Europe and the Soviet Union, and indeed, halting in defining their interests.

Japan is a different case, but with similar characteristics. There too, social change is going on very rapidly, and the Japanese are in the throes of re-examining their values and priorities domestically. With its strong and burgeoning economy, its limited political influence, and its military dependence on the U.S., Japan is also obviously searching for its role, its links with the other parts of Asia, and its relations with the United States and Europe.

171

The Soviet Union (and China) show some of the same symptoms. There are strains and stresses in the economy, and pressures of consumers and others for domestic change, especially in the Soviet Union, though they can be contained or channeled at least for some time. Both the USSR and China are re-examining to some degree what course to follow under the evolving conditions of international affairs. Both are pursuing a policy of détente and wider relations with the non-communist world. Such a policy currently serves their differing needs, even without assuming changes in basic outlook: the USSR needs trade, technology, and credits, and lower tension serves both its European purposes and its Chinese problem. China's fear of the Soviet Union has prompted it to break out of its earlier isolation and to establish better relations with the U.S., Japan, and the developing states. Thus, it is hard to judge whether these changes are more than tactical shifts. Nor do we know whether they would survive changes in leadership.

Hence, while cooperating with them is possible and useful, it is prudent to assume that rivalry or hostility continues to be a major element in their relations. After all, efforts at cooperation are not new. For fifteen years, the West and the USSR have been trying to understand and come to terms with the constraints (and imposed cooperation) inherent in their nuclear predicament, and have been making limited arms control and other agreements. This sort of cooperation is quite different, however, from that among the advanced nations of Western Europe, Japan, and the United States.

The United States, in its way, reflects similar aspects: (1) the domestic ferment resulting from Vietnam, internal problems, and generational change; and (2) ambiguity about what kind of an international order it thinks is emerging and what role it will play. The first Nixon term has not resolved this ambiguity. The withdrawal from Vietnam, and efforts to improve relations with China and the USSR, while useful or necessary, are only preliminaries to answers, and leave unclear the sort of order and the U.S. role. The actions taken have been greatly influenced by the special interests of the President in summitry and in dramatic steps.

The talk about balance of power really does not clarify our purposes or priorities. Indeed, it can serve as a platform for unilateralism as an alternative to the predominance of the U.S. since the war. In that period, while the U.S. may not have had an imperial urge to run other people's affairs, it was so much larger and stronger than most of its allies and clients that it became used to more or less calling the tune, and to having more freedom of action than others. As this position has eroded, one reaction has been to resist the constraints of interdependence by asserting more unilateral independence. This attitude has been manifested in various actions such as those of 15 August 1971 in the monetary field, and in the handling of the China trip. The balance-of-power concept fits into this mold: the balancer can imagine himself in the driver's seat playing off others and so remaining "dominant."

Whatever its appeal, the idea is inadequate as a strategy. The general notion of balancing power has, of course, some validity; since the war, the United States has clearly been offsetting or "balancing" the power of the Soviet Union and China. But that obvious fact does not mean that a balance-of-power system can provide the foundation for a stable and prosperous international order suited to the conditions of our times. In that quest, models from past history are not the appropriate place to begin.

II

As General Beaufre has said, a strategist should start by asking: what is "necessary"? What do the objective conditions require? The circumstances in which we find ourselves and their implications for international relations seem to be clearer than the state of mind of many of the actors.

The key factor of international life in our time is interdependence. It has reached its greatest depth and intensity with respect to the advanced nations of Europe, the United States, and Japan. This is obvious in economic affairs, whether it be the monetary system, trade, agriculture, investment, energy, or the multinational corporation. What each nation does has direct repercussions on the prosperity and economic welfare of the others.

Security is similar, though unequal. For quite a long time, certainly through the next decade, Western Europe and Japan will continue to depend on the American nuclear umbrella, and mutual interests will require cooperation to assure a collective system of defense. Even though the fear of military aggression may recede, the deterrent capacity of the United States (and its allies) will still be relevant in maintaining confidence and avoiding political pressure in the face of Soviet and growing Chinese power.

By the same token, the advanced nations share common interests in relations with the communist states—the USSR, Eastern Europe, and China.

These relations are still between "limited adversaries" that may agree to cooperate for differing motives and purposes. Concerning them, the approach and expectations are basically different from those implicit in the partnership among the advanced non-communist countries.

At this stage, the objective should be to foster conditions and constructive change that will expand the range of genuine cooperation. But this will be a long-term effort. In pursuing it, the advanced non-communist nations need to concert their policies in negotiations and otherwise.

Concerning the less developed nations, the advanced nations will be more effective if they work together. While the future of the less developed countries depends mainly on their own efforts, the advanced nations have an interest in their stability and progress, to which they can contribute with regard to trade, transfers of resources, investment, and technical assistance. Given the great disparity in power and capacity and inevitable sensitivity and resentment, these relations call for a compassionate and understanding approach by the advanced nations.

III

In seeking a viable international order, the advanced non-communist nations clearly have many common interests and needs. The nature of their relations imposes certain imperatives. That is the crucial point. Inevitably, their relations involve frictions and competition as well as joint interests and must be handled so that conflicts do not jeopardize common needs. They cannot be dealt with at arms length, for they involve continuing interactions that have to be managed by active collaboration. Such management requires more than summitry, though that has its place. It calls for day-to-day cooperation at many levels of government, among officials and experts, informally and through joint agencies. Moreoever, it requires that many domestic decisions of each party be taken in the light of the wider, or joint interest. In short, these countries must pursue parallel courses in many important fields, and do so over an extended period of time. Operationally, that means that their political leaders and officials have to be able to work together regularly in order to manage this sort of concerted policy.

This will not be easy to achieve among a group of democracies. At stake are matters that go deep into the domestic life and politics of each of these countries. In each the necessary decisions will impose burdens or hardships on individuals and groups that may be politically influential. For example, joint efforts to reduce trade barriers in order to serve the general interest in efficiency and productivity may force some firms to adjust output or cease to operate and require their employees to shift jobs or learn new skills, with significant effects on unions. Likewise, if the European Community does ultimately rationalize its agricultural policy, the impact will be felt by farmers in France, Italy, Germany, and elsewhere. Again, the efforts to combat pollution and to improve the quality of life have serious potential for skewing competition among the advanced countries unless they can keep in step on the measures they take, and on their timing.

For such collaboration, both political and bureaucratic, it is essential that the course of each of the parties reflects a reasonable degree of consistency: it has to be predictable, and it has to be reliable. If democratic leaders are to align their policies with one another, particularly the smaller ones with the larger ones, they must have confidence that if they do expend the necessary political capital to control domestic parochial pressure in the interest of wider cooperation, they will be able to count on parallel action by their partners and not find themselves out on a limb. And this means, finally, that whatever course is adopted has to be supported by parliaments and by the public, so that there can be a degree of consistency and coherence over a period of years.

IV

To carry out such a long-range policy together, the advanced nations will have to share and act on a common strategy in their foreign policy. First, they will have to set a course to which the various partners can rally, and which can provide a sort of navigational chart in carrying on their own domestic political activities; second, they will have to set priorities for choices in trying to deal with a changing world; third, they will have to enable political leaders and officials to work together, because it is they who know the general direction and the priorities. Finally, they will have to enable the partners to engage in a long-term coherent and cumulative effort, which alone can be effective in shaping the situation.

In concrete terms, the implementation of a policy of this sort by the United States will require substantial changes from the methods and practices of the last four years. It calls, in the first place, for a much clearer definition by the President of the strategy of U.S. foreign policy. What kind of order is the U.S. trying to bring about, and what are its priorities? The answers have been extremely unclear during the first Nixon term. The Foreign Policy Reports and the President's actions and various statements concerning balance of power have been confusing on these issues. If the purpose is to create an international order resting on cooperation among the advanced countries, it is essential to establish the priority of this aim and its relation to the other aspects of policy, such as relations with the communist countries.

Second, the Executive Branch outside the White House will have to be given more opportunity for participation in making and executing policy. The necessary cooperation with the other countries requires much more devolution of authority to the regular departments, agencies, and officials, and much better understanding of where we are going. In particular, it implies a much larger role for the State Department and for the leadership of that department.

Third, it involves much more systematic effort to involve Congress and to persuade its members of the necessity of the courses taken. Its leaders should have a participating role in formulating and carrying out our basic approach to international order and international relations. The support of the Congress will be essential in trying to resist parochial tendencies in trade and other fields, tendencies that can undercut efforts to carry out such a collaborative policy.

Finally, there has to be a much more systematic effort to educate the public, to deal with the press, and in general to explain what the imperatives are, and what our policy is.

This is a tall order. It would be difficult enough if the situation were static, and if the partners were all in a position to perform effectively. But neither is the case. The situation is changing rapidly and will continue to do so; and none of the partners is fully able to perform its required role.

The authority of the European Community is limited and its machinery cumbersome; at best, years will be required to achieve the political and economic unity needed for acting as an effective entity for its members. Japan is also slow to act and often indecisive. And the U.S. will doubtless continue to suffer for some time the consequences of the Vietnamese trauma and its effects on the economy and political processes.

There is also no doubt that the climate of détente strengthens parochial and local pressure groups and produces other political problems that were less likely to arise when fear gave a higher priority to security and alliance needs. Latent nationalism and unilateralism foster a resistance to subordinating special interests to a common purpose. In addition, the questions of relative roles and influence loom larger in Europe and Japan and cause resentment.

For the longer term there is another factor that is hard to assess. Through all these advanced societies there appears to be a growing *malaise* or at least unease among some groups about the sheer size of the society, its homogenized character, its impersonality, and about the loss of control over one's destiny. This often expresses itself in the form of resentment of large organizations and especially of distant government. Yet interdependence creates the necessity for coordination and action at levels even more remote from the average citizen. The effect will be to move one step further away the control over matters that people will quite properly feel are directly affecting their lives. Thus, there is a genuine tension between this desire for more participation, more control over one's destiny, and the imperatives requiring coordination on a global scale.

Coping with these dilemmas will demand political leadership of a very high order. The President and the prime ministers will have to expend considerable political capital in espousing and pressing for the necessary policy. It implies also a really serious effort to educate and to draw in diverse parts of their societies in order to make the policy effective.

The U.S. role remains central. While certainly not as dominant as in the past, the United States is still far and away the strongest among the advanced countries, having more capability for trying to do the things that need to be done than either Western Europe or Japan. It will have to take the lead in cooperation based on partnership and consent, rather than on any effort at dictation. It will have to be patient with the great difficulties in working with Europe and Japan as partners, and indeed will have to assist them as it can to overcome those difficulties. Meeting these responsibilities will tax the maturity of leaders and citizens.

Obviously the outcome is not foreordained. The great question is: will the democratic states be able to rise to the challenge of this period?

12

The Problem of Domestic Consensus

Leo Cherne

Let me begin by recounting a story. A minister was visiting a patient, terminally ill, who was receiving oxygen. The sad family was waiting outside, and the minister was seeking to provide some comfort during this difficult period. He kept pressing upon his parishioner questions toward that end: "Is there anything I can do that would bring you comfort? Is there any action we can take? Is there any message?"

All of this with no response, until the minister thought to take from his pocket a pad and pencil, gave it to the patient, and repeated the question, "Is there anything you would like to say, anything we can do?" The patient hastily scribbled a few words just before he expired.

The minister left to bring the unhappy news to the family, but with a sense of modest accomplishment; he had at least extracted the final words. And as he rejoined the family, he took the pad from his pocket and thought he had better read it first. It said, "You're standing on my oxygen tube!"

The oxygen of any demanding strategic policy is public opinion. This has been a repetitive theme throughout this conference. A German view heavily emphasized the *milieu* of détente in the Federal Republic, which has made Chancellor Brandt's government partially hostage to the actions of the Soviet Union. It was asserted by another participant that national strategy cannot be divorced from domestic perceptions and it was properly asked whether the Europeans are taking account of the changed domestic consensus in the United States. There were several references to the sharply reduced sense of danger presented by the USSR to its neighbors in Western Europe. One of our colleagues has said that mood and will are *the* decisive battlefront, adding that "these moods are seldom fatal." I would caution that once fatal is generally terminal.

Now there are certain moods, and even very distressing ones, that can be very difficult and yet have only transitory effect on national policy. Bill Moyers said about a year ago at the peak of our domestic distress: "Our country is passing a great big kidney stone; it hurts like hell, but you seldom die of it." And in a real sense, we have passed that great big kidney stone. There are all sorts of ways in which our national mood, the consensus, is manifesting a significantly reduced unease, distress, and discomfort. Now, what can be said of our mood, our consensus, and especially of those aspects that are genuinely relevant to the national security and strategic capability?

177

In an open society, no protracted effort, no burdensome preparation for national strength (I am talking about additional demands upon a community rather than habitual expectation), no costly involvement in the safety of others can ever be greater or more reliable than the public understanding of the need for such efforts. The will of the American people to sustain such very large efforts is crucial. That will not only requires the perception of a danger that is real, of perceived hazards that must be averted, but also exists in proportion to the confidence that is vested in those who conceive and guide these strategic purposes.

Now if the domestic consensus is to be shaped toward a supporting role in a comprehensive national policy, there must either be a clear perception of need or danger so unambiguous to public view as to require no further education, or there must be so clear and consistent an explanation of the national policy, and the strategy it pursues, as to earn the needed support for the effort, the costs, the sacrifices which may be required.

I must now make two observations that, if not totally inconsistent, will at the very least leave an unresolved paradox. I do not believe that a public consensus in support of the Nixon Doctrine presently exists. Nevertheless, I do believe it to be remarkably clear that there is overwhelming public support for the major foreign policy actions that have been taken by President Nixon and his surrogates in the White House, led by Dr. Kissinger.

The absence of a consensus in support of the Nixon Doctrine exists simply because that Doctrine is not widely understood. In fact, there does not appear to have been common understanding of that Doctrine even at this conference. There have also been some here who have gone even further and have questioned whether such a Doctrine exists.

To the extent that there is public understanding of any coherent conception, I believe the public sees the Nixon Doctrine as an honorable effort to delimit our responsibilities, to withdraw from overextended positions, to lessen our costs, and to reduce the prospect that the United States will be as exposed to hazard as we have been during these 28 years. To the extent that the Nixon Doctrine has a content larger than this public understanding, any additional commitments, costs or undertakings will still require the creation of public support.

Public support of President Nixon's foreign policies is largely retrospective, involving as it does fundamental approval of actions that have been taken, departures from previous policy that have been made and generally applauded. In one respect, this consensus of approval is not retrospective. It does of course provide approval of a man, his colleagues and their collective acuity, and, to that extent, represents a political account that can still be drawn upon within limits.

But the absence of popular understanding of the complex purposes upon which we are engaged is at least as important as the real approval of actions that have been taken. A new multipolar world and a foreign policy addressed to that world involve a national strategy that may require restraints, costs, obligations, even sacrifices—enthusiasm for which will be difficult to muster in the absence of a wider public understanding of that very much more complex forward foreign policy. If what is perceived by the public is a sequence of steps reducing our hazards, lowering our costs, and honorably withdrawing from previous obligations, such an understanding cannot long serve to energize a comprehensive national security policy, especially as intermittent difficulties appear to make our allies more difficult to live with than seems to be the case with our former enemies.

At one point in this meeting, our present strategic design was described as one that had foregone confrontation for a reliance on a balance of power. At that point, a panelist was asked whether the balance-of-power concept has any meaning in the Soviet Union, any background in their culture or political experience. His answer was a flat "No." Now, if they were seeking to muster a consensus around the balance-of-power concept, that I suppose would represent something of a problem to them. But I don't think they are.

I ask now whether the balance-of-power concept has any roots in the American experience. I suggest that whatever echo may be found will be largely negative. To the extent that there will be an American reaction to a balance-of-power doctrine, I think our responses will tend to be critical, suspicious, reminiscent of the European political struggles from which our people fled, and from which the long history of our earlier isolationism grew. I do not think, as useful as indeed balance of power may be as a strategic concept, it is one which can engage a popular support that readily provides any degree of energy.

Now, it may be a measure of our immaturity that as a people we tolerate ambiguity poorly, that our collective energy has required the perception of real and immediate danger, or a hostile ideology, or the driving force of an ideal. None of these three exists today with sufficient clarity. How can we indeed measure whether or not an affirmative consensus exists that is adequate to support the demands of a national security policy? I believe that the ways in which public support is extended or withheld in matters significant to a credible national strategy include most, if not all, of the following factors:

There should be an essential willingness to sustain a Selective Service system adequate to meet the manpower requirements of the Armed Forces or, alternatively, an adequate and continuing number of voluntary enlistments must be forthcoming either to supplement conscription or to meet altogether the manpower needs of the military. It is already clear that popular support for a Selective Service system is inadequate, and it is yet to be determined whether such public support will meet those manpower requirements through voluntary enlistments.

There must be a high level of career continuation in the Armed Forces by the graduates of the several Service academies sufficient to provide vigorous leadership for the Services. There is already some indication that this regeneration of management capability is in doubt, and that defections both in faculty and among the higher scholarship academy students is something of a problem.

There must be the willingness of both Houses of Congress to appropriate the funds essential to sustain programs central to the foreign policy. No significant Congressional aversion to explicitly military appropriation is yet visible. It is at least equally clear, however, that a number of the non-military programs and especially those involving military and economic aid are without adequate Congressional support. It must be a matter of the highest concern that Congressional pressure to pull our troops back from their posts in Europe grows at precisely the time when on-going negotiations with the Soviet Union suggest their presence.

There must be the willingness of the electorate to accept that level of taxation needed to finance such national security programs. If that level is anything beyond the present one, it is not likely to be forthcoming, and it is important to recall that the present level of taxation is less than it has been during large portions of this previous period.

Finally, and perhaps most importantly, there must be the ability and willingness of the periodical and newspaper press, and especially the electronic media, to understand the rationale for our national security policies. Significant portions of the press do not presently exhibit such an understanding, and a major portion of television expresses hostility.

Now how can such public support be generated? I believe there is no substitute for an adequate and reasonably continuous articulation of both policies and the means needed to implement those policies by the several instruments of the federal government involved in the conduct of the nation's foreign policy. These several, of course, include the Department of State, the Department of Defense, and particularly the Office of the President. These have as one of their fundamental responsibilities the maintenance of public support for whatever is our national security purpose.

On one level, that process of articulation has been especially forthright and remarkably detailed. The several public expositions by the President's National Security Advisor, Henry Kissinger, have, in my opinion, been models of public education. But I think I do them no injustice when I observe that they have served more to explain what it is we have done than to outline what our national security purposes will continue to require.

Precisely because our strategy is now complex, and the world now multipolar, precisely because relationships must be balanced and more must be left unsaid than can ever be exposed to public view, I have deep sympathy for those who carry the responsibility for the continuous maintenance of a public consensus of support. To understand the difficulty is regrettably not to eliminate the necessity. There still remains the need for a public understanding of the forward thrust of our national security policy and all that it may require if it is to be successful.

It is urgent that the Congress perceive that our foreign policy needs are so primary as to require the full implementation of programs designed to meet those needs at whatever cost to other national needs, or at least that the Congress understand that the funds required to implement the nation's foreign policies can be provided with no significant sacrifice to other essential needs. It is here that our dilemma grows daily. It is both regrettable and undeniable that the Congress in particular perceives our national security needs to be in conflict with internal needs. And this problem has been made no simpler by the fact that the President's party is in control of neither House of the Congress and the aggravating fact that the Office of the Presidency and the power of the Congress are currently in contest.

The final means by which adequate public support can be generated involves a sufficient understanding among the leaders of the private sector of America that national security needs exist, that the measures being advanced to implement them are responsive to those needs, that those responses are not in excess of actual requirement, and that the implementing actions are consonant with the international reality.

If these are the means by which a consensus can be fashioned, nourished, and kept vital, it is then important to understand the obstacles to the process. It is of course especially vital that the unusual or new difficulties that now exist be recognized.

Emphasis on the need for public understanding, for an education toward that understanding provided by the national leadership, for support of that understanding expressed in the Congress does in a sense suggest perceptions and actions that may simply not be available. A policy in transition is never the most easily articulated nor the most readily understood.

Such a national security policy that, in addition, exacts complex and sometimes painful accommodations from other nations or ourselves may be discussed with some candor by non-governmental specialists like those at this assembly, while imposing reticence among those who administer the policy. It is ironic but nevertheless true that this official inability to "explain" is frequently more exacting when changes in our policy involve nations that have long been friendly than when they involve other nations toward which an unmitigated hostility has been directed.

We are in precisely such a period. It is not easy for those responsible for the creation or administration of policy to discuss frankly with the American community the changes that have been introduced in the relationships with the Peoples Republic of China and the Soviet Union. It is not at all unlikely that ambiguity about those changes is itself one aspect of the effectiveness of the new strategy. As difficult as are such public expressions, ironically even more counterproductive are the frank expositions of whatever collateral changes these in turn produce for our allies.

To that extent, therefore, a public consensus in support of a significantly changing foreign policy or national security strategy is more difficult to nourish than were the understandings held by the American people during the period of unrelieved cold war. In a real sense, that public consensus must, during critical intervals, rest on faith, on a confidence vested in leadership, on an intuitive understanding that "they must know what they're doing." This fact is complicated by other present tendencies that involve significant portions of the American community.

There is the undeniable fact of fatigue. It would be remarkable if any nation expended what the United States did during World War II and undertook what it did by way of international obligation in the post-war period without finally producing a public impatience with "so much for so long." But then, in addition, two wars, each less than "satisfactorily concluded," have further taxed that willingness to assume continuing heavy burdens. Neither the Korean nor the Vietnamese experience have left the American community with an unequivocal conviction that the costs involved were worth the disappointing relationship between efforts undertaken and results achieved.

Other factors have complicated that problem of understanding, have made more difficult faith in the American leadership within the American community. The American intellectual community, whether burdened by an excessive sense of guilt or disappointed by the ever-present distance between the real and the ideal, has always been suspicious of "the establishments." Criticism is in fact the honored obligation of the student and scholar and a sense of some superiority an invariable byproduct. This has been expressed in different ways by Henry Adams, by T.S. Eliot, by the expatriates of the 1920s, Sinclair Lewis, or the majestic impertinences of Galbraith. If this is traditional, the size of that educated elite is not. The magnitudes of those who are students or faculty on the campuses of America is altogether new and introduces a new potency in what has traditionally been suspicion and criticism.

Simultaneous with this egalitarian thrust toward mass higher education are the peculiar attributes of America's most popular mass communications instrument—television. In my judgment, the criticisms of television that rest upon suggestions of bias, of elitism, of the metropolitan background of the major newscasters, have led us to focus on some existing problems that, in my view, are not the central ones. I cannot in these observations devote sufficient time to an adequate examination of the inherent differences between television and the printed press. Yet several must be emphasized. They do affect the public view of all of our institutions and particularly those governmental ones most concerned with the national security.

The essence of television is that it is a mass entertainment instrument. Its news and public affairs programs are as rigidly disciplined by the demands of audience size and audience interest as are any of the top ten programs in the television diet. It is extremely difficult for television to deal with the abstract. it is comfortable with the concrete and happy only with the visual. And yet, the public perception basic to the existence of a consensus in support of a national security strategy involves much that is abstract and virtually nothing that is visual.

If a particular section of a newspaper were in fact to be measured by how many read the particular page, there might indeed, some 25 years ago, have passed into oblivion the editorial pages of The New York Times. But newspapers and other forms of printed media do not in fact measure the balance they provide on the basis of what appeal that individual slice has for audience size.

Television does, and I will say it must. In addition to being entertainment, television is theater. The very nature of theater is that it presents a conflict perception of life, and it is inherent in television, not only as a visual instrument but as a theatrical instrument, that whatever it touches it advances with an adversary content—a conflict perception.

Television finds it difficult to deal with complex matters, and it is not an overstatement to suggest that nothing involving our Administration in international affairs is simple. Survey after survey gives unmistakable indication that television is not only the first choice of the public for the exposure to news, but is the most believed of all of the purveyors of news.

It is clear that these recent years have seen remarkable social changes. All of the industrialized nations of the world have been exposed to technological pressures and to social adjustments that have profoundly altered or at least strained a number of previous values. There is, I believe, a close relationship between the tension that has been imposed upon historically stable beliefs and the sharp drop reflected in the American public of its confidence in the leadership of all its institutions on which we have counted to protect our stability. The widespread loss of institutional confidence further burdens those who must sustain public support of institutional behavior.

One periodic survey demonstrates this dilemma most clearly. The Louis Harris organization has asked the American people, "Do you have confidence in the leaders of the following institutions. . . ?" The survey measures the relative degree of confidence or lack of it in the leadership of each of sixteen major institutions in American life. As recently as 1966, the American public expressed its confidence in more than half of these major organizations. One year and a half ago, only one of these sixteen institutions retained the confidence of a majority of the American people—medicine. All other organized segments of American life were well below the 50 percent confidence level. The result was so startling that the Harris organization was led to conduct the same study, previously taken at five-year intervals, after a lapse of only one year, in November 1972. There were changes. Now no institution has the confidence of a majority of the American people. Medicine still leads the pack, but it has joined the other establishments enjoying only minority support.

However, there are also favorable and, I believe, truly significant changes: five of the institutional groupings have lost further confidence. Two of them have remained stable, but nine have enjoyed some degree of recovery. And among the nine which have begun to recapture some confidence are several which are vital in the field of national security: The military leadership, in which only 20 percent expressed confidence in 1971, achieved a rating of 35 percent in 1972. The Executive Branch, which was at a 23 percent confidence level in November 1971, rose to 27 percent. The Congress, in which only 19 percent vested confidence in November of 1971, picked up an additional 2 percent a year later.

It is still early to extrapolate a vigorous return of institutional confidence from these figures, and yet I will venture a guess that the great kidney stone of which Bill Moyers spoke did pass some time within the last year, that the tide was turned before the end of the war in Vietnam, and that we are beginning to perceive the very slow return of something like confidence in our institutional forms.

These surveys present us with a number of troubling paradoxes. The public on the one hand expresses its greatest belief in the news that it sees on television, while on the other, the public accords the leaders of that institution almost as close to no confidence as any of these beleaguered establishments enjoy. The Executive Branch has the confidence of a little more than a quarter of the American people, yet the same people have registered near historic support for the head of that branch during the last election.

I will not pretend to resolve those conflicts. But it does seem clear, on the one hand, that many people still accord considerable faith to individuals while distrusting the impersonal entities to which they are attached. But the more significant observation with which I will conclude this aspect of my remarks is that this study cannot really be understood as an accurate measure of the *performance* of these separate institutions. If some enjoy the confidence of a majority and others do not, if some were going up while others were going down during recent years, one could assume that the disparate directions did in fact reflect a public assessment of performance. But when *all* of the institutions, though in different degree, have suffered a radical decline in confidence, we are, I think, dealing with an overriding fact of institutional revolt. And, if this is so, this is a major problem for those who must sustain a public consensus behind the institutions essential to a national security policy.

I conclude with an expression of minor regret about a phrase to which President Nixon returns frequently: "A generation of peace." To the extent that this phrase suggests the accomplishment of that goal, it may serve to devitalize public support for continuing demanding national effort. So much of what has been said here seems to suggest that substantial new energy must be applied, substantial accommodations must still be made, and some substantial costs must still be paid. If "a generation of peace" is understood to be a largely accomplished fact, it serves to make more difficult the continuing pursuit of our purposes. If it is in fact a concrete objective, the content of the requirements must be better understood. If it is a viable and not yet attained ideal, I believe that this must be made clear. In that event, in fact, it can be made useful as one of the traditional motivators sustaining public consensus behind strategic purpose.

Part VII:
A Strategic Synthesis

In the closing chapter, William R. Kintner synthesizes the strategic implications of the Nixon Doctrine for the process of change already evident in the structure of the international system. His view of international affairs includes assessments of regional trends as well as the domestic policy requirements of a responsible U.S. foreign policy. He emphasizes the need both for greater international cooperation in an increasingly interdependent world, and for placing top priority on U.S. relations with allies in an era of negotiations with adversaries.

Dr. Kintner is the Director of the Foreign Policy Research Institute and Professor of Political Science at the University of Pennsylvania. For many years Dr. Kintner has been engaged in research activities within and outside the U.S. government in the field of foreign policy and national security planning. He is a member of the Council on Foreign Relations, the Board of Foreign Scholarships, and the author or coauthor of many articles and books on American foreign policy and political-military problems.

13

The Emerging Nixon Doctrine: Toward a New International System

William R. Kintner

A Glance at the Chessboard

Conflict and Cooperation

In his second inaugural address President Nixon said, "As we meet here today, we stand on the threshold of a new era of peace in the world." This conviction reflects an assumption that has strongly flavored the 1970, 1971, and 1972 Presidential State of the World Messages (the Nixon Doctrine): the world is changing as a result of "the fluidity of a new era of multilateral diplomacy."

This vision of a new international milieu assumes the emergence of a five-power world as the People's Republic of China, Western Europe, and Japan supplement the Soviet Union and United States as major actors on the world stage. Concern for the preservation of the pentapolar system as a whole should prompt moderation in their dealings with one another and lead to the common acceptance of new rules of mutual restraint. This concern may, then, provide the foundation for an era of peace. Yet it seems more likely that the immense qualitative differences among the five presumed great power centers, the disparity in their relative strength, and the multitude of other actors will spawn countervailing difficulties for some time to come.

A five-power world does not exist in 1973 and may not come into being by the end of the decade. The fact that the United States and Soviet Union remain militarily far stronger than their nearest competitors suggests that we are still in a bipolar world. Moreover, the great and sustained increase in Soviet strategic and naval power threatens to disturb even the current bipolar power balance between Washington and Moscow.[1] Thus, the world is in a state of transition. We may be witnessing the conception of multipolarism without any clear knowledge of its delivery date.

If we are upon the threshold of a generation of peace, the cause is the growing interdependence of nations rather than any new global balance-of-power system. The central fact of our era is that the scientific-technological revolution—along with the industrial revolution, which both preceded and accompanied it—are together transforming human society in every region of the world. Notwithstanding rhetorical accusations directed at the "imperialists," ideologies conceived in the past have become largely irrelevant. Most of the conflicts that

189

have raged since World War II have been internal in character and, unless internationalized for reasons of great power competition, have remained so.

Despite evidence that the underlying world forces favoring international cooperation are growing stronger, all-encompassing ideologies are still proclaimed in both Moscow and Peking. Nor have all war-generating issues been muted. The leaders of both the Soviet Union and the People's Republic of China cling to the view of a world shaped in their own image after American power has eroded and one or the other of them has become dominant. Although the heavy-handedness of the past has given away to subtler tactics, *the Soviet objective is to win the struggle with the United States by dint of superior diplomacy based on superior strategy resting on predominant power.* The Soviet Union has achieved strategic parity with the United States (and perhaps incipient superiority) and is currently far stronger than China despite the Chinese development of an ICBM force. Moreover, the Soviets are conducting an encirclement strategy against their erstwhile ally. But China has passed beyond the point at which such a strategy could be feasible. As the basis of industrial and military growth, China has emphasized self-sufficiency in technology. According to Raphael Tsu, "one can expect for 1972 a [Chinese] gross national product of some $145 billion and the production of about 25 million metric tons of steel."[2] Tsu, a solid state physicist, concluded that China has developed a high-level scientific base and "is on the way to becoming an advanced industrial power."[3] Still, the Soviet Union will continue to pose a formidable threat to China through this decade. The return by China to an alliance with Russia seems virtually foreclosed, and a quasi-alliance between China and the United States is an even more remote contingency.

Flanked by a progressively powerful China, a dynamic Japan, and a resurgent Western Europe, the Soviet Union's long-term prospects for expanding its position in the Eurasian land mass are uncertain. On the other hand, the Soviet Union has yet to reach the peak of its absolute and relative power. Even so, the Soviet Union has, step by step, gained Western acceptance of the settlement in Europe that it sought at the end of World War II. Moreover, reliance upon power will continue to be the distinguishing feature of Soviet foreign policy. While the complexities of an incipient multipolar world may constrain the exercise of Soviet muscle, there is scant prospect that the Soviet Union during this decade will render major concessions to the United States. Moscow may tolerate residual American positions in both Europe and Asia for the sake of momentary self-interest, but such limited convergences of interests notwithstanding, the Soviet Union has no desire to see the United States continue as an equal competitor for influence in world affairs.

Although they will remain the tallest actors on the world stage, both the United States and Soviet Union will face a more complex world than that which marked the global system of the 1960s.

Part of this complexity derives from the unbalanced nature of the multipolarity that will emerge during this decade. The United States has accepted the diffusion of power, has based its policies on the likelihood that this diffusion will continue, and has encouraged greater independence on the part of its allies. Yet to the extent that the trends toward such a new global constellation are visible, they reflect as much a decline in relative American power as a waxing of Soviet power and the growth of China's strength.

The Contemporary World: Emerging
But Imperfect Multipolarity

The international system of the 1970s will be characterized by continuity but also by more fundamental change than at any time since the immediate post-World War II era. The widening of political participation in the democracies and the technological revolution in mass communications have opened diplomacy to continuous and intensive public scrutiny. In the generation after the Second World War, diplomacy operated in the predominantly bipolar environment of two cohesive alliance systems—an environment in which neither antagonist was prepared to accept the legitimacy of the other and, therefore, the legitimacy of the prevailing international system as a whole. The question is now: can either superpower accept a new multipolar system as legitimate? It could be argued that the Soviet leadership can adapt to, and exploit, the terrain of multipolarity more readily than the United States because of its systemic advantages of flexibility, tactical speed, and relative immunity from domestic public opinion in decision making. This may be true. On the other hand, some hard factors in Soviet political culture and behavior may prevent a Soviet acceptance of the legitimacy of the emerging international system. Soviet leaders have traditionally put great emphasis on the centralized and exclusive exercise of power and have shrunk from political relationships that they cannot fully control. Multipolarity demands, of course, the flexible manipulation of just such relationships.

By contrast, the United States may fare better in a multipolar world because its leaders are the products of a political system in which, at every step of their political ascent, they have had to deal with autonomous domestic political forces as these compete in the electoral arena. In the final analysis, the United States, accustomed to pluralism at home, can live with pluralism in international affairs far more comfortably than can the Soviet Union. Yet, this "advantage" can be exaggerated. The Soviets are becoming more sophisticated students of pluralistic processes. Thus, they have created institutions for intensive study of the United States and other nations, and are becoming more adept at interpreting, utilizing, and even manipulating pluralistic systems to their own strategic advantage. They may transfer this knowledge to the broader international stage.

Applying the Nixon Doctrine:
Selective Emphasis

The major problem posed for the United States by the emerging international system is one of transforming formerly dependent allies into partners, while changing its relationships with its adversaries. Stated differently, the problem is how to retain the assets of a bipolar world while taking advantage of whatever opportunities are presented by incipient multipolarity. There is little doubt that America's diplomatic surprises of 1971 tended, if anything, to throw the international system into confusion. Continuous change and excessive flexibility in foreign policies are incompatible with partnership. Yet, the restoration of viable partnerships with its allies remains the main prerequisite for America's ability not only to navigate its own ship of state successfully, but also to manage a multipolar world.

In this connection, it is necessary to observe that the three pillars of the Doctrine—strength, partnership, and negotiations—have been constructed unevenly. The result has been an overemphasis on bilateral negotiation with the Soviet Union, while the Western Alliance continues to decline militarily and experiences a series of monetary crises. In the Far East, the Administration's major spectacular event, the reopening of relations with China, substantially shook the U.S.-Japan Alliance.

Several East-West negotiations in the coming years harbor profound implications for America's future role in the Western Alliance and throughout the world: negotiations in SALT II, on Mutual and Balanced Force Reductions (MBFR) and the Conference on Security and Cooperation in Europe (CSCE). From these negotiations could issue results unfavorable to the United States and its allies if the United States acts as if a genuine commonality of interest now characterizes the U.S.-Soviet relationship. This approach often leads to agreements with the Soviets that damage relationships within NATO. Some *cognoscenti* believe that the United States, in dealing with the Soviet Union, appears to lack confidence in its ability to think a problem through rationally, reach a decision as to what it wishes to accomplish, and then hold fast to positions commensurate with its power and accomplishments.

In a situation where the United States feels that it can no longer shoulder the costs required to shape world events, it is going to be difficult to coordinate a global strategy with allies who define their goals and responsibilities differently. Thus, if the Nixon Doctrine reflects a conscious decision to limit the U.S. role in world affairs simply because previous commitments were costly, there is real danger that the Nixon Doctrine will lose its power as a guiding doctrine and will become a strategy of reactive pragmatism.

Guidelines for Policy Design

Recognizing the Driving Force

Mankind is about to realize that the excessive exploitation of the earth's resources will soon present the world with a series of problems that dwarf the issues of international relations we have confronted in the past. Behind this realization is the fantastic growth of world economic activity, particularly in the last two decades, as the result of an industrial-scientific revolution that has left no part of the world unaffected.

The technological revolution is introducing on a global scale the problems of resource scarcity, environmental pollution, and social justice. Although experts disagree as to the extent of resource scarcity and the scope of pollution, everyone acknowledges that our resources are finite. Finite global resources can support many more poor people than they can rich people. Population growth and energy consumption trends will make this problem—frequently dubbed the North-South gap—an inflammatory reality in our own generation. The stage is being set for the presentation of some revolutionary questions of just distribution of global resources for all members of the human family.

Finding answers to these questions will not be easy. Any successful international collaboration on those problems must offer something to the industrialized nations of all political persuasions and to the developing world as well. American policy should find means to balance national interests and international cooperation in all these arenas. A central issue, however, is whether Moscow and Peking will place the imperatives of essential cooperation above the pursuit of their parochial ideological ambitions.

The Diplomatic Challenge

Historically, the extension of democracy and the upholding of the principle of self-determination have been the central elements of the American national mission. After World War II, however, containment of communism became America's chief international purpose. Now President Nixon has restored the concept of self-determination as the basic principle of U.S. foreign policy. In his second inaugural address, he stated that "We shall support vigorously the principle that no country has the right to impose its will or its rule on another by force." At the same time, we will no longer "presume to tell people of other nations how to manage their own affairs." Applied with intelligence, the Nixon Doctrine will permit a more relaxed and effective diplomacy with the nations of the Third World. The United States should also seek to maintain better relations with both the Soviet Union and China than they can have with each other. But such relations should never be sought at the expense of our relations with regional partners.

Opportunities exist for taking fair advantage of the various linkages in international affairs. Thus, for example, the United States should make it explicit in the series of negotiations on European security and Mutual Balanced Force Reductions that progress in the MBFR preparatory talks is a precondition for the Conference on Security and Cooperation in Europe. Moreover, the creation of permanent machinery as a result of the CSCE should be made contingent on solid accomplishments in reducing the Soviet presence in Eastern Europe.

Soviet interest in American technology and in increasing East-West trade suggests possible American leverage *vis-à-vis* the Soviets in political and military sectors. The precondition for exercising this leverage, however, is a coherent strategy that recognizes and exploits the interrelationship of assets available to it.

Dealing with Ideological Barriers

The ideological arena is the one in which Soviet, Chinese, and American approaches are fundamentally irreconcilable. It is unlikely that there will soon be a convergence. At the dawn of the American Republic, Thomas Jefferson said, "Every man and every body of men on earth possesses the right of self-government." At the time of the Soviet invasion of Czechoslovakia, *Pravda* expressed a different viewpoint: that all rights, including that of self-determination, are "subordinated to the laws of the class struggle." Nikolai Podgorny, Chairman of the Presidium of the Supreme Soviet, notes that peaceful coexistence is "absolutely inapplicable ... in the struggle between socialist and bourgeois ideologies." And Mikhail Suslov, a senior member of the Soviet Politburo and the Party's most prominent ideologist, reaffirmed in January 1972 that "In our era of struggle between two world systems—socialism and capitalism—the ideological struggle permeating all aspects of social life, including even science, inevitably grows sharper."

Whether we like it or not, we remain engaged in ideological competition. In this competition, we have nothing to fear and should never be reluctant to stand behind the concept and practices of a free, pluralistic society. We should continuously strive to make our society a better model of our beliefs.

*Collaboration in Science and
Research and Development*

The major scientific and research and development establishments of the world belong to national governments. A large part of their efforts have been devoted to weapons systems. Collaborative defense R&D with our allies, despite acknowledged difficulties, appears particularly attractive because the costs for manpower and complex equipment have risen dramatically. Diminished available real resources and increasing costs make the elimination of duplicative research and development on costly weapons systems extremely attractive for both the United States and Europe.

Outside the defense sector there has been very little collaboration between either allies or adversaries in those areas of intrinsic common interest. If the world is going to cooperate in the solution of global environmental problems, for example, there is no way to avoid collaboration in research and development. Science cannot solve all the problems arising from the industrial revolution but it can mitigate the adverse effects of many. The United States, the recognized world leader in many branches of modern science, should initiate cooperative R&D wherever possible and beneficial, with both allies and adversaries.

The Military Balance

It is paradoxical that a world presumably on the threshold of a generation of peace is devoting vast resources for defense. According to ACDA (Arms Control and Disarmament Agency), 120 nations in 1971 spent $216 billion on defense—an increase of 82 percent over 1960 figures. In 1972 there was a $7 billion trade in international arms deals, little of which can be justified as contributing to regional stabilities conducive to peace. The record of the post-World War II years, however, would suggest that the time has not yet come for a universal transformation of swords into plowshares. Any strategy for creating a "generation of peace" requires appropriate military concepts, forces and deployments that will sustain the national will of the United States and its allies in meeting the many and varied challenges of the 1970s.

In our ideologically divided world, a fundamental prerequisite for the maintenance of international cooperation in the decade ahead is a rough equilibrium of military power between the Soviet Union and China, on the one hand, and the United States and its European and Asian allies, on the other. Both the Soviet Union and the PRC will maintain formidable armed forces during this decade for various purposes. The impressive Soviet military buildup in many spheres over the past five or six years is likely to continue despite the SALT I Agreement. A priority task for the United States will be to maintain strategic nuclear stability as the prerequisite to the orderly and beneficial transformation of the international system. This requires that the United States manage its technological strategy as efficiently as possible and that it adroitly conduct negotiations leading to mutual reductions in forces. At the same time, it will be more difficult for democratic governments to sustain a high level of military expenditures for conventional as well as strategic forces. Whatever the long-range implications of the end of the war in Vietnam and the re-establishment of a volunteer army, the example the United States sets in fielding well-equipped armed forces will be critical.

International Economic Expansion and
the International Monetary System

The expansion of economic activity has been very striking in those areas most ravaged by World War II—Western Europe, Japan, and the Soviet Union. Concurrently, in the Western world, monetary arrangements established after the war have just about disintegrated.

A number of factors have caused economic dislocations of Western capitalism. The dollar is no longer characterized by its early post-war stability. This is a result of consistent U.S. balance of payments deficits, in part caused by vast budget deficits related to U.S. foreign policy commitments. Also, with the growing strength of other national currencies, large speculative flows have occurred that capitalize on currency weakness by moving funds from one national currency to another.

With the demise of the Bretton Woods agreements, substitute measures have treated the symptoms of the problem but not the source. The Smithsonian agreements hammered out in late 1971 simply realigned currency values. These stopgap measures dealt with neither speculative flows nor with ways of dealing with the large international dollar accumulations. Other "dollar crises" arose in February and March 1973 as the result of speculations in Europe and a general lack of confidence in the dollar.

In both monetary and trade matters the United States has recently taken a more self-interested perspective geared to making the management of both fields based more on international (as opposed to predominantly American) responsibility and cooperation. In 1973 IMF negotiations, the United States is pushing for a system of automatic devaluations and revaluations of currencies based strictly on objective criteria relating to the trade account, thus eliminating national decisions in this field. In the current GATT rounds the United States is calling for the harmonization and institutionalization of all national non-tariff barriers to trade.

The Williams Commission, set up by President Nixon to examine world economic developments since World War II, concluded that U.S. economic ills were mainly attributable to political considerations:

Indeed, the Commission was impressed with the fact that many of the economic problems we face today grow out of the overseas responsibility the United States has assumed as the major power of the non-Communist world.[4]

In order to increase U.S. economic competitiveness, the Commission recommended a program including the removal of political constraints on economic decisions:

... such a program must include a new look at those U.S. policies, rules and regulations which tend to impede our exports—for example, in the fields of anti-trust, taxation, transportation, East-West trade and export finance.[5]

The postwar economic recovery of Europe and Japan and the emergence of newly industrialized societies in Korea, Singapore, Brazil, and elsewhere led to a weakening of the American economy in relative but not absolute terms in the late 1960s. This in turn has stimulated economic frictions in U.S.-Western Europe and U.S.-Japanese relations. A growing equality in economic relations is forcing the United States to protect some of its domestic industries as the result of political pressures and gives the Europeans and Japanese a greater flexibility in pursuing their own interests. The consequence is a serious growth of truculent economic nationalism. Such nationalism stems, in part, from popular pressure forcing national governments to play an increasingly active role in correcting prevailing macroeconomic deficiencies.

American unemployment remains relatively high. The pinch has also been felt elsewhere. In Canada, unemployment reached 6.5 percent at the end of 1971, the highest level in ten years. In Britain, unemployment passed the politically salient million mark in early 1972. Inflation has been every bit as serious a problem. Over the two years 1970-1971, the price deflator for OECD countries averaged 5.6 percent. Moreover, in most West European countries the Bank of International Settlements reported that wage payments were running ten to fifteen percent higher in mid-1972 than a year ago. The American balance of trade deficit reached a record $6.4 billion in 1972 and now appears likely to go even higher. Part of the trade deficit can be charged to the evolution of a largely service economy in the United States. But a good deal of it also stems from the lack of competitiveness and initiative now exhibited by some sectors of American industry.

The United States no longer dominates the Western world economically as it did since the end of World War II. The United States and its allies need to find reforms in the international monetary system that will inspire cooperation based on confidence rather than cutthroat competition derived from fear.

The Role of the United Nations

In the future, even perhaps in the context of monetary agreements, the United States should merge its foreign aid program into a multilateral effort supported by all the major industrialized nations, under the auspices of the United Nations. The restoration of war-ravaged Indochina, however, is the wrong place to begin. The United States will probably play the largest role in the rehabilitation of Southeast Asia, and indeed it should. The United States should make certain that any assistance provided to North Vietnam will be contingent on North

Vietnam's abandoning its expansionist designs against the South. Assisting North Vietnam on any other basis will mock American sacrifices in this long and bloody war.

The United Nations provides an excellent forum for seeking the solution to international problems through collaboration. However, it will be able to perform a major role in coping with international problems only if the larger powers cooperate with each other within its framework.

Domestic Support for U.S. Foreign Policy

A modicum of public support will still be essential for the execution of even the "lower profile" policy implicit in the Nixon Doctrine. Will it be forthcoming?

In 1971 public opinion survey experts Cantril and Roll designed a questionnaire that was to measure the strength of the oft-publicized inward-turning among the American people. In response to the statement: "We shouldn't think so much in international terms but concentrate more on our own national problems and building our strength and prosperity at home," over three-quarters of the American public agreed in 1971 and only 16 percent disagreed. Such results undoubtedly reflect the depth of American frustration over the protracted involvement in Indochina. The American public seems increasingly to recognize that our domestic purposes and our stature as a nation are intertwined and that neither can be achieved without the other.

Regional Trends and the Nixon Doctrine

Western Europe

Western Europe remains the primary area of U.S. foreign and security policy concern. In his press conference of February 1, 1973, President Nixon stated that "We must now turn to the problems of Europe. We have been to the People's Republic of China. We have been to the Soviet Union. We have been paying attention to the problems of Europe, but those problems will be put on the front burner."

Hopefully, this change in priority has come in time. The Atlantic Alliance is, at present, floundering. Economic and monetary tensions divide the United States and its European allies. Other wedges include oversimplified and euphoric reactions to détente and domestic pressures on both sides of the Atlantic against even the existing levels of defense spending. Perhaps most important of all are shifts in the balance of influence between the two superpowers in Europe and throughout the international system. The promise of political union in Western Europe also remains unfulfilled. Any movement in Western Europe toward greater political unity over the next decade is likely to be hesitant, fragmented, and continually subject to reversal—this despite the fact that the heads of government of the nine members of the enlarged European Community have solemnly agreed to strive for the creation of a loose political union by 1980. National bias and parochial concerns continue to beset the European community despite the need for further collaboration in the economic, political, technological, and defense sectors. The Europeans are pushed in this direction by the realities of the contemporary international system. But preoccupation with national sovereignty, *Ostpolitik*, and the deepening uncertainties about the American security guarantee (and the fear that a coalescence of Western Europe might speed an American retrenchment) act as sharp brakes to any meaningful unity movement. Public indifference to problems of security is widespread in Europe. This apathy may sharply restrict initiatives designed to strengthen military capabilities, especially if such initiatives entail increased public burdens or might endanger détente.

Paradoxically, European uncertainties and fears coexist with a general sense of optimism. These uncertainties stem in part from changes in the broader environment, particularly the contingency of a progressive American disengagement from Europe. Western Europe is experiencing an affluence that is unprecedented in the history of that continent, yet Europeans are still captives of an historical experience in which prosperity and tranquillity often have given way to economic dislocations and conflict.

It is illusory to look upon Western Europe as an "entity"—one that can shoulder the burdens of partnership with the United States, let alone take its place among the other "power centers" of the world. Western Europe still needs help, if no longer in the form of "grand designs" drafted in the United States, then at least in the "guiding impulse" toward political cohesion. Yet even should Western Europe muster political cohesion it is doubtful that it can become a truly independent security community for many years to come.

Indeed, disparate security perceptions in Europe are taking their toll. Anti-Americanism is widespread and the Soviet image is changing. There is a mellowing of attitudes toward Moscow, encouraged by an optimistic notion that the character of the Soviet Union has been fundamentally transformed, by fears of an American retrenchment, and by hopes of political profit and economic gain from dealings with the USSR and its allies. The forces that are pulling in this direction in Europe bank on the alibi that the United States pointed the way (which is *not* correct), and on the assumption that a large-scale American military withdrawal from Europe is inevitable. In reality, however, they are trading on a general public sense of security and well-being that permits their governments to undertake the kinds of "experiments" that would have been unthinkable even five years ago. Several key countries in Europe are governed by socialist parties that are under increasing pressures from vocal left-wing elements and generally bear a doubtful loyalty to NATO and its institutions. The problem is most acute in the FRG. The Social Democrats remain amateurs in foreign policy and strategy, but they have rejuvenated their party and learned modern methods of winning elections. Even if the FRG commitment to the Alliance remains ostensibly firm for the time being, the power of the left wing in Brandt's party is waxing and may yet dominate the next party congress of the SPD. And the rise in left-wing sentiments is marked in France as well.

For many years the stark need in Europe for rejuvenating and modernizing the European bureaucracy, especially in the making of foreign and defense policy, has been recognized. Until this is done, there will be few European strategists with whom we can really talk and with whom we can cooperate on strategy.

In the meantime, the drift of policies continues—in many ways abetted, wittingly or not, by the United States. West Germany's *Ostpolitik* is a prime example.

The first steps of *Ostpolitik* were supported, or at least accepted by the United States and the other allies, because they promised to release the Alliance from certain risks and obligations and to expand its freedom in exploiting the opportunities of cooperation with the Soviet Union. *Ostpolitik* has been a bargain of "recognition" of the status quo in Europe in return for the "milieu of détente," but it is an asymmetric bargain because recognition cannot be withdrawn as easily as détente. The climate of détente is largely in the control of the Soviet Union.

Further steps of *Ostpolitik* are oriented toward a "peace order" in Central Europe which implies a fundamental change from the Adenauer concept, which wanted to avoid any German national definition of interest in foreign policy and therefore strove to make the Federal Republic into an integrated part of the West. The *Ostpolitik* revives a national German definition of Germany's interests. This reflects to some extent the stagnation of the Alliance's central function of defining common policy.

Brandt's *Ostpolitik* portends that the domestic prerequisites in Europe for the reorganization of NATO according to the Nixon Doctrine are fading. In order to be implemented, the Nixon Doctrine must offer not only a concept of foreign policy, but also a strategy whereby the necessary domestic consensus can be created or revived in Europe. It requires not only America's leadership, but also a demonstration of America's membership in the Alliance.

*The Mediterranean, the Middle East,
and Africa*

The Nixon Doctrine implies the devolution of strategic responsibilities onto regional powers and the promotion of their self-reliance. In the Middle East, Turkey remains the cornerstone of U.S. policy—guarding the Dardanelles and the

Eastern Mediterranean. Turkey bears a deep, historically-rooted fear of Russia. Despite its antagonism toward Greece over Cyprus, the two countries cooperate militarily through NATO. The U.S. Sixth Fleet now uses Piraeus as a home port. It is of concern to the United States, therefore, to help reduce Greek-Turkish friction over Cyprus.

Iran, on the southern flank of the Soviet Union and bordering the oil-rich Persian Gulf, is another key state in the Middle East. The Shah is undertaking an increasingly independent and active foreign policy designed to insure Iranian predominance in the Gulf and perhaps even to extend its influence into the Indian Ocean. Although Iran experiences friction with neighboring Iraq, it has attempted to develop stable relations with Saudi Arabia. The United States has fostered good relations with both Iran and Saudi Arabia through economic ties and military aid and should seek to promote their cooperation in the interest of regional stability and economic growth. Both countries are also antagonistic toward the Soviet Union. Iran's potential move into the Indian Ocean would be directly related to fear of the Soviet naval presence there. But this fear should not be unduly exploited by the United States, as any resulting increase in the Iranian presence in the Indian Ocean might have the counterproductive result of leading the Soviets to establish a more active presence both in the Gulf and in Iraq.

The United States faces a difficult balancing act in North Africa in its relations with Morocco and Algeria. Although the U.S. has extensive military ties with Morocco, it is rapidly developing common interests with Algeria based on oil and natural gas. At one time, the United States feared that there would be a polarization between a U.S.-supported Morocco and a Soviet-supported Algeria, but Algerian determination to maintain its autonomy and the low-keyed U.S. approach have resulted in the development of complex and growing economic relations. The trend in U.S.-Algerian relations suggests that Algeria may turn out to be an important example of the Nixon Doctrine's emphasis on U.S. promotion of the self-reliance of Third World countries.[6]

Finally, the most difficult problems lie on the Arab-Israeli front. Israel maintains clear military supremacy, in part by dint of arms supplied by the United States. At the same time, the U.S. has provided the military and economic underpinnings for King Hussein's rule in Jordan and has striven to avoid a complete break with Egypt. American oil companies are engaged in production in Egypt and Libya. The United States is faced with the task of keeping hostilities at a minimum in order to deny the Soviet Union a role as champion of the Arabs. At the same time, the American commitment to Israel must be maintained while commercial relations with the Arabs expand. Any policy in this volatile region is fraught with danger. The application of the Nixon Doctrine to the Middle East is an extremely complicated and delicate operation requiring a subtle approach and a respect for the national interests of the local countries.

In non-Mediterranean Africa, the focus of the U.S. attention should remain on the four geopolitically strategic states of Africa: Nigeria, Ethiopia, South Africa, and Zaire (the former Belgian Congo). At this time, the "low profile" of the Nixon Doctrine seems particularly well-suited to the problems faced by the United States in Africa. Our policy interests in white-dominated southern Africa should reflect sympathy for the demands from our own citizenry and the black-ruled nations of Africa for racial justice. However, this should be tempered by recognition of South Africa's strategic importance and the necessity of having to deal with South Africa regardless of its form of government. The United States should continue to have as its primary objective in sub-Saharan Africa the support of "the African effort to keep free of Great Power rivalries and conflicts."[7]

The Pacific Basin

The elaboration of the Nixon Doctrine has coincided with, and in part helped accelerate, a number of highly important trends in Asia and the Pacific. The U.S. task in Asia is to help continue or adjust to these trends in order that they remain synchronized with fundamental U.S. interests in the area.

Japan and Europe now constitute two formidable economic poles of the emerging multipolar world. Over the 1970s, Japan will be devoting greater resources of economic assistance to the rest of Asia. Japan's anticipated role in the postwar economic rehabilitation of Indochina is another very encouraging sign. It is not likely, however, that Japan will play a major security role in Asia in the 1970s, although her defense budget will probably continue to grow.

While China has not renounced the use of force or support for "wars of national liberation," her entry into the United Nations and her new approach toward the United States, Japan, and other Asian nations are encouraging. China forms a potential pole in a multipolar global balance, although her influence is still largely psychological and diplomatic.

As initiated by the Nixon Administration and highlighted by the President's trip to Peking during February 21-28, 1972, the American-Chinese détente has had the effect of dampening considerably the incentives for continued communist-noncommunist confrontation in Asia. The détente is converting the old rationale for hostility into drives for negotiations, reduced tension and, hopefully, over the long run, cooperation. While the impact on our Asian allies of the American diplomatic about-face toward China was initially severe, they are now making some encouraging readjustments. The Sino-American détente has allowed China to be brought more directly into the Peking-Washington-Moscow triangular relations and has created additional leverage upon the Soviet Union. For China the détente has permitted her to improve relations with the United States, Japan, and other countries as the threat from the Soviet Union grows more ominous in Peking's perspective.

The Sino-Soviet rift has long since progressed past polemics into a racial, geographic, military, political, and diplomatic struggle just below the threshold of open hostilities. There have been periodic outbreaks of violence on China's northern border, where the Soviet Union stations over 1,000,000 troops. Both countries are diverting vast expenditures to defense measures against each other. In turn, the dispute is driving Moscow and Peking to compete for influence throughout Asia, South Asia, and Southeast Asia. The USSR's concept of an all-Asian collective security system is designed to encircle and contain the Chinese. The Soviets have taken advantage of South Asia's confusion and India's fear of China and suspicion of the United States. In turn, Moscow's overtures toward Tokyo and increased attention to the smaller states of Asia are calculated further to contain China. By contrast, China is attempting to find ways out of Russia's encirclement through better relations with the United States, Japan, and other countries. In these circumstances, it would be in the U.S. interest to seek to maintain better relations with both China and the Soviet Union than either enjoys with the other.

The Nixon Doctrine's most concrete step has been the selective withdrawal of U.S. military forces from forward operating bases in Asia. The "Vietnamization" program and the Vietnam ceasefire are the key indicators of the Doctrine's policy of reducing the U.S. presence and turning more of the responsibility for internal defense over to the indigenous countries. Similar U.S. military disengagements have also been underway in Japan, South Korea, Taiwan, the Philippines and other countries.

Indonesia is potentially one of the great nations of the Pacific Basin. Its large and dynamic population and vast natural resources will enable this country to become increasingly significant in the Pacific Basin subsystem. The willingness of Indonesia to play a role in the supervision of the Vietnamese ceasefire reflects a generally favorable political relationship with the United States and a desire to play a constructive role in the Asian region.

The late 1972 elections in both Australia and New Zealand reflect a growing disenchantment in both countries with too close a diplomatic identity with the United States. Since taking office, Gough Whitlam's Labor Government has protested the bombing of Hanoi-Haiphong, failed to criticize the docker's strike against U.S. shipping, recognized Peking, voted for certain Third World resolutions at the United Nations, closed down the Rhodesia Information Center in Sydney, ended conscription and released imprisoned draft dodgers. Prime Minister Whitlam may be the strongest figure to appear in Australian politics since Menzies. His actions represent a determined effort to make a public impact and express the pent-up frustrations of a party that spent twenty-three years in opposition. One needs bear in mind, however, that while the changes have been sooner and more dramatic than they might have been had the Liberal-Country Party coalition remained in office, the latter was also gradually moving Australia toward a more independent position. At the same time, the Labor government, while it may be expected to downgrade SEATO and to renegotiate the terms on which the U.S. has strategic installations in Australia, is nevertheless strongly attached to the American alliance and would not have been elected if it had not been. Post-election developments in New Zealand, where Norman Kirk was installed in a Labor Party landslide, generally parallel those in Australia. The U.S. continues to enjoy favorable relations with South Korea, Taiwan, Singapore, Thailand, and the Philippines. The first four of these nations continue to make solid economic progress. The general situation in the Philippines, however, appears to be regressive in both political and economic terms.

The Western Hemisphere

American encouragement of greater self-reliance coincides with important regional developments in Latin America. But the devolution of U.S. responsibilities has been difficult in a region of many weak states where the United States has traditionally played a powerful role. A notable exception is Brazil, whose emergence as the leading regional power requires special American attention.

The fifth largest state in the world in land area, Brazil occupies nearly half of the South American continent, bordering on all but two of its nations. Its population of 100 million may well double before the turn of the century. With resource reserves already among the largest in the world, Brazil's potential has long been acknowledged, but only in the past five years has it seemed possible to exploit it. A military-backed but largely civilian government has provided stability and direction to the country and has made an impressive showing in economic growth. Gross national product, at about 50 billion dollars in 1972, is already double that of its nearest South American competitor.

Continued American support for Brazil's growth could be of considerable assistance to regional stability, particularly if U.S. influence with the military-backed government can be maintained. This will require increased military assistance and sales to help reinvigorate military cooperation.

In contrast to Brazil, Allende's Chile has been experiencing economic throes. U.S. restraint in dealing with Chilean expropriations of U.S. investments has vitiated charges that external intervention is responsible for these failures. The "low profile" of the Nixon Doctrine there seems particularly appropriate in unmasking the failures of economic planning of doctrinaire Marxism. The Chilean example may reduce the attraction of similar experiments to other Latin American countries.

Although the United States, in the interest of promoting regional self-sufficiency, seeks to encourage the emergence of other centers of power, there are few candidates for such a role south of the Rio Grande. Mexico and Venezuela have that potential but are preoccupied with internal problems. Mexican economic growth has been, however, impressive in recent years.

The small Caribbean states will remain dependent on outside help for modernization, development, and occasionally security. Consequently, U.S. economic aid and military assistance will be required for the foreseeable future. Regional arrangements to resolve conflicts and strengthen the economies of Caribbean states should be encouraged. At the same time, Canada and the larger Latin American states should be induced to play a larger role in Caribbean economic development.

Successful implementation of the Nixon Doctrine in the Caribbean requires that the United States continue to take the lead in security issues. U.S. commitments in the Caribbean region differ from our commitments in South America. The Caribbean region is within the immediate Southern defense perimeter of the United States. As the only power capable of countering the Soviet military presence in the Caribbean, the United States must continue to take the responsibility for dealing with this strategic threat.

The possibility of eventual détente between the United States and Cuba should not be excluded, although the process would be complex and long. By dealing with Cuba at arm's length the United States has allowed Cuban policymakers and Soviet advisors to take full blame for the island's economic problems. Havana's response to détente overtures such as joint measures to combat hijacking could provide a possible basis for further U.S. diplomacy, including a discussion of such topics as trade and travel.

A low U.S. profile has also eased the difficulties in negotiating with the current nationalist regime in Panama over the Canal Zone. The United States should continue to assure Panama that bilateral relations—not complaints in international forums—provide the best basis for negotiating a new treaty for the canal that will satisfy Panamanian interests.

Elsewhere in the hemisphere, the United States can no longer take its Canadian neighbor for granted. Because the two neighboring countries must deal with many issues from different perspectives, many sensitive problems between them remain unresolved. Canada is cautiously diversifying its foreign policy and searching for new international roles. Behind this search is a growing concern that extensive economic ties with the United States make Ottawa excessively dependent on Washington. Ottawa recently formulated new guide-lines for U.S. investment, though Canadian nationalists believe more stringent measures are necessary. American concern with its balance of payments has also led it to seek more equitable trading conditions, through such measures as revision of the 1965 U.S.-Canadian automobile agreement. While Canadian-U.S. relations will require some important adjustments in the near future, there is no reason why they cannot be achieved through patient diplomacy.

Directions for Choice

The Broad Scheme

While it is impossible to predict the exact configuration of the emerging international system, it is most unlikely that a genuine multipolar world will emerge within the next decade. There is almost no prospect that five power centers roughly equivalent in economic and military strength will come into being. The chance of an enlarged European Economic Community becoming a true political and security community by the early 1980s appears remote. There are so many asymmetries among the would-be pentagonal poles that a rough power equilibrium between them is unlikely ever to emerge. For one thing, economic and political multipolarity must be expressed also in terms of a strategic-nuclear power balance if a truly pentagonal system is to function. Consequently, unless and until a politically unified Western Europe and Japan both reach for adequate independent strategic nuclear capabilities, multipolarity will be a slogan without substance. During the forthcoming decade both Western Europe and Japan will continue to shelter themselves under the U.S. security umbrella. As long as these relationships persist, the overriding aim of U.S. foreign policy must be the creation of a viable partnership with Western Europe and Japan. Unless we are successful in revitalizing the form and spirit of our mutually supporting transoceanic alliances, we face the prospect of seeing Western Europe fall under Soviet hegemony and Japan caught in the web of Soviet-Chinese rivalry.

The initial step toward a viable partnership should be the revitalization of the Atlantic Alliance. The prerequisite is a clear identification of common interests to which common action on the partnership principle can be addressed. Once this new foundation is laid for cooperation, the United States and Europe together must make a place for Japan in their councils and in their common actions. Around this triangular association other nations in every continent can cluster.

U.S., Europe and Japan in a
New Relationship

The U.S. will have to find new, inspired directions to reaffirm its abiding interests in a secure and healthy Europe and a vital and more independent Japan. To do so, the sum total of the policies which the United States pursues toward Western Europe, Japan, and its Soviet and Chinese adversaries must begin to comprise a coherent, reinforcing whole. Only then can the United States forge new links with Western Europe, Japan, Australia, and its other Pacific partners and bind them into a new Pan-Atlantic, Pan-American, and Pan-Pacific world.

The visible U.S. commitment to NATO in terms of diplomatic interest and military manpower has declined—or threatens to decline—at the very time when we have sought to weave a web of common interests with the only power that could conceivably threaten NATO—the Soviet Union. While we argue over monetary and trade policies with our European allies, we have worked out agreements for large sales of wheat to the Soviet Union at rates far below the world market price. In the process of fostering a climate of confidence with Moscow, we overlook the remarkable psychological transformation engendered in Western Europe. In the lands of our European allies, the conviction is gaining ground that the Soviet Union has become just another state, albeit one with a different—and not necessarily incompatible—social system. U.S. diplomacy has contributed substantially to this new Soviet image.

The policies we pursue toward Europe are frequently ambiguous and often contradictory. In NATO we talk MBFR in the hope that the Soviet Union will match force reductions of our own that are widely believed to be inevitable. Meanwhile, we threaten to pull back our troops unless NATO countries (primarily the FRG) meet our offset payments and render trade concessions to ease our balance-of-payments problem. In dealing with the European Community as if it were as economically aggressive as Japan, we overlook the sizable and favorable balance of trade we had with Western Europe until 1972. In pressing for monetary and trade adjustments with European countries, we pass lightly over the 60 billion Eurodollars (most of which the Europeans are holding) and the manner in which the Europeans have helped to finance the U.S. multinational corporations' invasion of European territory. We are not certain as to whether we should continue technological cooperation with Western Europe, and our uncertainty drives the European countries into seeking technological independence in those very areas that are at the top of our foreign money-earning list (aviation and enriched uranium).

What is to be done?

First, we must reconcile our policies and practices *vis-à-vis* the Soviet Union and the People's Republic of China with our alliance objectives. Under no circumstances should we give superpower negotiations priority over the task of keeping an alliance together. Militarily, diplomatically, culturally, and economically our ties with Western Europe are far more important to the future of the United States than accommodation with the USSR. The same is true of our relations with Japan relative to links with China that are today at best a promise rather than a fact. This truth requires constant reiteration and must be asserted in our diplomatic positions in the forthcoming multilateral negotiations (CSCE and MBFR) as well as any bilateral U.S.-Soviet talks (SALT II).

In SALT II the Soviet negotiators will emphasize the issue of "forward bases," a euphemism for NATO. They will also seek to stop transatlantic technological cooperation. The Soviets intend to render NATO—and by extension a new European center of power—impotent by attempting to force upon the United States in effect a priority choice between its own security and the relative security of its allies. To lull the Europeans, the European Security Conference was proffered in order to stall any new West European defense coalescence and to distract attention from the more important arena in SALT.

Under these circumstances, the United States should make certain that the results of SALT II will not be at the expense of NATO or Japanese security. The U.S. strategic posture should not be so reduced relative to that of the Soviets as to uncouple our strategic power from the NATO Alliance or our bilateral defense treaty with Japan.

In the CSCE, the United States should hew relentlessly to its position that the free movement of persons and ideas between East and West is the price the Soviets must pay for Western acquiescence in the legitimacy of the status quo in Eastern Europe.

Nor should we sign any MBFR agreement that does not result in security for NATO's members at least equivalent to what they now have. Our aim should be to secure an MBFR agreement in which the relative security now enjoyed by NATO members is achieved at a lower cost. The criteria utilized to estimate the "equality" of proposed mutual reductions should not be tied to any one standard—be it number of men, tanks, or aircraft. Rather the United States should first consider the overall security position of Europe and use the MBFR talks to bring the Western Europeans closer together, to coordinate European and U.S. positions on security issues, and to maintain the cohesiveness of the NATO Alliance.

U.S. trade deals with the Soviets or with the PRC may be as disruptive as security negotiations. Historically, the Soviets have turned several times to the West to overcome economic difficulties (the poor 1972 wheat harvest), to survive (lend-lease and Hoover famine relief), and to acquire necessary technology and/or management skills (N.E.P. and U.S.-Soviet exchanges, the latter heavily weighted on the scientific-technological side). Until recently, the United States has checked the desire of Western businessmen to make a quick mark, franc, pound, or dollar by trading with the East on the basis of liberal credits and the export of machinery and know-how at minimum costs. The thoughtless cupidity of the West has helped the Soviet Union to keep on top of a carefully controlled tide of rising consumer expectations at home while simultaneously devoting a constant portion of a steadily rising GNP to its defense forces and military, space, and atomic R&D.

For some time now, the Western nations and Japan have been in a rush to be first in line for trade deals with Moscow and Peking. In evaluating the potential impact of East-West trade, a distinction must be made between essentially short-term, tactical advantages that may accrue to the United States and the long-term implications of greater economic exchange. In the short run, diplomatic gains can be made by linking trade to other issues. Soviet eagerness to acquire Western and particularly American technology apparently helped induce the Soviets to a significant behind-the-scenes role in encouraging the North Vietnamese to reach a settlement of the war. Strategic considerations suggest that the United States and its West European allies coordinate some aspects of their trade with the Soviet Union.

In the longer term, it is doubtful whether increased trade will play more than a peripheral role in resolving the basic conflicts between the United States and the Soviet Union. In the past, Soviet interest in trade has been a function of Moscow's overall foreign policy line, not a determinant of it. While it may be argued that today the Soviet economy is in dire need of technological revitalization, there is no indication that the Soviets will compromise basic tenets of their ideology for the sake of increasing economic efficiency. When the leadership's legitimacy is so closely tied to the principle of one-party rule, there can be no liberalization of the system meaningful enough to alter U.S.-Soviet relations basically. Nor will the Soviets permit Western firms to "penetrate" Soviet society. A state trading agency will handle all Western companies and funnel their orders to Soviet enterprises. The latter will deal in most cases with the official Soviet agency rather than with individual Western firms.

Given these facts of life, "Allies First, Adversaries Second" could be the slogan denoting the overall policy the United States should pursue in the 1970s. Such U.S. policies will stabilize the psychological foundation of a viable U.S. relationship with Western Europe. On that foundation the United States should erect a comprehensive policy in which diplomatic, security, economic, and technological aspects are intertwined.

The U.S. needs to convince its European and Japanese allies that they rank first among American policy determinants. A new reaffirmation of U.S. policy toward Europe is needed—but to what end? U.S. support of a European union evolving into an economic, political and, ultimately, security community is one possible goal. Such a union is conceivable and may be attainable—except in security dimensions—by the 1980 date announced in the October 20, 1972 Paris summit meeting of the EEC Nine. Whether Western Europe by itself will ever be able to establish a viable security community is doubtful. But U.S. policy can help build the foundation for a unified Western Europe created within the framework of the expanded EEC. There can be an overlapping of an expanded partnership if U.S. policy aims to revive the concept of a broadened Atlantic Community and transform it into an Atlantic-Pacific Community in which the United States, Canada, and the emerging European union could be linked with Japan and other Pacific allies in a workable political-military framework. Because such a framework would encompass the older and newer components of Western civilization, this wider goal is the most attractive. It could only come about, however, if the American President made the creation of an extended Atlantic world the overriding task of his office.

For a long time to come, progress toward an independent European union and a yet-to-be-born Atlantic-Pacific world requires the confidence of assured security. Provision of this indispensable ingredient, therefore, must continue to be the priority business of both the United States and its West European allies. All transatlantic relations must somehow be reconciled with this imperative. Both the style and content of U.S. diplomacy toward Atlantic and European institutions, as well as toward individual European states, should manifest the integral character of America's political, security, and economic relations with Europe. Consistent U.S.-European consultation should become axiomatic before, during, and after all negotiations that, whatever their locale, affect the core Atlantic relationship. (U.S. consultation with European NATO countries during SALT I set a partial precedent. In SALT II, we must avoid obstacles to U.S.-West European technological transfer that will damage NATO's security posture.)

The U.S. should indicate that it will maintain in Europe that level of forces consistent with an agreed long-term alliance arrangement including mutual commitments of the majority of most essential members of the alliance. The commitment should not be pegged to MBFR negotiations, but should permit accommodation to MBFR reductions if those should materialize. We should embark simultaneously on a combined NATO modernization program, selecting the best weapons produced by R&D regardless of national origin. Weapons production would be allocated to the U.S. and the major European member nations of NATO under licensing arrangements.

In the economic field, the objective would be to establish over time a dynamic equilibrium between the U.S., the European Community, and Japan leading to a common market. We must continue the dialogue embracing the Atlantic-American-Pacific political complex. The policies adopted to achieve this end would result from jointly conducted expert discussions concerning exchanges in trade, repatriation of profits, monetary stability, and technological transfers.

Expanding the Northern Arc

Unless we are successful in revitalizing the form and spirit of our mutually supporting transoceanic alliances, we face the prospect of seeing Western Europe fall under Soviet hegemony and Japan caught in the web of Soviet-Chinese rivalry.

The initial step in this revitalization should be the restoration of the Atlantic Alliance—the wellspring of that Western civilization that has been so largely responsible for the creation of the modern world. The common interests we share must be clearly identified so that there can be common action in finding the roles of partnership between us. Once this new foundation is laid for cooperation, the United States and Europe together must make a place for Japan in their councils and in their common actions. To this triangular association other nations in every continent can be naturally drawn. Some obvious candidates include the former British dominions of Canada, Australia, and New Zealand, which share much in common with the United States. Korea, Vietnam, Thailand, Indonesia, and the Philippines, along with Japan and the United States, provide the building blocks for a new Pacific Basin system. Mexico and

Brazil are logical candidates for partnership in Latin America. Algeria and Morocco, along with Nigeria, South Africa, and Ethiopia, are likely to set the pace in Africa. Turkey, Saudi Arabia, Iran, and Israel should be the focal points of American policy in the Middle East. India will be paramount in the subcontinent, but despite her tacit alliance with the Soviet Union, the United States should find it possible to establish a tolerable relationship with her as well as with Pakistan and Bangladesh.

All nations are not alike or equal. U.S. policy should seek to associate us with those nations, in every region of the globe, that are actually or potentially the most competent and cooperative. As such nations learn the practices of partnership, the common problems facing all humanity can be more easily dealt with.

Conflict and Cooperation[a]

This paper has asserted three reasons why no simple balance-of-power strategy is adequate. First, because of the nature of the problems facing the advanced nations in particular, and because of the growing importance of global issues, there is need for collaborative problem-solving and the beginnings of a cooperative world system. Second, it appears that the eventual resolution of these problems will require fundamental transformation of the economic and political institutions of the present world system. Third, if such a transformation takes place, the collaboration of the great powers will be required to impose order and insure stability while the new order is emerging.

The pending energy crisis suggests the necessity of international collaboration. The crucial problem is how to ensure adequate supplies of energy over the next thirty years for North America, Western Europe, Japan, Brazil, and perhaps even for the Soviet Union, while simultaneously reducing attendant ecological hazards. The United States must commit major resources to this problem to meet its own needs and could assist the parallel achievement of a European as well as a Japanese solution. The energy question could become an example of "doing great things together" and thus provide a positive base for international comity.

The ecological problem must also be addressed in coping with the energy crisis. Dealing with the ecological byproducts of energy production and consumption requires both research and development and comprehensive and enforceable international and domestic laws and regulations. Such legislation must reconcile the desirable level of energy utilization with some consideration of the cost required for energy production and consumption.

---

[a]This section was in part prompted by comments made by Dr. Willis W. Harman, Director, Educational Policy Research Center, Stanford Research Institute, following the Airlie House Symposium on National Strategy in a Decade of Change.

The United States should perhaps take the lead in initiating a major international program in research and development concerned both with the unlocking of new sources of energy and the proper safeguarding of the ecology. All nations in the world should participate in this undertaking, including the Soviet Union, which has much to offer.

Tackled with imagination, with confidence, and with conviction, the energy problem may provide the impetus required to move the world into an era of cooperation. But for this to happen, people must see more advantages in working with each other than in trying to manipulate affairs on the old pattern of national gain.

Despite many reasons for being optimistic about the resolution of the energy crisis and the spirit of cooperation it may engender, caution must temper our expectations. The mutual benefits that will accrue to all may not be sufficient to overcome the factors that move men and nations to heed the sirens of economic nationalism, ideology, and racism. The formidable nature of these and other hurdles cannot be ignored. However, the world energy crisis is but one example of several issues that will afford the nations of the world the opportunity to work together for mutual benefit. Whether or not these opportunities will be seized or ignored remains to be seen.

The agenda for action is an impressive one. The 1970s present us with a "crisis of crises" of dwindling resources, threatening energy shortage, impure water and foul air, side effects of chemical fertilizers and insecticides, possibility of major famines, chronic unemployment, persistent inflation, unstable currency, unsolvable urban problems, a growing rich-poor-nation gap, and a disturbing political shift to the left. Are these symptoms of a fundamental dysfunction in the world system, a dysfunction requiring basic systemic change to bring them to a satisfactory state of resolution? If so, what is the nature of that change? Fundamentally, it is a recognition by all contemporary states, but particularly by the more powerful ones, that none of the important problems confronting mankind can be solved unilaterally. Yet few nations are willing to concede the obvious.

The communist-led countries are perhaps more intransigent on this point than some of the other nations. The Soviet leaders assert that regardless of improved relations between capitalist and socialist states, ideological peace—and hence genuine cooperation—is impossible. "Marxist-Leninists do not entertain any illusions in relation to the anti-people's essence of imperialism and its aggressive aspirations," General Secretary of the Soviet Party Leonid Brezhnev asserted in June 1972, following President Richard Nixon's journey to Moscow. He added that successes with respect to the doctrine of peaceful coexistence "in no way signify the possibility of weakening the ideological struggle"; instead, it is necessary "to be prepared that this struggle will intensify, will become a still sharper form of the antagonism between the two social systems."

We are now able to discern more clearly the greatest drama of the 1970s, a drama more complicated than that of the previous two decades but reminiscent of it nonetheless. It is the contest between two doctrines: the so-called Brezhnev Doctrine and the Nixon Doctrine. The first, as defined by *Pravda*, means the restriction of the sovereignty of those states allied with Moscow. The second means the expansion of the sovereignty of those states allied with the United States. On the global scale, the Soviet government's aims are transparent: hold what it has in Eastern Europe, confirm the decline in U.S. power through negotiations, and smother—by threat of force, by counterbalancing alliance, and by enervating negotiation—the emergence of the other three power centers in China, Japan, and Europe. In contrast, the United States is attempting to expand the role of its European allies, to negotiate a halt to tension and arms development with Moscow, and to encourage the return of China and Japan as significant international factors.

Moscow's view of things, well-expressed in the Brezhnev Doctrine's concept of limited sovereignty, is that the world should be a hierarchy, or succession of powers, with the Soviet Union and its allies more powerful than the rest. Washington would like to see a series of balances, with every group possessing the strongest stake in peace. In the last eighteen months, the different attitudes may be discerned in policy. While the United States worked diligently to prevent war in the Middle East and South Asia, the Soviet Union worked diligently to upset the balance in South Asia and to maintain a neither-peace-nor-war situation in the Mideast.

Despite attention given to comparative superpower strength and negotiations, the development of new "partnership" between the United States and its allies remains the most neglected part of the Nixon Doctrine, in theory and in practice. The strained state of U.S. relations with its allies is profoundly discouraging for the growth of partnership. The major threat to the would-be partners, the Soviet Union, is skillfully improving its political relations with the individual Western States and Japan while the partners themselves are engaged in nasty battles over trade and money.

If the United States, Western Europe, and Japan fail to resolve the monetary crisis amicably, if NATO's effectiveness is further reduced by U.S.-Soviet strategic agreements and ill will between the allies, if the Japanese conclude that American policies in the Far East detract from their security, then the vast assets created by the United States since the Second World War will be squandered. It is not only that the five-power world will not emerge as politically and militarily balanced, but also that the stability of the international political system will depend more and more upon those bilateral agreements now being reached between the United States and the Soviet Union. If these agreements make clear Moscow's "equality" with the United States, the center of gravity within the global system will then shift toward the Soviet Union.

This shift could lead to a catastrophe. The most precious possessions of the Western alliances—their representative governments and their civil liberties—are precisely those features of public and private life implacably opposed by Moscow as the most serious threat to communist rule. The urgent priorities of the Western alliances are not those which involve reduction of all tensions between East and West. These tensions are now as low as they are likely to be without substantial changes in the fabric of either free or communist societies, or both. Changes in both would imply a convergence in systems which at this point in time is simply unattainable.

Rather than searching for the impossible or the undesirable, the United States and its foreign friends and associates should revive the spirit of "doing great things together" that animated the leaders of the postwar world, on whose accomplishments we have lived so well for twenty-five years. Collaborative structures whose foundations were laid in necessity and nurtured by goodwill and successful experience can be modified, rebuilt, and expanded into the "partnership" proclaimed by the Nixon Doctrine. When they are completed, negotiations with adversaries can be pursued with less danger, but also in the hope that the necessarily cooperative multipolar international system can then be created. A dynamic Atlantic-American-Pacific alliance will be invincible. But should this innovative, expanded structure die stillborn, the United States and its allies will be more vulnerable than they have been since the late 1940s.

Institutional Improvements and Public Support

Bureaucracies have never been noted for their capacity for innovation. The new departures in our foreign policy probably could only have been achieved as they were—by Presidential decision and surprise execution. But in any modern industrialized state, bureaucracies are absolutely essential in the execution of the patient and time-consuming task of building a creative partnership among proud and diverse nations. The time has come to engage the skills and competence of public servants in many departments and agencies of the United States Government in this great enterprise. Only then will this undertaking deserve and obtain the sustained support of the Congress and ultimately the American people.

The policy machinery of the present Administration requires revamping if Administration policies are to be sufficiently well thought out to command broad support. The Nixon Administration has won its major foreign policy battles with Congress by varying margins and received a massive reelection vote. The concept of partnership, however, may require more U.S. commitment rather than less. The Nixon Doctrine's first-term operation is probably seen by the general public as mainly a withdrawal from Vietnam and a trimming of commitments elsewhere. It is possible that the Moscow and Peking trips and the trappings of "détente" have been interpreted at the popular level to mean less necessity for defense.

The looming Presidential-Congressional battle over the budget and national priorities also gives cause for concern. Yet the President's legislative supporters are highly skilled parliamentarians with a good grasp of issues. Furthermore, some Democrats enjoying key defense committee chairmanships are friendly to the President's foreign policy. Moreover, the House has generally supported Mr. Nixon's national security requests.

Despite these advantages, the President has yet to construct a bipartisan bloc for his foreign and defense policies. In any event, his Congressional relations will affect importantly negotiations with the Soviet Union as well as the creation of partnerships with Western Europe. The Nixon Doctrine will be seriously handicapped unless it gains wide support for its many constructive aspects.

Prospects for a New International System

A primary conclusion of this paper is that this decade is not likely to witness the advent of a genuine multipolar world. Consequently, the more important and practical problem is whether the emerging international system of the 1970s will feature more cooperation or more competition.

A number of factors suggest the likelihood of a more cooperative system. First, as industrialization has spread throughout the world, power has become increasingly diffused. Growing scarcity of resources occasioned by spreading industrialization may bring about cooperative efforts to insure their equitable sharing as well as more adequate compensation for their producers. The smaller nations will tend to favor cooperation among the major powers. Since in many cases they hold the key to stores of basic raw materials, their voice may be more readily heard. Economic interdependence, coupled with some kind of political multipolarity, may lead to greater diplomatic flexibility and maneuvering, which could create an increasingly intricate and interlocking web of relationships between the United States, the Soviet Union, Japan, China, and Western Europe. Such a web of vested interests might perpetuate an overall structure of relationships that would inhibit Soviet policymakers from reverting at some future date to an aggressive strategy. Finally, the geographic proximity to the Soviet Union of both Western Europe and China will act as an inhibiting factor on Soviet policymakers. Similarly, China will be restrained by the presence of the Soviet Union on its borders.

Americans tend to be optimistic. I have attempted to stress the fact that long-term trends do favor an international system in which cooperative behavior becomes the norm. On the other hand, to quote Lord Keynes, "in the long-run, we will all be dead." In the short-run, there are a number of difficult problems that must be solved. If a true partnership is to be created between the United States and its allies throughout the world, we must understand how our partners perceive the problems and prospects of our relationship, and we must assess clearly the trend of world events.

Of course, President Nixon deserves tribute for his bold and imaginative diplomatic maneuvers during his first term in office. The settlement in Vietnam came about because he properly perceived the conflict there as an element in the global confrontation rather than as an isolated event in the Southeast Asian peninsula. In both the Middle East and the Far East, President Nixon bargained for short-term advantages to be paid for in the long-range currencies of Great Power rapprochement. For this reason, neither the blockade of North Vietnam last spring nor the intensified bombing of Haiphong and Hanoi last December were seriously contested by either Peking or Moscow.

In Europe, the Soviet policy of détente has largely succeeded in obscuring the Soviet Union's military predominance, particularly in Central Europe, where Soviet military might is concentrated. At this point, the Western Alliance is totally bereft of either the parliamentary support, the defense schemes, or the political strategy necessary to deny the Soviet Union its minimum objectives: the increasing subservience of Eastern Europe and the growing neutralization of Western Europe. In West Germany, where the popularity of the Brandt government rests, in part, on its *Ostpolitik* with the Soviet Union, and in Yugoslavia, where the post-Tito era promises at least confusion, NATO has crucial challenges with less and less strength to meet them. There must come a point where a West German government will have to face the stark choice between Soviet displeasure and greater Western unity. There may also come a point when rival factions in Yugoslavia may embroil the Great Powers in a post-Tito succession crisis. If present trends continue, will NATO possess sufficient political cohesion and military strength to mount a credible defense of Western interests?

Stronger partnership between the United States and its European allies is indispensable in assuring the success of this undertaking. To obtain persuasive public support, the partnership concept must foster the vision of an alliance capable of achieving peace and security for all of the associated democracies. However, within the present mode and climate of competitive economic nationalism and general indifference to security issues among the European, American, and Japanese peoples, achieving transnational cooperation will be difficult.

The major task facing all of us is to put new life into an alliance that has served so well for a quarter of a century. Unless we set about doing this as soon as possible, the forces of cohesion may well give way to the forces of disruption preparatory to the establishment of a new world system under philosophies hostile to democratic representative governments.

Consequently, if in fact we stand on the threshold of a new era of peace in the world, the central question before us is not how shall we use that peace, but how shall it be built? There is much work yet to be done.

Notes

1. See John Erickson, "Soviet Military Power," Royal United Service Institute Paper, May 1971.

2. Raphael Tsu, "High Technology in China," *Scientific American*, December 1972, p. 13.

3. Ibid., p. 17.

4. *United States International Economic Policy in an Interdependent World*, Report to the President submitted by the Commission on International Trade and Investment Policy, July 1971, Washington, D.C., p. 7.

5. Ibid., p. 9.

6. William B. Quandt, "Can We Do Business with Radical Nationalists? (1) Algeria: Yes," *Foreign Policy*, Summer 1972, p. 131.

7. Richard M. Nixon, "U.S. Foreign Policy for the 1970's," U.S. Department of State *Bulletin*, March 22, 1971, p. 387.

Part VIII:
1973 Symposium Discussion

I. The New International Milieu

Change is endemic in both national and international affairs. Yet, as the name of this symposium suggests, this decade is witnessing changes both at home and abroad more fundamental and rapid than at any time in the post-World War II era. The present can rightly be called a period of transition between two eras. The familiar bipolar world of the era ending is evolving into a new amalgam of continuing nuclear bipolarity and an increasingly multipolar political and economic world. The United States has formulated a new, and fundamentally different foreign policy—the Nixon Doctrine—as a guide for defining and implementing America's role in the era which is emerging.

The formulation of policy and the structuring of the bureaucratic mechanism to make the new policy operationally specific require insight into the factors underlying the change. In dialectical terms, the international situation is one of persisting conflict but with new opportunities for resolution of conflict, the process being both complicated and facilitated by the multifaceted nature of the emerging international system. It is therefore appropriate to examine how the Nixon Doctrine differs in a fundamental way from past policy, and how it approaches the challenges and opportunities of the new milieu.

The thesis of the opening paper presented at the symposium is that implicit in the Nixon Doctrine is a radical approach to international relations—an approach based on a balance-of-power concept but one that requires an international structure based on agreement among all nuclear states that the inevitability of nuclear confrontation between them must be prevented by a new order of international politics. The Nixonian theme of a "generation of peace" is not rhetoric directed at U.S. public opinion and the devolution of American involvement in Vietnam, but is rather a positive and concrete goal for U.S. policy, based on the strategic necessity of preventing nuclear war—without either abandoning U.S. allies or surrendering U.S. interests via a retreat to pre-World War II isolationism.

In the 1960s the United States tended to overemphasize the quantitative aspects of strategy and to neglect the broader political context of international relations. In that era nuclear force was perceived as a negative element, i.e., a view of deterrence and arms control based on the assumption that, if the United States were persistent enough, nuclear weapons could be removed from political considerations and reduced to a strategic nullity. Quantifiable outcomes expressed in fatalities resulting from massive first or second strikes were the criteria of the nuclear equation; the quest for strategic options short of all-out city destruction was eschewed as inimical to the concept of deterrence and even dangerously destabilizing.

219

A major accomplishment of the Nixon Doctrine lies in Henry Kissinger's reintroduction of politics into the nuclear equation and in providing a basis for erecting a global order based on a new international politics.

The Nixon Doctrine essays to achieve a generation of peace by moving from an era of confrontation to an era of negotiation. In the process it must overcome a dialectical contradiction inherent in the three declared principles of the Doctrine: adequate U.S. strength; a vital partnership with allies; and a willingness to negotiate with adversaries. The problem is how to preserve partnerships— specifically and importantly, for example, the maintenance of a "coupled" strategic deterrent for the protection of Europe—while at the same time pursuing bilateral negotiations with the Soviets in such broadly influential areas as strategic arms control and trade.

This contradiction in U.S. policy is to be resolved by using U.S. strength as a synthesizing force: linking the areas of agreement reached between the United States and the Soviet Union on strategic arms and other matters with the overriding necessity perceived by both nuclear superpowers, that of preventing general nuclear war. The strategic umbrella resulting from this shared objective can then extend over Europe and sustain the Atlantic partnership. Likewise, in the future, the bilateral arena of the second round of strategic arms limitation talks must be specifically related to the multilateral negotiations on mutual and balanced force reductions and on security and cooperation in Europe. The joint declaration of principles between the United States and the Soviet Union in May 1972 obviously bears a direct relationship to multilateral negotiations.

The strategic nuclear deterrent equation has resulted in a situation of mutual assured destruction (MAD) should all-out nuclear war occur. MAD is essentially a negative concept but it does have positive implications: it sets limits on the use of military force—and therefore on the freedom for pursuit of expansionist aims; and it sets some benign limits on sovereignty, for example, acquiescence by each superpower to the right of the other to inspect national territory via surveillance satellites. These kinds of limits, under the strategic nuclear umbrella, affect the global balance of power. It is fundamentally different from that reached in the 19th century; the latter expired with its failure to prevent World War I. Similarly, the old Clausewitzian dictum that "war is an extension of policy by other means" is gradually being replaced in the nuclear age with a new concept of international relations, namely, that general nuclear war must be prevented by any means. This necessity to curb any expansionism which might draw the nuclear powers into a serious confrontation sets a requirement for new concepts of international politics: one such concept is that of mutual assured survival and security (MASS) as a goal of negotiations. It is based on a most primitive form of self-interest: i.e., for one adversary to say to the other, "I can only assure my survival by assuring yours." Such a concept is compatible with the currently perceived situation in which:

1. Neither side can expect to gain decisive strategic superiority over the other.
2. Basically, the United States and the Soviet Union are not on convergent courses, although there may be some convergent trends, e.g., in the technology of energy utilization.
3. Both sides apparently accept the staying power of the other's political, economic, and social systems.
4. Paradoxically, in order to retain the U.S. strategic coupling to Europe and to deny Soviet political coercion, it is necessary to introduce strategic options other than assured destruction.

Although the primacy of the U.S.-Soviet conflict of strategies, and the related pre-eminence of the U.S.-European alliance show that the new international milieu continues to have strong bipolar characteristics, the Nixon Doctrine is conceived on a broad and flexible basis, prepared to deal with the reality and the opportunities of multipolarity, i.e., that a more pluralist world can enhance the prospects for peace through a diffusion of power. There are three major negotiating elements, or areas of strategic concern, other than the main U.S.-USSR-Europe negotiating axis:

1. *Vietnam.* Although direct American involvement in the Vietnam war has been ended by the ceasefire agreement of January 1973 and the withdrawal of U.S. troops, a stable peace in Indochina requires further negotiations and agreement among the powers who have interests in that region.

2. *Eastern Europe.* The tendency of many East European countries toward neutralism in international affairs and their desire to formulate more independent foreign policies is being reinforced by East-West negotiations to broaden political, economic, and cultural contacts. This development may impinge on Soviet interests in this area.

3. *The Middle East.* The importance of the Arab-Israeli conflict is receding in the face of the impending world energy crisis and the consequent increased dependency of the industrial states on this region for vital oil supplies. This development will add new complications to an already unstable region.

It is in Asia that the emerging multipolar world is most in evidence. The rise of Japan, the Sino-Soviet dispute, the acquisition of nuclear weapons by China, and the President's trip to the PRC in February of 1972 have combined to produce a new set of relationships in Asia. As the Nixon visit showed, actions taken by one power toward another not only affect relations between the two directly involved, but also produce other reactions by other powers. Thus a series of interrelationships between and among the United States, the USSR,

China, and Japan have been both a product of and a catalyst to the evolution of this multipolarity.

In addition to Europe and the Pacific Basin, the effect of the new multipolar situation has extended to Latin America, the Indian Subcontinent, and Africa. In recognizing this development, the Nixon Doctrine provides a rational framework for reconciling conflicting policies, goals, and national interests.

The discussion that followed this presentation centered on the balance-of-power concept of foreign policy and the Soviet response to that concept. The Nixon Doctrine can be seen as a reversion to the classical balance-of-power approach of the 19th century, with some critical differences. The United States is trying to assist in the creation of a number of power centers on the assumption that they will be able to shoulder their own burdens, with occasional American help to prevent the balance from being upset. This approach recalls the British policy of the last century of subsidizing friendly powers with money and weapons in order to stop those who were not. The danger of applying the balance-of-power principle today, however, lies in the relative weakness of America's allies. Western Europe and Japan cannot build a nuclear force adequate to deter the Soviets by themselves. Without a major U.S. role in the defense of Europe and Japan, the will to be independent and to resist pressures implicit in a balance-of-power world is lacking in the non-communist world.

The Soviets have a very keen recognition of their self-interests. Thus, despite the superficial impression that the Soviets tend toward abstractions and formulate foreign policy on the basis of a dialectical view of history, their strength in fact resides in their pragmatism. Records of Soviet internal debates and discussions with foreigners—including Stalin's talks with de Gaulle in the Second World War and Brezhnev's with Dubcek in 1968—have shown the Russians are pragmatic to the point of brutality. By contrast, U.S. foreign policy is often clouded by elaborate theories and a weak consciousness of self-interest.

Yet the Soviets will have their own difficulties in operating in a balance-of-power world. The concept of the balance of power is foreign to Soviet tradition since it involves a recognition of the world state-system. Neither Soviet theory nor Soviet mentality lends itself to a recognition of the legitimacy of such a system. Besides, the Soviets are operationally uncomfortable when power is dispersed in such a way that they cannot control it. Their concept of power is basically monolithic. Even if the Soviets could adapt to the balance-of-power concept, their attitude toward it is less important than the "objective situation." The idea behind practicing balance-of-power politics is to limit the competitor's choices, to hem him in, so that his freedom of action is circumscribed regardless of his subjective desires. It is at this point that the balance of power becomes most tenuous as a guiding principle of U.S. foreign policy. If the other power centers are unwilling or unable to contest the Soviet Union, a multipolar world may prove more dangerous than the bipolar world. Soviet ambitions are restrained in some measure, however, by the geopolitical dilemma of the Soviets.

China is at their back, Western Europe is directly in front of them, and the United States represents a powerful threat from overseas. Whether or not the Soviets accept the concept of balance of power, they confront some of the problems of such a balance.

II. U.S.-European Partnership

Three European papers were solicited in order to receive a European assessment of the status of the Atlantic partnership at a juncture in history that all agreed was critical for both East-West and West-West relations. Serious concern was voiced over the extreme fluidity of the situation in Western Europe today. The virtual neutralization of the U.S. extended deterrent and the conventional military imbalance in favor of the Warsaw Pact have spawned new uncertainty in Europe. To re-establish an atmosphere of confidence, the United States must fashion a new and comprehensive policy toward Europe. In the absence of such a coherent U.S. policy, the danger looms that the alliance will topple under its own weight. A major threat to the alliance at present is a tendency on the part of some U.S. officials to place higher priority on economics at the expense of strategic questions. If trade and balance of payments problems are allowed to take top priority in U.S.-European relations, the strategic consensus of the Alliance may well crack under the impact of disagreements over secondary matters.

Once the U.S. Government has clarified its own priorities, the European participants at the conference declared, intensive West-West negotiations are required if the Soviet Union is to be deprived of the opportunity to exploit fissures within the Atlantic Alliance. The series of East-West talks now underway on strategic arms limitation, mutual and balanced force reductions, and security and cooperation have kindled apprehensions that a disorganized West may sacrifice key elements of its security through lack of coordination and consultation.

A French view emphasized that the European situation today, fraught with uncertainty, could lead to any of three possible futures, depending on whether the Europeans decide to take action and then coordinate their decisions. The most desirable outcome would be for Western Europe to become a unified entity—economically, politically, and strategically. An integrated Western Europe, according to this view, would be linked not only with the United States but also, in some manner, with the Soviet Union. The Soviets would otherwise be reluctant to permit Western Europe to assume the proportions of a rival superpower. A second possibility, from a French perspective, is that Western Europe will emerge from the present unstable situation as an economic unit but also as a U.S. *economic* protectorate or, in the event the United States abandons Europe, a Soviet protectorate. The third possibility, a variant of the second, is that the Soviets may use the current round of negotiations in Europe to exploit divergences within NATO and, by establishing political bridgeheads in susceptible countries, prevent Western Europe from ever becoming a political entity. This outcome is the most worrisome at this time. Having been screened off from reality for so many years by the existence of NATO, the West European nations must now confront the question of the kind of future they wish to have. Once the West Europeans have mustered the resolve to go through the taxing process of reaching agreement among themselves, they will then have to reach agreement with the United States—all the while not provoking excessive interference from the Soviet Union. Although difficult, in the French view, the first alternative was deemed the only one that is advantageous for both Western Europe and the United States.

To avoid the danger of the third alternative, Western states must enter the Conference on Security and Cooperation in Europe with positive plans that will blunt the Soviet effort to seize the peace issue for its own purposes. According to one French view, if the Russians can exploit the principles of non-aggression and non-intervention in the internal affairs of other states, there is no reason why the West cannot pick up the same issues and advance its own conception of a new collective security system. Such a Western initiative would not only demonstrate a positive approach to the Russians, but would also preempt a divisive maneuver by the Soviets within NATO's ranks. The basic obstacle to a dynamic Western policy, however, is that the Soviet Union seems to know its interests better than the Western allies know theirs. Under the circumstances, it is no small task for the West to take the initiative in negotiations with the Soviets. Moreover, the West must be aware that the developments that unfold on the central front in Europe will impact elsewhere around the globe, particularly in Asia, where the Chinese would be adversely affected by any East-West agreement freeing Soviet troops in Europe for redeployment to the Soviet Union's eastern borders.

On the military plane, the United States and Western Europe must take action to compensate for the weakening of the U.S. strategic guarantee, a gradual process of debilitation codified by the SALT agreements. Given the impossibility of defending Western Europe conventionally against an attack by the Warsaw Pact, the need is urgent to shift to a doctrine of early use of a new generation of tactical nuclear weapons and precision guided munitions within the framework of the flexible response strategy. At the strategic level, the decoupling of the U.S. deterrent from European security requires the strengthening of nuclear cooperation between the British and French with the ultimate purpose of creating an independent West European nuclear force.

It is debatable, however, whether the nuclear question should, at this time, be made the cornerstone of further European integration and defense cooperation since the control problem could be a source of divisiveness within the Alliance. The West Germans will be resentful if excluded from the control mechanism, yet the French and British harbor deep misgivings over West German participation. Moreover, the question may be asked why, if the credibility of the far larger U.S. deterrent has been reduced, the credibility of combined Anglo-French deterrent would be greater? National control of the British and French nuclear forces may enhance their credibility in defense of their national interests. But there is no reason why the West Germans should have more confidence in a French and British willingness to use their forces in support of a West German interest than they now have in the American resolve, unless the British and French are willing to share control of these weapons with the West Germans.

This question of an independent European nuclear force assumes special importance in the context of West German domestic politics and the uncertainties raised by *Ostpolitik*. According to a German view, the *Ostpolitik* bears a strong element of nationalism. While it is far from clear how the West Germans will ultimately choose between the relative priorities of *Westpolitik* and *Ostpolitik*, their decision is likely to hinge on the attractiveness of closer association with Western Europe. The domestic situation in the FRG, it was argued, bars the possibility of developing a consensus behind a policy of strengthening the Western alliance *if* that step threatens the policy of détente with the Soviet Union. Because the milieu of détente has become the basis for the consensus of the Brandt government, one German opinion affirmed, the Soviet Union now looms as a controlling factor in West German domestic politics. The growing influence of radical elements in the SPD and the necessity for SPD deputies in the Bundestag to placate them to win party renomination suggest the difficulty of forging a West German domestic consensus behind an alliance-oriented foreign policy. The absence of a consensus for such a foreign policy is underscored both by the CDU's origination of the *Ostpolitik* and by public opinion polls showing that one-half of all CDU supporters favor the Government's foreign policy.

The scope of Soviet influence over German domestic politics as a result of the Brandt government's *Ostpolitik* was subject to debate. The argument can be made that the Soviet Union wields significant leverage over the Brandt government because of its presumed ability to "control" the détente. On the other hand, it may be argued that because of border problems the Soviet Union's own policy of détente is "controlled" more by China and the United States than Brandt's *Ostpolitik* is controlled by the Soviets. Thus, President Nixon's political position, no less than Brandt's, might be seen as dependent on détente. Moreover, it was argued, the Brandt government is considerably more committed to a West European union than is either the Heath or Pompidou government. Finally, it cannot be maintained that Brandt's *Ostpolitik* is simultaneously nationalist and, with respect to the Soviet Union, capitulationist.

Nevertheless, to the extent the Soviet Union has acquired political leverage over Bonn, it will no doubt exert its influence to prevent the FRG from cooperating more closely with an incipient West European entity. The Soviets are now able to say to the West Germans, in effect: you cannot have an integrated Western Europe and an *Ostpolitik*; you must choose one or the other. Given this choice, no one can predict what course the West German government might take. As a result, a new factor of uncertainty hovers over the movement toward West European integration.

According to the German presentation, if Western Europe is to become an effective and autonomous entity *vis-à-vis* the Soviet Union, U.S. leadership toward this end is required within the framework of the Nixon Doctrine. The absence of that leadership in NATO in the past decade and the U.S. Government's eagerness to pursue its bilateral relationship with the Soviet Union helped spawn the revival within West Germany of a trend toward national definition of foreign policy goals. Although success in the domestic European struggle to develop a consensus behind an alliance-oriented foreign policy is a prerequisite for European security, U.S. leadership is also indispensable for success. For instance, a British view stressed that U.S. assistance is necessary if Europe is to have a credible nuclear capability of its own. The United States can aid in the formation of a combined European nuclear force based on existing and expanded French and British deterrents. Without U.S. assistance Western Europe cannot develop its own tactical nuclear weapons to bridge the gap between strategic and conventional defense. All the key weapons needed to make the flexible response strategy viable against a Warsaw Pact invasion are American. They include a new range of small tactical nuclear weapons, an improved airborne antitank capability, "smart" bombs, and medium-lift helicopters for infantry mobility.

In the political arena, as in the security field, there is no substitute on the horizon for U.S. commitment and U.S. engagement. The problem in Western Europe is broadly one of a malaise of the spirit. Europe needs assurance that the U.S. commitment is long-lasting. In the past the overarching principle of massive retaliation at a time and place of our own choosing provided a common strategic framework uniting the members of the alliance. If a new security concept can be found of sufficient simplicity to unify NATO, then the many issues and challenges threatening alliance cohesion can be overcome.

Disarray in the alliance is partly a function of the fact that policymakers are preoccupied with response to events and have little opportunity to relate their decisions to a coherent structure. The absence of a structured framework within the Atlantic world reflects Washington's current preoccupation with superpower relations and with the global manipulation of the balance of power—a preoccupation that has left U.S. policymakers insensitive to the need for establishing regional structures capable of being maintained over time.

One result has been that European-United States trade and monetary tensions have been allowed to spill over into the security area. The danger exists that if the issue of American short-term economic interests in Europe is allowed to gain ascendancy, the United States will become even less enchanted with European integration. We must restore the conception of the U.S.-European relationship driven by common political-security imperatives. If the United States, Canada, and the European allies can conceive a new transatlantic relationship and imbue the alliance with a new *élan*, then economic problems can be dealt with on the basis of a broad consensus on political and security policy. In this way, disputes over tariffs and exchange rates will not fracture the alliance.

An essential element in reinvigorating the partnership is a better West European consultative organization to conduct a dialogue with the United States. The Eurogroup, composed of a number of NATO's European Defense ministers, has begun to do for defense policy what the EEC needs to do in foreign policy and economic policy. The Eurogroup voted on its own initiative last year to spend an extra $5 billion to improve West European defense. Were France to join the Eurogroup, it might function as a defense advisory organization for talks with the United States. Two similar organizations within the EEC could be created to conduct talks with the United States on foreign and economic policy. The Davignon committee provides the nucleus for political consultation. The forging of a new, reinvigorated partnership would also blunt the Soviet campaign to drive a wedge between the allies at the current and upcoming sets of negotiations on strategic arms, mutual and balanced force reductions, and European security. In the absence of common purpose and a coordinated Western approach, the Conference on Security and Cooperation in Europe may turn into a conference on Soviet security and our cooperation. In this respect, two proposals should be rejected out of hand by Western negotiators. If the West were to accede to the creation of a nuclear-free zone in Central Europe, U.S. forward-based systems would have to be withdrawn from the area, leaving our allies to their own devices in the shadow of Soviet conventional superiority. One likely result would be the progressive Finlandization of Western Europe. A not dissimilar outcome might well ensue in a train of events flowing from a no-first-use pledge with respect to nuclear weapons.

Faced with these dangers, the new partnership must be based on a conception of European security as *Atlantic security*. The unilateral withdrawal of substantial numbers of U.S. troops from Europe would do irreparable damage to Atlantic security. Unilateral cutbacks are sometimes portrayed as a potential means of shocking European public opinion into an awareness that Europe must shoulder a larger part of the defense burden. But public opinion polls show that Europeans are increasingly disposed to believe that the Soviet Union is no longer a threat to their security. In this climate of opinion the withdrawal of U.S. troops could hardly be expected to produce the desired shock effect. In fact, it is difficult to imagine any circumstances that could result in the foreseeable future in Europe's becoming an equal partner to the United States, a partner capable of withstanding long-term Soviet threats to its existence. Given domestic political trends in Western Europe, particularly in West Germany, the options available to the "Atlanticists" will probably become increasingly narrow in the future. This means that now is the time for the United States to move in the direction of a new policy toward Europe consonant with the Nixon Doctrine's emphasis on strengthening relations with our allies.

In this connection the United States must be more aware that the conduct of negotiations with adversaries can threaten to impede the evolution of its partnership with Western Europe. Bilateral negotiations with the Soviet Union on strategic arms limitations and trade have provoked a degree of uneasiness in Europe with respect to U.S. global priorities. A full measure of mutual confidence and common purpose is required if the knotty problems of trade deficits and balance of payments are not to reverberate throughout the Alliance in a psychological climate of mistrust of the motives of each party. The positive goals of enhancing Atlantic security demand that the United States do what it can to nurture a stronger and more unified European entity that can participate as an equal partner with the United States in securing a new structure of peace.

In short, three problems above all bedevil the U.S.-European relationship: the threat of a trade war, the inadequacy of NATO's tactical nuclear strategy, and an apparent unwillingness on the part of the United States to listen to its allies. To prevent the outbreak of a trade war that could threaten common strategic interests of the allies, it is of the utmost importance to solve their economic problems. If a trade and monetary confrontation can be avoided, the West will have the possibility of recasting, through joint effort, the tactical nuclear strategy on which the survival of the Alliance hinges now that the Soviet Union has achieved strategic nuclear parity. Finally, the solution of both these problems—and many others—depends on the United States' learning how to listen to its allies. In the past the United States has been an effective leader but a poor listener. At a time when some would have the United States renege on its responsibilities, it is all the more incumbent that this country first become a good listener and then move on to assert vigorous and determined leadership.

III. The New Milieu: The United States and the Third World

If the situation in Europe is fluid, it would be only a slight exaggeration to characterize the Third World as a maelstrom. Virtually all the major crises, with the exceptions of the Soviet invasions of Hungary and Czechoslovakia, that have alerted the U.S. armed forces since the Second World War have occurred in the Third World. Moreover, the outlook for stability and economic growth in the Third World is generally discouraging. The discrepancy between the economic growth of the developed countries and the less developed nations has been increasing. Having failed to match results with expectations in its past foreign assistance programs, the United States now gives the appearance of having given up on the problem of promoting economic growth in the Third World. If U.S.

policy continues this trend towards "benign neglect," future U.S. trade and investment programs are likely to arouse increasingly unfavorable reactions in Third World countries. Unless the United States gives more attention to this kind of problem, expropriations or other forms of harassment of American corporations are likely to increase and the United States will face attendant political difficulties of the sort marring U.S.-Chilean relations.

The Mideast

The Mideast is one of the most unstable regions of the globe today, despite the diminished danger (resulting from the 1970 ceasefire and the expulsion of 20,000 Soviet military personnel from Egypt in July 1972) of an Arab-Israeli war and superpower confrontation. Preoccupation over the danger of a renewal of the Arab-Israeli conflict has obscured the fact that the Persian Gulf has emerged as the number one prize in the Mideast. Some 60 percent of the world's known oil reserves are located in the Persian Gulf. The increasing dependency of the developed states on oil presents the Soviet Union with the opportunity to take advantage of the West's and Japan's growing dependency on their sea lanes. By the end of this decade, about half of U.S. oil consumption is expected to depend on imports. Europe and Japan will be even more dependent, importing 70 to 95 percent of their oil needs. Under these circumstances, either the Soviet Union or the small states with large oil reserves might be tempted to disrupt oil supplies to the West and Japan. Interruption of oil supplies could take any of four forms: (1) willful disruption by suppliers or attacks on tankers by enemy submarines; (2) domestic turbulence leading to interrupted production; (3) the rise to power by a fanatical leader, such as Qaddafi in Libya; and (4) outside takeover by a relatively small military force.

In the coming struggle for power in the Gulf, the Soviets will have a strong position based on their geographical proximity, treaty relationship with Iraq, and naval presence in the Indian Ocean. The danger to the West stems from the Soviet opportunity to disrupt the flow of oil by controlling strategically critical sea lanes and from Soviet efforts to make its influence predominant in the Persian Gulf area. U.S. policy should aim at ensuring the independence of the area as a whole and at safeguarding the flow of oil for the next ten years while Western governments seek alternative sources of energy.

To prevent the Persian Gulf from becoming a Soviet sphere of influence, the United States must maintain a credible military presence in the area. There is some hope that after Vietnam the Arabs will increasingly come to see that, given the Soviet Union's traditional heavy-handedness and immediate proximity to the region, a U.S. military presence is preferable to American isolationism. The inability of Western Europe to protect its vital interests in the area seems to leave the United States with a larger role. In fact, Western Europe's failure to overcome its disunity in order to gain positive political influence in the oil-rich Moslem world dramatizes the extent to which the concept of Western Europe as one of the poles of a five-power world is premature.

Growing Soviet influence in the Gulf also demands that the United States and its allies bolster the stability of friendly governments in Saudi Arabia, Kuwait, and Iran. Further, expanding Soviet naval activity underscores the indispensability of maintaining U.S. naval superiority on a global basis as a direct effort to deny Soviet efforts to project their military power for political purposes in the Persian Gulf as they are doing elsewhere throughout the Third World.

The oil-rich states of the Mideast pose yet another problem for the developed countries. Some primitive governments will accumulate enormous capital holdings, raising questions of what they will do with the new capital. Their control of capital will give them a potential to disrupt the international monetary system unless the world's major economic powers can devise a strategy to handle the problem. It may be that specific inducements should be contrived to encourage them to invest in the West, and thereby transform a problem into an opportunity.

In general, the problems of strife in the Mideast are so vast and deep-seated in nature that there can be no easy resolution. The best that can be expected is that conflict will be kept under limited control. In the Arab-Israeli dispute the long-term prospect is for continuing conflict with only occasional lapses into cooperation. The Soviets can be expected to pursue a policy of neither peace nor war, since the latter would entail great risk, while the former would render the Soviet presence superfluous. Nevertheless, despite dim prospects for success at this time, attempts to bring about a lasting peace should be continued. Any settlement probably awaits the right psychological moment when both parties are ready to sit down together to end the strife. In dealing with this overall problem, the United States ought not to press the Israelis to make one-sided concessions, since the present situation is less urgent than in the past.

Elsewhere in the Mideast, the internal stability of the Northern Tier states of Turkey and Iran—long taken for granted—can no longer be assumed. Internal crises will likely beset Turkey, while Iran's political progress lags far behind its economic development. Iran has lately improved its relations with the Soviet Union, and apprehensions remain that Iraq may assist Soviet efforts to increase its influence over the Persian Gulf. Although close Soviet cooperation with Iraq may complicate its relations with Iran, it is not likely to pose a great problem.

The overall prospect, then, is for the Mideast to remain a source of instability in U.S.-Soviet relations as part of the grey zone belonging to neither camp. The situation is complicated by the fact that neither superpower is in control of events inside the area. Internal developments in one or more countries, rather than war, are most likely to upset the balance of power in the area.

The Energy Crisis

The energy crisis is a complex phenomenon, the nature of which is far from universally agreed upon. By the end of the decade the Soviets themselves could become a major oil importer because of rising automotive output and the need for oil to export to Comecon and Western Europe. This may actually put the Soviets in conflict with oil-producing states, since the latter will insist on being paid top prices in hard currency by the Soviets as they now are by Western oil companies.

Of course, the energy crisis facing the West is far graver. The Office of Emergency Preparedness has even stated that the energy crisis may replace the Cold War as the United States' most urgent problem. But it must be kept in mind that Western dependence on Mideast oil is a function of its low cost. If the oil producers push the cost up excessively, Western governments will seek alternative sources of oil and energy. Moreover, while there may be no substitute for large quantities of Middle East oil in the next ten years, in the long run alternative sources, whether fossil or non-fossil, can be made available. In the near future, however, the Soviets may try to play middleman between the oil-producing states and the West and so control the West's key energy supplies. In this situation, the United States would be compelled to rely on the unwillingness of oil-producing states to let the Soviets have the middleman's profits taken out of their revenues.

One possible step to ease the energy crisis in the United States would be to import oil and natural gas from the Soviet Union. But the high cost of Soviet fuels and the political uncertainties stemming from U.S. dependency on Soviet supplies make this alternative less than satisfactory. Instead, the United States should consider five other courses of action:

1. Develop alternative fuel and energy sources.
2. Provide economic incentives for new domestic exploration.
3. Turn to developing sources in Canada.
4. Adopt conservation programs, (e.g., differential taxes on automobiles according to their size).
5. Enlist the support of other oil-poor but underdeveloped countries that also will have to pay the producer countries' rates.

With respect to developing alternative sources of energy, a "nuclear neurosis" has contributed to the Plowshare energy-extraction program's going down the drain. Technical and economic problems with the use of nuclear explosions to produce natural gas are overshadowed by the problem of public unwillingness to accept the minute risks of slight impurities in the gas produced through Plowshare.

Finally, there is the possibility that oil-consuming states will group together to counter the Organization of Petroleum Exporting Countries. Although a recent U.S. initiative along these lines failed to win European or Japanese agreement, a new crisis may again place this alternative at the top of the agenda. Over the long run, however, the Third World's importance as a source of raw materials, including fuel, will decline since raw materials are wasting assets. Until that time, the United States is in critical need of an effective energy policy.

The Third World and the Nixon Doctrine

In some quarters in Asia and elsewhere, the Nixon Doctrine is regarded as an elaborate rationalization for a major U.S. withdrawal, the successful conclusion of the Vietnam War to the President's satisfaction notwithstanding. If this interpretation were to prevail, the implications would be ominous for the future of U.S. relations with adversaries and allies alike. While the United States does not attach the same importance to all Third World countries, it is questionable whether this country can afford to let the chips fall where they may in the ideological conflicts of the underdeveloped world.

In the Western Hemisphere, the emergence of Brazil is a factor of the first importance. At the same time that its Chilean neighbor is beset with severe economic problems, Brazil's GNP has reached $55 billion, with annual growth rates of approximately 10 percent. The United States, in choosing its priorities in the Third World and Latin America in particular, will find it necessary and desirable to pay greater attention to Third World nations that, like Brazil, are on the move.

The Third World is an important factor in the overall East-West confrontation and in its impact on specific issues as well. For example, decisions by Third World countries to produce or not to produce nuclear weapons will have important implications for the international milieu. Brazil, India, Israel, and a handful of other non-nuclear states may acquire nuclear weapons systems in the not too distant future. The U.S. government must weigh the consequences of nuclear parity between the superpowers in considering the implications of nuclear non-proliferation. Conversely, the reliability of U.S. security guarantees will have a critical impact on whether individual states feel compelled to acquire nuclear weapons. Psychological restraints on these countries are presently very great, but they may diminish with time.

Third World countries will have an increasingly pivotal impact in another field of growing importance in the future. The politicization of international scientific research and cooperation may impose increasing obstacles to efforts to take full advantage of the world's natural resources, particularly in the sea and the seabed. A marked dichotomy between North and South is developing in the field of oceanic research, often pitting the United States and the Soviet Union in the same group against an array of less developed states in the Intergovernmental Oceanic Commission that fear the technological exploitation of their resources by developed countries.

The principle of the freedom of the high seas is under challenge by those Third World countries seeking to expand their territorial waters. Third World apprehensions have also generated political movements to create nuclear-free bodies of water, for example, in the Indian Ocean.

The problems posed by the Third World, while they are not always matters of life and death, often have an important impact on the influence that the great powers may or may not exercise. Soviet and Chinese support of national liberation movements, the competition between themselves for the leadership of the international communist movement, and the resentments and apprehensions of Third World countries regarding great-power exploitation have combined to add a North-South dimension to the East-West conflict.

Against this backdrop the United States would seem to have three primary national interests to pursue in the Third World:

1. The prevention of a significant part of the Third World from falling under Chinese or Soviet influence.
2. The protection of free access to the raw materials and markets of the Third World.
3. The promotion of stable and, if possible, democratic governments in the underdeveloped world.

A number of factors complicate the realization of these goals. First, the underdeveloped states have the capacity to decide their own futures without U.S. assistance. Whether these states take the Brazilian or Chilean approach to economic growth and foreign investment, for instance, is in a sense less important than the fact that it will be they, not the United States or the great powers, who make the choice. A second complication is posed by the expanded political and military role of the Soviet Union, particularly in the Mideast and the Indian Ocean. While the threat posed by the Soviet presence in the Persian Gulf and Indian Ocean may not be a major cause for concern at this time, it is a growing problem. Third, limited U.S. resources and the differentiated nature of the Third World require the United States to choose some order of priorities in dealing with problems arising in Latin America, Asia, and Africa.

IV. The Emerging Balance in the Pacific

The Nixon Doctrine has raised a host of questions in the Pacific Basin stemming from uncertainty as to whether the United States is merely readjusting its relations or fundamentally altering its commitments. Although the U.S.-Japanese security tie has been the backbone of Pacific security since the Second World War, the President's overtures to the People's Republic of China have created doubts concerning the U.S. commitment to its Japanese ally, as well as to Taiwan, South Korea, and other countries in Southeast Asia. At the same time, the U.S. military withdrawal from Vietnam has kindled apprehensions in Southeast Asia that the resulting power vacuum will be filled by hostile political and military forces. Because the Nixon Doctrine stresses that America's allies must assume greater responsibility for their own defense, many Asians are increasingly uncertain whether they can count upon U.S. support. Not unlike the situation in Europe, the U.S. penchant for bilateral negotiations with adversaries has been destabilizing for relations with allies.

Significantly, at the symposium the two most pessimistic outlooks on the future of U.S. relations with its allies were presented by the speakers from Germany and Japan, the defeated states of the Second World War that have since joined the ranks of America's staunchest allies. The Japanese speaker affirmed the urgency of the United States' clarifying the meaning of the Nixon Doctrine for Asia. If it is merely an excuse for "bugging out" from U.S. responsibilities, the entire Pacific Basin will be destabilized. Although the Nixon Doctrine envisages a larger defense role for Japan in the Pacific, domestic and international factors constrain Japan from quickly and effectively expanding its role in maintaining stability in the Pacific.

The policies of the American occupation have left Japan a two decades-old legacy of pacifism powerfully reinforced by the constitutional prohibition on Japan's maintaining a defense establishment adequate to the task of serving as an instrument of national diplomacy. Alone among major nations Japan has been almost totally dependent on the United States for its security. Because of this traditional state of dependency, the Nixon Doctrine's emphasis on self-reliance for Asian nations poses a particularly acute dilemma for Japan. On the one hand, the United States appears eager to treat Japan as one of the five great powers in a new pentapolar world. On the other hand, Japan can be considered a superpower only in economic terms—and a highly vulnerable economic giant at that. Japan must trade to survive. With the world's third largest Gross National Product, Japan must import virtually all of its oil, coking coal, copper, manganese, bauxite, iron, and so forth. Aggravating this dilemma are not only the domestic legacies of the American occupation, specifically the prohibition against armed forces, but also the little-noted provisions of the international legal order. The Charter of the United Nations, implying that Japan is still an "enemy" state, impedes a more positive Japanese role in security matters and bears directly on the future of the American-Japanese alliance. Thus, although there is no questioning that Japan will play an increasingly central role in the economic development of East Asia, a number of factors constrain Japan from playing the more active defense role which the Nixon Doctrine implicitly requires.

Nevertheless, there are certain security areas in which Japan's Self-Defense Forces could play a more active part. Japan could increase its naval role in the Pacific to defend the sea lanes on which it relies for the imports and exports that assure its economic survival. Similarly in the military assistance field, Japan could play a useful role in supplying weapons and equipment to other Asian states.

Japan's options for the 1970s are, accordingly, not quite so narrow as they might appear. In the next six to eight years, Japan will probably develop an eclectic policy combining a growing multilateral East Asian defense with a predominant reliance on its ties with the United States.

Moreover, a number of factors may lead Japan to consider the nuclear option more carefully. The Soviet Union's achievement of nuclear parity with the United States and Asian perceptions of a declining U.S. commitment to the Pacific Basin may sooner or later lead in this direction. If the Soviet Union were to achieve strategic superiority through technological advances and the failure of SALT II, pressure would build on Japan either to produce its own national deterrent or to reach an accommodation with the Soviets. A growing Soviet naval threat to the sea lanes over which Japan imports 90 percent of its oil from the Persian Gulf and 10 percent from Indonesia might also nudge Japan in the direction of neutrality. Similarly, the People's Republic of China may over a longer time span achieve comparable leverage over Japan. Such a situation could develop if Taiwan and the Bashi Straits should fall under the influence of either communist power. In these circumstances, any delay in Japan's decision to develop the option of nuclear defensive measures—if not accompanied by a prolongation of the period before the Soviets or Chinese can obtain critical leverage over Japan—may compel Japan to forfeit the nuclear option for the future. Not to make a choice soon may mean no chance to choose in the future.

The politics of the Pacific Basin in some ways resembles a four-sided game. For the United States, the task is to forge a stronger partnership with its Japanese ally at the same time that it negotiates with its Soviet and Chinese adversaries. U.S. relations with Japan will continue to be buffeted by trade and monetary turbulence. For this reason it is essential that U.S.-Japanese relations be given top priority at the highest levels of the U.S. government.

Japanese-American relations must provide the cornerstone of peace and stability in the Pacific Basin, all the more since the U.S. and the Soviet Union are likely to remain in a state of guarded competition. The Sino-American *rapprochement*, the Soviet naval modernization program, and increased Soviet naval activity in the Indian Ocean make it unlikely that a relationship of complete cooperation will evolve between the Soviets and the United States. In fact, the problem for the United States is to perform a delicate balancing act to take advantage of the Sino-Soviet split without antagonizing either party.

The Sino-Soviet conflict forms the background against which many of these changes in the Asian international milieu are occurring. American contacts with the Peoples Republic have made it abundantly clear that China opted for improved relations with the United States in order to counter the Soviet Union. One of the most striking aspects of life in China today is the deep-seated hostility toward the Soviet Union and a pervasive fear of a Soviet attack on China. The Chinese see the Soviets as devious and malevolent beyond America's capacity to understand. Chinese hostility on occasion even takes the form of questioning why the United States is talking to the Russians at SALT instead of bolstering the NATO alliance. By contrast, the Chinese are surprisingly unconcerned about the future of Taiwan. They consider the Taiwan problem solved by the Shanghai communiqué and by Prime Minister Tanaka's concessions. They fully expect Macao, Hong Kong, and Taiwan to be restored eventually to the motherland and even welcome American investments in Taiwan because they are seen as ultimately investments in China.

Concern over Soviet intentions has caused a number of anomalies in Chinese life. The Soviet threat has created not only a strategic crisis but an ideological crisis and a problem of civil-military relations in the structure of power. For the last century and a half, the Chinese have not had to worry about their inner frontiers. The threat came instead across the sea, from the British, then the Japanese, and most recently the Americans. As a result, military forces were largely deployed near the population centers, and this gave the military a central role in governing China. Now, however, the Chinese must return to the Great Wall problem, the problem of guarding their land frontiers. This compels them to extract resources from the rest of the country and deploy them in the barren frontiers in the northwest and elsewhere. As a result, the administrative apparatus and the regional divisions of the country have been strained.

These problems, however, exist against a background of remarkable social and political stability in China today. The turmoil of the Cultural Revolution is clearly past. In its place the continuity in Chinese culture from prerevolutionary times has reasserted itself. Even the Chinese economy is reminiscent of the past. Although more industrialized today, it remains a "bicycle economy." The primitiveness of the economy dispels any illusion that it is at all comparable to the Soviet and American economies. Accordingly, the opportunities for expanding Sino-American trade are far more limited than was first hoped in the wake of the President's dramatic trip to the People's Republic.

The Soviet threat has contributed to an ideological paralysis in China today. Individual Chinese will assert that ideology is the most important part of their lives, and that their only ambitions are to serve the state. Revisionism is regarded as an implacable foe demanding ideological vigilance. But at the same time Chinese foreign policy can obviously be understood only in terms of pragmatic opportunism. There is no way the ideology can explain why the capitalist United States is now a friend while the Soviet Union is an enemy. Consequently, at the very time that the Chinese proclaim the supreme importance of ideology, it is fast losing its potency.

Many Chinese expect that the danger of a Soviet attack will crest six months to a year after Mao dies. For what other reason than an attack, the Chinese ask, have the Russians assembled a million troops on their borders? The Chinese also anticipate that during the Mao succession crisis the Soviets will play one Chinese faction off against another in the hope of bringing to power a faction inclined to restore friendly relations with them. The case of Lin Pao is cited as an example of a Chinese leader playing the pro-Soviet card, and the Chinese fully expect that something similar will happen after Mao is gone. These expectations suggest the possibility that the Sino-Soviet split might be patched up at some time in the future. The Sino-Soviet dispute, however, is now so bitter that this is unlikely. But the possibility must nevertheless be guarded against that the two communist powers will seek an accommodation—which, after all, would be in their mutual self-interest.

The future of Sino-Japanese relations is also uncertain. The Japanese and Chinese have established a remarkable relationship now that former Prime Minister Sato has left the Japanese political scene and the Chinese no longer need to compensate for their opening to the United States by snarling at the Japanese. Despite Soviet talk of an Asian collective security system to contain China, Chou En-lai is weaving a far-ranging and skillfully constructed web of political relationships designed to restrain the Soviets. Japan has an important role to play in this scheme, although Sino-Japanese cooperation will probably not extend to the level of entente or positive collaboration against the Soviets.

India, of course, is intended to play a key role in the Soviet scheme for an Asian collective security system. The Soviet-Indian Friendship Treaty, concluded shortly before the outbreak of war on the subcontinent, has raised their relations to a new level of cooperation, with India the distinctly junior partner. Despite the disparity in power between the two, the Indians will likely strive to maintain as much independence of action from the Soviets as possible.

Southeast Asia remains the most fluid area in the Pacific Basin in part because the United States is perceived as turning its back on the region. The United States is seen as creating a possibly serious vacuum, one that will be filled by someone. The question is, by whom? Little local concern is expressed that the Russians will move in as America departs. They are regarded with little affection and are viewed as being rather remote and heavy-handed. The Japanese, although widely resented for better or worse reasons, are regarded as a major economic problem, witness the scattering of small-scale boycotts organized against them recently. But they are not regarded as a political or military problem, although large-scale Japanese rearmament might well reverse this perception and provoke a full-scale crisis in the region. At the present, the concern in Southeast Asia is that the Chinese will fill the real or hypothetical vacuum left by the United States.

The balance of power in the Pacific will be affected by the balance of power in Europe. Any successful outcome of the MBFR talks in Europe will have an impact in Asia. An MBFR agreement will free Soviet troops now stationed in Eastern Europe or on the Soviet Western border for redeployment on the Soviet Far Eastern border. One can assume the Chinese are not indifferent to this prospect. They have already expressed themselves in favor of further European integration and have conducted a diplomatic campaign to warn the NATO allies against the duplicity of the Soviet propaganda campaign for détente in Europe. Moreover, West German delegations visiting Peking have been cautioned on a number of occasions as to undesirability of the *Ostpolitik* for these same reasons.

Nevertheless, China and the Soviet Union share a number of objectives in common, particularly with respect to weakening relations between Japan and the United States. Given this parallel objective, the United States jointly with Japan must devise a common strategy for Asia and the Pacific. Disputes over trade and other economic difficulties must not be allowed to overshadow the very real cooperation that forms the basis of this relationship. Nor must the prospect of normalizing relations with Peking interfere with the broader community of purpose that unites Japan and the United States. Japan's foreign policy is now at a crossroads as a result of the growing stature of China, the passing of the bipolar world, the ambiguity of U.S. commitments in Asia in the wake of Vietnam, and the emergence of Japan as a major economic factor at a time when the postwar monetary and trade systems have fallen into disarray. The sense of movement in Japan's foreign policy requires the United States to clarify the meaning of the Nixon Doctrine in concrete terms. Action speaks louder than rhetoric. The maintenance of U.S. military forces in the Far East conveys a firmer message than any verbal commitment to build a new structure of peace in the Pacific. By the same token, on the other hand, a shrinkage of the visible U.S. presence through large-scale troop withdrawals from, for instance, South Korea can only erode Japanese confidence in the U.S. security guarantee.

Finally, to demonstrate a continuing commitment to Asian peace and security, the United States must keep Japan informed as to its intentions and policy initiatives. As this country engages in triangular politics with the Soviet Union and China, care must be taken that Japan is not left as the diplomatic victim of American maneuvers.

V. Strategy of Implementation:
Resources and Economics

Partnership with allies and negotiations with adversaries are two pillars of the Nixon Doctrine in the international arena. Both partnership and negotiations, however, are doomed to failure unless the third pillar, represented by national strength, is buttressed by a greater commitment from the American people. The annual defense budget represents the embodiment of public attitudes toward the national defense effort and so reflects a tacit set of national priorities. The danger for the United States is that the proposed FY 1974 defense budget of approximately $81 billion will support, in comparison to U.S. forces in 1964, one-third fewer strategic bombers, three less divisions, five less tactical air wings, eight less aircraft carriers, and less than half the number of surface combatant ships. But at the same time, the proposed budget is under Congressional attack because it is nearly 25 percent higher in constant dollars than average defense spending before the Vietnam War. Because of this opposition to what is already a stringent budget, the two pillars of the Nixon Doctrine relating to partnership and negotiations may be unable to support the new structure of peace that the President seeks to create.

By many measures the proposed FY 1974 defense budget is quite modest. The entire U.S. Government budget is slated to increase in Fiscal 1974 by 7.5 percent while defense increases by only 6 percent. The proposed defense budget is the smallest proportion of the total budget in any year since the Second World War. In fact, if the United States committed the same proportion of the forecast 1973 GNP to defense as it did in 1944, the total defense budget would be no less than $520 billion.

Despite this, critics often do not recognize that a number of inputs into the defense budget have pushed costs up without increasing military capabilities. Inflation, the cost of converting to an all-volunteer army, and mounting military pension costs have driven expenditures up but obviously have not enhanced our military posture vis-à-vis the Soviet Union. An additional constraint on maintaining an adequate defense posture stems from the increasing importance of uncontrollable items in the U.S. budget. Items such as Social Security, Medicare, Public Assistance, Veterans Assistance, and so on made up 65 percent of the budget even in 1972. By 1974 the proportion of uncontrollable items is projected to increase to 72 percent. In other words, there is relatively less and less room in the budget for new discretionary programs to upgrade the U.S. defense effort.

A number of partial solutions to the problem of developing a strong defense posture were suggested. To earn Congressional support for the necessary expenditures, it is essential that the DOD budget not only *be* lean and tough but *look* lean and tough. The complete elimination of unnecessary personnel expenditures—whether a result of a top-heavy grade structure or other factors—would probably reduce the defense budget by less than a billion dollars, but failure to cut the fat helps destroy the consensus on which an effective defense program must be based.

More fundamentally, a consensus is needed on an overall scheme by which the American public can agree how large the defense budget should be. The competition for the allocation of resources within the budget is acute, and internal domestic politics greatly affects the amount allocated to defense. Without a scheme to develop a consensus, the tendency will be to cut the defense budget to a greater extent than social programs, regardless of defense needs. One possibility is to select a base period and then calculate increments, based on an agreed-upon formula, to that era's DOD budget (in constant dollars) in order to arrive at a suitable figure for the current fiscal year.

However, there are some difficulties with this approach. No consensus will easily form on whether to select as a base period an era of tensions or one of relaxation. Nor is it clear that an arbitrary formula of base amounts and increments can substitute for a realistic appraisal of the dangers and opportunities presented by the world situation in any given year. Thus, the requirements of the U.S. defense budget vary as a function of the Soviet overall effort in defense.

Attempts to compare the American and Soviet economies reveal both numerical and conceptual problems, and the results are necessarily approximate. Yet this comparison is necessary for knowledgeable judgments to be made in assessing the adversary's defense policy.

There is no doubt that Soviet production potential has moved appreciably closer to that of the United States during the last decade. The Soviet leadership has shown a strong propensity to devote a large portion of this expanding potential to national security requirements. The USSR has thus been able to improve and expand both its nuclear and conventional forces.

At the present time, however, the Soviet economy is in the midst of a difficult transition. Traditional Soviet growth strategy has involved mobilizing large increases in inputs of capital and labor to obtain continued growth in production. But the demographic pattern and the increased competition for capital by the consuming sector have combined to make this strategy unattractive. A new plan for growth is now being implemented. The new strategy alters output in favor of consumption to some degree and shifts more investment toward the production of consumer goods. It emphasizes productivity increases as a source of growth and therefore depends upon the modernization of technology and the improvement of management.

Trade has been assigned the role of easing the bottlenecks created by shifting to the new strategy and of aiding modernization by importing technology. If the modernization program through trade can be made self-financing, it will not have to compete with the military for funds for research and investment.

It is not clear whether the Soviets will be successful in making this transition, but the first two years of the latest five-year plan witnessed severe setbacks in agriculture that adversely affected other sectors of the economy and decreased the overall growth rate.

The U.S. economy is going through its own period of transition, characterized by inflation, a considerable degree of unemployment of resources, and adjustments to changing national priorities. The performance of the economy is improving, but there are three areas that present long-run problems: the effectiveness of the federal budget as an instrument for economic stabilization, the economic implications of changing national priorities, and the balance of payments.

In the area of international economics, the recent and continuing crises have called attention to the fact that trade and monetary policy is foreign policy. No longer can the United States afford to relegate economic policy to a secondary position in the making of foreign policy, for international economics is not merely a constraint on policy, but is also a determinant of that policy.

In the search for a solution to the current economic problems facing the international system, agreement on realistic rules and principles of conduct is needed. A new economic structure must be built that will help rather than hinder the search for peace, and that will become a source of stability rather than friction and acrimony.

The President has pointed out that as the danger of armed conflict between the major powers is reduced, the potential for economic conflict is increased. Thus economic policy becomes high foreign policy.

Achieving international economic harmony is made difficult, however, by forces that have lately arisen in the United States and are feeding the forces of economic nationalism. A new coalition of groups which previously supported a wide international role for the United States has joined together to propose restrictions on trade and investment that would force this country back in time to an inward-looking position. These economic and political forces reinforce the impact of those who see the United States as overextended in the world. Unfortunately, the trade position of the United States will not easily or quickly be improved. All developed countries desire a trade surplus, making for an incompatibility of each industrialized country's economic goals. Moreover, the mounting demand for energy in the United States makes it likely that annual energy imports will increase by a total of from $4 to $15 billion by 1980. Unless barriers to U.S. agricultural exports are lowered, the United States will face an uphill struggle in righting its trade and payments imbalances even after two devaluations of the dollar. Monetary and trade readjustments are required if the U.S. balance of payments situation is not increasingly to affect American ability to engage in international activities, whether in the form of foreign assistance or military security arrangements.

VI. Strategy of Implementation: Diplomacy and Domestic Consensus

In looking back upon the first four years of the Nixon Administration, it is apparent that the President was basically engaged in a "rescue operation" to conclude American involvement in Vietnam while healing the deep divisions in American society. In the preceding years the stature of the Presidency itself had been called into question—at the very time when the President needed public support for winding down the Vietnam War in a way that would safeguard the country's continued vigorous engagement in international affairs. Accordingly, the first years of the Nixon Administration were devoted to establishing the groundwork for a policy of engagement that would be sustainable at home.

At the same time, international relationships had undergone fundamental change. The strategic military balance *vis-à-vis* the Soviet Union had fundamentally changed by 1969 compared to the late 1950s and early 1960s. The Soviets had achieved nuclear parity and had modernized their naval and air forces. The end of American nuclear superiority and the profound effects both at home and abroad flowing out of the controversial Vietnam war had caused the relationship between the United States and its traditional allies and friends in Western Europe to undergo a general decline from their highpoint during the early postwar period. Even the nature of communism had been subject to enormous change. By the middle 1960s, it was no longer seen as a monolith controlled from Moscow. Moreover, the priorities of the Soviet state were rather different by 1969 from what they had been under Stalin.

In this extraordinarily complex situation, the Administration was legitimately preoccupied with the problem of reordering priorities in foreign relations and with preventing the forces of anarchy from deluging unstable regions of the world before the Nixon Doctrine could be made fully operational. The U.S. role of opposing the dismemberment of Pakistan in the Indian-Pakistani crisis in 1971 can be seen in this light as an effort to keep the delicate fabric of international order from unravelling before the institutional requirements of a "new generation of peace" could be fulfilled. Now that these necessary preliminary tasks have been accomplished, it is urgent for the United States to focus its energy on fashioning the institutional structure implicit in the Nixon Doctrine's affirmation of partnership with allies as the fundamental building block of peace.

In its first four years, the Administration, in introducing the Nixon Doctrine, has faced an internal dilemma: new directions in foreign policy cannot be charted *with* the full participation of the bureaucracy, but once enunciated the new policy cannot be implemented *without* the bureaucracy. Thus, ignoring the professionals at the middle level while policy initiatives are being formulated catches up with top-level decisionmakers at the stage of executing policy. The difficulty in sustaining necessary continuity in policy at a time of formulating new initiatives is particularly severe in the United States. Compared to the Soviet Union, Americans are amateurs in the field of strategy. In contrast to American dilettantism, the Soviet approach is thoroughly professional. What is needed on the U.S. side is a major effort to train and give proper responsibility to professional personnel.

Even given greater professionalism in its bureaucracy, however, it is doubtful whether a democracy can operate an intelligent, coherent foreign policy. Frequent changes in Administration raise barriers to continuity and render policymaking haphazard under the best of circumstances. This problem is particularly evident with respect to institutionalizing the Nixon Doctrine, a task whose accomplishment will require not only the full four years of the President's second term but also the first years of a new Administration.

An effective national strategy requires, in addition to strengthening the bureaucratic base, broad-based public support not only from the population but also from Congress. In moving from an era of confrontation to an era of negotiation, the United States faces new challenges in explaining to the public the rationale for its policies. Neither partnership, requiring patient day-to-day diplomacy, nor negotiations with adversaries, requiring a consistent pursuit of the national interest, can be sustained in the absence of public support. The Presidency, because of its visibility and authority, is the indispensable institution in creating an educated public consensus behind national policy. If public support is to be forged behind the Nixon Doctrine, it is essential that the President play a strong leadership role in articulating the nation's goals. The Vietnam War has fundamentally eroded public confidence in our government institutions (although there is some recent evidence that with the end of that war, this erosion is slowly being repaired). In moving away from the moral certainties of a policy aimed at enlisting the Free World in the containment of communism to the ambiguities of a policy designed to create a web of interdependence, the President must educate the American people to understand the inescapable international responsibilities of the United States and its allies. In this connection, it behooves U.S. policymakers to play down the rhetoric of "building a new generation of peace" until the institutional prerequisites have been established.

Those international responsibilities exist today in a milieu that is both fluid and unprecedentedly interdependent in a broad range of areas: trade and monetary affairs, agriculture, energy, and security problems. It is highly desirable, therefore, that the advanced countries concert their efforts to encourage the Soviet Union and China to move in the direction of greater cooperation, although the communist powers are not as yet ready for cooperation of the magnitude that holds the Atlantic world together.

The maintenance of a stable interdependence of the United States, Europe, and Japan makes difficult demands on their diplomacy. If democratic states are to pursue parallel courses, the officials and bureaucracies of these countries must work together at the operational level in a wide range of fields on a day-to-day basis. Thus, while summit meetings between heads of state play a role, particularly in dramatizing issues and mobilizing public support, they must be supplemented by broader participation if deeper, ongoing relationships among allies are to be sustained. A further prerequisite for a stable interdependence is determined leadership. With it, the parliaments and public opinion of America's partners will embrace a wider degree of cooperation than their parochial interests might otherwise incline them to accept. This, of course, requires that all partners to the cooperative enterprise set a course that is coherent and consistent and that can lead to cumulative results over the long term.

When the world is surveyed in these terms, it is clear that the United States and its partners fall short of the prerequisites of close cooperation demanded by the Nixon Doctrine. The essential political disunity of Western Europe, the uncertainties and changing priorities in Japan, and a tendency toward unilateral initiatives by the United States throw up critical barriers to the kind of partnership envisaged by the Nixon Doctrine. The demands of the Nixon Doctrine call for a number of changes in the way Americans do things. First, the Nixon Doctrine must be given concrete meaning. The President must define more explicitly the direction in which he seeks to move. The United States cannot ask its allies to follow its lead until U.S. priorities with respect to adversaries and allies have been clarified.

Second, there must be a devolution of authority in policymaking within the Executive Branch. The mainstays of any true policy, the bureaucracies, must be given the opportunity to participate more actively in policy formulation and implementation. This implies a larger role for both the State Department and Defense Department and requires the National Security Council to share its responsibilities to a greater degree.

Third, a more systematic effort must be made to involve Congress in the policymaking process. Legislative leaders and Congress as an institution must be convinced that they are participating in setting U.S. priorities in foreign policy. If the effort to involve Congress is not made, Congressional support for troop deployments overseas and for liberal foreign trade policies—to name only two crucial policy areas—is not likely to be mustered in the foreseeable future. Two factors, one temporary and the other chronic, have been impediments to closer Executive-Congressional consultation in the recent past. First, the Vietnam war often made close consultation impossible for reasons of military necessity. Second, and more importantly, the splintered jurisdiction of the Congressional committee system prohibited a discreet and effective dialogue. One helpful step would be a Congressional self-study leading to internal reorganization and the creation of a Select Joint Committee on National Security composed of leading members from the relevant committees to upgrade communication between the two branches. Not all problems in Executive-Congressional relations are susceptible to solution by institutional changes, but those that are should be dealt with at the earliest opportunity.

Finally, a systematic effort must be made to educate the public and press as to the imperatives of the international situation. In the absence of public understanding, it will be impossible to sustain any policy in the Congress. Nor will it be possible to sustain public support either for initiatives that a balance-of-power policy may increasingly demand or for a common approach by the United States and its allies in solving the international economic problems that threaten to undermine the more important security relations. Moreover, if the American public understands the Nixon Doctrine to be nothing more than a rationale for withdrawing from the responsibilities of the last twenty-five years, then the Nixon Doctrine cannot serve to energize the American people behind the comprehensive national security policy that a challenging decade of change demands.

Appendix: Report of 1972 Airlie House Conference: National Strategy in a Decade of Change

Appendix

Report of 1972 Airlie House Conference:
National Strategy in a Decade of Change

From February 17 to 20, 1972, the Stanford Research Institute (Strategic Studies Center) and the Foreign Policy Research Institute sponsored a symposium on the general subject of National Strategy in a Decade of Change. The symposium brought together scholars, analysts, and governmental officials, both civilian and military, who were experts in a number of substantive areas in the national security field. The general purpose of the symposium was to examine the changing world environment and the U.S. role in this new milieu. In particular, the symposium examined the new American foreign policy—the Nixon Doctrine—as to its compatibility with conditions of the world system, and discussed the necessity for and opportunity for attaining a national consensus to support the new policy.

It was anticipated that another conference, involving among others most of the participants at the February 1972 meeting, would be convened to discuss this same general subject either at the end of 1972 or sometime during the first few months of 1973.

The subsequent conference would examine the validity of the general findings of the February 1972 conference at Airlie House. It would take into account the impact of such impending events as the Presidential visits to Peking and Moscow, the signing of various international agreements, such as those resulting from Bonn's *Ostpolitik* and the Strategic Arms Limitation Talks, and other important developments affecting the structure of international security.

This report has been prepared to preserve for the participants of the 1972 symposium the sense of the 1972 discussions and to provide a basis for further thoughtful consideration of the complex issues involved preparatory to the next session.

Richard B. Foster
Director
Strategic Studies Center
Stanford Research Institute

William R. Kintner
Director
Foreign Policy
Research Institute

I. The International Milieu of the 1970s

The 1972 symposium began by recognizing consensus that the international system of the 1970s is and will be characterized by both continuity and change. Although nearly every year in recent times could be called a year of transition, nevertheless there is a degree of change taking place now which is more

249

fundamental and significant than at any time since the immediate post-World War II era. Change has been a major theme in the foreign policy statements of President Nixon. While the outlines of the new international system evolving out of this period of transition are not yet clear, there are elements visible of both the familiar bipolar structure and a new multipolarity.

Militarily, the world is still bipolar. The United States and the Soviet Union are the only two nuclear and military superpowers. But even the relationship between these two powers has been changed—by the advent of Soviet nuclear parity, and by changing mutual perceptions. The Nixon Doctrine, recognizing this new relationship, can be characterized as undertaking a sustained U.S. effort to alter the Soviet-American strategic competition in nuclear areas to less dangerous forms of competition. There is a new acceptance by the United States of realistic limits to U.S. power and influence, and a new recognition of the importance of the strategic interaction process between two superpowers that conduct their national strategies in different ways.

There is room for debate about the degree and form of the new multipolarity emerging from the old bipolarity. Japan and the European Economic Community are important centers of economic power, and the People's Republic of China, having acquired nuclear weapons and an enhanced political status as a member of the United Nations Security Council, is potentially a major power. Thus there is increasingly frequent reference to a pentapolar world (the United States, the Soviet Union, Japan, China, and Western Europe). But there is uncertainty as to whether there will be five, six, seven, or more power centers. India, Indonesia, Brazil, and others may merit inclusion in a multipolar milieu. A complicating factor in any perception of multipolarity is the weight to be accorded to each power, depending upon whether the criterion is strategic nuclear power, conventional military power, political influence, economic strength, or such intangibles as the quality of leadership and cohesiveness of national will.

Some have characterized the Nixon Doctrine as a U.S. policy based on a balance-of-power concept. In 19th century Europe, the Treaty of Vienna was followed by 100 years of general, if intermittent, peace. But it may be doubted whether, with so many changed factors, a new multipolar balance of power can be expected to achieve the same goal in the last third of the 20th century. And, if it could, would such a limited goal be responsive to the desires and aspirations of the Third World? In making an assessment of what the United States seeks to gain from the concept of balance of power, it is important first to define U.S. national interests; this is a task for the Administration, the Congress, the media, the academicians, and ultimately for the American people. However, there is a problem as to whether, in today's U.S. domestic climate, the people are willing to accord sufficient trust and support to their leaders to allow them to engage in the actions that balance-of-power diplomacy requires.

In the Europe of Metternich, instability in great power relations resulted from potential shifts in alignment. Diplomacy in this setting was designed to maximize a state's potential for maneuver, and for taking advantage of opportunities afforded by shifting alignments. All the key actors shared an interest in preserving the international system as necessary for their own security. Moreover, traditional diplomacy operated in a milieu in which domestic politics were largely separated from foreign policy.

Today's conditions of diplomacy are radically different from those of the 19th century. The spread of political participation and the technological revolution in mass communications have subjected diplomacy to continuous and intensive public scrutiny. In the generation after the Second World War, diplomacy was predominantly bipolar and was based on two cohesive alliance systems. These disparities limited the interchangeability of roles. Further, bipolarity was characterized by lack of mutual acceptance of the legitimacy of the international system. Neither superpower considered the preservation of the other as essential to preserving the system.

Against this background, it is apparent that the emerging international system of the 1970s has characteristics of both postwar bipolarity and the 19th century multipolar diplomacy. One difference between today's international system and that of 19th century Europe is the great disparity today in power among the key international actors. These disparities limit the interchangeability of roles between the emerging power centers, making it far more difficult to pursue a completely flexible foreign policy. Nevertheless, the Nixon Doctrine seeks to develop a new international system in which diplomacy can play a greater role in the accommodation of differences among nations than was possible under the bipolar system of the post-World War II period.

Interaction between nations is a key element of the emerging international system. However, there are great differences in the motivations and the capabilities of nations for taking advantage of the system. The Russian political culture is dominated by administrative power, and because of the relatively slight importance of domestic public opinion, the Soviet leadership enjoys sharp advantages of flexibility and tactical speed in multipolar international relations. However, these advantages may serve to prevent the Soviet leaders from either understanding U.S. concepts of emerging multipolarity or accepting the legitimacy of the resulting international system. Further, the attributes of Soviet political culture and behavior may lead to Soviet leaders taking destabilizing actions in the diplomatic-political environment.

The tactical flexibility of the Soviets allows them to deal with capitalist or fascist governments when it suits their purposes. They have shown some sophistication in manipulating balance-of-power perceptions in their efforts to Finlandize Europe. The Soviets seem also to be acutely aware of the political advantages available to a nation that deploys an all-ocean navy.

Nevertheless, there are some difficulties the Soviet Union may be expected to encounter in competing in a balance-of-power world. The Soviet Communist

Party has traditionally put great emphasis on centralized and exclusive exercise of power and has shrunk from political relationships that it cannot fully control. For example Russian frustration with Sadat in Egypt and Castro in Cuba has reinforced their feelings of aversion for allies they cannot fully manipulate or control.

By contrast, the United States may fare better in a multipolar balance-of-power world, since its leaders learn the techniques of dealing with autonomous domestic political forces as they compete in the electoral arena. In the final analysis, the United States probably can live with pluralism in international affairs far more easily than can the Soviet Union.

Study of the Soviet system shows that it has a sophisticated, professional methodology for formulating and carrying out national strategy. The Marxist dialectic of history provides the Soviet political leadership and their military intellectual establishment with a general methodology for explaining the past and projecting the future. They have set up institutions for intensive study of the United States and other powers and are becoming more adept at interpreting, utilizing, and even manipulating American domestic politics to their own strategic advantage. If the United States is to operate in a new era of negotiations as stipulated by the Nixon Doctrine, there is a great need for developing a sophisticated methodology for understanding, predicting, and controlling future U.S.-Soviet interactions; further, there must be a body of competent people—including experts in independent research organizations—to undertake this important development. Finally, and perhaps most importantly, the governmental institutional structure must be strengthened and streamlined for the most effective policy formulation and implementation.

International affairs analysts do not agree as to whether in a new balance of power system the United States could or should manipulate successfully either the Soviet Union or China. One view is that the two communist powers will themselves be seeking to manipulate each other and the United States and will not play purely passive roles. Another view is that the United States is now in a position to have better relations with both China and Russia than either can have with the other, but this view is in conflict with the belief held by some that the common element in Chinese and Soviet communist ideologies makes it unlikely that the United States could ever be closer to either than each is to the other. However, it does appear reasonable that given the Soviet-American strategic confrontation, it would be unwise for the United States to follow the normal balance-of-power rule and ally with the weaker power against the stronger. In the first place, China is not yet a global power; moreover, because of the nuclear confrontation with the Soviet Union, U.S. interests in limiting the arms race necessitate maintaining stable relations with that nation.

Consideration of the progress that has been made in certain areas of arms control causes some analysts to warn that such progress should not lead the Western public into supposing that Soviet goals in other areas have necessarily changed; for example, the Soviet leadership is in the midst of a political offensive in Europe to divide NATO and reduce the U.S. presence while it clamps down at home on political dissent.

Another concern is that the emergence of a multipolar world—when coupled with the Nixon Doctrine, as some people understand it—might signal a general U.S. retreat from its international responsibilities. If the United States reduces its deployed conventional forces, weakens NATO and its other alliances by stressing excessively the concept of multipower military burden-sharing, and puts more of its nuclear forces at sea, the effect could be a drift back into a massive retaliation doctrine. However, it seems clear that such developments are neither intended by the Nixon Doctrine nor, if they occurred, would they be compatible with U.S. national interests.

II. U.S. Relations With Allies

In implementing the Nixon Doctrine, it is important to maintain the confidence of allies in an era of negotiations with adversaries. The United States can retain the confidence of allies only by honoring its commitments to them. While professions of continued American support are useful, there is no substitute for concrete actions in conveying the reliability of U.S. assurances.

However, as a realistic consideration, it is still problematic whether the United States can build a new structure of global relationships in which all nations, friends and adversaries, participate and have a stake. The Nixon Doctrine represents only a first step toward such a new international consensus, which stresses the need for changed relationships between the United States and its allies and potential partners if the international system of the 1970s is to be viable.

The problem posed by the new international system is one of transforming allies into partners while undertaking negotiations with adversaries. Stated differently, the problem is how to retain the assets of a bipolar world while taking advantage of whatever opportunities multipolarity presents. Thus the Nixon Doctrine may be seen as an attempt to implement partnership while at the same time securing the advantages of diplomatic maneuverability in a multipolar world. Whether the need for rapid change and flexibility in foreign policies is compatible with partnership is a major problem which American diplomacy will have to confront in the future.

There does seem to be fairly general agreement that partnership relations require U.S. actions on several fronts. First, it is necessary for the United States to maintain a defense posture providing diplomatic leverage in relations with both allies and adversaries. If the United States were to permit the Soviet Union to gain or appear to gain strategic nuclear superiority in some areas, and to achieve a significantly enhanced capability to deploy conventional capabilities abroad, the credibility of U.S. guarantees could be eroded. A weakened U.S. defense posture would convey the message that this country has neither the will nor the means to play a significant role in the world.

Second, the United States must maintain essential defense links with its allies as they assume a greater burden for their own defense and adopt a more independent stance in foreign policy. If contemplated U.S. force reductions in various regions are not based on close consultation and negotiation, they may serve to undermine the confidence of our allies in U.S. treaty commitments. Unilateral force reductions in Europe, moreover, would be interpreted as a major weakening of U.S. resolve in support of its NATO commitments.

Third, U.S. alliance interests must not be undermined by diplomatic initiatives toward adversaries. American diplomacy in the remainder of the 1970s faces a real dilemma in this regard. The secrecy and surprise of the U.S. initiative to the People's Republic of China seriously jarred U.S.-Japanese relations, which are the cornerstone of international stability in the Pacific. Future negotiations with adversaries require greater mutual understanding between the United States and its allies.

Fourth, the United States should consult as fully as possible with allies in preparing diplomatic initiatives toward adversaries. Full consultation with allies is an essential element of American diplomacy in an era of negotiations. The United States consulted extensively with NATO countries on issues raised at the Strategic Arms Limitation Talks, but in other respects the U.S. record has been spotty. As the U.S. initiative to China continues to develop, there is a clear need for intensive consultation with America's Asian friends and allies.

Fifth, the United States must take carefully weighed steps to encourage allies to strengthen their own defenses. Related to this point, it is essential for the U.S. Congress to understand that U.S. force reductions in various regions of the world may be less likely to stimulate greater burden-sharing by our allies than to convey the mistaken impression that the United States has downgraded the adversaries' military capabilities.

There is understandably some concern about the ambiguity of the Nixon Doctrine's assurances as to how the United States will discharge its commitments; i.e., that commitments will be kept, but at lower cost and less effort. The danger is whether less effort will be adequate—and whether allies will perceive it as adequate—to deal with those commitments regarded as vital. Allies are more likely to judge the Nixon Doctrine by concrete actions than by rhetorical reassurances.

III. Regional Impact of U.S. Policy

Europe and the Middle East

In light of the strengthening of the Soviet military posture in Europe, there is little cause for the optimism prevalent in some European circles concerning

Soviet intentions. In the past some observers cited Soviet intentions in order to highlight the unlikelihood that the West would ever have to deal with Soviet capabilities. Today, by contrast, some analysts point to Russian capabilities as a factor demanding caution in estimating their intentions. For although a Soviet-led attack on Western Europe is no longer considered likely by most analysts, the Soviet Union may hope to extract political gains from its conventional superiority in an era of strategic parity.

In the event of an actual Russian attack, NATO's conventional forces would probably prove no match for Warsaw Pact armies. Under the flexible response doctrine, there would be a delay before resort was made to nuclear weapons. At that point, some analysts believe, the United States would be compelled to choose between nuclear retaliation or capitulation. This dilemma, under conditions of nuclear parity, can be seen as the flaw in U.S. strategy; stability is maintained in this circumstance only because a Russian attack runs so great a risk that they have no incentive to find out how fatal the flaw is.

But some observers believe that the Europeans have not thought through the concept of deterrence. Europeans say they want deterrence but have given insufficient consideration to the elements of defense and to the strategy for use of tactical nuclear weapons. They believe that Europe cannot be defended below the level of strategic nuclear war. If this be true, it raises the question as to how this belief squares with the strong European desire to retain 300,000 U.S. troops and 7,000 tactical nuclear weapons in Europe. A further inconsistency in the thinking of Europeans is that while they increasingly support early use of tactical nuclear weapons, they also have serious misgivings over any strategy that might result in large-scale civilian casualties. Thus NATO strategy is fraught with illogicalities.

U.S. policy in Europe will be confronted with two other major problems in this decade. Both problems are related to the prospect of complete or partial U.S. military withdrawal not fully balanced by Warsaw Pact cutbacks. First, it is not at all apparent that Europe would respond to U.S. troop cuts by taking greater responsibility for its own security; it is possible that Europeans might seek an accommodation with the Soviet Union, which might redound to the detriment of U.S. interests.

Second, if the Europeans respond to U.S. force reductions by taking more vigorous defense measures, Europe may, over a period of years, move away from the United States, ultimately occupying a position of neutralism between the two superpowers. One solution to both problems would be to work toward greater economic integration of the United States and Europe.

Optimism is still in evidence, however, in the view that the concrete benefits of a U.S. military presence in Europe will, in the final analysis, outweigh contrary considerations based on the amorphous sentiment that the United States is somehow "overextended". Holders of this view maintain that most of those Senators speaking out for withdrawal are doing so not because of irresistible pressure from constituents but because of vague feelings of overcommitment.

Although there was not sufficient time during the symposium to deal with the Mideast as a discrete problem, its relevance to Europe was recognized. The increased Soviet naval presence in the Mediterranean was seen, at least in part, as an effort to turn NATO's vulnerable southern flank. Political instability in Greece, Italy and the Balkans may present Moscow with an opportunity to make strategically important political gains in the future. The Mideast, and particularly the Persian Gulf, is vitally important to Japan, since the Japanese economy is heavily dependent on oil from this area.

Asia and the Pacific and Indian Oceans

Soviet interests in the Indian Ocean should be interpreted in the light of their interests in Asia and the Pacific generally. From the military standpoint, most of the Soviet vessels in the Indian Ocean are from the Pacific fleet. Politically, the Soviet-Indian Friendship Treaty and Indo-Pakistani War point up Soviet interests in strengthening their hand on the southwestern border of China. The impression that the Soviet Union is engaged in an active effort to encircle China is reinforced by recent high-level visits between Moscow and Tokyo and by mounting Russian interest in Malaysia and Singapore, as well as in the Philippines and Thailand. It may be that the Soviets have sensed, more correctly than many Americans, that a key feature of the Nixon Doctrine is the gradual decontainment of China. Accordingly, the Russians have found it expedient to step in and contain China to the north and west as American pressure to the east and south slackens. While the Sino-Soviet conflict antedates the proclamation of the Nixon Doctrine, the massive Soviet military buildup on the Chinese border and the military clashes there coincided with the Doctrine's proclamation and early implementation.

With respect to Sino-American relations, although some analysts believe that the United States has made major concessions to China and has approached the Chinese as a supplicant, this is not necessarily the case. The Chinese have changed their policy, too, and no longer put primary stress on wars of national liberation. It should also be remembered that the tremendous Soviet military buildup on the Chinese border probably has helped move the Chinese toward the accommodation with the United States.

The Russian response to the Sino-American *rapprochement* can be seen as a willingness to yield small concessions to the United States, as at the Strategic Arms Limitation Talks (SALT), and to attempt to slow a Japanese move for *rapprochement* with China. A four-power balance may be developing in the Far East, with the United States hoping to take some of the Soviet pressure off Western Europe by complicating its position in Asia.

It is possible that, in the future, the Soviet naval presence in the Indian Ocean may increase far more than is now commonly thought. This presence may be assisted by greater Indian accommodation to Soviet needs, particularly with respect to naval facilities. One response might be to increase U.S. naval presence there. However, overall reduction in the U.S. naval forces, and a possible adverse domestic political reaction in the United States to such a move, makes a large American presence appear unlikely in the near future.

There is some apprehension that new United States policies will result in the further watering down of its commitments to states in the Pacific and Indian Ocean area. It may be that U.S. planners should give greater consideration to the possibility of creating a Pacific and Indian Ocean Defense Agreement in order to forestall such a development.

Regarding the future of U.S.-Japanese relations, the "Nixon shocks" of last summer not only embarrassed the Sato government but, more importantly, demonstrated to the Japanese that the United States, in matters that affect its national interests, will act unilaterally. If this is the case, many Japanese argue, the United States may also act unilaterally with respect to its security guarantee. As a result, the U.S. nuclear guarantee has lost credibility in the eyes of some Japanese, with potentially profound implications for future U.S.-Japanese relations. This new uncertainty may, for instance, lead Japan to develop its own nuclear weapons now that certain political constraints, such as the reversion of Okinawa, are being removed. President Nixon's visit to Peking has also taught the lesson that membership in the nuclear club confers international political status.

Nor should Japanese interest in the security of their sea lanes to the south be minimized in Washington. The Japanese are concerned that free passage be maintained not only through the Taiwan Straits but also off the east coast of Taiwan and off the east and west coasts of Okinawa. If these lifelines were to be threatened, Japan would be faced with the alternative of either increased military involvement in the area or negotiated accommodations in neither their interest nor the U.S. interest.

Latin America

U.S. interests in Latin America, if they are to be protected, require resolution of the conflict between U.S. perceptions of hemispheric interests and Latin American perceptions of those interests. The United States has concentrated on security interests in the area and on protecting U.S. trade and investments, while Latin America has been more concerned with its independence from the U.S. and its own economic development.

According to this view, the main challenges to the United States are political, psychological and economic rather than security-related. Moreover, the challenges come from within Latin America rather than from outside.

U.S. political and psychological interests in Latin America derive from three main sources: a tradition whereby Latin American countries support the United States on most international issues; the U.S. sense of obligation to them as members of the hemispheric family; and their status as developing countries.

Economically, the United States acquires raw materials from the area, invests large amounts of capital, and engages in extensive trade with Latin American countries.

Militarily, U.S. security will probably not be challenged from the area by an increased Soviet military presence, for several reasons. Although Soviet missile submarines or land-based rockets in Latin America can complicate the global nuclear balance, they cannot decisively alter it. Soviet conventional capabilities in the area will increase, primarily because of a larger naval presence, but this change will not be decisive locally since U.S. conventional power will continue to be far superior. Psychologically, an increased Soviet military presence could have a deleterious impact if it goes uncontested. But this problem can be turned to the U.S. advantage by a countervailing psychological factor. The mere presence of the Soviet Union in a country like Cuba provides a vivid demonstration to other Latin American countries (provided the United States does not succeed in obscuring the demonstration) of how much worse it might be for all Latin America to be dependent on a power other than the United States. The Soviet presence also shows its economic and political system in a bad light. These could be important lessons for a Latin America that sometimes seems to North Americans to be irrationally hostile to the United States.

IV. International Economic Cooperation

The strengthening of multilateral economic and financial cooperation in the free world will be critical to a successful theory and practice of international relations in the 1970s.

Unlike many other aspects of U.S. foreign policy, a policy of economic cooperation enjoys a consensus of support both at home and abroad. The large array of international institutions supporting this goal includes, *inter alia*: the International Monetary Fund, the General Agreement on Tariffs and Trade (GATT); the Organization for Economic Cooperation and Development; the World Bank; and the Inter-American, Asian, and African Development Banks. U.S. trading partners, U.S. allies, and a large part of the Third World favor this kind of cooperation. The fact that institutions promoting such cooperative activity already exist provides an incentive for continued cooperation in the economic sector.

The economic base for U.S. leadership in the world is suffering some erosion, although less than the recent emphasis on attrition of U.S. power would lead one to believe. The United States Gross National Product, now about 40 percent of the total GNP of the non-communist world, is back to about where it was in

1938, having steadily declined from a peak of about 52 percent in 1953. Trade, of which the U.S. portion is only 15 percent, exhibited a similar pattern. This combination of a large imbalance between the share of GNP and trade is not a good one for stabilizing the world's economy, or for exerting economic and political leadership. U.S. overseas investment is a more potent base for international leadership than U.S. trade, but unfortunately, investment is a less viable base for leadership than trade.

America performs an important world role as a supplier of "public goods"; i.e., goods that cannot be charged for, such as military security, or a sound financial climate in the free world. As the United States takes a lower profile in world affairs, its ability to sustain former levels of supplying public goods probably will shrink. Others, such as the group of nations comprising the European Economic Community, will have the capability to produce compensating amounts of public goods, but it is not yet clear that this will take place.

Restructuring the international monetary system is a vitally important goal for the immediate future. In order to accomplish this restructuring, one suggestion is that intensive negotiations be resumed among leading countries, and that the tempo and effectiveness of multilateral cooperation with respect to common economic and financial problems be stepped up. In order to link more effectively the economies of less developed countries with those of industrialized states, a more generous and effective multilateral development program is needed. Trade barriers should be lowered in industrialized countries for the products and services of less developed countries.

There is also the need for the United States and its partners to maintain an adequate rate of economic growth. The importance of continued U.S. leadership in the economic sector consonant with the U.S. economic position was emphasized. A passive and limited U.S. economic role is a recipe for failure.

In consideration of actions to support the importance of trading and monetary relations in protecting U.S. political and security interests in the world, the following six measures would serve to promote a more effective international trading system:

(1) The elimination of all tariffs among the advanced industrialized countries over a period of ten to fifteen years.
(2) Comparable action to liberalize trade in agricultural products, implying modifications in internal support programs which give rise to restrictions.
(3) Where countries face internal stresses as a consequence of this liberalization, trade adjustment assistance programs should be established. Where import restrictions are necessary for political or other reasons, they should be tolerated for limited periods of time, e.g., three to five years, and then phased out.
(4) Elimination or reduction of nontariff trade barriers as well as tariffs, with the United States participating in the process.

(5) Liberalization of trade barriers to imports from less developed countries.

(6) A review of the terms of the GATT, modifying those provisions which do not fit current realities and strengthening the institutional and procedural arrangements for implementing the agreement.

In the long range view of international economics, one of the major issues that will face the United States in this decade is the gap between rich nations and poor nations. There is no easy solution to this problem, and some experts believe that the United States, while helping less developed countries, should not assume responsibility for their success, which ultimately depends on their own political and economic program.

V. Strategic Military Alternatives

An important task of the symposium was to consider a number of alternative military strategies, nuclear through conventional, in the light of historic developments and the new milieu in which the Nixon Doctrine must operate. Analysis of the problem does indicate that both history and the framework of the Nixon Doctrine narrow the range of alternatives open to the United States and the free world. While it can even be argued that the Cold War is not yet ended, the international environment undoubtedly is changing, and change calls for strategies different from those pursued in the past. The clearly defined opposing blocs of the Cold War are evolving into more diffuse sets of several interacting centers of power. These interactions take place under the umbrella of a continuing bipolarity, characterized by an approximate strategic balance between the United States and the USSR. For the United States there are neither resources available nor a political consensus to support a return to the previous heavy responsibility for free world security. Strategic military alternatives for the future will be constrained by two realities: (1) Americans want to spend less for defense; and (2) Americans want the allies to bear a larger share of the free world defense burden.

It seems generally agreed that the one strategic military alternative clearly not feasible is to turn back the clock to the Cold War approach, even though it can be demonstrated that Soviet (and Chinese) military power is growing. This constraint seems to point in the direction of smaller, but better, U.S. military forces, drawing on the benefits of high technology to stress quality over quantity. This inevitably means also that fewer U.S. forces can be deployed, and that it will be necessary to consider regional priorities in deciding where an American military presence is essential.

Consideration of the regional impact of the Nixon Doctrine raises the question as to whether there ought to be a regional approach to strategy. There is historical precedent for the concept of regional priorities; i.e., that U.S.

interests differ in various regions, and that it is logical to pursue a regional approach to strategy. But one can take exception to this view, and maintain that to become preoccupied with regions may result in overlooking an important area or the relationship of one area to another, e.g., the interdependence of strategies in Europe and the Middle East. However, even accepting the importance of this latter point, it seems inevitable that regional considerations will continue to have relevance to military strategy.

Europe and the Atlantic Alliance continue to demand top priority in the U.S. defense posture, with the East Asian (or Pacific Basin) area next in order of importance. But analysts differ on what is a necessary or feasible posture in the large area lying between these two priority regions; i.e., the Middle East-South Asia-Indian Ocean area. It is a universally accepted concept that the Indian Ocean and its littoral is a strategic entity, that the Soviets seem to regard it as such, and are pursuing a maritime strategy to establish their presence and promote their political influence there. On this point, the British never regarded the Indian Ocean as an entity when British power was predominant between Suez and Singapore. As to the American strategy in this area, although the U.S. Pacific Command's geographic area now extends westward to the Arabian Sea, the problem is whether sufficient naval forces will be available to maintain a credible American presence in the Indian Ocean.

Strategic parity between the United States and the Soviet Union has aggravated problems of regional security and the American defense posture in general by reducing the credibility of the U.S. nuclear guarantee. The United States therefore cannot afford to accept anything less than genuine strategic parity with the Soviet Union. A doctrine of strategic "sufficiency," pegged at a level below true parity, is potentially dangerous in its impact on U.S. allies, who may prefer accommodation with an adversary over the uncertainties of the U.S. commitment. The Soviets have not accepted a posture based only on the doctrine of assured destruction, making it doubtful that the United States can conclude arms control negotiations to limit each side's offensive strength to an assured destruction capability. In fact, Soviet thinking includes consideration of the possible efficacy of a first strike to preempt what they would perceive to be an imminent nuclear attack on them.

Whether the United States should develop a counterforce capability is controversial. If there were no budget constraints, such a course might be strategically sound. But within the share of the budget allotted to defense expenditures, a counterforce program would place severe limits on the extent to which tactical nuclear and conventional capabilities could be sustained and enhanced. Nevertheless, it must be recognized that the Soviets will lack a strong motive to eschew their counterforce posture in the absence of, at least, an effort by the United States to develop some counterforce capability.

There is little controversy over the premise that the United States must increase its expenditures in military research and development. Soviet military

R&D has been increasing rapidly at the same time that American R&D has been cut back. A fundamental corollary of the Nixon Doctrine is that while the American presence abroad is given a lower profile, a vigorous program must be pursued to maintain U.S. leadership in the historically decisive field of technological innovation.

Another critical corollary of the Nixon Doctrine is a meaningful military assistance program. Having attained strategic parity, the Soviets are now able to engage in local war in various regions of the globe. As a result, U.S. military assistance needs to be expanded in coordination with economic aid programs to deal with the threat of wars of national liberation. The scope of the problem is demonstrated by the graph in Secretary Laird's FY 1973 posture statement portraying the relative impact of the conflict in Southeast Asia on defense expenditures by the United States and Soviet Union to support their respective allies. The U.S. expenditures were disproportionally high because of direct U.S. participation. The Soviet Union—and China—managed to equip local communists for a tiny fraction of the expenditures made by the United States. As a result the Soviet Union has had a larger proportion of its defense budget available for its own strategic buildup than the United States has had for corresponding programs. The problem for the United States is to keep a low "expenditure curve" on its efforts to enable allies and friends to defend themselves. An increased military assistance program offers the best hope of solving this problem.

With respect to Europe, the Soviets are seeking to decouple U.S. strategic power from European defense. A strategic arms limitation agreement[a] limiting ABMs but not offensive weapons would have the effect of eroding the credibility of the U.S. guarantee to Europe by freezing the United States into a position where it must accept destruction of U.S. territory in order to defend Europe. Further, the United States must be wary of other agreements with the Soviet Union that would have the consequence of reducing the U.S. commitment to Europe. Although there is no magic number of U.S. ground forces necessary to NATO defense, it is critical that in the future the monumental achievement represented by NATO not be undermined by hasty disengagement.

Arms Control

The strategic arms control problem remains essentially bipolar, although the multilateral agreements—on nonproliferation, biological and chemical warfare, the seabed and space—have been significant. Nevertheless, the U.S.-Soviet nuclear confrontation remains the key problem. Very probably the Soviets will have great difficulty in coming to the point of actually reducing armaments.

---

[a]A Treaty on Strategic Defenses and an Executive Agreement on Strategic Offensive Weapons was signed by President Nixon and General Secretary Brezhnev in Moscow on May 26, 1972.

Their continuing fear of the Chinese will inhibit decreasing either their nuclear or their conventional capabilities. The Soviets, having gained a position where their nuclear and conventional strength can be translated into political dividends, will be reluctant to dilute this advantage through arms control.

The Chinese seem now and for the forseeable future to be outside the realm of arms control negotiations. China fears not only Russia, but probably also Japan. The extent of Chinese fear of Japan's military potential in Asia is difficult to assess; it could be quite high, linked to the Marxist view of Japan in China, i.e., that it is impossible for the Japanese to become strong economically without becoming militarists; and, if economically strong and militarist, Japan must become imperialist.

Arms control continues to be one of the tools available to help create a stable world political environment; the bipolar attempt to deal with strategic arms is a key stage in the progress in arms control made over the past several years.

Nuclear Proliferation

Further nuclear proliferation could have a critical impact on the nature of the new international system of the 1970s. Despite the Non-Proliferation Treaty it is quite possible that Japan, India, and Israel could go nuclear, and there are other countries, including Brazil, that might well do the same if they decided that such a step was necessary for their survival. The creation of a Japanese and a European nuclear force would complicate substantially the task of Soviet strategic targeting. In an age of strategic parity between the Soviet Union and United States, independent nuclear forces may enjoy greater credibility as a deterrent to Soviet threats than an American nuclear force whose use in behalf of an ally would invite retaliation directly against U.S. territory.

On the other hand, the formal establishment of a European nuclear force (EUNUFOR) and the nuclearization of Japan might lead the Soviet Union to seek a *rapprochement* with China. In any case, the U.S. strategic nuclear commitment and conventional military presence in both Europe and Japan are important factors restraining the Europeans and Japanese from going nuclear.

Critical questions regarding proliferation are, whether the United States can do anything to prevent the nuclearization of Japan, and what the U.S. should do if the Japanese make the decision to develop a nuclear capability. One approach could be called "nuclear neutralism"; i.e., the United States should not encourage Japan to go nuclear but neither should this country actively seek to discourage Japan from such a step, and if in the future Japan decides to acquire nuclear weapons, the United States would be well advised to accept the decision. An argument in favor of this policy is to recall the worsening of Franco-American relations that resulted in part from American opposition to the French nuclear program in the 1960s. A repetition of that experience should be avoided in the Far East.

The U.S. attitude toward proliferation should make sense from the standpoint of the particular regions involved and the kind of world structure the U.S. wants to see evolve. With respect to Europe, for instance, U.S. assistance in the creation of a European nuclear force is related to the kind of Europe America wants to see evolve. Any policy aimed at preventing the development of such a force would in fact require denuclearizing the Europeans. The existence of independent nuclear forces in Britain and France is an important reason for taking a positive attitude towards a European nuclear force.

Alternative Strategies

Among the strategic military alternatives possible under the Nixon Doctrine, there is no single preferred strategy for the decade of change into which the United States and the world have entered. If it is true, as has been argued, that the current nuclear posture of "U.S. strategic support of integrated forward defense" is no longer a sustainable strategy from the standpoints of cost or credibility, other strategic alternatives are possible, such as (1) a supranational strategic capability, with national strategic forces under the control of the U.N. or some free world body; (2) regional strategic nuclear capabilities; i.e., national strategic forces coordinated for a regional defense on the NATO pattern; (3) independent national solutions.

The first of these is possible but impractical, since no nation is likely to turn its nuclear trigger over to a supranational body. The second strategy is at least feasible, and a number of variants are possible within this concept. It would seem to lead to a multipolar nuclear situation, and probably to some proliferation of nuclear capabilities; e.g., a free world nuclear grouping in the Far East, probably involving nuclear weapons for Japan and Australia. The third "go-it-alone strategy" would lead to considerably greater nuclear proliferation, especially if confidence in the U.S. nuclear umbrella is perceived to be declining.

Thus, among these three strategies, the second alternative would seem to be preferable; it could be described as "independent regional defense capabilities," to include strategic, tactical nuclear and conventional forces. This strategy would substitute "controlled proliferation" for what could be a random and probably excessive proliferation if a go-it-alone strategy were adopted. Survivability of strategic forces would be emphasized by maintaining a mix (ruling out a "blue-water" strategy), and by taking protective measures. The strategy would include highly mobile, technologically advanced, ready-response forces to deal with conflicts beginning on a lower scale. The U.S. strategic forces under this concept should have a reasonable counterforce capability to overcome the moral and psychological limitations of a strategy based only on assured destruction of cities and people.

Another alternative is a maritime strategy. In view of the spread of Soviet influence internationally, the maritime arena can be seen as the principal area of future U.S.-Soviet interaction. The peacetime posture of the United States under a maritime strategy would involve forward deployment of U.S. forces to demonstrate U.S. interest and resolve in meeting its commitments. The U.S. overseas presence should be sufficient to have political impact. Adequate forces in being, particularly naval forces, would be necessary to deter the Soviets in crisis situations. Under this concept the strategic triad would be retained, but would give greater future emphasis to sea-based deterrence. NATO would continue to be of primary importance in regional strategy, but with a gradual shift of ground force responsibility to European allies. A U.S. military presence in the Pacific theater would rely heavily on sea-based and air forces. Overall, a "surge" capability for reinforcement at a crisis spot would be an essential element of strategy. While this strategy would place strong reliance on the partnership concept in conformity with the Nixon Doctrine, nevertheless the United States should retain unilateral decision prerogatives and force capabilities.

An examination in broad terms of the relationship between national strategy and the perceptions of the American people regarding what is necessary for future national security indicates to some analysts an erosion of the national will. Consistent with this trend, the current public antagonism to all things military would be seen as a product of both apathy and misinformation. The policy to reverse this situation would not, however, lie in radical movement in new directions; while it is proper to examine and discuss bold new strategies that may well be applicable in the future, prudence suggests that careful thought be given to the values of existing strategies, as to how well they have served in the past, and how they might be modified and strengthened for future validity.

No consensus emerged from the symposium on what would be the best military strategy to implement the Nixon Doctrine. To place primary reliance on assured destruction in future strategy appears philosophically unsound in that the Soviets have never accepted this doctrine in their strategic thinking. The implied nuclear inferiority in the assured destruction strategy has the very serious flaw that inferiority surrenders a usable political advantage to the enemy. Nuclear parity is therefore a political necessity, from which point both sides would see the wisdom of preventing nuclear war and of pursuing the goal of arms control in a mode that would assure survival rather than destruction. In choosing an effective U.S. strategy for the future there must be a better integration of military power with the many other elements of national strength—economic, social, cultural, psychological—into a rounded composite of total "political" power for peace. Further, besides the integration of U.S. strength, there is a necessity to marshal comparable allied strengths for a free world partnership approach to the challenges lying ahead.

VI. A New Domestic Consensus on Foreign Policy

The absence of a domestic consensus in the United States on the ultimate goals of American foreign policy is a significant constraint on the effective conduct of the country's foreign relations.

There are many signs that the internal values of the American people are changing. This change is taking many forms in many areas: civil rights, black power, women's liberation, and ecology. There are also evidences of a public retreat from the responsibilities of power, a lessening of national will, a growing doubt that the system will work and a lessening belief that classical, traditional American goals represent anything worth fighting for. Although the growth in the "attentive public" brought about by the mass media and mass education and the perceived growth in the subjective competence of the American citizen can be seen as healthy signs in the long run, the immediate result has been that American society has become highly fragmented. Each of the various sectors of American life have their advocates and their opinion leaders, and each exerts tremendous lobbying pressure on Congress.

These changes in the internal values of the American people are, indeed, influencing the sense of national priorities. It is becoming increasingly difficult to justify the U.S. defense budget to the American people in terms of the Cold War. Competing international influences are affecting people's lives and, more importantly, their pocketbooks. If priorities are viewed as what has first claim on resources, then it can be statistically demonstrated that changes in attitudes are having an adverse effect on U.S. international posture.

Besides the changes in values, there is evidence to show that during the 1960s the country's priorities changed. Priorities closely related to the U.S. international posture—national defense, research and development, space exploration and aid to developing nations—received less support. Programs relating to health, education, and welfare in the public sector received greater priority, in terms of percent increase of GNP. All visible signs point to a continuation of this trend.

Allocation of Resources

It is possible to analyze the shifts in American priorities according to how the dollars, public and private, are being spent. Areas making increasing claims on resources include private plant equipment, transportation, health, education, and public assistance. Spending in a new category, environmental protection, is also rising. Spending has been decreasing for urban facilities, national defense, research and development, foreign aid, and agricultural support. It is interesting to find that in spite of the claim often heard that Americans are less interested in the symbols of affluence, they continue to spend about five-eighths of their income for private affluence.

By the use of an econometric model to project potential GNP, one can identify the factors that condition economic growth in the future. Projection analyses show that to achieve a 4 percent growth rate and a 4 percent unemployment rate over the rest of the decade, it would require a doubling of government expenditures for goods and services. Or, to put it another way, by holding to a relatively constant defense budget, and even with exponentially rising non-defense government spending, the model indicates that the unemployment rate would rise rather rapidly over the decade, accompanied by sizeable inflation. It is probable that if Americans faced a choice between high unemployment, say 6 to 7 percent, and some inflation, say 5 to 6 percent per year, they would choose inflation.

The resource allocation problem can be related to two sets of values, the terminal and the adjectival. The former, representing the old and basic values—preservation of the state and the American system—can evoke sufficient sacrifice for adequate allocation of resources for their preservation. The adjectival values—related to changes in contemporary life styles—are more controversial and thus it is harder to obtain a consensus on spending for them. Thus there is dissent about priorities. In the post-industrial (or mass consumption) economy, there may be less inclination to give enough weight to the terminal (good) values to sustain adequate support. There is a budgetary dilemma in manipulating the defense and non-defense sectors: some 80 percent of non-defense expenditures are fixed by law, while only about 10 percent of defense expenditures are fixed. This leaves most of the discretionary spending in the defense area. It is possible to change the non-discretionary spending, since laws can be changed, but it would require a long and controversial political process. Thus defense spending tends to bear the brunt of budget cutting, unless an extremely strong case is made to the people to keep the defense budget up.

If one raises the question of why national security priorities and domestic social priorities cannot exist side by side, without undue shifting of either, the answer of most economists would be that the only way both areas can receive the support desired by advocates of each is to increase taxes; i.e., transfer resources from the private consumption sector to the public sector. This problem is a basic part of the search for a new American consensus. What may be needed is an analysis from the bottom up of resources required to support alternative strategies. This would mean, in the budget sense, a baseline review of all programs to permit reallocation of resources to those programs having the highest priority. Also needed is more effective and flexible federal interagency cooperation, although a major governmental reorganization probably is not required.

The Institutional Framework

In the search for new mechanisms to create a workable consensus, the institutional framework and organization of the U.S. government are important considerations. A problem is that the national security-foreign policy community of the United States is in a state of institutional crisis. This crisis appears to exist on all planes—the relationship between government and governed, between the executive branch, and the Congress, within the executive branch, and within the national security community itself.

The multiplicity of "foreign offices" also affects the conduct of foreign policy. The proliferation of Congressional committees and figures involved in Congressional oversight of American foreign policy has engendered confusion. Senator Humphrey's suggestion that a joint committee on national security be established in Congress could be one possible solution.

Another institutional problem is the tendency in the U.S. government to compartmentalize the conduct of foreign relations, leading to an inability to integrate the economic, the strategic-military, and the political factors into a coherent whole. The strengthening of the National Security Council would be one means of resolving this problem.

Other means of establishing consensus are possible. The various intellectual establishments can play an important role in influencing the communications media. They are a powerful force in developing or retarding the establishment of a new consensus in foreign policy goals.

Final Session: "A New Consensus?"

General Charles H. Bonesteel III:

After two days and three nights of attentive listening to our discussion, which to my mind has pretty well covered the waterfront, I have decided that I best can contribute, if at all at this late date, by taking a rather simple approach to this complexity that confronts us. In this vein I am going to impose on you and read a few definitions.

The Soviets and the Chinese have a complete and precise lexicon, and they know whereof they are speaking when they use a particular word or phrase. In our pluralistic society, I am sure each of us fully understands these definitions, but sometimes when we hear these words frequently in reports, our views are a little diffuse.

So using Webster's Collegiate Dictionary as my authority:

"Objective: an end or aim of action."

"Policy: a definite course or method of action selected from among alternatives and in light of given conditions to guide and determine present and future decisions."

"Doctrine: a statement of fundamental government policy, especially in international relations."

"Strategy: the art and science of employing the political, economic, psychological and military forces of a nation or group of nations to afford the maximum support to adopted policies in peace or war."

So much for the lexicon.

Today, this country has a broad policy, expressed publicly in three volumes, over three years, and an authoritative doctrine enunciated by our President. This doctrine may have caused some symptoms of future shock, but I suggest that we look at it in the sense that it has many perceptive features. It is perhaps broader and hopefully has more content than some of us allege.

Our objective according to the doctrine is a generation of peace. The Administration is clarifying its strategy to reach this objective to gain for it the maximum support possible under conditions of peace and war.

This doctrine according to opinions at this conference is realistic and was carefully selected from among alternatives. It is sensitive to the many meaningful changes that are taking place in the world, in our Western culture and in our democratic and pluralistic society; and it hopes to channel some of these changes in a constructive way.

This is our official policy.

We are not here to write on a *tabula rasa* a new and fresh policy. This is not done too simply in the real world. But we are here, I believe, each in his own responsible way, to see how we can be helpful with regard to that policy or one which—in our individual estimation—has greater content or meaning.

The foreign policy and doctrine of a great power such as ours will not remain credible or viable unless it has the loyal and responsible support of a preponderantly significant segment of the citizenry, and of our allies. It can only hold this support if it has integrity and persuasiveness—a persuasiveness of its hopes and its proofs of success, and an integrity to support itself against its critics and our adversaries. It obviously must be both sensitive to the times and also have staying power.

I suggest that we include these particular criteria, among others, as we later evaluate the constructive content of the reports of our working groups in our overall search for the basis of a national consensus to support such a policy for the coming and possibly decisive decade or more of change ahead.

Parenthetically, I would hope that we will not let a search for perfection be the enemy of the good.

It is also obviously true that what will really make our policy manifest is not its declaratory words, but how it is carried out in action. And this will depend, in large part, on the strategy derived to support the doctrine. In this regard, I would like to take a trip to China, which is a rather popular thing to do and, begging your indulgence, go back 2,500 years or so to reiterate our old friend Sun Tzu's elements of strategy.

As I repeat them, in brief, may I ask you to translate his word "war" as the Soviet definition of "peaceful coexistence," its comprehensive meaning as a protracted competition between the different social systems, with its just wars, and definitely involving the power element.

Sun Tzu says:

Generally in war the best policy is to take a state intact. To ruin it is inferior to this. To capture our enemy's army is better than to destroy it. To subdue the enemy without fighting is the acme of skill.

Thus, what is of supreme importance in war is to attack the enemy's strategy. Next best is to disrupt his alliances. Next best is to attack his army. The worst policy is to attack his cities. Attack cities only when there are no alternatives.

Your aim must be to take all under Heaven intact. Thus your troops are not worn out and your gains will be complete.

This is the art of offensive strategy.

We all know that Mao Tse-tung is a deep student and disciple of old Sun Tzu. But I would like to submit that, at least as a hypothesis, allowing for the passage of 2,500 years, the growth of nation-states, the explosion of technology, the awesome existence of nuclear weapons, and the declared conviction of all Soviet leaders that their ideology or, if you will, their socio-economic system, will not converge with ours, it would then appear that the Soviet policy-makers adopted much of the essence of Sun Tzu's strategic thinking and have been testing his strategic priorities on the non-communist "all under Heaven."

To me, at least, I think you can make the reasonable argument that a great deal of their total strategy is aimed at defeating our strategy. Therefore, I suggest that at least one hypothesis to determine the criteria by which to evaluate the effectiveness of a strategy in the future, that we test these strategies comprehensively against the essence, modernized, of old Sun Tzu. If they cope successfully with such a hypothetical strategy, then I think we can move on to their perfection or their increased subtleties.

That is all that I feel I could contribute in my small way to our overall discussion.

Group 1: Dr. N. Frederick Wikner:

Our particular working group was most congenial, and had many common points of interest which I will try to report accurately here.

First of all, my group noted that the past twelve years have seen something which many thoughtful men understood throughout their lives: that the phrase, "We will pay any price and share any burden," articulated at the Inaugural Address of President Kennedy, really was not a statement reflecting great insight; instead, except in extreme cases, the United States and its population was not willing to pay great prices for involvement overseas.

Ambassador Kohler very carefully reminded us that the average Congressman and Senator, as well as our body politic, has an interest in assisting peoples throughout the world, but they would much rather see this assistance levied on them through modest increases in taxes rather than the commitment of their sons to combat in causes in which they frequently do not see their own home interests clearly reflected. The panel reached a consensus that one of the underlying causes for the articulation of the Nixon Doctrine is the recognition of this essential point.

Our working group also noted two things that came out clearly in this meeting. We all generally agree that the Soviet Union has achieved essential nuclear parity with the United States, and that it has developed military forces that are now evident on a worldwide basis. We also cannot help but notice that China is emerging on the world scene.

The second factor is, of course, very significant: throughout the 1970s, it is our feeling that there still will be a dominant superpower consideration to keep in mind, and it will be the relationship between the United States and the Soviet Union.

Nevertheless, it is going to be to our advantage, and certainly to our best interests, to observe the greater expanding polarities of the world, and to encourage them. Our political and other relationships throughout the world give us a significant advantage over the Soviet Union. We are better prepared to deal with a multipolar problem than it is.

Many members of the panel were agreed that it is essential for a successful foreign policy to have the understanding and support of the American public.

We also need to have a good understanding of the conditions of the American priorities system, and those other conditions which seem to change rapidly with time. Here we all felt that Professor Trager's brief summary statement the other evening was very fine.

The U.S. has derived its serious values from its Judeo-Christian culture, as evolved and developed in 17th, 18th and 19th Century Europe, which as Professor Trager said, gave us terminal and adjectival values that were very important. Whatever our dissatisfactions might be with the state of our society, we still want to have a political, economic, and social system that allows the pursuit of life and liberty and opportunity, and we do not want this taken away from any of us.

The adjectival values, as Trager presented and talked about, do change. As H.L. Mencken has so beautifully observed, it gives a sort of carnival atmosphere to life in the United States on occasion. We can become very distressed with this, or we can enjoy it.

Another major point that the group made was not only should we try to remember the qualities of U.S. society that determine our foreign affairs, but we should also have a very clear and realistic view of the nature of our adversaries. Here we should note that the Cold War did not end with the Cuban missile crisis. It continues today. The Soviets call it peaceful coexistence, and we are greatly aided in understanding what the Soviets mean by that term by reading what the Soviets have to say about it.

We all wished, in our group, that more attention in this meeting could have been given to this, and particularly to a problem that we all face, that is: how can we describe the nature of Soviet intentions as well as capabilities that may match these intentions in terms that are more acceptable to the public and the Congress.

Finally, there was unanimity between members of the State Department, former Ambassadors as well as retired military, that as we consider the changes that are coming in this country and how they impact on our foreign policy, we should not forget the need to have adequate military power, and to have meaningful and secure alliances.

The Nixon Doctrine, as articulated and as I understand it, insists on the United States' maintaining adequate military forces, and it restates, as forcefully as anyone can, that we will continue to maintain significant military alliances throughout the world. We may change the character of these somewhat, but we certainly are not going to abandon them.

Sy Weiss, of the State Department, wanted me to state that one of his fears, and a fear of a number of his colleagues, is that we may reduce our military strength too rapidly, thus leaving the State Department and our Ambassadors overseas in the position of not having adequate military presence to back up and sustain the policies that we are trying to promulgate around the world.

Group 2: Mr. Fritz W. Ermarth:

Gentlemen, one need not dwell here on the difficulties of summarizing the debates of a group as varied in background as those members of Group 2. The value of the discussions themselves far exceeds that of my own poor efforts to distill them.

In retrospect, rather surprisingly to me, our deliberations gave scant attention to the substantive content of national security policy demanded in the decade before us, and to which the bulk of formal conference proceedings were devoted. This apparent lack of concern, I submit, resulted from far-reaching tacit agreement, at least within our group, on the most general imperatives of national security policy in a decade of change.

We were, I think, largely agreed that something akin to balance-of-power politics in a heterogeneous, multipolar world is going to be the name of the game; that we are faced with the conflicting requirements to sustain old alliance ties while exploring new relationships with two mutually hostile opponents. We also agreed that the new world will continue to demand of us formidable military power of great variety—too little, rather than too much of which may be provided by the continuation of present trends.

Although perhaps of only minimal prescriptive value, the substantive elements of policy on which I believe we tacitly agreed are in no way uncontested propositions in our society, which brings me to the primary subjects of our discussion, all of which deal with the problem of the political consensus that must underlie viable national security policy.

Our first general theme was: how should we think about the consensual demands of viable national security policy, and I should point out that we used the term "consensus" in the broadest sense as applying to the sources of public support for policy, to relations between the Executive Branch and the Congress, and to understanding and coherence within the Executive Branch of government.

We were, not surprisingly, agreed that we need more consensus at all of these levels than we have.

Another major point of agreement was that, as one member put it, "We can't go home again." It will be nigh impossible in the future to recreate the atmosphere of bipartisanship and public support that characterized the era of engagement in the 1940s and 1950s. Some pointed out, I think correctly, that we tend to exaggerate the degree of policy consensus that actually prevailed in those supposedly halcyon days.

To my own surprise, there was rather general agreement in our group that the kind of dissent with which, at best, we shall have to learn to live is not necessarily a bad thing. Pervasive consensus on goals and means in any policy arena may be a recipe for serious errors and oversights.

One of the areas where we were not able to agree, it seems to me, was in defining in some sort of meaningful way the degree of consensus at various levels demanded for policy viability. Some of the group—notably public officials—took the view that the present lack of consensus is a serious constraint on national policy-making by the Presidency. Striking a somewhat different note, others—myself included—tended to believe that the President retains great and underexploited power both to mold policy consensus and indeed to pursue policies in the face of vigorous overt dissent.

Another important point on which we tended to agree, aided by the equilibrating perspective of Secretary Fowler, was that important areas of foreign policy—notably much of foreign economic policy—do enjoy necessary support among critical publics. It is primarily in the definition of levels, character, and application of military power, as well as foreign aid, where the problem lies; and these are happily not the entirety of our foreign affairs.

Our second major concern was whether the Nixon Doctrine, as articulated to date, can provide a basis for generating required consensus at all relevant levels.

Here it was agreed that, on the most general plane, the Nixon Doctrine does respond to inexorable pressure of the external and internal national security environment, but it remains, in our view, a seriously deficient set of instruments for leadership in national security policy.

I am not being unjust, I think, in detecting even in its defenders among us a sense that sloganeering rather than substance characterizes much of the Nixon Doctrine. For planners and executors of policy in government it lacks much of the operational guidance demanded of it, and indeed claimed for it, by its authors. For interested publics, of whatever persuasion, it is a poor means of structuring expectations.

As one member of our group argued, the Doctrine should at least give us a clue about what should not happen. The Nixon Doctrine allows for a great many momentously different futures, all of which are disturbing to sizable critical publics.

This leads me to our final area of concern. Leaving aside the substantive imperatives of policy, by what political and institutional procedures are leaders in national security to garner the necessary degree of consensus in the public and the government?

Unfortunately, limitations of time, discipline, and I daresay candor on our part, precluded a comprehensive attack on this problem.

On one point we were largely agreed: however childish, irascible, even malign are some of its Congressional opposites, the Administration must show a good deal more effort and forbearance in cultivating Congressional support for the involvement in national security policy decisions. This is, I would judge, very much a matter of style, but one on which the gravest security and even Constitutional issues may hinge.

Beyond this, we engaged in a lot of complaining. The apportionment of responsibilities within the Executive Branch is unhealthily concentrated in the White House, conflicting at the very least with the overt structure of government. The Nixon process leaves much to be desired, a point on which Kissinger, I suspect, would agree.

Understanding among engaged levels and agencies in government is inadequate, while communications are voluminous. Although its implications remain obscure, this theme was constantly on our minds. The way we conduct the business of making and executing national security policy has got to be scrutinized and quite possibly reformed.

Group 3: Dr. Philip H. Lowry:

I am extraordinarily impressed by the fact that all five groups seem to have tackled this problem from complementary points of view; in the sense that Group 1 dealt with philosophy, Group 2 dealt with structure, and Group 3, because of the accidents of statistics—if its selection was a quasi-random process—dealt with substance.

Our first creation was to find a major gap in the proceedings. We felt that insufficient attention had been given to the strengths of the United States and the Free World. Everybody is so bemused by the weaknesses of the future, that it is a miracle this country even exists today.

Our pluralistic society is in fact a great strength. It is better able to handle multipolarity, and it is far more adaptive to change.

The United States' demonstrated capacity for abrupt change when the crunch comes—I am thinking of Korea and Pearl Harbor—is a major deterrent to the other side. They never can be sure of the U.S. reaction.

U.S. industrial productivity and the rise of Japan has demonstrated the failure of socialist theory. I do not think that thought ever has appeared in a public statement, although the converse appears in every party congress on the other side. The industrial base of the Free World serves as a deterrent to less than general war. If the United States in particular is not destroyed, any overt aggression by the Pact risks a radical change in priorities and a major jump in military budgets.

Another problem deals more with the execution of foreign policy. Can we structure our policy, our doctrine, our strategy and our tactics, on our strengths? We must do this if we are going to have the initiative. Otherwise we are shoring up weaknesses, which tends to diffuse our efforts and makes us not quite strong enough anywhere.

Our second major point concerns regional priorities. We noted that the conference was not entirely helpful. Going through the various papers, we noted that Europe is "essential," the Middle East is "inescapable," the Atlantic is "crucial," the Pacific is "critical," the Indian Ocean is "vital," and the Mediterranean is of "immediate concern."

Our conclusion is that all of these regions are, in fact, interrelated, and a regional approach to formulating policy is probably a bad thing.

On military priorities, we had—I would not say "vigorous," but "determined"—discussion. We concluded that this conference had not given sufficient attention to military assistance as part of the military priorities.

An additional gap, that was alluded to by Andy Pierre and others, was this: What should the policy of this country be in the event—and the very likely event—that some of our allies who are now non-nuclear will become nuclear powers? Is this something that we should encourage? In particular, I can report a complete consensus that if Japan should elect to become a nuclear power, we should not make the same mistake we made with regard to France.

Group 4: Mr. George D. Hopkins:

I want to thank all the members of Group 4 for their conscientious participation in our deliberations, but especially I want to thank Dean Edmund Gullion of the Fletcher School, who put together this paper which seems to summarize most of our thoughts well.

He entitled the paper: "Some Reflections on Consensus, the Nixon Doctrine and the Balance of Power."

The need for consensus in foreign policy is obvious and especially so in a democracy. We have enjoyed a rough consensus in this country since 1947 that was inherent to the wartime cohesion and because of a continuing threat commonly perceived by the population.

In the sense that foreign policy involves goals, the means of attaining them, the detailed conduct of foreign affairs, a choice of defense strategy and tactics, agreement on costs and risks to be accepted, and an agreed scale of priorities— such conditions do not now exist in this country.

Consensus has been the victim not solely of the Vietnam war, but also the crushing weight of cumulative trials and burdens: fatigue after a generation of hard toil in the foreign field; a considerable degree of success that has served to diminish the perception of danger; the pressure of a new generation to whom the struggles of their fathers is merely history; concurrent domestic crises; and the acting out on the American scene of social revolutionary trends that are secular and worldwide.

Such consensus as still exists is diluted or possibly masked by the fight between the Senate and the Executive on their responsibilities for foreign affairs, and by the minority role of the President's party in the Congress.

There does, no doubt, exist an American consensus on priorities about peace, national survival, territorial integrity, continuance of the American way of life, and fidelity to our obligations, probably in about that order. There is probably also a majority belief, but not a consensus, that we are over-extended and ought to concentrate more and spend more on domestic needs. But the majority would begin to break up at questions of the best location for our defense lines, or of how much we should spend on defense.

There is no consensus in the new foreign policy in any meaningful sense, or even a consensus in the proposition that some old foreign policy, familiar to the general public, is out of date, unworkable or abandoned.

President Nixon probably would be right in thinking that there is a lowest common denominator consensus on the very general principles of the Nixon Doctrine as enunciated in a Presidential broadcast to the nation on November 3, 1969. The United States will keep its treaty commitments, provide a shield to allies and countries deemed vital to our security, but will look to nations otherwise situated to assume the primary responsibility of providing manpower for their own defense.

If we try to translate that Doctrine into specifics of who, what, where, when, how long, with what, who first and at what cost, the Doctrine raises more questions than it answers. The unfolding of the future and of the budget choices will inevitably bring answers of a kind, but others that go to the heart of intentions will remain.

Will we in fact keep all of our commitments? To Taiwan, for example, to Pakistan, to CENTO? If some of our alliances become outdated, what will we do about it? Can we find the additional tax money to afford the kind of armament the farflung alliance network requires?

How do we reassure our allies and our own people about our intentions when we seem to court our enemies? How do we convince peoples that we are standing firm when they actually see us pulling out? Will our deterrent remain credible? What is our answer to the worldwide Gaullist-type doubts? These are a few of the questions which press for resolution.

It has, however, been revealed by the Administration, and here at Airlie, that a multipolar world and a balance-of-power theorem exist, and that its manipulation will presumably be the mode by which the Doctrine will be applied.

The more sophisticated public will understand the balance-of-power considerations, while others may rid themselves of the feeling that these are somehow immoral. But there is far from being a consensus on how to operate a balance-of-power policy or upon its merits and demerits.

Balance of power means playing one party off against another. We see nothing wrong with that if the American leadership can do it, and if our people do not get the impression that it warrants a massive withdrawal from commitments and forward defense.

A balance-of-power condition assumes, among other things: first, a concept or paradigm of world order and legitimacy shared by the constituent powers; a weight and balance reasonably known or constant for each power; and a reasonable constancy in leadership and political principle.

To operate a balance-of-power policy requires, among other things: sophisticated leadership and consummate skill in summitry, against a more historical expectation; a willingness on the part of people to entrust power of great discretion to professionals—soldiers and diplomats; an aptitude for secret diplomacy; an open-minded commitment on the part of the people to foreign entanglements even in the face of what may be bewildering changes in companions and in destinations; a showing that the volatility of the combinations in pursuit of balance does not increase risks in an atomic age; and finally, a credible willingness on the part of a nation possessing power to place it where it is needed—for example, by the United States in Asia if required.

In other words, the optimum operation of the balance may require a supply of statesmen like Bismarck and a people as disciplined as the Prussians.

Whether the American people understand and accept these implications is questionable. Nevertheless, whether we like it or not, this may well be the way things are, and this may be the name of the game.

It is also true that new factors in technology and "correlation of forces" dictate considerable revisions in deployment, weaponry, and strategy.

Our point is merely that the ingredients of an informal consensus do not yet exist and should not be certified to exist until they do. It is not enough merely to bring the words "balance of power" into the open or to acknowledge multipolarity. These are not enough to constitute a policy on which consensus can be sought.

As suggested at this conference, there is widespread apprehension or, depending on one's point of view, anticipation that multipolarity coupled with the Nixon Doctrine is only a rationale for vast retreat. We believe it is none of these things, and cannot be, but many of our own people and our allies do believe it.

The laying down of burdens always appeals to people. We fear that the Nixon Doctrine can be falsified by an uncontrollable chain reaction into some kind of neo-isolationist result. This is why we believe it is premature to claim a consensus without seeing clearly what it involves. We hope, of course, that the American people will pursue unity, if not consensus, even while uncertainty continues.

The Administration can doubtless do much to persuade worried foreign leaders that the Nixon Doctrine is not a formula for disengagement. It may be harder to convince the Americans, including Administration opponents who claim to see the Doctrine, the China visit, and other actions as a move into their camp.

It is also high time, as we have been urged at this meeting, for the majority of the so-called opinion molders—educators and others—who are persuaded that the Nixon Doctrine does not mean dismantling collective security to spread that message. But people believe what they want to believe, and this will not be an easy job.

We do not presume to say how this can be done, especially in an election year. We should take heart in our resources and our record. What is lacking here is not the means, but the will. The nation still retains major strengths, and these strengths will be required to maintain a strong defense while a new consensus emerges.

We still have firmly-rooted national traditions, including one of success. We are favored still by our geographic position, wealth, and our unparalleled technology. We have a good record. We seem to be heading toward a trillion dollar economy with only moderate inflation at something approaching full employment. We have the means.

If the Nixon Doctrine is to be successful, the moral factor will have to outweigh the material factor by an even greater margin than it usually does.

Group 5: Dr. James E. Dougherty:

Our group had the same problem with the tyranny of terms as everybody else, I suppose. We began by asking whether multipolarity, whatever that is, including some vestiges of the Cold War, is better than the old bipolarity, whatever that was. Burt Marshall reminded us that there never was a time after World War II when the United States, even when it was apparently vested with a kind of international omnipotence, was really able to manage this unruly world with any semblance of efficiency. He said we would have to beware of overglamorizing "the good old days."

Recent history, to paraphrase Voltaire, is a bag of tricks the older generation plays on itself by exaggerating the successes and forgetting the failures of the Truman-Eisenhower years.

One of our members, Len Weiss, urged us to recognize that non-military factors may become of increasing importance. He saw such factors as national morale and resolve, the social and political cohesion of the society, and the way people and leaders behave under stress as being more significant than the precise military-technological equation. Not all of his formulations met with the agreement of all present, but I deem it only fair to report what Len had contributed.

One of our members was struck by the fact that this conference seemed to accept not necessarily with enthusiasm but with a certain amount of equanimity the idea of independent nuclear forces in Europe and Asia. He also noted that there were few demurrers from the proposition that the continuation of the Atlantic alliance and the U.S. military presence in Europe is a prime goal, but tactical nuclear weapons are needed in the NATO force structure, and that we should take a sensible cut at mutual and balanced force reductions (MBFR).

If this is indeed an era of negotiations, then we ought to be seeking agreements which produce symmetrical effects upon the security of all parties concerned, and which leave none of them feeling psychologically disadvantaged. We should also attend to the maintenance of those capabilities which will enable us to achieve and preserve equitable symmetrical arrangements.

Thus, when we start negotiating Phase 2 of SALT, or the linkage of SALT to MBFR and a conference on European security, we ought to emphasize in NATO consultations our insistence upon symmetrical reductions, such as a tradeoff of quick-reaction aircraft for tanks, as an earnest of our continued commitment to the alliance.

We should be ready to reach a bargain on anything, but we should not give up assets without a *quid pro quo*.

Our informal session last night helped us to come to grips with the problem of national consensus in relation to the Nixon Doctrine. What seemed to come out of that discussion was that the level of international activity that we sustained in the past may be less necessary in present circumstances, even though we shall as a nation continue to do what we deem necessary to defend vital interests, which are always hard to define in advance of actual challenges.

The Doctrine envisages a less kinetic attitude in foreign affairs, a lower profile, greater local self-help with a renewed U.S. assistance program, and a sort of calculated pause during which we adjust U.S. foreign policy commitments down to a level that will command support from a public suffering from crisis fatigue, disenchanted with the role of "world policeman," and frustrated by the ethical, psychological, and fiscal ambiguities inherent in a policy of guns *and* butter during a protracted, distant, and poorly understood war.

Undoubtedly, the Nixon Doctrine owes its genesis to the domestic situation and to new international conditions. As David Jordan put it last night, the President seeks to cool the country, so that the nation can bind up its wounds. If the Doctrine serves its purpose, it will hopefully create the conditions in which a national consensus on foreign policy objectives can be slowly restored. It cannot be quickly manufactured, nor can it be imposed. It has to reemerge gradually, especially among the policy, communications, and intellectual elite, who were more disunited and uncertain than the population at large.

We too agreed that the Doctrine does not mean retreat or neo-isolationism. After a period of relaxation and consensus building, the President could shift back to a renewed policy emphasis on strength and commitment. The Doctrine does not mean, in our view—nor would the public be willing to tolerate an admission—that we are now ready to let Vietnam or any other country in Southeast Asia go down the drain. In fact, one of the assumptions on which the Doctrine is based is that the international conditions make that a bit less likely to occur now, and that a timely modification of our posture might enhance the prospects of holding, in the long run, what otherwise might have been lost.

I would end with one personal comment. The psychopolitical texture of the international system today is what it is in no small degree because of our decision to go into Vietnam in the mid-1960s. If there is something slightly incredible to us about the President's trip to Peking, it probably would have been even more incredible had we and the world not experienced all the various effects of Vietnam on our strategic posture, on domestic and foreign attitudes, on Sino-Soviet relations and so forth.

We should hesitate, then, to conclude that Vietnam has been a failure of national policy. We can look at it as a kind of U.S. holding operation, an effort to establish a quasi-equilibrium in Asia, while the implications of the shift toward multipolarity were becoming a bit clearer.

Perhaps Walt Rostow was right in suggesting that this has been Asia's world war of the great powers, which could lead first to containment and subsequently to a sort of mutual deterrence in Asia, as happened in Europe 25 years ago. The Soviets were neither able nor willing to counter the Lin Piao strategy; we had to try to make its application too costly. The Chinese could not deter a Soviet nuclear attack, but without having had to utter a threat, the mere existence of the U.S. strategic force and the uncertainty of what a Sino-Soviet World War would lead to eventually may have helped to deter such a war.

Thus the United States, I think, has contributed toward drawing Asia into a global balance system in which the future of political-strategic equilibrium on that continent will be integrally related to the strengthening and extension of mutual deterrence in the world as a whole.

As Burt Marshall noted, who would have thought two years ago that Cambodia could still be hanging on today? For this intervention, the United States has paid a heavy price, but perhaps our postwar disillusionment while the war is still going on will eventually give way to a fuller appreciation of the magnitude of what we have wrought at tragic cost, to ourselves, and, even more, to the people of Vietnam.

Our group ended its dialogue last night on a note of quiet confidence, I think.

We said that this nation, as a nation, still has important things to achieve in the world, and we had confidence in the ability of this people to survive what we have been through and to regain a balanced and hopefully more mature perception of our future role in the world.

Dr. William R. Kintner:

Most of my commentary will concern the papers prepared for the conference. Before discussing them, I would like to share some of the background of this conference. Both Dick Foster and I, working in the national security vineyard for many years, became aware of the Nixon Doctrine during its formulation. We viewed it as a serious effort to restructure American foreign policy and looked around to colleagues in our respective worlds and found that few seemed to attach proper importance to it, particularly within the bureaucracy. As one reason for this, Dr. Edmund Gullion pointed out that, beyond the level of philosophy, the Nixon Doctrine could be interpreted a thousand ways. It can be all things to all people. Yet philosophically, the Nixon Doctrine does command respect, both from the people who are disenchanted with the American role in the world and those who believe the United States still has an active and constructive role to play.

Consequently, one aim of the Conference on National Strategy in a Decade of Change is to search for a new consensus on American foreign policy. At a time when the United States is undergoing a crisis of confidence in its institutions and its basic values, it becomes desirable to search for a common purpose and to achieve some general agreement on our foreign policy goals. The Nixon Doctrine, which seeks to establish broad guidelines for an American role in leading the world toward a generation of peace, could provide a framework for this new consensus.

Some of us have heard Dr. Henry Kissinger describe the Nixon Doctrine as "not a cookbook." This is as it should be, for the Doctrine is a general statement of principles. The task is to better apply the general principles of the Doctrine to the more specific foreign policy problems of the present decade. Our conference should contribute to this end.

A recent editorial from the *Wall Street Journal* addressed this issue:

. . . . each of the foreign policy statements the President has issued these past few years, makes it clear enough that he wants badly to turn loose of the global arrangements . . .that have served so well since World War II but now seem increasingly undermined by the passage of time and events. Mr. Nixon wants to join with others, both allies and adversaries, to construct a new world order.

While it is impossible to say exactly what this new global arrangement will look like, it is evident Mr. Nixon is not trying to preserve the tightly-knit military-economic-political blocs that have divided the world for the last quarter of a century. Rather, he believes that beneath the umbrella of strategic balance of power, there can be a looser, more relaxed economic and political interplay among the nations of the world.[1]

This is also a fair statement of the gist of the deliberations of the conference.

Several common themes emerged from the papers that I read. There was an almost universal acceptance of the fact that we are now in a period of great change, both international and domestic. These changes were discussed by Mr. Leon Sloss and several others. The United States is perhaps changing more rapidly than any other major power. Mr. M. Mark Earle, Jr.'s paper suggested that if we are in fact moving into the postindustrial era, which is to culminate around the year 2000, then the next ten years will be the most critical, both from the point of view of our own internal development and the impact of this transition on the world at large.

Concern was expressed about the internal situation in the United States in almost all of the papers. Such phrases as "The U.S. is slipping collectively, but better off individually," "decadence in the American spirit" and "self-flagellation" were voiced by several participants. General S.L.A. Marshall noted the low esteem in which our armed forces are currently held, particularly by the media. On the economic side, Professor Henry C. Wallich analyzed the decline of American predominance in the area of trade and in the international monetary system.

The dark side of our history is being scanned by those critical of our society. Many participants expressed concern with the arguments made by the revisionist school concerning the Cold War and by those who believe the United States is arrogant in its use of power.

Dr. James N. Rosenau discussed what he called the first American adaptation transformation. The United States is now moving from a promotive relationship to the world to a preservative one. The last twenty-five years of our history have been abnormal. We had never before been so deeply engaged in the world outside, but for the twenty-five years of the postwar period the United States did try to shape the world somewhat along the lines of its own desires. This period is now coming to an end and, as Dr. Rosenau suggests, we are now trying to preserve what we have, both internally for the people within our own society, and externally by trying to find a new balance in our relations with the rest of the world.

In the conference presentations there were a number of allusions to the role of diplomacy. Mr. Richard B. Foster's paper, for example, noted that the role of the diplomat has increasingly emphasized efforts to influence—directly or indirectly—the domestic policies of the host nation. This is not a new phenomenon—communist states have been practicing it for years—but it has become more important because if they can influence internal attitudes, they may determine the external. It is quite clear that Hanoi's policy toward the United States is not limited to the battlefield but focuses on opinions in Washington and throughout the United States.

Dr. Robert L. Pfaltzgraff's paper analyzed diplomatic summitry as embracing not only meetings of heads of government but also the centralization of foreign policy machinery in the offices of the heads of government. In his view, summitry in the first sense is not fully compatible with maintaining and strengthening relations with U.S. allies, since the rapidity of change sometimes resulting from summitry may undermine the confidence of our partners. Summitry can be criticized, as George Ball did so eloquently in the *New York Times*, but the fact remains that it is being practiced by every major leader in the world. The key issue is how to keep the drama of summitry alive for certain useful effects without destroying the patient and studied diplomatic interaction that has to take place at the working level. If the requirements of diplomatic professionals are ignored, summit meetings may produce diplomatic disasters.

A number of papers argued that the United States must exercise care lest the new contacts with our adversaries should destroy the bonds of trust and confidence with our friends. This is of particular importance in relation to those nations of Asia with which the United States has had long and deep associations, including Taiwan. In the flush of the new relationship with Peking, the United States must insure that early concessions affecting the interests of our allies do not leave us negotiating from a position of weakness.

We need to give greater consideration to psychological and political warfare. This is not a new idea. It is something that we have discussed but neglected for the past twenty-five years, but in the era we are now entering it becomes even more important. Dr. Richard L. Walker's paper on the Asian areas stressed this point. At a time when the President can visit Moscow and Peking, it is important to draw moral distinctions between the Western and the Communist worlds and to transmit our values to the uncommitted.

Although the potential and actual threats which United States strategy and the Nixon Doctrine must face were not the direct subject of the conference, many participants did allude to danger areas. Participants presented papers on four such areas: Dr. David C. Jordan on Latin America, Dr. Walker on the Pacific, Dr. Alvin J. Cottrell on the Indian Ocean, and Dr. Laurence W. Martin on Europe. For example, Dr. Martin's paper was concerned with the dangers that will confront Western Europe if the United States does not inspire greater cohesion in NATO. In the event of American withdrawal from Europe, the probable failure of the Europeans to pick up the slack would result in the Soviet Union's enjoying a tremendous military preponderance and concomitant political influence. Dr. Morton A. Kaplan noted the difficulty of assessing Soviet strategies on issues of arms control and European security and outlined three competing strategies supported by various groups in the Soviet Union. He also noted that most problems of security and arms control will be subordinated to the more general political and military relations between the two superpowers, at least through the present decade.

Similar worries were voiced with respect to other parts of the world. Dr. Jordan's paper made the very informative point that the erosion of the land base of America's seapower is a major goal of Soviet strategy. They are simultaneously trying to build up their own land base to support the worldwide use of their own seapower. In the geopolitical sense, the United States is an offshore island of the Eurasian-African land mass. Until the present, the United States has enjoyed free access to the peripheries of Europe and Asia and has denied others access to all of North America. Now the Soviet Union is beginning to play in our waters while we are losing the capacity to play in theirs.

The four papers devoted to specific geographical regions stressed the need for the United States to maintain its regional commitments. Just as NATO remains the keystone of European security, Japan, the Republic of Korea, and the Republic of China remain the keystone of Asian security. Major General Alexander M. Haig, in his address to the conference, asserted that the United States was indeed maintaining its commitments. But in actual fact, the strength that underlies these commitments is declining. For example, when I was in Korea in June of last year, we officially had 40,000 men stationed in that country. I was told at that time that the actual figure was much lower. In the 1972 posture statement by the Secretary of Defense, the figure is still carried at 40,000, yet there have been two troop reductions that have taken place in the past year. This dichotomy between what we say we are doing to keep our commitments, and what we are actually doing, tends to undermine confidence among our allies.

Striking a somewhat different note, it seemed to me that Dr. Cottrell, in his suggestive paper on the Indian Ocean, has overlooked the fact that we are in a period of retrenchment. He recommended that the United States enter the Indian Ocean in strength as rapidly as possible, particularly with maritime forces, in order to maintain a degree of stability in that region. His argument is based on an important fact—namely, that 90 percent of Japan's energy sources must travel through that region, as does 65 to 70 percent of Europe's energy sources. Moreover, unless the United States finds alternative energy sources by the 1980s, we will have to import 50 percent of our oil from the Middle East. To avoid this would require the discovery of reserves equivalent to Libya's every year. Since this is unlikely, the question becomes, as Dr. Cottrell notes, whether the United States is going to permit the Indian Ocean area to become vulnerable to increased political pressures emanating from the growing Soviet naval presence? On the other hand, however, it must be doubted whether the present mood of the nation permits us to undertake such a new commitment.

General Richardson and others contributed valuable analyses of the nuclear question. The general consensus seemed to be that "nuclear neutralism" is the best policy toward Japan. If the Japanese decide that our umbrella is getting too thin, the most disastrous move we could make would be to oppose their acquisition of nuclear arms. It would do irreparable harm to the U.S.-Japanese link. Likewise, in Dr. Martin's paper, it was argued that a united Europe could not acquire a sense of confidence based on greater autonomy without coming to grips with its own concepts of nuclear defense.

In my view, the United States should realize that some of the ideas of the early 1960s, to the effect that all nuclear proliferation is bad and should be opposed, need reassessment. It is the Soviet Union, rather than the United States, who should be most concerned about our allies acquiring nuclear weapons. To the United States, some limited proliferation would be a source of strength. Several participants also recognized the necessity of incorporating tactical nuclear weapons more fully into European defense strategy, primarily as a deterrent.

Many recommendations were made for better adapting national strategy to the exigencies of the present decade. Dr. Andrew J. Pierre suggested that America's present and future interests and commitments be reappraised, primarily by the Congress, on a region-by-region basis. Other participants made similar proposals. One may legitimately question whether the some forty-four different alliances (with the commitments implied in them) to which the United States subscribes will serve as best in the future. Can the United States count on some of the benefits of the multipolar world to relieve us in part of direct responsibility for global security?

Few of the papers took the view that we are already in a multipolar world at this early date. One major question we face is how to move toward the emerging new order to our maximum advantage with improved stability in the global system. We are now witnessing some of the birth pangs of multipolarity but have yet to reap the benefits. To date, American power has declined more quickly than it has been replaced by the new centers of power.

In many of the papers the importance of leadership was underscored. Do we have the staying power for a prolonged contest with totalitarian opponents? How can we insure discipline within our bureaucracy so that any President can announce his policy to the bureaucracy without having it prematurely publicized in the newspapers the next day? As Dick Foster observed, the Soviet Union has a highly professional cadre of strategic planners. Can our own divided bureaucracy continue to compete successfully? This is one of several organizational problems that require our close attention if foreign policy and security policy are to be made more effective.

The papers presented at the conference were uniformly excellent. I would hope—if all works out well—that we can perhaps convene this group at the end of 1972. In the interim, I hope the authors of the papers will reflect on them in the context of the interaction they had at the conference, as well as on world developments during the year. Then perhaps we can produce a volume that could be made available to the public, addressed to whomever the next President of the United States may be. I believe that the transmission of the ideas of this conference to the public at large would be a fruitful endeavor.

Those who are concerned about national security have difficulty in making their points of view known to the public. I attended a conference about two weeks ago that was called together by former Senator Joseph Clark for the National Urban Coalition. At the beginning of the conference Senator Clark mentioned that there were several hundred active peace groups in the United States. Peace is a banner we all seek to serve. Yet I do object to the fact that the peace groups that tend to ignore the needs of security seem to own the title. If we advocate a sound national security policy we should also be able to claim the peace title. Unfortunately, there are only a few active groups in the United States who are informing the people at large about the legitimate claims of security.

Last year, Joe Fowler tried to help bring such a group together nationally and perhaps the effort should be revived. I share the opinion that has been expressed here—that between now and November we are going to be listening to, and living in, the national election circus in which it will be difficult to move toward any new consensus. But when the final count is in, each of us must work toward this end. The support of the American people must be enlisted in behalf of whoever has the responsibility for leading our country into the 200th anniversary of our birth as a nation.

Mr. Richard B. Foster:

I would like to start out by thanking you all; you are a very hardy group. From the schedule we have followed, it looks as if this meeting had been designed by a group of Puritans with the work ethic of 1620 who looked on winter's weather as a challenge and a spur. Perhaps in some sense we are trying to recover a part of that work ethic and other elements of the Puritan tradition. My own ancestry goes back to the group of men who were the original Puritans. As part of the Puritan tradition, the colloquy was a requirement. My father's monologues led me to realize how important it was to do a bit of study so that I could make it into a dialogue. It took many years before he acknowledged my existence as a member of the dialogue, but it finally happened.

Our meeting is thus in one of the oldest and greatest of American traditions, to enter into a colloquy about matters of great import, and to voluntarily associate out of concern for the common weal. I think it is in this sense of our traditions that the organizational pattern and principle of voluntary association is best expressed in the type of symposium we have held here.

This symposium had another aim—that of research. You are participating in a relatively new type of process—the interdisciplinary team approach to complex social and political problems. I believe we have the basis to produce a research product that no person or single group—at a research institute or inside government—could have produced.

In my paper on "Strategic Interactions," I brought up the intellectual challenge to America laid down by the Soviet Union. Such a colloquy as this, in which we make an attempt to think through very complex issues, a step at a time, with patience, through participation, is the beginning of an answer to that challenge. We have given all of you copies of the latest 1972 official state documents of our government relating to national security. Whoever is President in 1973 will have to live with these documents; he won't be able to change policy abruptly. He will need to live with the policies of his predecessors, just as this President has had to live with the policies of his predecessors. In a great nation there can only be an evolutionary change of national security policy and doctrine.

As to the threats to our nation's security, we deliberately avoided inviting papers on this subject. These threats are summarized in President Nixon's Foreign Policy Report to Congress and in the annual report of the Secretary of Defense. Mr. Baroody's statement that these unclassified documents "tell it like it is" means that there are no "top secret" documents and other higher categories of classification that have more valid information. This is an open government and these documents contain the facts on which we base our policy. The actual world situation—including the military balance—is as portrayed in these two documents and in other open U.S. State papers.

In this sense, we are doing something, I think, of a magnitude of greatness that has very seldom been risked in human history. We are making available to our adversaries—to the Soviet Union and China—the material about our forces, about their forces, and the comparison of relative strengths that neither the Russian nor the Chinese government make available either to us or to their own people. For example, in the SALT negotiations the negotiating numbers and characteristics of Soviet weapons are unilaterally provided by the United States, at great cost and expense to us. The ICBM we have termed "SS-9"—a term which our Russian colleagues use—is a U.S. term. We don't know what the Soviets call their ICBMs—and you may be interested to know that the Soviet research groups with whom I have had discussions are very anxious to find out from me what military forces their own government has deployed. With the open U.S. official sources—together with data from the London International Institute of Strategic Studies, I can say to my Russian research colleagues "now we have something we can talk about, since my government has provided you with the assessment of your strengths as well as our own."

This must be the answer to the question of "credibility" of our own government. The dilemma posed by stubborn Soviet secrecy was resolved by the United States unilaterally in a most extraordinary manner. We forget how great a moral strength and conviction of the worth of our open society this act takes. It is a strength of the U.S. system that we seldom reflect on.

The timing of our colloquy is fortuitous. The three official U.S. documents you have were just published. The President is in China. Many of our guests from government are somewhat exhausted from turning out these documents and preparing for the President's trip to China. We are happy to have this balanced attendance from the Government and private sectors, a balance of military and Foreign Service officers, of active researchers, of professors from academia, of men from the world of business. We can, however, improve on our participation. For example, we have very little or no participation from minority groups.

We plan to keep in touch with you as a group. A consensus, even if it is limited, once reached, is a very precious thing from a voluntary group. With all our differences, we recognize the necessity of getting together on problems of national security and national survival. We have tried to avoid politics and polemics. I think we have succeeded. Sometime after the November elections, perhaps in December or early next year, we will reconvene.

The Nixon Doctrine I take to be a guide in our search for a national consensus. It is based on an open approach, on open literature. Matters that once were treated with greatest secrecy within Defense and State are now available for public discussion and debate. It provides the basis for a centrist strategy and for a political centrism that constitutes what we used to call bipartisanship in foreign policy. Our national strategy must have an appeal to a large enough section of the populace so that it does in fact enjoy the support at least of a majority of the Senate.

We cannot allow ourselves to be picked apart by our adversaries. If we fail because of lack of will to reach a consensus, we will in fact fulfill the prophecy of our enemies who predict our demise by internal dissolution, not by war. I am not afraid of a preventive nuclear war launched by the Soviet Union. I am concerned, and I think we all should be, of the use they make of their intelligence, of the skill of their strategists, of the great conviction that they have about the moral rightness of their cause. In the last analysis, they are thinking men with a common experience and a common dialectical logic—not doctrinaire fanatics or slaves of computers.

I think one of the great problems we have to overcome is the notion that we can think of the Russians as "fatalities"—"120 million Russian fatalities" balanced against "120 million American fatalities." We have to start thinking of them as thinking men in terms that General Bonesteel outlined—men who are trying to discern and to defeat our strategy. In terms of "all things under Heaven," to take us intact by political means, not defeated and destroyed in war.

The modern purpose of military arms is the indirect manipulation of strategy and policy—not a direct means of waging war. I think we will soon have an agreement with the Russians reflecting the fact that the competition in nuclear arms is too dangerous. We and the Russians are trying to alter the means of competition in arms to a less dangerous form. In fact, if the Nixon Doctrine means a shift to an "era of negotiation," we really have a chance to change from a very dangerous form of nuclear confrontation to a less dangerous form of social-economic-political-diplomatic competition. I think we should all welcome this change to peaceful competition. This is something we can win, and win very effectively if we put our minds to it. Thus, the Nixon Doctrine will be less a matter of rhetoric and statements of high purpose, such as those included in Mr. Kennedy's 1961 Inaugural Address, and more a matter of thinking through and working out the very complex problems of our contemporary era, both domestic and international. Slogans alone won't do that job.

I want to thank now all of you who did participate.

General Bonesteel:

I think we shall call it quits here. It is not my mission to try to derive any consensus from our discussion today, but if there was one, or two, I think they come out pretty loud and clear.

The first one that seems generally held is that it is a shame that the internal values of the American people and perhaps of the West seem to be changing in a way adverse to our position in the world, and I think derivative from that is an explicit or implicit consensus that the situation demands not only a rise in perceptive policies, doctrines, strategies, and action, but perhaps most of all, inspired leadership to try to put the world values in a more balanced perspective.

As a final note, I had a most interesting experience in Korea when the North Koreans were trying to stir up a miniature Vietnam War. I found in my strategic discussions with the ROK leadership, the South Korean leadership, that a quotation from Shakespeare was very useful. It goes something to the effect that:

"Our doubts are traitors, and oft forbid us the good we might have won, by fearing to attempt."

This is from *Measure For Measure*, and I think that there is great meaning in this quotation, and it can serve as an approach to the future. I would hesitate to have any of you look up the context, however, because it is a statement, as I remember it, of a brother who is condemned to death in a new Blue Law campaign taking place in Vienna; he is trying to get his sister to seduce the ruler of Vienna so as to abort the death penalty on him. I am not quite sure whether the context applies to the international situation today.

I think that it is certainly my duty to express, on behalf of all of us, our appreciation as participants to the co-hosts, and to the multitude of people who have worked hard to provide an environment for this discussion, whether the discussion was fruitful or not. I personally think it was very fruitful.

Index

Attendees: Symposia on National Strategy
in a Decade of Change

Dr. David M. Abshire
  Center for Strategic and International
  Studies
  Georgetown University
Dr. Benson Adams
  Bureau of Politico-Military Affairs
  U.S. Department of State
Dr. Harold M. Agnew
  Los Alamos Scientific Laboratory
Capt. Dickson W. Alderton, USN
  Office of the Chief of Naval Operations
  Department of the Navy
Dr. Robert J. Alexander
  Rutgers University
Mr. William B. Ammon
  Martin-Marietta Corporation
Mr. Charles B. Anderson
  President
  Stanford Research Institute

Col. James C. Barnes, Jr., USA
  Office of the Deputy Chief of Staff for
  Military Operations
  Department of the Army
Dr. Frank R. Barnett
  National Strategy Information Center
Mr. William J. Baroody, Jr.
  Assistant to the Secretary and Deputy
  Secretary of Defense
Gen. André Beaufre
  French Institute of Strategic Studies
Mr. Gordon R. Boe
  Stanford Research Institute
Brig. Gen. Robert D. Bohn, USMC
  Assistant Deputy Chief of Staff (Pro-
  grams), U.S. Marine Corps
Gen. Charles H. Bonesteel III, USA (Ret.)
  Stanford Research Institute
Dr. Robert R. Bowie
  Harvard University
Maj. Gen. Leslie W. Bray, Jr., USAF
  Office of the Deputy Chief of Staff, Plans
  and Operations
  Department of the Air Force
Miss Donna Brodsky
  Foreign Policy Research Institute
Mrs. Sally G. Bunting
  National Water Resources Association

Maj. Gen. Frank A. Camm, USA
  U.S. Atomic Energy Commission
Dr. Robert W. Campbell
  Indiana University
Lieut. Col. Robert D. Carpenter, USA
  Office of the Deputy Chief of Staff for
  Military Operations
  Department of the Army
Mr. William M. Carpenter
  Stanford Research Institute
Dr. Daniel S. Cheever
  University of Pittsburgh

Mr. Leo Cherne
  Research Institute of America
Cdr. William A. Cockell, USN
  Office of the Chief of Naval Operations
  Department of the Navy
Lieut. Gen. Robert E. Coffin, USA
  Office of Defense Research and Engineer-
  ing
  Department of the Army
Ms. Judy Cole
  Foreign Policy Research Institute
Capt. Frank W. Corley, Jr., USN
  Office of the Deputy Chief of Naval
  Operations (Plans and Policy)
  Department of the Navy
Dr. Donald R. Cotter
  U.S. Atomic Energy Commission
Dr. Alvin J. Cottrell
  Center for Strategic and International
  Studies
  Georgetown University
Lieut. Gen. Donald H. Cowles, USA
  Department of the Army

Col. Clarence M. Davenport, Jr., USA
  (Ret.)
  Stanford Research Institute
Lieut. Gen. John J. Davis, USA (Ret.)
  Stanford Research Institute
Col. William J. Davis, USMC
  Office of the Deputy Chief of Staff (Plans
  and Programs)
  U.S. Marine Corps
Dr. Anton W. DePorte
  Department of State
Dr. James E. Dougherty
  Saint Joseph's College
Dr. Joseph D. Douglass, Jr.
  Advanced Research Projects Agency
Rear Adm. D.J.J. Downey, USN
  Office of the Deputy Chief of Naval
  Operations (Plans and Policy)
  Department of the Navy
Dr. Waldo H. Dubberstein
  American Enterprise Institute
Col. Ray A. Dunn, Jr., USAF
  Office of the Deputy Chief of Staff,
  Plans and Operations
  Department of the Air Force

Mr. M. Mark Earle, Jr.
  Stanford Research Institute
Dr. Samuel D. Eaton
  Planning and Coordination Staff
  U.S. Department of State
Mr. Frtiz W. Ermarth
  RAND Corporation

Miss Dorothy Fosdick, Staff
  Subcommittee on National Security and
  International Operations
  U.S. Senate

Mr. Richard B. Foster
  Stanford Research Institute
Col. D.M. Fowler, USA
  The Brookings Institution
Mr. Henry H. Fowler
  Goldman Sachs and Company
Mr. Norman Furth
  Stanford Research Institute

Lieut. Col. Cornelius J. Gearin, USA
  Office of the Deputy Chief of Staff for
  Military Operations
  Department of the Army
Dr. Harry G. Gelber
  Yale University
Dr. Stephen P. Gibert
  Georgetown University
Maj. Gen. Edward B. Giller, USAF
  Atomic Energy Commission
Dr. Roy O. Godson
  Georgetown University
Col. Carlton D. Goodiel, Jr., USMC
  Office of the Deputy of Staff (Plans and
  Programs)
  U.S. Marine Corps
Dr. William E. Griffith
  Massachusetts Institute of Technology
Dr. Lawrence Grinter
  Foreign Policy Research Institute
Rear Adm. Charles B. Grojean, USN
  Office of the Chief of Naval Operations
  Department of the Navy
Dr. Edmund A. Gullion
  Fletcher School of Law and Diplomacy
Dr. Andrew Gyorgy
  George Washington University

Gen. Alexander M. Haig, Jr., USA
  Vice Chief of Staff, Department of the
  Army
Dr. Fritz C. Hallowell, Jr.
  Advanced Strategic Systems Program
  Department
  General Electric
Lieut. Col. Charles W. Hansen, USA
  Office of Deputy Chief of Staff for
  Personnel
  Department of the Army
Dr. Willis W. Harman
  Stanford Resarch Institute
Col. James E. Harrell, USMC
  Office of the Deputy Chief of Staff
  (Plans and Programs)
  U.S. Marine Corps
Mr. John M. Hennessy
  U.S. Treasury Department
Dr. Harold C. Hinton
  George Washington University
Col. Harold L. Hitchens, USAF
  Department of the Air Force
Lieut. Col. Richard W. Hobbs, USA
  Office of the Deputy Undersecretary
  of the Army
Dr. Johan J. Holst
  Norwegian Institute of International
  Affairs

Mr. George D. Hopkins
  Stanford Research Institute
Dr. Alfred J. Hotz
  Augustana College
Dr. Samuel P. Huntington
  Harvard University

Lieut. Col. Francis A. Ianni, USA
  Office of the Deputy Chief of Staff for
  Military Operations
  Department of the Army
Col. Harald W. Ingholt, USAF
  Stanford Research Institute

Mr. Jerome E. Jacobs
  Hughes Aircraft Corporation
Dr. David C. Jordan
  University of Virginia
Dr. Wynfred Joshua
  Stanford Research Institute

Dr. Werner Kaltefleiter
  Social Science Research Institute
  Konrad Adenauer Foundation, Bonn
Mr. Jack Kangas
  Office of Assistant Secretary of Defense
  for Systems Analysis
Dr. Morton A. Kaplan
  University of Chicago
Miss Doris King
  Stanford Research Institute
Dr. William R. Kintner
  Foreign Policy Research Institute
Ambassador Foy D. Kohler
  University of Miami
Mr. Henry L.T. Koren
  Deputy Under Secretary of the Army
  (International Affairs)
Mr. Sven Kraemer
  National Security Council
Mr. Arnold Kramish
  The Office of the U.S. Permanent
  Representative to UNESCO

Dr. Walter Laqueur
  Institute of Contemporary History and
  Wiener Library, London
Dr. Leonard A. Lecht
  National Planning Association
Mr. Raymond G. Leddy
  Consultant, Department of Defense
Mr. Jon L. Lellenberg
  Stanford Research Institute
Brig. Gen. William L. Lemnitzer, USA
  Office of the Deputy Chief of Staff
  for Military Operations
  Department of the Army
Ambassador William Leonhart
  National War College
Mr. Avraham Lif
  Embassy of Israel
Brig. Gen. George G. Loving, USAF
  Air University
  Maxwell Air Force Base
Dr. Philip H. Lowry
  General Research Corporation

Dr. Stephen J. Lukasik, Director
  Advanced Research Projects Agency
Brig. Gen. Robert P. Lukeman, USAF
  Office of the Chief of Staff of the Air
  Force
  Department of the Air Force
Maj. Darwin D. Lundberg, USMC
  Office of the Deputy Chief of Staff
  (Plans and Programs)
  U.S. Marine Corps

John O. Marsh, Jr., Esq.
  Attorney at Law
Mr. Andrew W. Marshall
  National Security Council
Dr. Charles Burton Marshall
  Johns Hopkins University
Col. Donald S. Marshall, USA
  Office of the Assistant to the Secretary
  and Deputy Secretary of Defense
Brig. Gen. S.L.A. Marshall, USA (Ret.)
  Birmingham, Michigan
Dr. Laurence W. Martin
  King's College, University of London
Dr. Kenneth McLennan
  Deputy Assistant Secretary for Policy
  Development
  U.S. Department of Labor
Mr. R. Daniel McMichael
  The Scaife Family Charitable Trusts
Dr. Roy M. Melbourne
  National War College
Air Vice-Marshall S.W.B. Menaul
  Royal United Services Institute for
  Defense Studies
Mr. John H. Morse
  Deputy Assistant Secretary of Defense for
  International Security Affairs

Col. Brooke Nihart, USMC (Ret.)
  Stanford Research Institute
Dr. William A. Niskanen
  University of California, Berkeley

Mr. William H. Overholt
  Hudson Institute

Miss Gail A. Patelcuis
  Stanford Research Institute
Mr. Richard Perle
  Subcommittee on National Security and
  International Operations
  U.S. Senate
Dr. Vladimir Petrov
  George Washington University
Dr. Robert L. Pfaltzgraff, Jr.
  Foreign Policy Research Institute
Dr. Andrew J. Pierre
  Council on Foreign Relations, Inc.
Dr. Richard Pipes
  Harvard University
Col. Joseph E. Pizzi
  Army War College
Dr. James G. Poor
  Atomic Energy Commission
Dr. Stefan T. Possony

Hoover Institution on War, Revolution
  and Peace
Dr. Lucian Pye
  Massachusetts Institute of Technology

Mr. Sheldon Rabin
  Stanford Research Institute
Col. Burr J. Randall, Jr., USA (Ret.)
  Stanford Research Institute
Brig. Gen. R. Charlwood Richardson III,
  USAF (Ret.)
  Alexandria, Virginia
Col. James T. Reitz, USA (Ret.)
  Stanford Research Institute
Dr. James Rosenau
  Ohio State University
Mr. David Rossiter
  Legislative Aide for Foreign Affairs to
  Senator Edward Brooke
Ambassador Francis H. Russell
  Fletcher School of Law and Diplomacy

Maj. Gen. Adrian St. John II, USA
  Office of the Deputy Chief of Staff for
  Military Operations
  Department of the Army
Dr. Virgil Salera
  California State University at Hayward
Dr. Ron R. Scheuch
  Stanford Research Institute
Dr. Jack M. Schick
  Center for Naval Analyses
Dr. William Schneider
  Legislative Assistant to Senator James L.
  Buckley
Brig. Gen. Henry J. Schroeder, Jr. USA
  Office of the Deputy Chief of Staff for
  Military Operations
  Department of the Army
Mrs. Harriet Fast Scott
  Stanford Research Institute
Dr. Paul Seabury
  University of California
Mr. Richard E. Shearer
  Department of Defense
Dr. Harvey Sicherman
  Foreign Policy Research Institute
Dr. Gaston Sigur
  The George Washington University
Dr. Max Singer
  Hudson Institute
Mrs. Marianna Slocum
  Stanford Research Institute
Mr. Leon Sloss
  Bureau of Politico-Military Affairs
  U.S. Department of State
Capt. John Smith, USN
  National War College
Lieut. Col. William P. Snyder, USA
  Army War College
Dr. Helmut Sonnenfeldt
  National Security Council
Mr. Ronald I. Spiers, Director
  Bureau of Politico-Military Affairs
  U.S. Department of State
Gen. Berton Spivy, USA (Ret.)

Stanford Research Institute
Ambassador John M. Steeves
  Center for Strategic and International
    Studies
  Georgetown University
Lieut. Gen. Richard G. Stilwell, USA
  Deputy Chief of Staff for Military
    Operations
  Department of the Army
Mr. Howard T. Stump, Jr.
  Sandia Laboratories
Mr. Gerald D. Sullivan
  Advanced Research Projects Agency
Brig. Gen. Gordon Sumner, Jr., USA
  Office of the Assistant to the Secretary
    and Deputy Secretary of Defense

Mr. Paul W. Thompson
  Foreign Policy Research Institute
Dr. Frank N. Trager
  National Strategy Information Center
Dr. Jun Tsunoda
  National Diet Library Associate
  Tokyo, Japan

Dr. Richard L. Walker
  University of South Carolina
Dr. Henry C. Wallich
  Yale University
Dr. Gus W. Weiss, Jr.
  Council on International Economic Policy

Executive Office of the President
Dr. Leonard Weiss
  Bureau of Intelligence and Research
  U.S. Department of State
Mr. Seymour Weiss
  Planning and Coordination Staff
  U.S. Department of State
Dr. Nils H. Wessell
  Foreign Policy Research Institute
Mr. Robert J. Whalen
  Vice-President
  Martin-Marietta Corporation
Dr. N. Frederick Wikner
  Office of the Director of Defense
    Research and Engineering
  U.S. Department of Defense
Mr. James M. Wilson, Jr.
  Deputy Assistant Secretary of
    State for East Asian Affairs
Dr. Paul D. Wolfowitz
  Yale University
Dr. Paul Wonnacott
  University of Maryland
Mr. James Woolsey
  General Counsel
  Senate Committee on Armed Services
Dr. Yuan-Li Wu
  University of San Francisco

Capt. W.K. Yates, USN
  Naval War College

About the Authors

William R. Kintner, a leading American authority on national security, U.S. foreign policy and international affairs, is Director, Foreign Policy Research Institute, Editor of ORBIS and a Professor, The Wharton School, University of Pennsylvania. His career has spanned the governmental, military and academic worlds. He is currently a member of the Board of Foreign Scholarships.

Richard B. Foster is the founder and Director of the Strategic Studies Center, Stanford Research Institute. He has been engaged in extensive analytical work over the past two decades in the field of strategy and national security policy, especially in politico-military policy, arms control, missile defense, and tactical nuclear weapons policy. He has pioneered in the development of a channel of intellectual interaction with research organizations in the nations of Western Europe and in the Soviet Union. He is author and coauthor of many SRI studies performed for the U.S. Government in the field of national strategy. Mr. Foster is a graduate of the University of California at Berkeley, with degrees in engineering and philosophy.